EVERYONE LOVES YOU
WHEN YOU'RE DEAD

OBITUARY.

Lowell.—On the 12th August, the hon. James Russell Lowell, aged 72.

Raikes.—A home telegram of 24th inst. records the death of the hon. Cecil Raikes, Postmaster-General, aged 53.

Wesley.—In May, Mr William Wesley, the well-known bookseller and publisher of Essex-st., Strand, aged 77.

Dean.—On 13th May, at Southsea, Mr George Alfred Henry Dean, head of the well-known publishing firm of Dean & Sons, aged 69.

Turner.—In June, in London. Dr. Turner, missionary, aged 73. He was the author of *Samoa a Hundred Years Ago* and *Nineteen Years in Polynesia.*

Cunliffe.—On 20th June, Mr Thomas Cunliffe, proprietor of the Bolton *Guardian.* Mr Cunliffe was one of the best-known men in Bolton, and a prominent temperance worker.

Henderson.—On 22nd May, at Ipswich, Mr William Henderson, senior partner in the music-printing firm of Henderson & Spalding, (formerly Henderson, Rait, & Fenton), aged 60.

Salmon.—In June, at Stockport, at the age of 71, Mr James Salmon, head of the firm of James Salmon & Son, and one of the best-known members of the printers' engineering trade.

Reed.—On 9th June, aged 73, Margaret, widow of the late Sir Charles Reed. Lady Reed was the youngest daughter of Mr Edward Baines, founder of the Leeds *Mercury* and for many years member for Leeds, and was younger sister of the late Sir Edward Baines, who died last year.

Byles.—On 17th June, in his 84th year, Mr William Byles, senior proprietor of the Bradford *Observer*, with which paper he had been connected from the issue of its first number on the 6th February, 1834. He was one of the best known and most respected men in Bradford, and is said to have «made his mark on its religion, its philanthropy, on its educational character, on its politics, and on its commercial reputation.»

Fothergill.—A home telegram of 1st August reports the death of Miss Jessie Fothergill, whose works—*Probation, The First Violin*, and others—are among the best English novels of the past decade. She was born in Manchester, where her father was engaged in the cotton trade. He belonged to the Society of Friends, but had to withdraw from that body on account of his marriage with a member of the Church of England. He died in 1864, and Mrs Fothergill removed with her family to Littleborough, near Rochdale. In this country home, in the wide wind-swept moors, and in the quaint rustic population, the future novelist took delight, and while hating lessons, she developed a passion for knowledge. Always delicate in health, the free country life strengthened and revived her. Like another Lancashire authoress, Frances Hodgson, she exhibited rare powers of observation and memory, and developed the story-telling faculty in early childhood. From the first, her published works were a success. Of late years she has lived in a pretty home in Manchester, but has had to winter abroad.

An English telegram of 23rd Sept. records the death of Wilkie Collins, the well-known novelist and dramatist, in his 66th year.

A cable message dated 23rd September, notes the death of Mr Henry Farnie, one of the most facile and industrious librettists of the century. He possessed a marvellous facility for rhyming, and could set words to anything in the way of music. His opera librettos are innumerable, and among other feats he adapted words to all of Dan Godfrey's waltzes. His name came prominently before the public in a divorce suit a few years ago, and since that time not much has been heard of him.

Mr Henry Samuel Ward, one of the oldest members of the Craft in Melbourne, died on the 14th July. He was born in 1824 at Clapham, and learned the business in his father's office. He afterwards obtained a situation on *The Times*, and in 1857 came to Australia in the *King of Algeria* as one of «the Forty» who came out under engagement to the *Argus.* He worked subsequently on the *Herald* and the *Age*, and held a frame on the latter paper to within three months of his death. He leaves a widow and two sons, one of whom is on the staff of the *Age.*

Bassett.—On 14th December, 1892, John Bassett, proprietor and editor of the *Printing World*, aged 29.

Sherrin.—On 9th January, at Auckland, R. A. A. Sherrin, an old journalist and parliamentary correspondent.

Smart.—A London telegram of 10th inst, records the death of Hawley Smart, a well-known novelist.

Higinbotham.—On 31st December, George Higinbotham, Chief Justice of Victoria, aged 65. He was associated with the London press prior to his call to the bar in 1853; and after emigrating to Victoria, joined in 1856 the staff of the Melbourne *Argus*, which paper he edited for several years.

Alabaster.—On 18th November, at Richmond, Surrey, aged 86, James Alabaster, of Passmore & Alabaster, printers and publishers. The firm was established in 1853, and its business consists entirely of printing and publishing the sermons and other works of the late Rev. Thomas Spurgeon.

Kemble. On the 16th January, at London, aged 83, Frances Anne Kemble, the famous actress, and author of interesting books of reminiscences. She belonged to an illustrious family of actors, being grand-daughter of Roger Kemble, daughter of Charles Kemble, niece of John Philip Kemble and of Mrs Siddons, and sister of Adelaide Kemble.

Jackson.—On 1st January, at Nelson, Mr H. D. Jackson, a well-known bookseller, in his 66th year. Mr Jackson was a native of Leeds, and arrived in Nelson with his parents in the barque *Phœbe*, in March, 1843. The family had their full share of the heavy pioneer work which fell to the lot of the early settlers. Mr Jackson was on the staff of the Nelson *Examiner* in its earlier years. He was promently connected with public institutions and local bodies. He married in 1854, and has left a widow and seven children.

A telegram from New York, dated 12th September, records the death, from yellow fever, of Professor R. A. Proctor, at the age of 51.

La Typologie-Tucker records the death on the 6th July, at the age of 64, of M. Pierre Alexander Chapelle, Paris,—a notable type-founder and designer of many popular ornamental styles of letter.

We regret to see by the Rangitikei papers that Mr Isaac Down, a half-caste, who was apprenticed to the printing business in the same office in which the writer served his time, has been found drowned. The meagre paragraph before us does not give us the date or any particulars of the accident nor the name of the locality; we gather that an inquest was held on the 17th inst., and an open verdict returned. Deceased, who was a son of the late Mr. Down, of Wairoa, was at the early age of seven years placed at the printing business with the late Mr H. L. Yates, in Napier, late in 1861 or early in 1862, and was subsequently apprenticed. His career in after life was somewhat chequered. He acted as telegraph lineman, native interpreter, and occasionally as compositor. In the latter capacity he was employed for some time at the Government printing office, where his knowledge of the Maori language was of value. Some years ago, having married, he took a small farm at Kaikoura, Hawke's Bay, but did not find the venture a success. He leaves a widow and two children.

The *Printers' Register* records the death of the oldest member of the craft in the United Kingdom—Mr William Scott, who died on the 29th June, at the age of 95. At the age of eleven he entered into the service of Messrs Eyre & Strahan, afterwards Eyre & Spottiswoode, of which firm he had been a pensioner for thirty years—thus furnishing an instance, probably unique, of a printer eighty-four years in the pay of a single firm.

American papers record the death by suicide in Kansas of Howard R. Hetrick, a reporter who has done some of the best newspaper work in the county. He had given way to drink, and all efforts to reclaim him were fruitless.

Mr Henry Anderson, who has been suffering for some months from cancer in the throat, died in Wellington on the 20th July at the age of 50. Mr Anderson was a trenchant and able writer, and at times fiercely personal. In the course of his chequered career he has been connected with nearly every newspaper in Wellington. He leaves a widow and family.

M. Louis Alauzet, a noted manufacturer of printing machines, died at Paris on the 12th May, in his 36th year.

In Dublin, on 5th March, was buried Mr Pattison Jolly, aged 104, probably the oldest printer in the world. He served his time at Ballantyne's in Edinburgh, and pulled the first sheet of the *Edinburgh Journal* over seventy years ago.

An English telegram records the death of Mr Justice Johnston, of the Supreme Court of New Zealand. Judge Johnston was the author of certain legal works, one of which, the *New Zealand Justice of the Peace*, is a standard text-book, and has passed through several editions.

Mrs Proctor, wife of «Barry Cornwall,» and mother of Adelaide Anne Proctor, died on the 5th March, at an advanced age, having been born about the beginning of the century. Mrs Proctor was a brillant conversationalist, and was on intimate terms with three generations of leading English authors.

Mr Arthur Stewart Ramsay, late of the Government Lithographic Office, died on the 15th inst., from the effects of a severe cold. Mr Ramsay, who had been 17½ years in the Government employ, had to retire last February, on account of retrenchment. He had latterly been in a very depressed state, being unable to obtain other employment. He leaves a widow and three young children.

A correspondent writes: Frederick William Cooke died at Auckland early in this month. He served his term in the office of the *Illustrated London News*, and arrived in the Auckland district early in the 40's. He was a well-read man, and many regrets are expressed at his decease. He worked for many years at the *N. Z. Herald*, and died in harness. He was a bachelor. «Death has locked up his mortal form.»

Mr Robert Savage, a regular contributor to the *Argus* and *Australasian*, and a graceful writer, died last month in Melbourne.

Dr. Johan H. Zukertort, a well-known chess-player, and editor of the *Chess Monthly*, died in Charing-Cross Hospital on 20th June, aged 46. As a player he had few superiors, and as a chess-writer, none.

An English telegram of the 8th May, reports the death of the celebrated statistician, Professor Leone Levi, at the age of 67.

Mr George Toulmin, an able and conscientious journalist, for many years proprietor of the *Preston Guardian* and other papers, died on the 17th February, in his 75th year.

Oscar Pletsch, the unrivalled German artist of child-life, has recently died, in his 37th year. His drawings have been a feature of all the children's magazines for the past fifteen or sixteen years.

Mr David Payne, of the firm of Payne & Sons, printers' engineers, Otley, died in November last.

An English telegram of 7th January, records the death of Mr Halliwell Phillips, Shakspearean critic.

An English telegram of 24th January, records the death of Pellegrini, the caricaturist of *Vanity Fair.*

We regret to have to record the death, on the 5th January, of Mr T. G. Smith, youngest son of Mr J. T. Smith, printer, Christchurch, aged 33 years.

We regret to note the death, on 23rd December, at the age of 59, after a painful illness, of Mr Lawrence Oliphant, diplomatist, and author of works chiefly of a philosophical and mystical character.

Mr Charles Hardwick, the historian of Preston, (in his youth apprenticed in the Preston *Chronicle* office), died on 9th July, at the age of 71.

Mr R. K. Burt, senior partner in the printing firm of R. K. Burt & Co., Fetter Lane, London, died on 10th July, aged 62.

Eneas Dawson, until lately senior partner in the firm of Dawson & Sons, stationers, Cannon-st., London, died on 24th July, aged 70.

Australian papers record the death, in her twenty-eighth year, of Mrs Boon, *nee* Dumas, a well known writer and essayist, whose domestic stories under the name of «Louise,» were marked by originality and pathos, and were an attractive feature in more than one Australian serial. She had been only one year married.

Mr Samuel Raynor, paper-maker, New York, died 8th May, in his 78th year.

Miller.—At Dublin, on 10th September, Mr Robert Miller, of the firm of William Miller & Sons, typefounders, Dublin.

Virtue.—On 24th September, at Bayswater, Mr John Virtue, aged 67, and for more than half-a-century connected with the *Art Journal* office.

Morton.—On 14th August, at Launceston, from injuries received in a trap accident, Mr John Morton, editor of the *Tasmanian*. He was a native of Berwickshire, and only 29 years of age. He went out to Tasmania in 1882. He leaves a widow and two children.

Miller.—On 14th September, at Islington, Mr W. Haig Miller, aged 79. His wife had died on the preceding day, and he passed away in his sleep. He had for many years retired from business, and devoted himself entirely to Christian work. He assisted in the foundation of the *Leisure Hour* and the *Sunday at Home*, and was the first editor of the former journal.

Sands.—At Baltimore, on 21st July, in his 92nd year, Samuel Sands, the oldest printer in the United States, and probably in the world. He was apprenticed in 1811 at the Baltimore *American* office, and in his long and active life was connected with many and various public institutions. In 1814 he set up from the freshly-written manuscript the national song of «The Star-Spangled Banner.»

Lytton.—On 24th November, at Paris, Lord Lytton, G.C.B., G.C.S.I., C.I.E., LL.D., British Ambassador, aged 60. He was the only son of the late E. B. Lytton, the most versatile literary man of the century, and no man of the present generation has had a more distinguished career. He entered the diplomatic service of the Crown at the age of 18, as attaché at Washington, and after long and honorable service as ambassador in various European capitals, was in 1876 appointed Viceroy of India. On resigning this office in 1880, he was appointed Ambassador in Paris. His published volumes, in prose and verse, under the pseudonym of Owen Meredith, indicate literary gifts of a high order, but never attained such wide popularity as the works of his late father.

Dr H. Monk, well known as the musical editor of *Hymns Ancient and Modern*, died on the 1st March.

A cable message of 7th May reports the death of Count Tolstoi, the celebrated Russian novelist, and a man of mark as a social reformer.

A London telegram of 10th inst. records the death of the Rev. Lord Sidney Godolphin Osborne, at the age of 81. The deceased has for many years past been a contributor to *The Times*, on social and philanthropic questions, under the signature of «S.G.O.»

Mr William F. Jackson, the oldest printer in Manchester, died on the 12th March, aged 89. He went into business on his own account in 1832, and remained in business as printer and stationer until his death. He had been three-quarters of a century at the trade.

Mr W. F. Tillotson, founder of the Bolton *Evening News* and the *Journal*, died at Bolton on 19th February, at the age of 44, after four days' illness, from inflammation of the lungs. He was remarkable for his business energy and methodical habits. He had established a «Fiction Bureau,» and induced many prominent novelists to publish their stories in the first place through newspaper columns. He had recently extended his operations to America and the European continent.

CANONGATE

Edinburgh · London

Glanville.—On 9th August, Dr. Doyle Glanville, F.R.G.S., a noted traveller, artist, and press correspondent, who had seen service in South Africa, Mexico, South America, the West Indies, China, Egypt, and New Guinea. He was correspondent of the *Graphic* throughout the Zulu War, and afterwards in the Sudan, whither he had accompanied the Australian contingent.

Bradlaugh.—On 30th January, Charles Bradlaugh, M.P. for Northampton, aged 57.

Plumptre.—On the 2nd February, Dr Plumptre, Dean of Wells, a celebrated theological writer, aged 69.

Carlile.—Accidentally drowned at Woodville, on the 30th January, Mrs Carlile, wife of Mr W. W. Carlile, formerly editor and part proprietor of the Hawke's Bay *Herald*.

Jarrold.—In November, at Norwich, in his 43rd year, Mr Samuel J. J. Jarrold, of the publishing house of Jarrold and Sons, Norwich and London.

Selous.—In October, at the age of 87, H. C. Selous, a Royal Academician of many years' standing. He was an able and vigorous artist in black and white, one of his best known works being a series of twenty fine plates illustrative of Charles Kingsley's «Hereward,» issued by the Art Union of London in 1870.

Reynolds.—On the 31st January, at Wellington, Ernest Reynolds, of the lithographic department of the *Press*, aged 18. He had taken a three weeks' trip to his parents' home at Clareville, Wairarapa, for the holidays. He was not very well on his return to work, and a week afterwards, becoming seriously ill with typhoid fever, was removed to the hospital, where he died. Mr Reynolds was a clever and efficient workman, and in private life was highly esteemed.

Meissonier.—A home telegram of 2nd February records the death of Jean Meissonier, the famous painter, who was born at Lyons in 1812. Of West, a contemporary epigrammatist wrote : He knows that bulk is not a jest, and gives us painting by the acre.» As West might have painted for Brobdignag, so Meissonier might have been artist for Lilliput. His works were in miniature, finished with photographic delicacy and minuteness, and were so highly esteemed that they realized higher prices than were ever before paid for the productions of a living artist.

Nicholson.—On 18th December, at Fielding, John Nicholson, of Christchurch, aged 24. Deceased was formerly employed as compositor on the Christchurch *Press*, but had to relinquish his duties on account of failing health.

Knowles.—On 3rd December, at Wellington, John Knowles, aged 68, a very old New Zealand journalist. He was born in London on 4th December, 1823, and arrived in Wellington in the *Gertrude* in October, 1841, at once entering into the service of the New Zealand Company. He took an active part in the pioneer work of colonization, and filled several important and responsible public offices. He edited the Wellington *Independent* from 1855 to 1864, and contributed largely to other leading New Zealand papers. From 1864 to 1869 he was New Zealand correspondent of *The Times*. He took an active interest in religious and educational matters; and was, in the early days, on the Wesleyan preachers' plan. For over 35 years he was an office-bearer of the Congregational Church, and for over 50 years Sabbath School teacher and superintendent. He leaves a widow and a grown-up son and daughter. No resident of Wellington was held in more general respect or esteem. The immediate cause of death was weakness of the heart, complicated with a cold taken a few days before his death.

M. Alkan, sen., a bibliographer, died near Paris on the 18th June, aged 84. It is not many months since he published his last work, *Les quatre Doyens de la Typographie Parisienne.* He was a frequent contributor to the trade journals, and as far back as 1838 started a periodical, *Les Annales de la Typographie*, which did not long survive.

Mr John Heywood, the well-known printer, publisher, and typefounder, died on the 10th May, after a fortnight's illness, at Stretford, near Manchester, aged 56.

Mr T. H. Potts, an old Christchurch resident, died suddenly on the 27th July, aged 60. Mr Potts was a prominent citizen and an enthusiastic naturalist, and was widely known by his series of papers entitled «Out in the Open.»

Mr Henry Littleton, head of the music-publishing firm of Novello, Ewer, & Co., died at Sydenham on May 11th, aged 66. He entered the business in 1841 as office-boy, and in 1866 became sole proprietor. Having made a considerable fortune, he retired last year from active participation in the business.

Field.—Home exchanges record the death of Mr Abraham Field, of the late firm of Field & Tuer, now trading as the Leadenhall Press.

Collier.—On 14th May, Mr T. Collier, R.I., one of the most prominent members of the Royal Institute of Painters in Water-Colors. In landscape he was unrivalled. [Owing to a misreading of the cable message, colonial papers in May—our own among the number—erroneously reported the death of the hon. John Collier, the celebrated portrait-painter.]

Weld.—A home telegram records the death of Sir F. A. Weld, G.C.M.G., aged 68. He came to New Zealand in 1844; filled many responsible offices, and in 1864 became Premier. It was a time of great difficulty, and he ably filled his post, initiating what was known as the «self-reliant policy.» Since leaving New Zealand he has held several colonial governorships.

Manley.—A home telegram, at Wellington, Mr B. N. Manley. For about ten years he was manager of the Wanganui *Herald*. Removing to Wellington, he joined Mr Ffrost in the rubber stamp business. He took great interest in chess, and in 1887 started the *Chess Chronicle*, which had a very brief existence. He was twice married, and leaves two children by his first wife.

Johnston.—We regret to note the death, in his 65th year, of Mr S. Reed Johnston, superintendent of the house of J. Eichbaum & Co., Pittsburg, Pennsylvania, and one of the best printers in America. He was best known through his skill in color-work and as the inventor of the «Owltype» process; but like all really artistic printers, he excelled in plain work, which he considered the true test of skill.

Munson.—At Honolulu, on 9th May, Mr John Munson. He arrived at Hokitika in 1865, and went into business there with his brother, Mr Job Munson, the present proprietor of the Buller *Miner*. When the Westport *Times* was started by Mr Job Munson and Mr John Tyrrell (the present proprietor), deceased joined the staff. He afterwards went into the stationery business, and later occupied the position of mining reporter to the Inangahua *Times*, fulfilling the duties very efficiently. Having been successful in mining ventures, he retired. A few months ago he went on a visit to America, and was his way back to New Zealand when he died.

EVERYONE
—LOVES YOU—
WHEN YOU'RE
DEAD

(AND OTHER THINGS I LEARNED FROM FAMOUS PEOPLE)

by NEIL STRAUSS

Sayers.—On the 31st August, at Melbourne, Mr J. N. Sayers, one of the early Victorian printers. He was born at Essex in 1808, served his time in London, and coming out to Melbourne in 1851 with a good printing plant, established himself in business in Little Collins-st., where he remained until his retirement in 1880.

Williams.—On October 7th, at Kensington, Mr John Williams, M.A., aged 52. He was principal editor in Cassell's publishing-house, with which he had been associated for 23 years. Besides the general supervision of the editorial department, he found time to edit many important works, including the *Encyclopædia Dictionary*.

The Rev. Horatius Bonar, D.D., best known as a hymn-writer, died at his residence, Edinburgh, on the 31st July, in his 81st year.

An English telegram of 26th September records the death of Eliza Cook, the well-known poet, at the age of 71.

*In memory of Johnny Cash, Curtis Mayfield, Alex Chilton,
Nusrat Fateh Ali Khan, Ike Turner, Lucia Pamela,
Ernie K-Doe, Antoinette K-Doe, Arthur Lee, Mark Linkous,
Timothy Leary, Jimmy Martin, John Hartford, Otha Turner,
Rick James, Raymond Scott, Patrick Miller, Josh Clayton-Felt,
Chet Atkins, Rick Wright, Ali Farka Touré, Roger Troutman,
and Bo Diddley, all of whom died between the time of
being interviewed and the publication of this book.*

And for all those who are going to die afterward.

WARNING:

Do not skip through this book looking for your favorite artists.

Each interview connects to the one before and after it.

So read this book from front to back.

After all, that is how books work (unless they're instruction manuals, in which case no one reads them at all).

If you succeed in doing this, send a blank email with the subject heading WINNER to readingreward@gmail.com, and you will receive a prize for following directions.

If you fail, send a blank email with the subject heading LOSER to readingpolice@gmail.com and you will receive your punishment. It won't be pretty.

As through this world I've wandered,
I've seen lots of funny men;
Some will rob you with a six gun,
And some with a fountain pen.

—Woody Guthrie, "Pretty Boy Floyd"

EVERYONE LOVES YOU

(WHEN YOU'RE DEAD)

[A COMEDY IN TEN ACTS]

[PRE AMBLE]

I've shot guns with Ludacris, been kidnapped by Courtney Love, made Lady Gaga cry, shopped for Pampers with Snoop Dogg, gone drinking with Bruce Springsteen, tried to prevent Mötley Crüe from getting arrested, received Scientology lessons from Tom Cruise, flown in a helicopter with Madonna, been taught to read minds by the CIA, soaked in a hot tub with Marilyn Manson, been told off by Prince, and tucked Christina Aguilera into bed.

This is my job.

Since I was eighteen, I've been under orders from magazines and newspapers to step into the lives of musicians, actors, and artists, and somehow find out who they really are underneath the mask they present to the public.

Yet for two decades, I've been doing it wrong. Newspapers and magazines are service industries, catering to the daily or monthly needs of a public that wants to be told what's new, what they should know about it, and what they should think about it. And in catering to that need, I didn't do justice to reality. Because no matter what happens during an interview, once it ends, a writer's loyalty is to the pressure of an immediate deadline, the style and tone of a publication, and the priorities of an editor. And an editor's loyalty is to a publisher. And a publisher's loyalty is to stockholders and circulation figures and advertising revenue. Somewhere along the way, the subject gets lost.

So to put this book together, I went back to my original interview recordings, notes, and transcripts and selected the best moments from the three-thousand-something articles I've written over the years. But instead of looking for the pieces that broke news or sold the most magazines or received the best feedback, I searched for the truth or essence behind each person, story, or experience. Often it came from something I'd previously ignored: an uncomfortable silence, a small misunderstanding, or a scattered thought that had been compressed into a soundbite. Other times it came from something more dramatic, like an emotional confession, a run-in with the police, or a drug-induced psychosis.*

Although I spent weeks working on some of these stories, what I realized is that most of the time I was waiting for just one moment of truth or authenticity. After all, you can tell a lot about a person or a situation in a minute. But only if you choose the right minute.

Here are 233 of them.

---

* Note that all quotations in footnotes, except where otherwise indicated, are also from these interviews.

ACT ONE

— OR —

THE WORST INTERVIEW EVER

— SYNOPSIS —

ENTER THE STROKES, *who do not want to be recorded,* THOUGH SNOOP DOG WANTS TO BE BOOTLEGGED, DESPITE HAVING GOTTEN HIGH WITH MADONNA, who claims nobody dies,

THOUGH JOHNNY CASH BEGS TO DIFFER BECAUSE HE VIVIDLY REMEMBERS **LOOKING DEATH IN THE EYE** AND LIKING WHAT HE SAW, &C.

[THE STROKES]
SCENE 1

When I met Strokes singer Julian Casablancas at 19th Hole, a dive bar near his apartment in Manhattan, he was wearing the same outfit he'd worn for the past week: a green work shirt with the words "U.S. Garbage Company" over the pocket and faded black pants. On his wrist were three fraying colored paper bracelets: one from a Kings of Leon concert a week earlier, another from a Stooges show two weeks ago, and a third from a Vines show who knows when.

As he ordered two beers for himself, he announced with evident pride that he'd finally come up with a press answer to "the Nigel Godrich question." (The band had hired Radiohead producer Nigel Godrich to work on its latest CD, but then quickly parted ways with him.) When asked what his great soundbite was, Casablancas said he would tell me when we began the interview. The tape deck was dutifully started. And so began . . . the worst interview ever.

JULIAN CASABLANCAS: I'm drinking myself back into the game.

I've noticed that people tend to think you're drinking and out of it. But the truth is that you're ultra-aware of everything going on and everyone's motivation—
CASABLANCAS: That's your opinion.

And what's yours?
CASABLANCAS: I don't see myself that way. If you see it that way, cool, thanks.

So how do you see it?
CASABLANCAS: I see myself out of my own eyes, which means I have no idea what's going on the other way around. I just think I try to be a good person—and I fail.

Casablancas reaches over the table and presses stop on the tape deck. Then he immediately starts it again.

CASABLANCAS: I'm sorry.

I don't care. Do what you want.

He turns the tape recorder off; I turn it back on.

Let's talk about the music instead.
CASABLANCAS: Fuck music.

All right, good. So let's talk about your shirt. You have a whole closet full of—

He turns the tape deck off again. I look at him. He looks at me. Then I turn it back on.

CASABLANCAS: Talk to me.

Okay, so what's your stock answer to the Nigel Godrich question?
CASABLANCAS: Fuck you. I'm not answering that question.

What the hell?
CASABLANCAS: Next question.

It's interesting. People's true personality comes out when they're drunk . . .
CASABLANCAS: You're too nice, man.
RANDOM WOMAN AT NEARBY TABLE: What's he like when he's sober?
CASABLANCAS: Sober he's a fucking asshole.
RANDOM WOMAN: So what is he right now?

Half sober, half drunk.
CASABLANCAS: And when he's tired, he's a rapist. (*Looks warily at the tape recorder, then speaks into the microphone:*) Rape is bad. Very, very bad.

Honestly, this has to be the worst—
CASABLANCAS: —the worst interview ever?

Oh man, good times.
CASABLANCAS: Good times. "Whoa-oh-oh-oh, for the longest time." (*Starts singing the Billy Joel song to the tune of the Clash's "Spanish Bombs," which is playing on the jukebox.*) It's the exact same melody.

He leans over and turns off the tape deck again, then sits in his seat, swaying and staring.

[*Continued . . .*]

[SNOOP DOGG]
SCENE 1

Despite rumors that Suge Knight wanted him dead for leaving Death Row Records several weeks earlier, there were no security gates, armed guards, or electric fences at Snoop Dogg's house in Claremont, just outside Los Angeles. There was just a sweatsuit-clad Snoop, who pulled me into the living room and pushed me into his home studio. Above the door, a sign read, "Home Honey, I'm High."

SNOOP DOGG: I want you to hear a few songs first. (*Presses* PLAY *on a DAT machine, and leaves the room while thirteen songs he's just finished recording blare from the studio speakers. As soon as the last song ends, he bursts back through the door.*) Well, did you tape some of it?

Of course not.
SNOOP DOGG: You should have.

What?!
SNOOP DOGG: Didn't we talk yesterday about taping pieces of the album and leaking them on the Internet?

Yeah, but most rappers try to avoid leaking their music, because then no one will buy it when it comes out.
SNOOP DOGG: Fuck it, just bootleg that motherfucker. Come on, man. I'll give you the ones you want.

Should I just leak it on the Internet, or do you want radio too?
SNOOP DOGG: All of it, man. That's what I want you here for. I ain't never done that shit before. (*He plays three songs, and watches diligently to make sure I record them.*) Cool. Can we use your wheels? I gotta go get Pampers.

For real?
SNOOP DOGG: It's cool. We can ride and do the interview. I always do interviews riding and shit. I remember I used to be riding with guns and shit all in the car with me, getting into this gangbang bullshit.

Let's try to avoid the gangbanging.

SNOOP DOGG: It was cool, though (*lights a joint and puffs*). Life is a motherfucker.

Is it true that you got high with Madonna?

SNOOP DOGG: I met her with Tupac. It was before he went to jail, before he got shot or anything. It was my first time doing *Saturday Night Live*. He came to see me because he was my nigga back then. He brought me a gang of weed and we all kicked it and smoked. Pac was a cool motherfucker, though, man. Death Row turned him out. Man, I feel bad.

[*Continued . . .*]

═══ [MADONNA] ═══
SCENE 1

We know her as Madonna. But her staff refers to her simply as M. And M was sitting in a private plane, which had just taken off from a Royal Air Force base south of London. She was en route to Frankfurt, Germany, where a helicopter was waiting to fly her to a television performance in Mannheim. For sustenance, M, her manager Angela, and her stylist Shavawn were all carrying bags of popcorn.

When's the last time you were in a helicopter?

MADONNA: I went in a cheap helicopter the day after I fell off my horse. I was on morphine, so I couldn't tell what kind of danger I was in. But because it was my birthday, I was like, "I'm going to Paris. I don't care if I'm injured." It wasn't until the morphine wore off the next day—I only did it for twenty-four hours, don't get excited—that I realized how scary the helicopter was.

How was the morphine?

MADONNA: It was pretty good. I'm a lot of fun on morphine. At least, I think I am. But I'm not fun on Vicodin.

ANGELA: Okay, do you know the story of Dr. Jekyll and Mr. Hyde? I've never seen a transformation like that in my entire life.

MADONNA: I only tried Vicodin once. I was in a lot of pain, and nothing killed the pain. Not even morphine, to tell you the truth. And everyone kept telling me to try Vicodin, but they kept saying, "Be careful. It's so amazing. But if you take it for more than ten days, you're going to get addicted to it." So I called five people to get advice before I took it, and they all told me I was going to love it. Whatever. So I took it.

SHAVAWN: She went on a walk with me, and it was really scary.

MADONNA: Drugs have a weird effect on me. They do the opposite with me. I just chewed the entire inside of my mouth. I bitched at everybody. And I was in *more* pain. It was terrible: the worst experience of my life.

At least you didn't get addicted.

MADONNA: I'm happy to say that none of my pharmaceuticals—and I've had a plethora of them given to me—have influenced me.

I don't like pills anyway. It's a control thing.

MADONNA: I just like the *idea* of pills. I like to collect them but not actually take them—just in case. When I fell off my horse, I got tons of stuff: Demerol and Vicodin and Xanax and Valium and OxyContin, which is supposed to be like heroin. And I'm really quite scared to take them. I'm a control freak too. And any time I've taken anything in my life, as soon as I take it, I'm like, "Okay, I want it out of my body." I just start guzzling water. I want to flush it out, fast.

Do you ever think about—

MADONNA: Do I think about dying? Is that what you were thinking about asking?

No, but that's a better question than what I was going to ask.

MADONNA: Real death is disconnecting, but the death where your physical body is no longer functioning, that's not real death.

What is it then?

MADONNA: Death is when you disconnect from God—or when you disconnect from the universe, because God is the universe. I think anyone who's disconnected is living in a serious hell. They can medicate themselves or live in serious denial to convince themselves they're not in hell, but sooner or later it's going to catch up to you.

[*Continued . . .*]

[JOHNNY CASH]
SCENE 1

There are some interviews that you look back on after the artist has died, and they bring tears to your eyes. Tears that, like Johnny Cash's life and music, are both joyful and tragic.

I notice that when you sing about sin, it's usually followed by guilt and redemption. Do you think that's how it always works?
JOHNNY CASH: I see that in my life a whole lot stronger than I guess a lot of people do, because I've been through so much—and I walked lightly and poetically on the dark side often throughout my life. But the redeeming love and the grace of God was there, you know, to pull me through. And that's where I am right now. Redeemed.

That's a big—
CASH: But I don't close the door on that dark past or ignore it, because there is that beast there in me. And I got to keep him caged (*knowing laugh*) or he'll eat me alive.

A lot of times people think that the idea of the man in black is nihilistic, but there's a positive side to it as well.
CASH: That's the whole thing. I've not been obsessed with death. I've been obsessed with living. It's the battle against the dark one, which is what my life is about, and a clinging to the right one. But, you know, I've, uh, in '88, when I had bypass surgery, I was as close to death as you could get. I mean, the doctors were saying they were losing me. And I was going, and there was that wonderful light that I was going into. It was awesome, indescribable—beauty and peace, love and joy—and then all of a sudden there I was again, all in pain and awake. I was so disappointed.

Disappointed?
CASH: I realized a day or so later what point I had been to, and then I started thanking God for life. You know, I used to think only of life, but when I was that close to losing it, I realized it wasn't anything to worry about when that does happen.

WALK ON THE DARK SIDE

COME SEE

RENO CIRCUS

Beast in the CAGE

So did you always believe that when you die you go somewhere else?
CASH: Yeah, but I didn't know it was going to be that beautiful. I mean, it's inde-
scribably wonderful, whatever there is at the end of this life.

[*Continued . . .*]

[NEW YORKERS]

Sometimes, if you listen closely, a neighborhood can have just as much of a personality as an individual. I used to live in New York's East Village, but before it was
cool and trendy—when it was just dangerous. One night, I heard a guy being held
up at gunpoint outside my window. Another night, three guys kicked the shit out
of me just for fun. Those experiences, along with the following things I overheard
in the area at the time, contributed to my decision to save up and move to a neighborhood with a more stable personality.

Overheard on Avenue B, two men talking:
"Just because I killed someone doesn't mean I'm an expert."

Overheard on the same block, a man talking to a woman:
"I'm not a jealous guy, I'm just violent."

Overheard on East Seventh Street, a man talking to a lamppost:
"I'm gonna break your face, sucker."

**Overheard at the Odessa Restaurant near Tompkins Square Park, the owner
talking to an anarchist squatter:**
"I think you guys should go start another riot for me. I need the business."

Overheard on Avenue A, two well-dressed white men talking:
"I'm not a racist or anything, but have you ever beaten up an African-American?"

Overheard at the bar 7B, two women talking:
"He's a total fox, so I love him. But he completely has no personality and doesn't
speak a word of English."

Overheard on a building stoop on East Sixth Street, a man talking to the apartment supervisor:
"You can't *always* go calling the coroner ten hours afterward."

Overheard in Tompkins Square Park, two homeless men talking:
"What's the point in pretending like I'm sane anymore?"

Overheard on Avenue D, two men talking, and I don't know what this means but it's scary as fuck:
"I don't take a life, I bury a soul."

[SNOOP DOGG]
SCENE 2

By the time I realized the situation I was in, it was too late because we were already on the highway in my cheap, well-dented Pontiac. The situation was this: Sixteen months ago, Tupac Shakur was killed in a drive-by shooting while in the passenger seat of a car. Ten months ago, Biggie Smalls was killed in a drive-by shooting. And one month ago, Snoop Dogg left Death Row Records, angering perhaps the most dangerous man in rap, the label's imprisoned president Suge Knight. So driving around Southern California with Snoop Dogg riding shotgun was, well, just stupid. Unless you *wanted* to die.

What label are you gonna find to put out this new record?
SNOOP DOGG: No label will want to put it out. That's why I've got to do it myself. If I get some distribution, I would take it. But this album right here is so on the edge that the average record label wouldn't want to put it out because of certain shit I say and the way I say it.

Snoop starts rolling another joint in his lap.

You're talking about that "Death Row Killa" song?
SNOOP DOGG: Mm-hmmm. (*Sings:*) Death Row, snitches wanna be gangstas / You niggas is bitches / Death Row, snitches wanna be gangstas / You niggas is bitches / Death Row killa / Death Row killa / Fuck all y'all.

He bends down until his head is almost in his knees, and surreptitiously lights the joint.

What do you mean by "snitches"?

SNOOP DOGG: I'm just knowing there are some snitches around Death Row. That's why there's niggas in jail. That's why there's niggas getting looked at real funny by the FBI. 'Cause niggas is telling on niggas. I don't give a fuck about niggas snitching on me because I ain't doing shit wrong. I smoke my chronic, what are you gonna do? Take me to jail for smoking chronic? I'm down to go to jail for that shit.*

What do you think's gonna happen once that song comes out?

SNOOP DOGG: I'm gonna make a whole lot of money off this album. I don't need them.

You're Death Row's biggest cash cow, so aren't they fighting or trying in some way to keep you from leaving the label?

SNOOP DOGG: They're not trying to take me to court and I'm putting out records right now without their permission, so they must know they can't beat me in court. But it ain't about that. It's about all I asked for is what I asked for, so let me move forward. Don't hold me down because you're locked up and you feel everything is against you. I'm not against you, homie. I just gotta take care of my family and Death Row can't provide for me right now.

What did you ask Death Row for?

SNOOP DOGG: A lot of shit. Man, I ain't never been accounted for. At all. As long as I've been rapping for Death Row Records, they never accounted for me. I never received statements on my money or none of that, man. They bought a nigga gifts and shit.

What gifts did they get you?

SNOOP DOGG: A Rolls-Royce, a penthouse suite on Wilshire, a motherfucking Hummer, gold chains, Rolex watches, diamond earrings, hotel suites, anything a nigga wanted. Anything to keep your mind off your money. They bought me this and bought me that instead of giving me my motherfucking money. [. . .]†

---

* Four years later, Snoop Dogg pleaded no contest to marijuana possession, and received a fine and a thirty-day suspended jail sentence.

† [. . .] denotes missing dialogue or a jump in time, generally because what occurred immediately afterward was boring, wordy, or off-topic, or because the theme was further explored in a different part of the interview. See the key on page 513 for a guide to symbols used in the interviews.

Didn't Death Row freeze your assets because of it?

SNOOP DOGG: Man, they haven't paid me since October. That's why I don't give a fuck about Death Row right now. I don't give a fuck about going on the record. I'll say it on TV and in public: "What y'all niggas gonna do to me? I made y'all. Nigga, I don't wanna wear your jacket no more. Y'all should just let me go. If you had let me go, I would have never said, 'Fuck Death Row.' But y'all don't even wanna let a nigga go. You wanna hold onto me like I'm a slave or some shit. This is 1998. This ain't 1898." [. . .]

When Dre left Death Row, did he ask you to go with him?

SNOOP DOGG: No, he didn't ask me to leave. He didn't say nothing. He just packed his bags and left. If he had asked me to leave, there would have been some violent shit, 'cause niggas will be niggas. But, I mean, I had fun and shit on Death Row, man. I can't say I didn't. I just hate that it ended like it did, man. I can truly say to all the little rappers coming up in the game: Money is a motherfucker and don't believe the color, know what I'm saying. You might see a black record label and be like, "I'm gonna sign with this label 'cause they ain't gonna be fucking me and the white labels just be fucking us." Man, niggas will fuck you over faster than white folks will.

So for all the young rappers coming in, get you some attorneys. Even if you ain't got no money, you gotta get attorneys so you can read over them contracts and know what you're signing so you won't be in the situation I'm in, where I gotta fight these niggas to get my shit back.

Pull over here, I wanna get some diapers.

Snoop leaves the car, and returns three minutes later carrying a bottle of barbecue sauce.

No luck?

SNOOP DOGG (*to the tape recorder*): I had a diaper run. Had to get some diapers for my baby. The store didn't have none; them motherfuckers was too small. We're just smoking on this motherfucking bomb-ass orange weed from my homeboy Chopper.

[*Continued . . .*]

[KENNY G
SCENE 1]

Kenny G was not merely on time for this interview: He was half an hour early, standing alone on the edge of a seaplane dock on Manhattan's East River, his hair tied back in a curly ponytail. At his feet lay a crumpled brown paper bag full of navigation maps he had bought for the journey we were about to take. Not just a light-jazz saxophonist but also a light-aircraft pilot, Kenny G ushered me into the cockpit of a seaplane and flew over the Statue of Liberty to Port Washington, Long Island for lunch.

Have you ever tried any drugs?
KENNY G: Oh, I'm not a drug user at all.

So you wouldn't just try them, even though you told me five minutes ago that you're the first guy to try anything new?
KENNY G: I'm not interested at all. I would only try something that's good for myself. No, I'm not. Not interested.

Not even tempted?
KENNY G: No. I mean, I go into one of those restaurants in Seattle and get one of those microbrewery beers on tap. After one of those, I'm happy. That's about all I can take. That's good enough for me. I don't think drugs are necessary. If you want to have an out-of-mind experience, there are a lot of different ways I think you could do it. If you sat by yourself on a mountaintop for two days, I think you'd be there. I know that's a little harder than taking a little shot of something and then you're high for a few hours.

So drugs are just lazy enlightenment then?
KENNY G: That's the perfect way of putting it. For me, if I want to get my spiritual stuff, it's flying my seaplane to some mountain lake, turning the engine off, and sitting there. That's awesome. I can't tell you what that feels like. You're totally alone and there's no one around. You're in a place where maybe a man wasn't supposed to be. Whew, it's so great.

Have you learned any important life lessons from other celebrities?
KENNY G: Do you mean about drugs?

[*Continued . . .*]

[CHRIS ROCK]
SCENE 1

Chris Rock sat alone in his room at the Ritz-Carlton in Philadelphia, where he was staying under the pseudonym Jimi Hendrix. CNN played silently on the television set. When a headline about investigators finding images of child pornography at Pee-wee Herman's house scrolled across the screen, Rock shook his head. "One of the funniest guys who ever lived," he sighed.

So many of your jokes and characters revolve around crack.
CHRIS ROCK: Basically, whatever was going on when you started getting laid will stick with you for the rest of your life. So crack was just a big part of my life, between my friends selling it or girls I used to like getting hooked on it. White people had the Internet; the ghetto had crack. It's weird, too. Crack and the VCR and the portable handheld camera—all this shit just came out at the same time.

And how are they connected for you?
ROCK: That whole being-able-to-tape-shit came out around the same time as crack. So you saw all these weird images of like guys' mothers blowing people on video for some crack. Or you go over to your friend's house and there's a porno tape of a girl you used to date blowing eight guys. That's crack.

I remember this rich kid from high school smoking crack in a cheap motel and hiring hookers off the street to smoke with him.
ROCK: That's crack too. I have never been to war, but I survived that shit. I lost friends and family members. The whole neighborhood was kind of on crack—especially living in Bed-Stuy [in Brooklyn], man.

And at the same time, in the end, what does this produce? Gangsta rap. This is one of the things that goes into the misogyny of rap. You see all these young guys with this weird distorted view of women because these women they used to hold on a pedestal are now doing all this nasty shit.

Especially in LA: It's the home of the groupies, so then it's also got to be the home of the normal guys getting left behind. So you combine that and crack, and you see a bunch of guys with real fucked-up views on women. That's how you get N.W.A. That's how you get a record like "A Bitch Iz A Bitch." That's how you get Tupac saying crazy shit on record.

So did you ever try it?
ROCK: The closest I ever got to doing crack was selling crack. Me and a friend of mine, we took these jobs at a camp just to get money. We were going to get paid a thousand or two thousand at the end of the summer, and then take that money and buy some crack to sell. But of course he got hooked on crack before we could go out and do it. And then right after that, God brought comedy into my life.

I wonder what would have happened if you'd started selling it?
ROCK: Who knows what would have happened? I would have been dumb to have done it. I'm not saying, "If it wasn't for comedy, I'd be selling crack." But I remember sitting with my friends, cutting up coke like it was yesterday: cocaine, lactose, vitamin B12. Cook it up—crack. I am so lucky I never tried crack. The most I did was put some coke on my tongue.

What gave you the strength and the resources to avoid it?
ROCK: I don't know if it was the strength and the resources. One of my brothers is an abuser of . . . things. So he kind of saved my life, by his example. People always get mad at athletes for getting high. I'm happy for every one. Dwight Gooden saved my life, Darryl Strawberry saved my life—because they always get punished. It's not like they get caught doing drugs and then they get a raise.

What did you mean earlier when you said that God brought comedy into your life?
ROCK: It's not even about bringing me into stand-up. It was just about getting me out of Brooklyn, especially at night. Brooklyn's fine during the day. But at night, man, I would probably have eventually tried some crack, just out of boredom.

[Continued . . .]

[PATRICK MILLER]

Patrick Miller was a legend, as far as I was concerned. Better known as Minimal Man, he was a pioneer of electronic and industrial music with at least six albums to his name, and had played with many legendary experimental and alternative musicians of the eighties.

But when I met him, he had fallen on hard times. He was living on the Upper West Side of Manhattan and, outside of the Dominican drug dealers in the neighborhood, I seemed to be the only person who visited his basement apartment.

I would stop by every other day and he would regale me with stories of punk, industrial, and new wave musicians.

On his wall, alongside prints by Bruce Nauman and Dennis Oppenheim, hung his own paintings. I recognized them from the covers of his albums, which I played regularly on my college radio show at the time. They were all variations on one image: a featureless head, usually wrapped in strips of bandages that were peeling off to reveal a discolored, decomposed face.

One afternoon during my junior year of college, I came by to accompany him to a rock-industry convention, the New Music Seminar. But after an hour of puttering around his house, he didn't seem to be any closer to leaving.

PATRICK MILLER: I want to find that guy from Play It Again Sam [Recordings] and make him pay me. You know, that's all the seminar is: musicians looking for record executives who owe them money.

Are you ready to go yet?
MILLER: I'm thinking of building a holding tank here.

For your cat?
MILLER: No, for drug dealers. . . . I feel like there are ants under my skin. I need to get high if I'm going to have to deal with this.

If you do that, we're never going to get out of here.

Miller walks into the kitchen and continues talking as he scrapes white powder out of a pot on his kitchen counter.

MILLER: For some reason, pharmacologists, doctors, and nurses are always attracted to my music. That's how I got started. They'd invite Minimal Man to play all these parties, and then feed us coke. (*Drops the powder into the end of a glass pipe.*) I invented Minimal Man as this wild person, and then I actualized it and took all kinds of drugs and stuff because I felt guilty for not living up to this fiction. For a while I was shooting an eightball a day. That's like a hundred shots. It got so crazy that I thought I'd take something to cool me off, so I got into heroin, thinking that it would help me free myself from drugs. Do you know how heroin works?

More or less.
MILLER: Your body is in pain every second of the day. Every molecule of air that is hitting it is causing a pain reaction. But because the body produces its own opi-

ates, it blocks the pain. So when you take heroin and get those opiates externally, your brain stops producing its own painkillers. That's why it's so hard to withdraw, because when you stop, you feel all the pain you never did before.

I try to distract him to keep him from smoking the crack he's heating in the pipe.

Ever heard of that band Lights in a Fat City?
MILLER: Shh.

He takes a deep drag off the pipe. Seconds after he exhales, his eyes start darting around, as if there's something hiding in the shadows of the room. He snatches a flashlight from his desk and turns it on, even though the lights in his house are already shining. He then begins scanning the room, looking for something, as he backs into a corner. Suddenly, he pulls a chair in front of him, crouches behind it, and grabs the book Rush *by Kim Wozencraft off his desk.*

MILLER: Is there a fly around? I can't stand flies. I'm prone to hallucinations. As soon as I see a little thing buzzing around in front of my eyes, forget it. Kill those fuckers.

He begins batting at the air with the book, as if invisible flies are trying to attack him. As he does this, I look up at one of his paintings—the bandaged, decomposed head that stares fearfully from his album covers—and realize: It's a self-portrait.

The following day, Miller sells the painting to me for forty dollars and checks himself into rehab. Several weeks later, he returns, clean-shaven, well-nourished, and wearing newly bought clothes. The first thing he does is buy the painting back from me. As for his paranoid reaction during our last encounter, he explains . . .

MILLER: I have a feeling I just staged that so we wouldn't go out.

After relapsing later that year, Miller moved near his family in Los Angeles to clean up. We remained friends until he died in 2003 of hepatitis C, a blood-borne disease that he most likely contracted from a used needle.

THE STROKES
SCENE 2

Dude, what are you doing? If you don't want to do this interview . . .
JULIAN CASABLANCAS: One day maybe I'll be able to communicate it better. But it's not where we're at right now. I just don't have anything deep to say. I'm trying to do it. I don't know.

I don't expect anything deep from you. I just want you to be yourself.
CASABLANCAS: I've got nothing to hide. But what I meant a few minutes ago, if I can even recall what I was saying, is just that there's so much shit to do and so little time. And everything I have to say is not going to be in this one *Rolling Stone* interview.

I hope not.
CASABLANCAS: There's a lot of stuff to do and it's going to be a long, hard road. If anything, it's just the beginning. And I'd like to get our foot in the door, and just get to a point where maybe we can say something that will be matterful. That's definitely not a word, by the way. And I look forward to the future, blah, blah, blah, blah. (*Stops the tape; I start it again.*) I mean, really, no one wants to hear what I have to say. No one cares.

Fine. Let's have a regular conversation, not an interview, and just leave the tape recorder running.
CASABLANCAS: Okay, here's the thing. It's not time yet. God, or whoever it is that controls things, is telling me not to say anything. People don't believe in us yet. They don't think we're serious or real or whatever. And I can't say anything until we've done something undeniable as a band.

Strokes manager Ryan Gentles enters the bar.

RYAN GENTLES: How's the interview going?

We've got seven minutes of tape so far.
GENTLES: Seven minutes is all you have? (*To Julian:*) You need to do this.
CASABLANCAS: What are you working for, me or *Rolling Stone*? It's like there's an angel on one shoulder and a devil on the other, and then a gay manager on my sleeve.

Your picture is going to be on the cover. Most people with pictures on the cover talk inside.

CASABLANCAS: You are a complainer. You've got enough. Work with what you've got. You're a professional. God bless America.

Casablancas picks up a bottle of beer, downs three quarters in one gulp, and slams it to the table. He mumbles something about RCA Records president Clive Davis speaking "like a gay chorus girl," stands up, and walks to the video game Golden Tee Golf. He turns around and addresses the bar.

CASABLANCAS: Anyone want to play Golden Tee?

When no one responds, he plays alone. Four minutes later, he returns to the table.

CASABLANCAS: Never play Golden Tee when you're drunk.

He then sits on my lap, kisses me seven times on the neck, and makes three lunges for my lips, connecting once. Before I can wipe dry, he is out the door, rolling himself home in an abandoned wheelchair he finds outside.

[Continued . . .]

[LEE GREENWOOD]

If you met the man who composed one of America's most patriotic songs, what would you ask him?

At halftime one Sunday at the Adelphia Coliseum in Nashville, Tennessee, country singer Lee Greenwood ran out to sing the anthem he had written eighteen years earlier, "God Bless the U.S.A." The stadium thundered with the sound of tens of thousands of voices singing along, "I'm proud to be an American."

As Greenwood trotted to the sidelines afterward, a photographer pulled an American flag out of his satchel and asked him to pose with it. "I don't want to seem cheap or disgrace the flag," Greenwood responded, declining. "I don't even sign them anymore."

Is there ever a moment when you don't feel proud to be an American?
LEE GREENWOOD: You mean that I don't believe the lyrics of my own song?

In the moment. Like if you sing "I love my wife" in a song, there might be a moment when you don't feel that.
GREENWOOD: No, I don't. I mean, we'll have arguments like everybody else, but very few and that's what keeps our union strong. But no, when I'm singing, I believe everything I sing.

What if there's a president who's not making decisions you agree with?
GREENWOOD: I don't . . . You know, the song first of all is not political. And I may not agree with a Democrat who's in office, but you know, if they ask me to sing at the White House, I'd sing in a heartbeat because he's the president. Anybody who has military service, I recognize and respect for what they've done.

Some people have criticized you for singing about how you'd defend America, but not serving in the Vietnam War.
GREENWOOD: When I went to join the service in the sixties, I had two children. And so I wasn't picked until they got to my number and it was too late. So that was the reason I didn't serve. But my father felt it necessary to join the war in 1943. I was a year old and my sister was three. At that time, I guess the government didn't consider it a threat or a liability if you had children. But when he joined the Navy, my mother never forgave him and divorced him because of it. So I think that's an issue for me.

So there must be something that bothers you about this country?
GREENWOOD: Inasmuch as . . . I guess it's capital punishment that bothers me. We don't want to be barbaric, but at the same time, it used to be an eye for an eye. You killed a person, and you went to jail or you went to the chair. Then you had to kill two or three people to go to the chair. And now it's mass murder. How many do you have to kill before you have to give up your life? It diminishes the value of one person's life. That's why our view on capital punishment, I think, weakens us in the eyes of other nations.

Then there are other countries who think we're barbaric for even having the death penalty.
GREENWOOD: Yeah, well, I like what the Marines say.

Which is?
GREENWOOD: "It's up to God to judge bin Laden. It's up to the Marines to make sure he keeps the appointment."

[MADONNA]
SCENE 2

After her television performance in Germany, Madonna sat on a couch in her dressing room, wearing a puffy silver jacket and matching boots, discussing the reasons she preferred living in the United Kingdom to America. "English people, they're not God-crazy like Americans are," she said. "If I became a born-again Christian, people in England wouldn't be comfortable with it, but people in America would." Suddenly, the members of Green Day, who'd also been flown in for the show, filed into the room and her demeanor changed.

Madonna has an unusual way of relating to strangers. She will ask questions—lots of questions. She will pay attention closely and ask good follow-up questions, yet you will get the uncomfortable feeling that she isn't so much listening as she is allowing you to speak. And so long as you are interesting or able to offer something she wants to learn, she will keep allowing you to talk. But as soon as she's gotten what she wants or her status as queen is threatened, she will turn ice cold.

"Do you have any kids?" she asked, peppering Green Day with questions.

"Have you ever seen *Napoleon Dynamite*?"

"What do you do for fun?"

"Do you like dancing?"

To this last question, Green Day singer and guitarist Billie Joe Armstrong replied that the only dance he knew was the "drunken sailor dance."

"What's that?" Madonna asked.

He stood up and demonstrated by slouching forward, letting his arms dangle, and swaying drunkenly from side to side. When a string of drool began dribbling out of his mouth, Madonna let him know that she got the point.

It was all fun and games until Madonna decided that it was time to fly back to London and one of the show's producers told her, "Green Day are going to have to leave before you." Instantly, her mood changed.

"Why?" she asked coldly. "We were supposed to leave first."

"Their cars are here, and yours are waiting elsewhere because you stayed backstage longer than you said you would," the producer explained.

"Well, I'll just fly back with them," she said, flustered.

"But they're taking a car to Frankfurt."

"Oh," Madonna replied, suddenly relieved, her status as queen restored. "We're in a helicopter."

Here's Madonna on life before she was queen . . .

MADONNA: When I first came to New York, I was a dancer for years, but I didn't know about nightlife. I had no friends. I didn't have a social scene or anything, and it was very lonely. It wasn't until I discovered clubs that things changed.

How did you first get introduced to the scene?
MADONNA: I just went by myself. I thought you had to get asked out to go to a club and that you couldn't dance unless someone asked you to dance with them. But I discovered in New York you could go out on your own and you could go to a club and you could dance by yourself. You didn't have to have an invitation, and to me that was really liberating.

So what was the first club you went to?
MADONNA: I was kind of a geek when I moved to New York, and I loved to read. You never know when you're going to get stuck in a room or on the subway with nothing to do—and I hate wasting time. So I always used to bring books everywhere in case it was going to be a drag or things got boring.

So the first club I ever went to was this club called Pete's Place. It was kind of like a restaurant-bar-disco. And all the lounge lizards were hanging out there. And everybody was so fucking cool. The guys all had forties suits on and porkpie hats. And the women were so glamorous: They all had red lipstick and black eyeliner and high heels. And I felt so dull. Because I was kind of embarrassed, I just sat in my corner and read my book.

What book was it?
MADONNA: It was an F. Scott Fitzgerald book, *Jazz Age Stories*. I was like, "Okay, I don't fit in. I don't know what to do with myself. I'm not dressed appropriately. There's nothing cool about me. I'm going to go read a book." So, yeah (*pauses*). Did you read *The Power of Now*?

No.
MADONNA: You haven't? How about *The Four Agreements*? I can only remember three of them: don't take things personally, always do your best, and be impeccable with your word. I love that one. I remember the fourth one was a repeat of the others, and I wasn't impressed with the fourth one.

The book editor probably thought the three agreements didn't sound as good for marketing.
MADONNA: Did you read that book?

No.
MADONNA: So you haven't read *The Power of Now* and you haven't read *The Four Agreements*. You must be really busy.

[CHRIS ROCK]
SCENE 2

When the news ends and a golf tournament begins, Chris Rock grabs the hotel television remote. "In case you say I was watching golf," he explains.

As Rock switches channels, he discusses the differences between comedians and rappers. "At the end of the day," he concludes, "comedy is some nerd shit."

CHRIS ROCK: I remember the last time I saw Tupac. It was after the MTV Video Music Awards. I had just done [the HBO comedy special] *Bring the Pain*. And at the last minute, MTV called me up to present. I wasn't quite big enough to host yet.

So I get up onstage, I present some award, I try a couple jokes, and then I see Suge Knight in the audience. I said, "Hey Suge, don't kill me."

And the audience laughs, right? There was that kind of tension. And later on, remember, they had the after-party at Bryant Park?

I'll never forget that party. Tupac was walking around with this parade of thugs who were carrying Death Row signs and posters. It was really aggressive.
ROCK: Yeah, it was a weird night. First, Eric B. comes up to me. He goes, "Yo, man, I don't know if you should have done that joke about Suge, man." He's like, "The spot is hot right now."

It was Eric B., man—the original thug life. Eric B. is from around my old way. Eric B. was driving a Rolls-Royce before he ever put out a record. That's all I've got to say. With rims. Nobody else was even talking about rims. My man was gangsta. And he's telling me this.

Then Hammer comes up and tells me the same thing. "Yo, man, don't mess with Suge." And Hammer is gangsta, man. Have you ever been around Hammer?

Are you serious? Hammer?
ROCK: Hammer ain't no punk, man. Hammer is more gangsta than all these guys. He rolls with the hardest crew, because it's a combination of jail guys and military

guys, because Hammer was in the Navy or some shit. When those motherfuckers rolled up, you fucking listened.

Then Tupac comes up to me. And he says, "Hey, man, that was kinda funny what you did." He shook my hand, and he had really clammy hands. Like he soaked them in Camay or some shit.

And he said, "I saw you on HBO, saying that 'niggas and black people' shit." He had half a smirk. I got the feeling that Pac was a minute away from punching me—or trying to punch me.

His voice had a tone of menace to it?
ROCK: Yeah, but because I roll by myself and I don't wear gold or nothing, it actually keeps me out of a lot of trouble. Whereas if I rolled like Eddie Murphy '88—if I had the shades and the leather and I had ten guys and a diamond ring over my gloves—I'd be getting into fights.

Literally three days after that MTV party, Tupac was shot.
ROCK: What's weird is, a week after that, I had to go to LA to do videos. And everywhere I went, people were like, "Yo, man, you shouldn't have said that shit about Suge." I've never seen people fear a guy so much in my life. It was like the whole world had become high school. And these were gangstas—not just punks like me.

That guy made some great records though. Suge Knight's name is on some of the best records ever.

I remember interviewing Snoop Dogg right after he left Death Row, and he had no bodyguards, no security, nothing.
ROCK: Maybe it was like the end of *Donnie Brasco*, where Al Pacino knows he's going to die. But he doesn't blink. He just takes off his watch and all his rings and he goes down to his death.

That may be. Snoop recorded these songs about how Suge Knight was responsible for Tupac's death. And he wasn't scared.
ROCK: The weirdest thing about being really successful is that you are kind of ready to die. Especially now that I've got kids. I mean, I want to live. Don't get me wrong. But I'm not in fear of dying. I've made my mark. Death is the enemy of my family—of my wife and my daughters. But to me as an artist, it's actually my friend.

(*Looks at tape deck.*) It better be working. You're getting some good shit.

[SNOOP DOGG]
SCENE 3

SNOOP DOGG: I heard what Suge said about me in *The Source* magazine. What'd he say, that Tupac didn't like me or something?

No, he said that you and Tupac had a falling out after the MTV Video Music Awards.
SNOOP DOGG: Yeah, we had a falling out because I didn't feel it was right for him to bring everybody involved into his feud. If he had a problem with Biggie Smalls or Puffy Combs, he was a grown man. He should have been able to handle that shit on his own. Don't bring all of us into some shit that you can handle on your own. From what I was looking at, them boys didn't want no problem. Puffy and Biggie never said, "Fuck Tupac, fuck Death Row, bring it on." They always was like, "We wanna be peace, we wanna make it happen." And I'm a grown man. If a motherfucker don't wanna quarrel with me or don't wanna shoot-out with me, why am I gonna force the issue? All I'll say is this: Gangstas don't talk, they take care of their business.
   Watch that left turn right there.

What happened to your relationship with Tupac after that?
SNOOP DOGG: We didn't speak after he left New York. But I went to see him when he was in the hospital all shot up, because I had love for that nigga and I love him to death to this day. I look at myself as a real friend: A real friend is gonna tell you the motherfucking truth. There's certain shit that Pac told me that hurt my feelings and made me mad, but I loved him for it because he was real and he told me the motherfucking truth. And Suge Knight can't speak on me and Pac, because our relationship was genuine, the same way his and Pac's was. Like I can't speak on how he had Tupac in the car with him doing stupid-ass gangbang shit in Vegas. That's on him. That's their relationship. If he had been with me, he probably would have been playing a video game, smoking on some weed, and fucking a bitch or something. Doing all that stupid-ass Mafioso shit—stupid shit.

Do you think it would have been better for Tupac if he was never on the label?
SNOOP DOGG: He probably should have just did songs with us and been down with us but not been signed to us, because the influence was too much. You become too infatuated with it.

Snoop Dogg

SMOKE  SHACK

FULLY STATE LICENSED MARIJUANA CLINIC

FREE MEDICAL EVALUATIONS

DOCTOR ONSITE ★ RECEIVE SAME DAY PRESCRIPTION

OPEN MON – FRI

1PM-11PM

SAT – SUN

3PM-12AM

75¢

SPECIAL

15519 CRENSHAW BLVD., SUITE 187

Bust a left. If I go in here, I'll have to sign eight thousand motherfucking autographs and take eighteen pictures.

We pull into a grocery store parking lot, and Snoop sends me inside to buy Pampers while he waits in the car. Afterward, we return to Snoop's studio.

What happened to the famous armored van you got to protect yourself?
SNOOP DOGG: It used to be on the side of my house, but I got rid of it. My armored van is God, man. He gonna get me through everything. 'Cause if he ready for me to go, that armored van can't do shit. I could be getting out of the armored van and get blown the fuck up.

People think that now you're living behind barred windows, surrounded by armed security guards—
SNOOP DOGG: Man, you're here. When you pulled up this morning, I let you in. When we went to the store, it was just me and you. Man, I'm chilling. Niggas know where I'm at. I ain't bringing no problems to nobody. If you say something about me, I'm gonna say something about you. If you steal on me, I'm gonna steal on you. If you jack me, I'm gonna jack you back. That's just the way I do it. I'm defensive, man. I'm not offensive no more. I'm not the type to go out there and just beat up a nigga for nothing. I'm just kicking back watching to see what you're trying to do to me.

Snoop rails against Suge Knight and Death Row for another hour, makes sure I have the cassette with his new songs, then lets me leave. On the way home, I notice that Snoop's Pampers are still in the backseat of the car, along with his bottle of barbecue sauce. I drive back and leave them in front of his door.

[*Continued . . .*]

[JOHNNY CASH]
SCENE 2

I wanted to ask what you thought of gangsta rap.
JOHNNY CASH: You know, I don't know. I was about just coming onto the music scene when they wouldn't shoot Elvis Presley below the hips on *The Ed Sullivan Show*. And I was working with Elvis when all these older people were saying that he's leading our kids to hell. I thought that was the strangest thing I'd ever heard. I was born in the Bible Belt and raised up in it. And Elvis is such a good person

and loved gospel music, a Christian. And that hurt him. And I thought it was just terrible that people would say things like that about him. Then all the rock artists that came along, they said that about them, too. But it doesn't bother me. Maybe gangsta rap does have some influence on young people, but damn, I think the six o'clock news is probably the most violent thing we hear today.

The reason I was asking was because a lot of people point to your lyric, "I shot a man in Reno just to watch him die"—
CASH: Fantasy.

Yeah, and they point to it as the first gangsta rap lyric.
CASH: It's a reflection of (*coughs*) the society that we're living in, just like the movie *Natural Born Killers*. It's grossly overstated and the most violent thing I have ever seen, but I couldn't walk out of the movie because it's so riveting. And it's throwing our violence right back at our face. You look at what's going on in this country as far as crime: It's hypocrisy to blame somebody for some violence because of a song lyric. I don't know if that's right. I wrote, "I shot a man in Reno just to watch him die," over forty years ago and I don't know of anybody that's gone out and done that just because I sang about it.

I was wondering, only because you deal a lot with it in your music, has your relationship with God changed over those forty years?
CASH: I think it's stronger than ever. You know, there were times when I was taking prescription drugs and was addicted. My addiction was really flowering and, um, I put God way back on the back burner. 'Cause with taking drugs, I had an awful, awful big ego. And you think you're invincible and bulletproof. I was always a believer, but during those times I just didn't bother to give God the credit for anything, or to really try to live the way I know I have to live to survive. I just thought I was invincible—until I bottomed out again. And every time I bottomed out, I realized how far away from God I'd been. So I started walking the walk again and trying my best as best I know how.

And how do you do that?
CASH: Now we have a minister of the gospel traveling with our show. He goes with us everywhere we go. He keeps me off the streets and counsels everybody on the show who might have a problem, no matter what it is, whether it's a spiritual problem, personal problem, family, marriage, drug, alcohol, whatever.

When I introduce him at the end of the show as being part of our group, he always sticks around to talk to anybody who might want to come see him about various problems they might have in their life. He's a recovering drug addict and alcoholic as well as a minister. He's always just a few rooms down the hall in case we need to talk to him. He keeps me centered and focused, you know.

For—
CASH: For survival.

Why do you think it is that people are most attracted to your darker songs, by seeing the beast in the cage, as you put it?
CASH: I mean, these themes are eternal. Most everybody goes through that once in their life, at least. "Delia's Gone" is a, you know, a folk song.

Though you rewrote some of the lyrics . . .
CASH: Well, one of the verses is original. Like, (*sings*) "First time I shot her / I shot her in the side / Hard to watch her suffer / But with the second shot she died." The American musical culture is steeped in songs of violence and murder. Disaster, train wrecks, floods, cyclones. Um, but then there's the spiritual, gospel side of the albums, too. That is so much a part of me: You know, gratitude and thanks and praise for life itself.

In 2003, Johnny Cash died of complications from diabetes. He was seventy-one.

KENNY G
SCENE 2

As Kenny G chattered happily during lunch, wearing a black leather jacket and an off-white turtleneck sweater, I realized that he was no less credible than the more dissonant jazz artists I admired. Like them, he plays what he feels. And perhaps if everybody were as gentle, pleasant, and meek as Kenny G, the world would be a much better place. Though the radio would suck.

Do you ever lose your temper or get in a bad mood?
KENNY G: Well, I was a little bit less than my, uh, jovial self yesterday, because I knew that I had to do something I really didn't want to do. I'm so spoiled. I pretty much do what I want to do when I want to do it. So when I have to do something I really don't want to do, I get a little bit, uh, not so happy.

What did you have to do?
KENNY G: The last thing I wanted to do yesterday was fly to New York and wake up at six in the morning to do *Regis*. I was playing with my son in the morning,

and I told him I had to go upstairs and pack to go to New York. He said, "Dad, why do you have to go there?" I said, "Because it's my job." He asked what my job was, and I had to think about it. I told him, "My job is to play the saxophone." He said, "Well, then, what's my job?" I told him, "To learn as much as you can and to be happy. That's your job."

That's great advice.
KENNY G: The biggest thing I could give to somebody is my respect. Love as well. But respect even more. Love you can just kind of get . . . I don't know.

Maybe love comes after respect. You have to respect someone to love them.
KENNY G: If you want to sustain the love, you have to sustain the respect to keep the love. If you lose the respect, the love's going to start to fall. That's it. Respect first, love next. But you have to keep the respect to keep the love.

That sounds about right.
KENNY G: Hey, Neil, you and I should write a book: *Love and Respect*. It could work. We'll go on a book tour. And inside the book will be like a scratch-and-listen. You scratch it and you hear a little saxophone playing. But we'd have to change our names. It can't be like Strauss and Gorelick. It's got to be like Deepak Chopra. Something mystical.

I like Strauss and Gorelick.
KENNY G: Strauss and Gorelick sound like doctors. "Dr. Gorelick, Dr. Strauss, you're wanted in surgery at six in the morning."

[THE STROKES]
SCENE 3

The following evening, Julian Casablancas called and promised to sit still for a normal interview. An hour later, he was waiting obediently at the Gramercy Cafe. You know what he was wearing; only the smell had changed.

JULIAN CASABLANCAS: I promise not to touch your tape deck.

Okay, I just want to ask a couple questions and make sure I got everything.
CASABLANCAS: It's no problem, man. I don't mind. I mean, I didn't want to not talk to you last night.

I know. I felt like you were putting too much pressure on yourself to say something interesting.
CASABLANCAS: I knew that I was . . . I was going to say something I was going to regret.

I appreciate you doing this again, because I know you hate interviews as it is.
CASABLANCAS: I don't hate doing them. I just get to the point sometimes where I feel like what I say never comes across. I just need to practice more. I don't know if it was because the tape was on, but I acted differently.

I was pretty discouraged after last night.
CASABLANCAS: I was so hungover. I mean, more than the night we fucking hung out until ten in the morning. Days and days of just fatigue. I was like, "The goal is just, like, don't die." I felt terrible. Oh God, all this bad news from [our record label] RCA, and we were just overworked.

Yeah, you were pretty wiped out that night. You were saying—
CASABLANCAS: I was saying what's the point of doing interviews when . . .

. . . you haven't done anything undeniable yet.
CASABLANCAS: Uh-huh. I just feel like it would be nice if people thought, "Wow, this is something really special," and then learned about the band from there instead of reading about a guy they've never heard of talking about all this fucking crazy, intense, over-the-top stuff. I was always bad at selling the band, you know.

You're not expected to, though.
CASABLANCAS: I still can't believe that you're doing a cover story on us. I'm still waiting for someone to say like, "April Fools." I'm sure a lot of people are going to be looking at *Rolling Stone* like, "Who the hell are these guys?"

Didn't you tell me one night that you used to practice *Rolling Stone* interviews in the shower?
CASABLANCAS: It was more like a grand monologue. It was never, you know, like, "So how is the pressure?" "What happened in Hawaii?" Because no one is listening, your mind is a lot better than it is when you're being interviewed in front of someone.

So what *was* your stock answer to the Nigel Godrich question?
CASABLANCAS: Yeah, it makes me nauseous explaining. It's not even good. It's like a run-on sentence, with little reference parts to lead to the next part. So . . . yeah, we just work differently. We got along great. All our parts need, you know, specific personalities, and the band comes in, plays live, and then he does his thing. And so we try to do it more hands off, blah, blah, blah, and that kind of thing.

That's it?
CASABLANCAS: I said it in the wrong order. I started with the working differently thing and I should have ended with it. And the whole thing is just a run-on sentence.

Do you mind if I go outside for two seconds to smoke a cigarette?

*A few minutes later, he stumbles back. The conversation turns to his drinking problem . . .***

When your girlfriend left you and people didn't want to be around you anymore because of the drinking, did it affect you at all?
CASABLANCAS: Yeah, definitely, especially when you are hungover. It's just weird, because you get this built-up stuff and it comes out when you're drunk. And you think afterward, "Yeah, maybe I was an asshole, but I said what was on my mind and that's what they hated about it." I would like my friends to be happy, but then, obviously, I'm like drunk and being very aggressive, so it probably makes them feel that . . . Yeah, it's not cool. You can't act like that on a consistent basis.

When was the first time you got fucked up?
CASABLANCAS: The first time was probably when I was ten and there was a dinner party. There were drinks on the table and I think I just downed all the drinks, and I was like, "Whoa. What the hell is this? This is great." My body immediately enjoyed it. It was like, "Life is actually fucking amazing in every single way."

After nearly three hours of talking . . .

If you had kids, would you want them to be musicians?
CASABLANCAS: If you're a musician, probably the fear is that your kid is going to be a shitty musician. Like if you're Bob Dylan: I can imagine him coming in and

---

* Ozzy Osbourne on alcoholism, from a press conference at his home: "I'll tell you what my drinking problem is: I've only got one mouth."

saying, "Turn that music down." And his son says, "No, you don't understand my music, Dad." And he says, "Yeah, I do. I'm Bob Dylan, and it's shitty."

My phone rings.

Hello?
ALBERT HAMMOND [**Strokes guitarist**]: It's Albert. Is Julian there?

Yeah. He doesn't have his own phone?
HAMMOND: No. I'm at the video store. Can you just ask him if he wants to watch *Fletch* tonight?

[PINK]

Here's a simple law of pop physics: An interview with Pink is as good as the number of Corona Lights she drinks.

PINK AFTER BEER ONE: "I always get nervous before interviews, because I don't think you should have to be interesting to make music."

PINK AFTER BEER TWO: "I used to think that they should pass out ecstasy in school lunchrooms so we'd actually learn some useful things. President Bush should try some ecstasy, that's for damn sure."

PINK AFTER BEER THREE: "[Producer] Linda Perry had heard of me, but she didn't get me. Of course, I didn't really get me either. Nobody does." (*She drops a piece of popcorn she's eating on her thigh. Then she bends down, positions her lips over her thigh, and sucks the stray piece of popcorn into her mouth like a vacuum cleaner.*)

PINK AFTER BEER FOUR: "I change my mind so much I need two boyfriends and a girl. I need an East Coast guy, a West Coast guy, and a girl."

PINK AFTER BEER FIVE: "Take your shoes off!" she orders me. "I want to lick your toes!"

PINK AFTER BEER SIX: "I realize that you can do a lot more on drugs than you can do sober." (*Janis Joplin's version of "Me and Bobby McGee" comes on the jukebox and she leaps up, strikes a rock pose on the sawdust-covered floor, and struts across the bar, belting the entire tune at the top of her lungs in front of a dozen befuddled patrons.)*

[SNOOP DOGG]
SCENE 4

The month our interview appeared on the cover of *The Source* magazine, Snoop Dogg emerged onstage during a concert by the rapper Master P, wearing the uniform and shouting the slogans of Master P's Louisiana record label No Limit. Evidently, he'd found a new home for his music—and a new mentor.

When I returned to his house for a follow-up article, a completely different Snoop greeted me at the door, wearing a gray hooded sweatshirt and a gold No Limit medallion studded with diamonds.

SNOOP DOGG: It's li'l head Neil! You wanna beer, Neil?

Sure, thanks.
SNOOP DOGG: They was tripping off that interview we did in *The Source*. Motherfuckers be tripping off that shit.

Oh shit, did you get in trouble over it?
SNOOP DOGG: I got a good response, but motherfuckers was tripping off why I was so mad. They had never seen me so mad before. The shit you brought across was good because you had me explain the ins and outs as to why the nigga was mad and whatnot. Some motherfuckers were mad and didn't like what I said, but they'll learn, they'll live, they'll forget. It's all part of life.

You seem like yourself again. What made you go from being angry to being at peace?
SNOOP DOGG: It's a part of growing up, getting strong mentally and physically, and getting my shit all the way together with where I have a faith in God and God makes everything happen. He put me in that situation with Death Row and he took me out of it. All I gotta say is that it was fun. It was all love. I enjoyed it and I wouldn't trade it for nothing in the world. It's like a marriage. When the divorce comes, you're mad. But after the divorce, you still love them. You can't stand to see anybody else with them, but you gotta accept it.

So you're cool with it now that you're in a new relationship?
SNOOP DOGG: That's what it's like.

The phone rings. Shante, his wife of one year, answers it and speaks to two No Limit rappers, who tell her they're flying in from Oakland that night to crash at Snoop's house.

So did you go to No Limit or did they approach you?
SNOOP DOGG: I did. Wanna go in the studio? Bring that beer with you. (*Walks in the studio, where four producers are smoking a blunt and playing a Madden football video game.*) Man, that shit smells good. Can I hit that shit? Goddamn, let me hit some. (*Sings:*) Let me hit some.

Come on over here, li'l head Neil. Whose drink was that, Goldie's? You want some chicken I made?

Sure.
SNOOP DOGG: My studio done got fresh. (*Walks out and brings back a drumstick.*) Can I get another hit off that blunt?

Last time we talked, you said you'd release your music independently unless a label was willing to give you fifty percent of everything you make. Did you get it from Master P?
SNOOP DOGG: I'm signing, ain't I?

That doesn't mean you got it.
SNOOP DOGG: Master P treats me good. It's not about fifty percent. It's about treating me like I'm supposed to be treated, putting me on the level of a superstar, promoting my shit and making people anticipate it. And putting me back in a position where in my heart and my mind I feel like I'm the best rapper in the world and can't nobody touch me. That confidence that he gave me is something no other label could have given me.

What does it take to give you that confidence?
SNOOP DOGG: Wisdom. Respect and wisdom.

Respect, wisdom, and publishing?
SNOOP DOGG: Especially publishing.

In what ways has Master P helped you?
SNOOP DOGG: In every way. The most important way was mental. I was lost. I was basically crazy out here: on my own, no support, me for me. I felt like the label left

me for dead. I was angry at Suge, because he was all my inspiration and I didn't have him. And everybody was going, "It's him. He's the one." And I was like, "Oh shit, it is him." But I look at the situation now, it wasn't him. He was there for me; it's me. That's why I'd like to holler at him so we can have a face-to-face and I can tell him what I need to tell him to his face like a man. Hopefully through these interviews, he'll see what demeanor I'm on and read through the lines and see that I didn't really mean what I said, but I said what I meant.

Are you worried at all that Master P will do the same things Suge did?
SNOOP DOGG: Master P saved me. I was broke, like couldn't-pay-my-bills broke. He's a motherfucking genius and I love him, because I realize he loves me. It's a cold expression, but love is a motherfucker. A lot of motherfuckers can say they love you, but they only love what you do for them. To love a motherfucker is to love him uncut. (*To the producers:*) What's up? Can the weed spend some more time on this side of the world? Boy, you all sure got it locked up on that side.

Did Master P meet with Suge to get you off the label?
SNOOP DOGG: I don't know and I'm really not concerned. I just know that it's official. I'm a No Limit soldier, and it's the start of a new generation.*

Who's managing you now?
SNOOP DOGG: I'm managing myself.

What happened to all those songs you played me at your house?
SNOOP DOGG: I didn't even put that shit on my album. All that shit has gone down the drain because I was on a bad vibe then. I had a lot of anger in my person. Me and P thought it would be best not to come from that vibe, just come all the way new. I don't have no personal thing against nobody at Death Row. It was more me not knowing or taking time to learn the business. It wasn't anybody's fault but my own, so I'm not angry at anybody over there. I don't have no grudges, no attitude.

Good thing I didn't leak them.
SNOOP DOGG: Why didn't you?

---

* Four years after this interview, Snoop Dogg left No Limit Records. The following year, No Limit filed for bankruptcy.

I didn't want to get involved in whatever was going on between you and Suge.
SNOOP DOGG: I'm glad I did those songs though. It was really good for me to just get it off my chest because I wanted to talk to somebody. I didn't have nobody to talk to. So I was talking to the music.

Did you hear that [alleged Tupac killer] Orlando Anderson was shot?
SNOOP DOGG: Yeah, I heard.

Think it was connected to Tupac?
SNOOP DOGG: Don't know, don't care, don't wanna know.

Did that night at the Universal Amphitheatre have anything to do with your attitude toward all this now? *
SNOOP DOGG: That night was a crazy night, and I forgot about it really (*laughs awkwardly*).

I heard someone from Death Row warned you not to talk about it anymore.
SNOOP DOGG: I can't speak to that, but I'm here at the house doing an interview with you.

Did Master P have to teach you how to say "uhh" † **in order to record for him?**
SNOOP DOGG: No, he didn't teach me that. He can't sell me that. I taught him how to say "bi-atch."

Can you teach me?
SNOOP DOGG: I can teach you how to say, "Woof motherfucker, woof motherfucker, bow wow wow yippie yo yippie yay."

You've improved your old hook.
SNOOP DOGG: I'm back, I'm back. (*Puff puff.*) That's some good shit here, man.

[CURTAIN]

---

* A business associate of Suge Knight's had told me that after a Master P show at Universal Amphitheatre, one of Knight's henchmen slapped Snoop and warned him to keep his mouth shut. When Snoop went to the police, they smelled marijuana and arrested him. The source said that the detainment was a way of saving Snoop's life.
† Ref. "Make 'Em Say Uhh!," largely forgotten Master P song, *Billboard* #16 single, 1998.

[ACT TWO]

OR

FLYING SAUCERS, ZOMBIE SLAVES, and AUTOPSIES on the THIRD STAGE

SYNOPSIS

Enter Russell Targ from the CIA, who has something mysterious in his pocket, which is used to trick Britney Spears into a psychic experiment, which doesn't faze a guy known only as "?" because he insists he's from Mars and totally sane, which Ben Stiller also claims, despite acting cagey about being in therapy, something Bruce Springsteen readily admits to and Lady Gaga says will destroy her, &c.

[PSYCHIC SPIES]
SCENE 1

Russell Targ is by all appearances a stereotypical nerd genius, with pants pulled past his belly button, mop-like gray curls, thick black-framed glasses, and a high, pinched voice. In the 1950s, he made his reputation by helping to develop the laser. But in 1972, his life took a turn for the surreal when he and another physicist found themselves with a contract from the CIA. For the next two decades, he was at the forefront of one of the strangest chapters of the Cold War: psychic espionage.

This is not a conspiracy theory, like the rumor that the military covered up a UFO crash in Roswell, New Mexico. This is actual fact: For twenty-three years, the U.S. government funded the research and development of teams of psychic spies trained in a type of ESP known as remote viewing, in which, with pen, paper, and brain, they attempted to tune into events taking place in locations and times outside ordinary sensory perception.

These spies claim to have psychically penetrated Russian nuclear laboratories, visited hostages in the American embassy in Tehran, and scoured the globe for secret terrorist camps. Asked after his presidency about unusual events during his term, Jimmy Carter recalled an incident in which a psychic in the program found the location of a downed Russian spy plane.

Sitting with Targ in, of all places, a casino in Las Vegas, I began interviewing him about the program, with a healthy dose of skepticism. But then, suddenly, he asked . . .

RUSSELL TARG: Have you ever done any types of psychic things?

I'm not sure. I don't think so.
TARG: I can try to show you something psychic. You'll need to use your pen and your notebook.

What do I have to do?
TARG: I have an object in my pocket. It's not an ordinary kind of thing that you would find in your pocket. And what I'm inviting you to do is try and describe the shapes that come to mind. But don't try and guess my object.

I don't know. Maybe it's a little loud for this?
TARG: If you were going to draw a shape associated with this object, what would you draw? (*I draw an uneven circle on the paper.*) Now what words do you associate with that object?

Uneven shape? Lustrous in parts?
TARG: Good. Take a breath.

I'm probably thinking too hard, right?
TARG: I just want you to get back into that mood. If you go back to that object that you saw, what else comes to view?

Um, parts are gray or black. And maybe it's rough on the outside.
TARG: You can write all that down. You are in contact with the object. Now you just want to draw the object that I'm about to show you.

Should I try to put my mind inside your pocket or just let it come to me?
TARG: Just let it come to you. You can look into your immediate future, because I'm about to lay this in front of you. (*I put the pen to the paper and let my hand relax. I start to sketch a circle, but at the bottom left, for some reason, I draw a small shape jutting out of its side.*) What did you just draw here?

I felt there was something protruding on one side of it.
TARG: Did you look at the thing in your hand? What did it look like?

Shiny.
TARG: You can write that down.

You probably have, like, a wallet or a pencil in your pocket.
TARG: Now tell me, without naming the object, what is the overriding property? Without naming the object, what are the recurring things you're experiencing?

Well, I feel like there's a circle with something poking out of one side. And I still feel like it's lustrous in parts but not all of it.
TARG: Well, that's all entirely correct. Would you like to see the object?

There's one more thing I want to write down. I feel like maybe it's a tool. I don't know. Maybe I'm going too far.
TARG: What made you think that? What did you experience?

Because when I thought it had a protrusion on it, I made an inference that it would be a handle for an object that has some sort of practical use.
TARG: You can write that down if you want to. I think that's excellent. Not ideal conditions here. Are you ready to see it?

He pulls a round black object out of his pocket, with something jutting out of the side, and places it next to my sketch. It matches perfectly. The object is a magnifying glass in a black, round, rough-surfaced case with a small protruding handle used to pull the shiny magnifying lens out.

How did you do that?
TARG: I have a background of thirty years in physics. So I wouldn't be doing something that didn't actually work.

So what's the secret?
TARG: The secret is that there isn't really any secret. It's an ability we all have.

A friend of mine was videotaping the interview, and we later showed it to a professional illusionist named Franz Harary to see if there was any magic trick involved.

FRANZ HARARY: With the experience you just showed me, there is no way magic could be involved.

Maybe Harary was protecting trade secrets. Maybe he didn't know this particular trick. Maybe I just got lucky. Or maybe . . .

[*Continued . . .*]

[BRITNEY SPEARS]
SCENE 1

Shortly after my experience with Russell Targ, I was interviewing Britney Spears. As recounted in *The Game*, the interview was going nowhere. Each question received a short, indifferent response. So I decided to do something I still feel bad about: trick her.

I told her about remote viewing, then asked her to think of someone she knew. I explained that I would guess the initials, and then proceeded to do a mind-reading illusion I learned while researching *The Game*. Of course, I messed it up. The following is a more complete transcript of the scene summarized in the book.

BRITNEY SPEARS: If you get this, I'm going to shit.

What was the person's initials?
SPEARS: G. C.

Okay, turn over the paper.
SPEARS: C. C.! That's weird. That's really close. I can't believe you did that!

Eighty percent of the time I can nail it if someone's open.
SPEARS: I probably have so many walls in front, so that's why you didn't get them both. Let's try it one more time.

This time, why don't you try it?
SPEARS: I'm scared. I can't do that.

I tell her I'm going to write down a number between one and ten, and she has to psychically guess what it is. On a piece of paper, I write "7," which is the number people guess most of the time, and hand it to her face down.

Now tell me the first number that you feel.
SPEARS: What if it's wrong? It's probably wrong.

What do you think it is?
SPEARS: Seven.

Seven? Okay, now turn over the paper.
SPEARS: Maybe I chose too fast. (*She slowly turns over the paper, then screams when she sees that the number is seven.*) How did I do that? (*She jumps off the couch, runs to the hotel mirror, and looks at herself in it.*) Oh my God, I did that!

That's amazing.
SPEARS: Whoa, I did that! (*Returns to the couch, still excited.*) I just knew that it was seven! Oh my God, I can't believe I just did that. That's weird.

See, you already know all the answers inside. It's just that society trains you to think too much.
SPEARS: You already know the . . . Oh my God. Cool interview! I like this interview! This has been the best interview of my life. This is cool. (*Fans herself to calm down.*) Can we stop the tape recorder?

I turn off the tape recorder, and she talks about psychology, spirituality, writing, and escaping her family. When I turn it on again, a much better interview ensues.

SPEARS: I'm writing a book right now.

What's it about?
SPEARS: I don't want to say because I want to come out and whatever . . . But it's like I'm going inside myself like I've never gone before. It's really kind of cool. And I never thought that I would just pick up a pen and start writing. I didn't think I would do that. But something is happening and I can't stop.

It's hard to write about yourself.
SPEARS: It is weird writing about yourself. But I'm not writing about myself. I'm looking at the bigger picture. I want people to read this and not think of Britney Spears when they read it. And I'm really opening up with it. Like you know when you read *Conversations with God* and it's like this channel that's going through him, but it's not about him. It's just like about the bigger things. That's what this is.

I know exactly what you're talking about.*
SPEARS: Because I don't like stuff about me. I could never do an autobiography about my life. I think that's so lame and cheesy and self-serving. But this thing I'm writing is just like trying to help people.

---

* I don't.

A year later, Spears scrapped her idea for a self-help book and asked me to write her
autobiography with her. That book didn't happen either.

[*Continued . . .*]

[? AND THE MYSTERIANS]

When it comes to one-hit wonders, the group ? and the Mysterians (pronounced
Question Mark and the Mysterians) stands at the head of the pack. In 1966, the
band's first single, "96 Tears," came out of nowhere and topped the charts. The
organ-drenched song is not only still played on the radio today, but is renowned as
a garage rock classic and an important precursor of punk rock. Before this interview, all I knew about the artist known as ? was that he was a skinny, leather-clad
Mexican-American who had supposedly never removed his sunglasses since the
sixties.

You said you originally wanted to be a dancer, so how'd you end up becoming
a singer?
?: The first time was in Flint, Michigan. I asked if I could sing a song after one of
my dance routines. Then my parents got me a tape recorder, and I started singing
songs like "96 Tears" into it when I was ten.

You composed it when you were ten years old?
?: Yes, and then I wanted to learn to play an instrument so I could make the music in
my head come alive. I went to the music store, and this girl said that her dad knew
how to play piano and could teach me. So I went to the nice side of town. I thought,
"This is what it must be like to be rich." Everyone wondered what I was doing there.

I asked her dad, "Could you teach me how to play the music in my head?" He
said, "You got to go to the beginning with 'Mary Had a Little Lamb.'" And I said,
"I ain't got no time for that." I sang "96 Tears" for him, and he played it. But then
he said the lessons would cost ten dollars a week, so I knew I wasn't going back
there. In the back of my head, I said, "Forget it."

But eventually you formed your own band?
?: Yeah, we recorded with no headphones, no acoustics, no separation—just a two-
track machine. We recorded "96 Tears," then made up the B-side. I had remembered a lot of the words I'd written, but I'd forgotten some of them, too. Eight
months later, it was number one.

How did you end up getting signed?
?: I needed a record label, so I went with Cameo Records because their records were orange and it's my favorite color. If I had known the Beatles were on Capitol when they approached me or Elvis was on RCA, I would have gone with them. And then I got mad and felt like getting off the label when our record came out and it wasn't orange.

What do you think of the term garage rock?
?: It was just rock and roll. After "96 Tears," rock and roll died. Hendrix and everyone were great musicians, but they weren't playing rock and roll. They called it rock. So what happened to rock and roll? I call our music the new age of rock and roll. I got ESP, too. I don't use it all the time, though.

As in extrasensory perception?
?: Yeah, at first the press said I was a gimmick, but how can I be? I'm a real person. I was born on Mars many eons ago. I was around when dinosaurs were around. I've always had dreams of T. rex chasing me, and he got me. I discovered this week that they just found footprints from when the dinosaurs were around and they weren't ape footprints. I said, "See, I told you I was around then. We hid so we wouldn't get eaten." Since then, I've lived many different lives. And even though I was born on Mars, I'm not an alien. I hate when people call it Mars, because it's not really Mars anyway.

What is it then?
?: It's just a planet, do you know what I'm saying. It's part of the universe. That's man's ignorance: They have to label everything. They have to call us Martians just like they call the blacks niggers. Who is mankind to do that just because they feel more superior?

Why do you never remove your sunglasses?
?: I never take my sunglasses off. Somebody instilled that in me, gave me that power and ability to have that. I have so much knowledge. When I return in another lifeform, I may be a tennis player or a basketball player because I'm very athletic today.

How do you know you're going to be reincarnated as a human?
?: Well, I myself am going to come back in the year ten thousand and I'm going to be singing "96 Tears." And people will know it's me in this other body.

How will they know?

?: Because I will say a unique phrase that no one in history has said before. And I've only told it to a few people. But for right now, I'm just going to rock and roll.

Can you tell me the phrase?

?: No.

[BEN STILLER]
SCENE 1

It took a lot of work to get Ben Stiller to agree to an interview. He was worried that he'd be portrayed as neurotic, like the character he plays in the movie he was promoting at the time, *Greenberg*. And he was upset that Alec Baldwin was rumored to be on the cover of *Rolling Stone* instead of him. After several weeks of negotiations with Stiller's publicist, I finally met him in the entranceway to the International Center of Photography in Manhattan. He was slumped in a black overcoat, with unkempt hair and a wiry gray goatee growing uncomfortably on his chin. A far cry from the outgoing, extroverted characters he usually plays on screen, in conversation he was guarded, as if imagining how every word was going to be used against him.

Your publicist called and said you were worried that all we'd talk about is whether you're as neurotic as the character you play in *Greenberg*. Don't you think that would actually make you seem that neurotic?

BEN STILLER: Yes, but I didn't know that happened, though I take responsibility for it as a person who has a publicist. I honestly didn't. A lot of times, publicists do things like that.

I looked at your top Google searches, and one of the top searches is "Ben Stiller bipolar."

STILLER: I said it once to a writer in jest, and the irony in those things sometimes doesn't come out. I learned my lesson, too, which is don't joke about bipolars. It isn't fair to people who have bipolar disorder.

So let's put the rumor to rest once and for all: Are you bipolar?

STILLER: No.

And you're not taking any medication?

STILLER: No.

You go to therapy, probably, but not for that?
STILLER: I have in my life, yes.

But you're not in therapy now?
STILLER: I have in my life.

I don't think it's a bad thing.
STILLER: I don't think it is, either. It can be really helpful. I think self-examination is a good thing, and it can take many forms. To be aware in some way is a good thing.

So the comment was totally out of context?
STILLER: Yes. Maybe you should talk to that dude, maybe he'll pull out some freakin'—

That's a good idea. What was his name?
STILLER: No, no. I think it was just said in jest.*

Part of comedy is exaggeration, so obviously that should have been understood.
STILLER: I think comedy is also context and inflection. A lot of times in an e-mail or letter, you can say something that has an ironic sort of underpinning that doesn't come across, thus the birth of the emoticon—and there's another level of irony about the ridiculousness of emoticons.

The other big search was "Ben Stiller height."
STILLER: How interesting. That's really weird. Wow. And I thought *I* was wasting my time on the Internet.

[*Continued . . .*]

[BRUCE SPRINGSTEEN]

You can tell a lot about musicians by how they arrive at an interview. Some come with a manager, a publicist, bodyguards, or a retinue of hangers-on. Bruce Springsteen came to this interview alone. He drove himself from his home in Rumson,

---

* The writer responded, "First of all I gotta tell you that since that particular issue of *GQ* hit the newsstands in the blighted month of September 2001, your note is literally, I believe, the first feedback I've ever gotten on it. I don't think my mother even mentioned it. Racking my brain a little to remember the context, I'm pretty sure this was more in a humorously exaggerated self-deprecation vein than it was actual self-diagnosis. He meant: 'I can be complicated,' not 'I'm sick.'"

New Jersey, to the Sony Music Studios in Manhattan in his black Explorer—and arrived early.

Sitting in solitude with his back to the door in a darkened conference room, a mass of flannel and denim with a glinting silver cross earring, he didn't need much prodding to be talked into heading to a nearby bar, where he ordered a shot of tequila and a beer, and gave the waitress a two hundred percent tip.

I hadn't planned to ask this, but have you ever been in therapy?
BRUCE SPRINGSTEEN: Oh yeah, absolutely. And I found it to be one of the most healthy experiences of my life. I grew up in a working-class family where that was very frowned upon. So it was very, very difficult for me to ever get to a place where I said I needed some help. You know, I stumbled into some different very dark times where I simply had no other idea of what to do. It's not necessarily for everybody maybe, but all I can say is, I've lived a much fuller life. I've accomplished things personally that felt simply impossible previously. It's a sign of strength, you know, to put your hand out and ask for help, whether it's a friend or a professional or whatever.

So do you still go regularly?
SPRINGSTEEN: Long periods of time will go by when I'm not [in therapy], but it's a resource to call on if I need to. You know, it helps you center yourself emotionally and be the man you want to be. I mean, it's funny because I simply never knew anyone who'd had that experience, so initially you go through a lot of different feelings about it. But all I can say is the leap of consciousness that it takes to go from playing in your garage to playing in front of five thousand, six thousand, seven thousand people—or when you experience any kind of success at all—can be very, very demanding.

Unlike most musicians I've interviewed, you've managed to avoid letting success cause you to lose your perspective and grounding.
SPRINGSTEEN: It's interesting, because when I started out making music, I wasn't fundamentally interested in having a big hit right away. I was into writing music that was going to thread its way into people's lives. I was interested in becoming a part of people's lives, and having some usefulness—that would be the best word. I would imagine that a lot of people that end up going into the arts or film or music were at some point told by somebody that they were useless. Everyone has felt that. So I know that one of the main motivations for me was to try to be useful, and then of course there were all those other pop dreams of the Cadillac or the girls. All the stuff that comes with it was there, but sort of on the periphery.

In some way, I was trying to find a fundamental purpose for my own existence. And basically trying to enter people's lives in that fashion and hopefully maintain that relationship over a lifetime, or at least as long as I felt I had something useful to say. That was why we took so long in between records. We made a lot of music. There are albums and albums worth of stuff sitting in the can. But I just didn't feel they were that useful. [. . .]

What kind of advice would you give the young Bruce Springsteen now?
SPRINGSTEEN: Two things. One, I would tell him to approach his job like, on one hand, it's the most serious thing in the world and, on the other hand, as if it's only rock and roll. You have to keep both of those things in your head at the same time. I think I took it very seriously. And while I don't regret doing so, I think that I would have been a bit easier and less self-punishing on myself at different times if I'd remembered that it was only rock and roll.

What do you mean by self-punishing?
SPRINGSTEEN: Beating up on myself physically (*laughs*). For me it was mostly mental and, you know, you drift down your different self-destructive roads at different times and hopefully you have the type of bonds that pull you back out of that abyss and say, "Hey, wait a minute." When I was twenty-five, I was in London and there were posters of me everywhere in this theater that were making me want to throw up and puke. I was disgusted at what I'd become, and then someone in the band would say, "Hey, do you believe we're in London, England, and we're going to play tonight and somebody's going to pay us for it?"

So I was lucky. I had good friends and a good support network that assisted me along the way. In retrospect, I look back on those times now and they just seem funny, you know.

And what advice would the young Bruce Springsteen give you?
SPRINGSTEEN: Louder guitars.

Should we head out of here?
SPRINGSTEEN: Well, damn, we've had a good time. I'm stoned.* Let's not stop now.

Springsteen emerges from the dark cavern of Hannah's Cocktail Lounge into the warm April sun of the city.

---

* Drunk, not high.

SPRINGSTEEN: Oh, man, it's the summertime. What a day.

A police car screeches to a stop in the middle of the street, and two officers step out. It is not the first time Springsteen has been approached by fans in law enforcement that day.

POLICE OFFICER: Hey, big guy.
SPRINGSTEEN: Hey, guy.
POLICE OFFICER: How you doing, buddy?
SPRINGSTEEN: Very good. Just having a good time. Enjoying the day.
POLICE OFFICER: A beautiful day out for walking around, huh?
SPRINGSTEEN: Fabulous.
POLICE OFFICER: How'd that concert go the other day?
SPRINGSTEEN: Good. Good time. I really enjoyed it.
POLICE OFFICER: Do you mind signing this for me?

Holds out his ticket pad. Springsteen autographs the ticket.

[LADY GAGA
SCENE 1]

Backstage at the LG Arena in Birmingham, England, Lady Gaga was preparing for her show. Bruce Springsteen's *Born to Run* blared on vinyl as she danced around her dressing room, wearing a blue bandana around her head in tribute and an un-buttoned studded vest with a black bra underneath. She was at the height of her fame, and consequently had done very few interviews. Fortunately, completely by accident, when I'd met her backstage in Nottingham the previous evening, I passed a crucial test by insisting on a seat to the concert there, which she didn't want me to see because it was a scaled-down "B show," as she called it.

LADY GAGA: You're going to get a good interview because when I met you yesterday, you wanted to see my B show. Are you kidding? We might as well have had sex by now. I mean, you came in my dressing room and said, "Please, I know it's a B show. I know you're hard on yourself. But I just want to see it once before I interview you tomorrow."

Well, good. Because I'm going to start with a hard question.
LADY GAGA: Go ahead.

I have a theory about you.
LADY GAGA: Should I lay down?

You might need to.
LADY GAGA: We don't have enough couches to lay me down.

Have you ever been to therapy, by the way?
LADY GAGA: No. I've like spoken to spiritual guides and things.

But never a straight-up psychiatrist?
LADY GAGA: I'm terrified of therapy because I don't want it to mess with my creativity.

That's interesting.
LADY GAGA: What's worse: being normal or being abnormal? I don't know.

So the question is: Do you think if you'd never gotten your heart broken five years ago, you wouldn't have become as successful as you did afterward?
LADY GAGA: No, I wouldn't. No, I wouldn't have been as successful without him.*

So here's the thought . . .
LADY GAGA: You made me cry (*wipes tears from her eyes*).

Do you think that all that love you directed toward men now goes toward your fans instead?
LADY GAGA: Well, I've really never loved anyone like I loved him. Or like I love him. I will say that the relationship really shaped me. It made me into a fighter. But I wouldn't say that my love for my fans is equated to my attention for men. But I will say that love comes in many different forms. And I sort of resolved that if you can't have the guy of your dreams, there are other ways to give love. So I guess in some ways you're kind of right.

Did he contact you at all after you got famous?
LADY GAGA: I don't want to talk about him.

---

* When she was a struggling, drug-addled musician on the Lower East Side, Lady Gaga fell in love with a bartender and heavy metal drummer, Luc Carl, who broke her heart. And sometimes it seems as if her music, her stage show, and her fame—in other words, Lady Gaga herself—were formed in response to that heartbreak.

Okay.
LADY GAGA: I'm sorry. I want to, but he's too precious to talk about.

I'm surprised. I thought you'd be out of it and over it by now.
LADY GAGA: Out of where?

Emotionally out of it. You seem to still be emotionally attached in some way.*
LADY GAGA: Into what?

In that experience or that relationship.
LADY GAGA: Oh, I love my friends and my past, and it's made me who I am. I didn't just like wake up one day and forget how I got here. In fact, I'll always have one high heel in New York City. I live in Hollywood, but you can't make me love Hollywood. I'll never love Hollywood.

Okay, you kind of dodged that, so one last thing: Do you think with that guy, it was obsession or love?
LADY GAGA: Love. But, you know, I don't really know very much about love. But I suppose if I knew everything about love, I wouldn't be good at making music, would I?

I don't know. Some artists make their best music when they're in love.
LADY GAGA: I'm terrified of babies, though.

Because?
LADY GAGA: I think, creatively, as a woman, you change once you give birth. I'm totally not ready for that.

Did you ever have any resolution with your father after he cut you off during your wild days?
LADY GAGA: It's just recently that I've been healed in a way because my father had this heart surgery that he was supposed to have since I was a kid. The fear of losing the man of my dreams, such as my dad—there's fucking Freud for you—was terrifying. So the biggest fear of my life passed.

---

* Indeed, at the time of the interview, Lady Gaga was in the process of rekindling her romance with him.

Do you ever feel like you're fulfilling your dad's unrealized rock star ambitions?
LADY GAGA: Yeah, sure I do. I love my daddy. My daddy's everything. I hope I can find a man that will treat me as good as my dad.

[*Continued . . .*]

=== **[CHRISTINA AGUILERA]** ===
SCENE 1

Christina Aguilera marched into her publicist's New York office, loudly smacking chewing gum. She was wearing baggy green army pants, a gold-chain necklace reading *Christina,* and a faded jean jacket over a navel-exposing T-shirt emblazoned with the word *Rockstar.* Her lips were glossed too pale, her eyes shadowed too blue. She plopped into a chair and splayed her legs over the armrest. Without stopping the music blaring on her headphones, she ordered, "Could you put Hot 97 on the radio?"

The next stop for the pop princess: a greasy feast at Houston's restaurant, where she insisted that everyone plunge each tortilla chip into all three dipping sauces—spinach-artichoke, sour cream, and salsa—for optimum flavor.

I'd been assigned to spend a week with this seemingly spoiled-rotten nineteen-year-old for her first *Rolling Stone* cover story. And only an hour into the experience, I was already regretting it.

How did the photo shoot go?
CHRISTINA AGUILERA: Everyone was like, "She's going crazy during that *Rolling Stone* photo shoot." They're so afraid that I'm going to be too sexy, you know what I mean.

Sexy in what way?
AGUILERA: I was doing some crazy stuff and my publicist was like, "Christina, don't do that! Christina, don't do this!" But I like being a little provocative.

Of course to the record label, you're not a person, you're an investment.
AGUILERA: Exactly. She's like, "I wouldn't care so much if you didn't have such a great voice." She was becoming an alcoholic at the shoot, pulling her hair out and asking for more red wine. She was finally like, "Put your hands on your crotch, I don't care!"

So what were you doing exactly?
AGUILERA: It was crazy. I had my Walkman on for a couple of poses and I put it right, you know, where my crotch is. And I was looking at the camera kind of full on and strong, and head down a little bit and sassy. Just doing that suggestiveness. It was interesting. . . .

To just vamp it up a little bit?
AGUILERA: Yeah, you need that release sometimes.

I think that's part of the pop music tradition, to walk that line between innocence and sexuality.
AGUILERA: Sexuality is a part of how I perform onstage. It's something that I'm playful with and flirt with, and that's flirting with disaster sometimes. It's just part of my nature and I can't help that. I'm not crossing the border too much, yet. But . . .

But what?
AGUILERA: I just don't think I can hide who I am much longer.

As the week passes and I travel with Aguilera to Toronto, where she's rehearsing for a tour, her teeny-bopper façade begins to melt away and reveal something much more real and vulnerable. At dinner one night, while her band and dancers get drunk and rowdy, Aguilera sits quietly near the corner of the table, talking with her choreographer, Tina Landon. In her hotel room the next morning, she apologizes for her introverted behavior.

AGUILERA: Yesterday was a weird thing. I was in a bad mood about something that happened. I was pulled out of rehearsals, and I didn't want to be. There was drama. I was talking with Tina about that—and about my love, my first love. I fell in love for the first time this year. I'm kinda like going through it.

That's a great thing to experience.
AGUILERA: It's crazy. I've never felt like that before. It's a little bit scary. I'm used to being this independent chick like not even really thinking about boys, and all of a sudden—whoa—like, this guy takes over everything. Well, not everything. But my focus is suddenly about this guy. It's made me vulnerable, and I don't like to be that way. [. . .]

Do you think you're experiencing it because you're at an age now where you're open to those feelings, or is it real chemistry with him?
AGUILERA: What do you mean chemistry?

When you're drawn to this one person and they're drawn to you, and there's this electricity and you can't logically figure out why.
AGUILERA: Yeah, it's like, why am I so crazy over this person? It's so crazy, so crazy. It's beautiful. It's tough, though, to really maintain a relationship while doing what I'm doing. You have to deal with his insecurities about who I am and all the *I'm not good enough* ideas in his head, which don't matter to me at all.

At least it's a person from the normal world.
AGUILERA: Are you saying it's not someone in the business?

I'm saying it's not a pop star. It's someone who works for you.
AGUILERA: How did you know?* [. . .]

Do you have dreams about him?
AGUILERA: Ooh, I've been dreaming some weird stuff. I dreamt that I had just come back from a trip to some foreign country and he left a message on my phone for this other girl. He didn't even know it. It was like he pressed speed dial and it went to the wrong number. And he's all like, "I'm really feeling you now and I miss you and I love you." And he was really pouring his heart out to this girl and it was not supposed to be for me. I woke up and I cried. I haven't cried over a dream since I was like . . . in years.

Did you tell him about it?
AGUILERA: I didn't tell him about it.

You should, because then he'd know that you have insecurities too.
AGUILERA: I'm going to tell him.

Fifteen minutes later, in the midst of discussing how she was upset that she didn't get writing credit for her breakthrough hit "Genie in a Bottle," she blurts out of the blue . . .

---

* From what she'd said so far, he was clearly not someone high-profile. The rest was just a guess to see how she'd respond.

AGUILERA: Let me ask you one question: Who do you think is the cutest one of my dancers?

Girl or guy?
AGUILERA: Guy. Just out of curiosity.

I don't know. All your dancers have great energy.

As we discuss her dancers, she begins to get impatient, until . . .

AGUILERA: What about Jorge?

He's cool. He's got a good body.
AGUILERA: I think it's interesting to hear other people's opinions.

She leans back in the couch, satisfied she's covered that one up pretty well.

[*Continued . . .*]

BEN STILLER
SCENE 2

I talked to a number of people who've worked with you in the past, and I wanted to get your reaction to some of the things they said.
BEN STILLER: Uh-oh. Okay.

One of the former writers on *The Ben Stiller Show* said there was a joke among the writers that if they wanted to make sure their sketch would be used, they included a scene with you taking off your shirt. Have you ever heard that?
STILLER: Oh my God, no. Jesus Christ . . .

Was that not true?
STILLER: You're not going to tell me what writer said that, of course. I have no response to that, but they were probably right. That's great.

Someone else you worked with described you as competitive and afraid of failure.
STILLER: I've obviously failed at that. I don't know if fear of failure is necessarily a bad thing. On the other hand, the ultimate fear of failure would be paralysis and not doing anything. I guess somehow if that's there, which I'm sure it definitely is, I don't want that to be what stops me from trying something.

"Micromanager" was another word that came up a lot.
STILLER: That's one of the hard things. I'm working on it. I've attempted to mi-
cromanage many things. And I feel like I'm in a place where I know that's not
bringing me happiness. Maybe it's because I'm getting older and too tired to do
it all. [. . .]

**People also say that you're one of the hardest working people they know, that
work is an addiction for you.**
STILLER: The first part of getting rid of an addiction is acknowledging that you
have it, and I acknowledge that I enjoy working. I think anyone that's kicked heroin will tell you they enjoyed it until they realized it was screwing up their life. I
haven't hit my bottom yet. But I've gotten to a place where I realized it's out of
balance, and I've adjusted that. The area of my life that I have no question about is
my commitment to my family and how much I love my family. And I think that's
the implication when people ask, "Oh, why do you work so much?"

**They didn't say it as a judgment like that. But maybe your perspective comes
from being raised by parents who were entertainers and not around a lot.**
STILLER: It's all valid stuff. I grew up with parents who needed to work to take care
of their family and also enjoyed working, too. They were great parents and also
weren't perfect parents. I'm all of those things, too.

[LADY GAGA]
SCENE 2

**You know, they say that most workaholics are that way because it's an addiction
and a way to avoid other things.**
LADY GAGA: In so many ways, my music also heals me. So is it heroin, and I need
the fix to feel better? Or is it that music is healing? I guess that's the big question.
When you work as hard as I do, or you resign your life to something like music or
art or writing, you have to commit yourself to this struggle and commit yourself
to the pain. And I commit myself to my heartbreak wholeheartedly. It's something
that I will never let go. But that heartbreak in a way is my feature. It's a representa-
tion of the process of my work. As artists we are eternally heartbroken.

That is total Rilke.
LADY GAGA: That's Rilke right here (*shows tattoo of a passage from* Letters to a
Young Poet *by Rainer Maria Rilke on her upper arm*). It's in German.

I didn't mean to get so deep so early . . .

LADY GAGA: I'm deeper than you thought (*laughs*). And we didn't talk about my favorite wacky outfit.

I was going to ask if you thought workaholism was a way of avoiding intimacy and the vulnerability that comes with that.

LADY GAGA: Well (*hesitates*), sex is certainly not like a priority at the moment.

Sex is different than intimacy.

LADY GAGA: I guess I view sex and intimacy as the same. But I'm at a different place in my life now than I was two years ago. So I guess I'm a woman now.

In what way do you mean?

LADY GAGA: I just . . . I don't know when or why you realize that you've become a woman, but I'm a woman. I think different. I feel different. And I care less and less about what people think as the hours go by. I feel very strong. But (*whispers*) I don't know.

A lot of times you seem to choose good-looking guys who are dumb to sleep with, because your heart is safe that way . . .

LADY GAGA: I've done that.

Whereas with intimacy, that's being able to show someone who you are and your vulnerabilities, and them being able to do the same, and both of you knowing you're safe.

LADY GAGA: Well, there's very few people I can do that with. I do it with my fans. I'm very intimate with my fans. I mean last night onstage, I told them about my grandpa [being hospitalized].

But now that you've sworn off romantic love in your life, you do treat the audience kind of like a lover. Like last night, you were telling them, "No pop star's gonna treat you like I treat you." It's what you might say to a boyfriend you don't want to lose.

LADY GAGA: I see that now. That's interesting. But there's some things I keep sacred for myself. And as someone who has written two albums about it, I have the right to choose whether or not I want to be a celebrity and I don't want to be one. And I feel that I'm relatively clever enough to control that people pay attention more to my music and to my clothing than they do to my personal life. Trust me, I'd much rather people write about what I wear and what I'm singing and what I do in my videos than writing about who I'm fucking. I mean, that, for me, is the kiss of death.

Do you feel like you're sacrificing certain parts of yourself and your life for your art and career?

LADY GAGA: It's kind of good for me, though, isn't it? Because what if we want to date? We're not gonna tell anybody. And we're gonna lie profusely that we're not together. And if you're like, "Why don't you want people to know?" then I know you're with me for the wrong reasons, so I'm like, "Fuck off."

But the danger of lying is that you're seen as hypocritical, like when Britney Spears said she was a virgin.

LADY GAGA: Okay, I'm not a virgin. The cat's out of the bag.

The point being that the more you try to hide things—

LADY GAGA: I guess what I'm trying to say is, this is show biz for me. It might not be show biz for the rest of you, but for me, this is show biz. If I were to ever, God forbid, get hurt onstage and my fans were screaming outside of the hospital, waiting for me to come out, I'd come out as Gaga. I wouldn't come out in sweatpants because I busted my leg or whatever.

And that's what Michael [Jackson] did. Michael got burned and he lifted that glittered glove so damn high so his fans could see him because he was in the art of show business. That's what we do. Some people don't. They want to relate in a different way. I don't want people to see I'm a human being. I don't even drink water onstage in front of anybody because I want them to focus on the fantasy of the music and be transported from where they are to somewhere else. People can't do that if you're just on earth. We need to go to heaven.

[*Continued . . .*]

[ALANIS MORISSETTE]

In 2002, Alanis Morissette released the first album she'd ever produced by herself. As part of this emancipation, she sang about one of her earliest experiences of exploitation in the music industry: when she was pressured at age fourteen into having a relationship with her twenty-nine-year-old producer. The song, "Hands Clean," became perhaps the first single explicitly dealing with statutory rape to hit the top forty.

I'm surprised that your record label let "Hands Clean" come out as the first single, since it's so controversial.
ALANIS MORISSETTE: Some people at the record label knew exactly what it was about and others actually didn't. But I think once I explained it to them, it made a little more sense.

How much did you tell them about it?
MORISSETTE: I told them everything other than the identity of the person.

Had you been wanting to write about it for a long time?
MORISSETTE: I've been wanting to face the truth about it with my own self for a long time. I believe there is a distinct difference between privacy and secrecy, and for a long time I [put] them both into the same category. But then I realized that secrecy is actually to the detriment of my own peace of mind and self, and that I can still sustain my belief in privacy and be authentic and transparent about it at the same time. So it was a pretty revelatory moment. I also do know in the same breath that I have a little ways to go, particularly with that subject (*pauses, laughs*). I have a ways to go in every other department, too, that's pretty obvious.

Did the experience affect your trust of other people in the music business?
MORISSETTE: Yeah, absolutely. I've had trust issues up until, you know, about thirteen seconds ago, to say the least. It's formed my view of not only the industry, but society in terms of patriarchy and power struggling and all of that.

Do you think of what happened as statutory rape?
MORISSETTE: Basically it could be categorized as that, but at the same time, I'm not one to really categorize. I'm the kind of person that will say "a person that I've been spending time with in a romantic way" rather than saying my boyfriend. So I'll say "someone that I was romantically linked to at a time when I was emotionally not necessarily prepared for it" as opposed to qualifying it as, like, statutory rape.

How did you end up getting out of the situation?
MORISSETTE: I left. Yeah, I moved. I remember my twin brother turning to me one day and saying, "You're so unhappy. Just go." And I remember pointing to a record of mine. It was leaning up against the wall in the corner of my room and I said, "But I don't want to let go of that." And he said, "You don't have to. Just go." And that was a really sweet moment.

Has the person the song's about contacted you since?

MORISSETTE: No, not yet. I'm sure I'll speak with him at some point. But there's not that much to say, other than that I'm sharing my experience and I will always respect his privacy as I did with the person that "You Oughta Know" is about and as I did with many of the songs.

What would be your advice for a teenage girl trying to make it in the industry today?

MORISSETTE: If I were to have a daughter who wanted to engage in this type of industry, I would make sure I had her back. I just feel like there was this illusion that I had to pick between two doors: this complex kind of dynamic with older men and younger women in the industry, or no music being expressed. But I realize as I get older and have more experience that there's always a fucking third door, you know.

[AT THE DRIVE-IN]

When spending an extended amount of time with someone for an article, previously guarded secrets often tend to surface. In the case of At the Drive-In, a posthardcore band that became the next big thing in rock music before imploding, it was a secret so dark that it felt necessary to call At the Drive-In guitarist Omar Rodríguez-López afterward and prepare him for its disclosure.

This portion of the interview took place before an At the Drive-In show at Universal Amphitheatre in Los Angeles. Rodríguez-López and drummer Tony Hajjar were discussing working with producer Ross Robinson.

When I've seen Ross produce other bands, he's had them regressing to their childhood and on the floor crying like babies to get something emotional out of them. Did he get into any psychotherapy with you?

TONY HAJJAR: I haven't talked about this, but I remember recording "Invalid Litter Dept." The song is about all the women that were murdered in the Juárez area. And the thing that happened was that in that song, Ross brought up my mom. She passed away in 1988, and it was a poignant time. That's what he got out of me on that song, that's for sure. And I haven't figured out whether that was good or bad.

How did she pass away?

HAJJAR: She died of cancer—on May 25, 1988.

And now you forever associate the song with her?
HAJJAR: I don't know if I should have gone that far when we were recording. Now, every time we play it, I do associate the song with my emotions about her.
OMAR RODRÍGUEZ-LÓPEZ: You obviously have an emotional link when you make music, but I think he embedded it that much deeper.*

Did he do that with you, too?
RODRÍGUEZ-LÓPEZ: For me, the emotional links he made with all the songs worked. I did a lot of camping when I was younger to work on my issues as an incest survivor. And there are plenty of things, like breath therapy, that I learned but had never thought to apply to music in the studio.

So it was like finding a way to get something constructive out of a destructive experience?
RODRÍGUEZ-LÓPEZ: Exactly. I definitely went through a time of searching and dropping out of high school and hitchhiking for a year and eating out of garbage cans and shooting all kinds of things into my arm and getting into really fucked-up situations just for the sake of experiencing them. And self-mutilation. That's not to say if we do our next record with someone else, I'm going to sit there with them and talk about all this stuff that happened to me. But now I know I can be conscious of it and use it as a tool for myself to get a better performance.
HAJJAR: I think we came out of that experience probably stronger and closer than we ever were, and I consider us five a really, really close band because we care about each other's thoughts and emotions and respect each other.† It was just an amazing time. I can't believe that it happened.
RODRÍGUEZ-LÓPEZ: We had sex (*laughs*).

Rodríguez-López brought up incest so casually that I assume it's a commonly known fact about him. But afterward, I can't find a single reference to the incident. So before the article is published, I call to warn him.

You mentioned in passing that you were an incest survivor, and I wanted to let you know that's going to be in the article.
RODRÍGUEZ-LÓPEZ: Yes, I know I said it.

---

* Ross Robinson on working with Jonathan Davis of Korn: "For one of the songs about how much he hates his ex-girlfriend, as usual, I put a picture of her on a pillow on the floor and put a microphone on top of it. Then I had him kneel in a fetal position over it and sing. I stood above him, and every time he wasn't giving it his all, I dug my fingers into his neck as hard as I could—on his pressure points, like Mr. Spock."
     Vanilla Ice on working with Ross Robinson: "A lot of people didn't know that I was an abused child. My mother was almost killed by whoever it was that made her pregnant with me. Ross has a way of getting things like that out of you. And now I feel like I'm free, because I put it on tape."
† Three months later, the band broke up.

Are you comfortable with it being in the story?
RODRÍGUEZ-LÓPEZ: I don't know. I think I trust your judgment.

The magazine wanted me to ask if there was a possibility of a lawsuit from the person who did it.
RODRÍGUEZ-LÓPEZ: No way.

Why is that?
RODRÍGUEZ-LÓPEZ: Because of this person's career, they wouldn't want to associate themselves with that.

Does anyone else know about it or could anyone testify that it happened?
RODRÍGUEZ-LÓPEZ: My close friends know about it.

The call ended awkwardly, but five hours later, Rodríguez-López phoned back.

RODRÍGUEZ-LÓPEZ: Thanks for calling about it. I had a long talk with my friends, and I'm ready for the information to be out.

[CHRISTINA AGUILERA]
SCENE 2

After dinner one night, Christina Aguilera climbed into a chauffeured van, sat in the backseat, and stared out of the window in silence for the entire ride, interrupted occasionally by the ringing of her cell phone. Her Discman earphones were over her head, but no music was playing. She was simply shutting off.

This seemed to be a frequent habit of hers: She would stare out a window or at a ceiling, and her mind would drift somewhere. You could yell her name, tap her on the shoulder, set her shoes on fire—and chances are she wouldn't respond. At the time, little was known about Aguilera's past other than her stint on *The Mickey Mouse Club* with Britney Spears, but gradually it became obvious why this habit began.

I notice a lot of times you seem to be zoning out.
CHRISTINA AGUILERA: I'm never zoning out. I told you I was a deep thinker. My mind is always thinking. I'll think about really crazy things, like being on top of that pole up there (*points to a flagpole outside*). Or I'll get a lot of different weird visions. It's like my own little world. My life just revolves around putting myself out there for people, and giving and giving. So whenever I get those five minutes

in a van or limo or wherever, those are special moments to just zone out and think and dream. I just love being able to do that. It's funny that you notice that.

Shortly afterward, she discusses wanting to be a role model. It seems like a strange thing to say, especially considering her conversation after the photo shoot about wanting to be more sexual and rebellious.

It's interesting how you want to be sexually provocative, yet a role model at the same time.
AGUILERA: Where the whole role model comes in for me is that it's cool to touch people and to make a difference in a positive way as far as, um, maybe getting the word out more about issues concerning domestic violence and child abuse and other issues that I'm really really adamant on trying to help with my status and everything. That is something I promised myself I would do before I even got signed. Deep down I want to have others benefit from my success. I want to be able to help others, open up shelters and visit them.

Was there something that happened in your past that makes you passionate about those particular issues?
AGUILERA: I've been around situations. Domestic violence. It's so sad. It's a topic that's so kept quiet. It's in the home and no one wants to get involved.

Do you mean your home?
AGUILERA: Yeah, I think the reason why my drive was so strong and I was so passionate about music was because I grew up in an environment of domestic violence. Music was my release to get away from it all. I would seriously run up to my bedroom and put on that *Sound of Music* tape. She [Julie Andrews] was free and alive, and she was playful and rebellious against the nuns. I know it sounds really cheesy but, um, that was my escape. I would open up my bedroom window and I would just imagine the audience. I would just sing out. As far as the past, I got myself out of it. And I promised myself when this happened, I would try to help others who were in the same situation.

Why do you think it took your mom so long to get out of the relationship?
AGUILERA: People don't know domestic abuse unless they're in it. It's not only physical abuse, but it's the damage inside—mental abuse. It's a sad thing to go through and watch. They play with your mind and make you feel bad about yourself and (*trails off and doesn't speak for several seconds*) . . .

So now you want to help others in the same situation?
AGUILERA: Yes, one thing would be to go to different schools and talk to kids about different personal experiences of my own and try and help them in some way. Get them to come out about their own experiences.

As far as your relationship with your father now, did he ever apologize?
AGUILERA: Yeah, he's apologized. I think he had a lot of guilt.

Did he apologize after you got successful or before?
AGUILERA: Actually before. I also lived around other situations. Next door to where we lived, I heard what was going on. There was so much domestic violence going around when I grew up, with my dad traveling in the military. It's so sad. So sad. I wanted to be so strong for everybody—for my mom and everyone. That's why I'm so girl-empowerment oriented (*laughs uncomfortably*). Even "Genie in a Bottle" is about making a guy work for it.

[*Continued* . . .]

[IKE TURNER]

A year after Ike Turner's 1975 performance in New York City with the Ike & Tina Turner Revue, the floodgates of his life burst open. Tina Turner walked out on him, claiming emotional and physical abuse; his studio in Inglewood, California, was razed in a fire; and he began logging more arrests (eleven) than legitimate solo albums (one). Then there was the Tina Turner biopic *What's Love Got to Do With It*, which portrayed him as a domineering, temperamental, career-obsessed, wife-beating cocaine addict. A few years after emerging from prison for cocaine possession in the mid-nineties, Turner decided to play his first concert in New York since that 1975 performance. With some reluctance, he agreed to an interview before the show.

When you were growing up, you saw a man shoot twenty-six other men?
IKE TURNER: Yeah, when I was a kid. It was in Mississippi. In those days, it was almost like if you was black, you was just like a roach or an ant or something they step on and never even think about it. I've seen them put blacks in bails of tar. You know, they take a guy and dip him in a hot bail of tar, and then put feathers on him. That's the way it was in those days.

Did that create a lot of resentment in you?
TURNER: You know, I never carried any malice in my heart for nobody, because otherwise I would never meet guys like you or nobody, man. You have to meet people for what they are themselves. It never had no bearings on me. My father was killed by a group of whites. The same thing, man, but anyway, I'm pretty open. I wish the public would be better open with me and with my career. Because movies can make people anyway they wanna make them.

Why haven't you performed in New York in so long?
TURNER: You know, like when Tina and I broke up, I don't know, I got insecure and started doing drugs and things. Man, I just didn't . . . I was afraid of rejection from the public, you know, because everybody knew that she did the singing. But I did all the choreography, the songs, the music, the arrangements. I did everything. But the public never knew what I did, because I wasn't interested in being the front of the show. So I just got insecure, man. And I didn't really get myself back together until I went to jail. I started performing some in jail, and putting groups together and shows together in jail, and then that's when I got my confidence back.

What kind of opportunities did you have to perform in jail?
TURNER: Once every two or three months you can put together a show, and we were dressing guys up like Ikettes. Everybody was dancing like girls onstage, and we just had a lot of fun.

I wonder if they're going to contact you for a job when they get out.
TURNER (*laughs*): For a fact, some of 'em have.

What instruments did you have in jail?
TURNER: They gave me a piano when I was in jail and they gave me two guitars. I was living in a dorm, and so I would put it under the bed and stuff. I never was mistreated in jail, man. I was earning five hundred dollars a week while I was in jail selling coffee, candy, and cigarettes. I saved up thirteen thousand dollars the seven months I was in there, because I had went down to zero financially.

You know, I got a call from some group that says they're going to protest the show—
TURNER: What?!

You haven't heard about that?
TURNER: No, no. You know, they really misled the public about me in this movie. The movie ain't really about Tina, it's about me. And I've never seen the movie

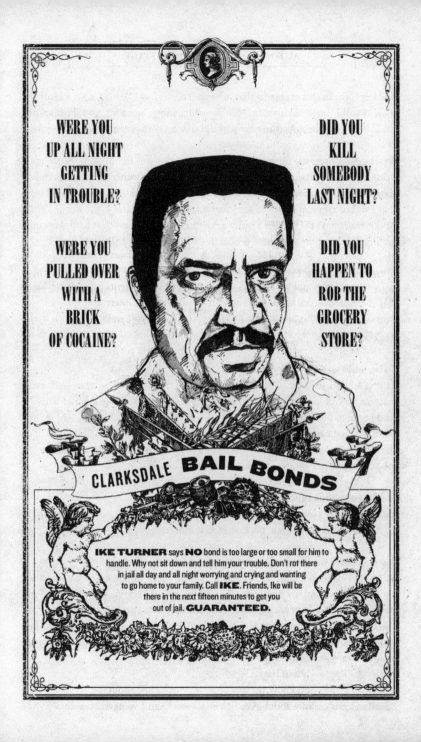

yet. But Tina, in this magazine that just came out called *Elle* magazine, admits in there that she never was a victim, that the whole movie was a lie. And she said she could've left anytime. And anyway they did that movie like that to sell the movie.

So why didn't you sue the producers?
TURNER: My attorney was supposed to be a friend of mine and Tina's, and I signed this contract for him. And it was four years later, man, when I found out that I signed away my rights to sue them if they portrayed me in the wrong light. And it really hurt me a lot. It's really a downer, man. It's making it harder for me getting my career because some people think I'm really like that movie.

A lot of people don't realize you had an impressive career before Ike and Tina with "Rocket 88" and all these incredible sessions that helped form rock and roll.
TURNER: No, they don't. I used to hide Elvis Presley behind the piano back in Arkansas.

So he could watch?
TURNER: Yeah, we were playing a black club and they don't allow whites in there, just like they don't allow blacks in white clubs. He used to drive a gravel truck.* And I used to slip him behind a piano in those days. And Little Richard—he wrote the first three pages in my book and said his style came from me. You know, it's the same thing with Jerry Lee Lewis—he's a copy of me. Prince is a copy of me. A lot of things that are out are copies of me and what I do.

Maybe your book can help set the record straight.
TURNER: But it's only being published in London. I tried all over America, and I hit a lot of stone walls, man. Because of that movie.

Separate from the movie, do you have regrets about anything?
TURNER: No, no, no, man. Today, man, my life is great. I'm proud of the way that I was with Tina and my kids. I don't do nothing that I regret, man, because I'm not the one that they made me out to be in the movie. It's like Tina always said: "If you knew Ike, you'd love him. But if you don't know him—if you just look at the way he looks onstage"—because onstage, I be into my music and I ain't thinking about how my face is looking . . .

---

* Elvis followed in his father's footsteps as a truck driver when he was nineteen. Though Turner says it was a gravel truck, this hasn't been confirmed, though Elvis did drive for the Crown Electric Company.

So you think your reputation comes from the way your face looks onstage?
TURNER: I don't know. I have no regrets of the past. I'm really happy with my accomplishments. I'm sorry that it had to get down to where they have to down me to launch her career. I think they could've did it without it. But anyway, I'll get over it.

In 2007, Ike Turner died in his home in Southern California at the age of seventy-six. The cause was a cocaine overdose.

LADY GAGA
SCENE 3

The moment Lady Gaga's concert in Birmingham ended, she rushed from the stage to the tour bus, covered in stage blood. As the bus lurched out of the back-stage parking lot, she heard a crowd screaming her name outside, then yelled to the bus driver: "Hold on, will you stop the bus? I'm just going to say hi to my fans."

Her bodyguards looked disapprovingly at her, then relented. She walked to the door of the bus and opened it to see hundreds of fans stampeding toward her. The bodyguards quickly ordered the driver to shut the door. As the bus pulled away, Lady Gaga smiled, pleased, and walked back to continue the interview.

You have a lot of things in your behavior that are signs of someone who had a traumatic experience in adolescence or childhood. Is that something you would ever discuss publicly?
LADY GAGA (*gasps*): Probably not.

When Christina Aguilera began talking about the dark issues in her past, there was no negative response to it and it ended up informing her work.
LADY GAGA (*hesitates*): I feel like I tell this story in my own way and my fans know who I really am. I don't want to teach them the wrong things. And you also have to be careful about how much you reveal to people that look up to you so much. They know who I am. They know how they can relate to me. I've laid it all on the table. And if they're smart like you, they make that assessment. But I don't want to be a bad example.

A bad example in the sense of being a victim?
LADY GAGA: Yeah, and I'm not a victim. And my message is positive. My show has a lovely naïveté and melancholy to it: a pop melancholy. That's my art. If I

told that other story in that way, I don't know if that's the best way I can help the universe.

Because if you did talk about it, then the things you do would be misinterpreted and seen through that experience?
LADY GAGA: Yeah. Maybe if I was writing my own book or something. I guess it's hard to . . . If I say one thing in our interview right now, it will be all over the world the day after it hits the stands. And it would be twisted and turned. And it's like you have to honor some things. Some things are sacred.

I understand.
LADY GAGA: There are some things that are so traumatic, I don't even fully remember them. But I will say wholeheartedly that I had the most wonderful mother and father my whole life. I was never abused. I didn't have a bad childhood. All of the things I went through were on my own quest for an artistic journey to fuck myself up like Warhol and Bowie and Mick, and just go for it.

That's interesting that you have this idea that the artist has to expose himself to these dark parts of life.
LADY GAGA: You do, but all of the trauma I caused to myself (*pauses*). Or it was caused by people that I met when being outrageous and irresponsible. I guess what I'm trying to say is that I like to, within moderation, respect that I'm not Mick Jagger or David Bowie, and I don't just have fans that are a certain age. There are, like, nine-year-olds listening to my music, so I guess I try to be respectful of who's reading *Rolling Stone*, if at all possible.

You do talk about cocks and pussy all the time, but I know what you mean.
LADY GAGA: I do, but cock and pussy is not the same as the things that I could talk about.

We can talk about something more positive. You seem to have become more religious or spiritual in the last year or so.
LADY GAGA: I've had a few different experiences. I'm really connected to my Aunt Joanne and she's not with us anymore. And then there was my father's surgery. And also my life has changed so much. It's hard not to believe that God hasn't been watching out for me when I've had such obstacles with drugs and rejection and people not believing in me. It's been a very long and continuous road that I love, but it's hard to just chalk it all up to myself. I have to believe there's something greater than myself.

Like a higher power?
LADY GAGA: Yeah, a higher power that's been watching out for me. Sometimes it really freaks me out—or I should say it petrifies me—when I think about laying in my apartment [in New York] with bug bites from bedbugs and roaches on the floor and mirrors with cocaine everywhere, and no will or interest in doing anything but making music and getting high. So I guess I've come a really long way and I have my friends to thank for that—and I have God.

[*Continued . . .*]

[ALI FARKA TOURÉ]

According to Ali Farka Touré, the world-famous African bluesman, spirits are at the root of all art. And if the spirits love a human being, they give him power. However, at the time of this interview, he had little time to spend in the spirit plane. After winning a Grammy for an album he recorded with Ry Cooder, which spent a record-breaking sixteen weeks at number one on the *Billboard* world music chart, he had to cancel a North American tour to stay home and protect his family from attacks by Tuareg nomads, who were fighting with the Malian government. Some of that hostility may have carried over into our interview, which was conducted through an interpreter when he was in Paris shortly afterward. It may also be worth noting that he was given the nickname Farka, or donkey, shortly after birth because of his stubbornness.

Is everything okay at home now?
ALI FARKA TOURÉ: There was nothing, okay. It was just a little incident.

Is this the first time you've left since the attacks?
TOURÉ: It's the first time I've left. There is no problem now.

Are you planning on doing a new record with Ry Cooder?
TOURÉ: No.

How about a record of your own?
TOURÉ: Oh no. I mean, yes, I have started my own recording already.

Are you collaborating with anyone on it?
TOURÉ: Hey, hey, that's enough of that. No more elaboration.*

---

* His next record didn't come out for another four years.

Were you disappointed that you had to cancel your American tour?
TOURÉ: Not at all, at all, at all. But in all sincerity, what really pissed me off was the guy who we were working with was a real asshole.

Are you playing any other shows in the U.S.?
TOURÉ: No!

Are you touring anywhere else?
TOURÉ: In Africa. I've almost done all of Africa. I'm very proud of this. My favorite place is Mali.

Do you think that the spirit of the blues is stronger there?
TOURÉ: That's very true. Where you are, you may call it the blues, but here, where I live, it's much purer than that. It's the African tradition.

Were you influenced at all by American blues?
TOURÉ: It was only from Africa, but why does one need to be influenced? Should you not be able to understand who you are by yourself, first?

Do you know yourself?
TOURÉ: Yeah!

When did you find out who you were?
TOURÉ: I was born in it. I grew up with it, and I evolved in it. My music is pure tradition. It's what I know. I don't know American music or French music or other music.* I know only my art, the geography, the sources, and the roots of my country. And I know them perfectly.

If it's traditional, then it must have influences in the past.
TOURÉ: Well, listen, what influences my personality or my music is really only my own business. I'm not forced to reveal it.

Do you consider yourself more a farmer than a musician?
TOURÉ: That is a hundred percent the truth. Agriculture is much more important than music. Why? Because if you can make music, it is a given that you have a full stomach. The one who doesn't have a full stomach can not even make music.

---

* Besides collaborating with American musicians like Taj Mahal and Ry Cooder, in his formative years in the sixties, Touré met John Lee Hooker when the bluesman visited Mali.

Some say you have the power to see into the future. What do you think?
TOURÉ: It's certain that if I do have the power to see in the future, it is a secret,
which I will hold and nurture inside myself.

*In 2004, Ali Farka Touré was elected mayor of Niafunké, his hometown in Mali. He
died two years later of bone cancer. He was sixty-six.*

[VON LMO]

On November 27, 1981, after playing a concert at Max's Kansas City, the no-wave
guitarist and singer Von Lmo disappeared. In his wake, he left behind countless stories (like the time he challenged Keith Moon to a drum battle backstage at a Who
concert), legendary shows (his group Kongress, fronted by a magician, was banned
from CBGB after nearly setting the club on fire), and a noisy style of guitar playing
that inspired bands like Sonic Youth. His *Future Language* album soon became a collector's item, due not just to its seminal avant-garde pop metal but also to its cover,
which featured five grown men wearing moon boots and cheap silver spacesuits.

Almost ten years after Von Lmo's disappearance, one of his former bandmates
spotted him driving a gold Cadillac down a one-way street in the wrong direction.
Von Lmo was officially back.

Where have you been the past ten years?
VON LMO: I was in a transition period. Everyone thought that I was dead, but I
was just in suspended animation. Being in suspended animation, I gained a lot of
incredible knowledge and lost twenty years off my life. I rejuvenated myself while
I was gone. I'm in the body of a teenager now. If you look at pictures of me from
1980 and if you look at me now, you can see the enormous change.*

Is there any truth to the rumor that you're a vampire?
VON LMO: I used to be into vampirism. I still am, sort of. I'm a member of the Z/n
Society, which is goddesses and vampires. However, whether I'm a vampire or not,
it's nobody's business.

You also claim to be a psychic?
VON LMO: I do have extrasensory perception. I've always been psychic since I can
remember. I do believe that this year will hold true to the new sound. That new

---

* A toupee.

sound is going to come forth and generate throughout millions of people. What Hendrix was to the sixties, I can be to the nineties. If not this year, it will be the tip of next year. People are ready for a change, and I have that facility. I have the setup and the technology. The Von Lmo band is here to give people the opportunity to make that change, to open up the mind and step into the next dimension.

You always tell your audience to enter the blacklight dimension. What or where is it?

VON LMO: I believe strongly in psychedelia. I'm into the psychedelic form of life, which is the blacklight dimension. When people ask me where I was born, I tell them I was born in the blacklight dimension, which is a dimension other than what most people are used to. It's very colorful, it has many interchangeable parts, it's flexible, and it can enhance your mind way beyond any other dimension. [. . .] Without my music, you can't get to these other dimensions. Music is everything. Music is life. Without music, there is only one thing and it's called death.

It's like your song "Leave Your Body."

VON LMO: It's the same idea, but "Leave Your Body" was written for a friend of mine, a girl who was actually a groupie of the band, who was going to commit suicide in 1979. I tried to help her by telling her that she's going to have to leave her body, get out of that present state, and just find herself. That's how I derived the lyrics to the song and helped her not to commit suicide, and it worked. I'm not saying that it can work for everyone. I'm not saying you can just pop in this song and it's going to help, but it can't hurt to try.

I actually first saw your *Future Language* album in a record bin with a sticker that said "Worst Record of the Decade" on the cover. . . .

VON LMO: Sometimes people just aren't advanced enough for my music.

In 2007, Von Lmo disappeared again: According to his former collaborators, he didn't go into suspended animation but to prison. A search of inmate records at the time revealed a prisoner in Sing Sing with his given name.

PSYCHIC SPIES
SCENE 2

Lyn Buchanan is a genial, easygoing man with prematurely gray hair, a George Lucas beard, and a well-established paunch. He has spent most of his life working on guided-missile and computer systems for the military, and nothing seems to surprise or unsettle him. That's why, when he was assigned to work in a special army unit at Fort Meade in Maryland, it took him years to realize that something was unusual about his job. This revelation occurred en route to Russell Targ's research laboratory at Stanford University.

LYN BUCHANAN: I was on a plane, looking at all the business people and secretaries, and I thought, "I wonder what they would think if they knew that I was a government agent training psychics."

How did you get involved with the remote-viewing program?
BUCHANAN: Most of it's still classified, but I was in the army and I was writing a highly complex computer program. There was a jealous sergeant who wanted my job, and he would sabotage my code. So on the day when I had to present the code to the commanding generals of twelve different countries, I was in the bathroom getting ready—fixing my hair and straightening out my clothes. And when I returned, I saw the sergeant walking away from my computer. When I hit one of the keys on the computer, the screen just went blank and the guy said, "Gotcha."

I got flaming mad. I've always had PK [psychokinesis], and so the whole computer network on the base just blew up—ninety-six computers and billions of dollars in damage.

How did they trace that to you?
BUCHANAN: There was a general named [Albert] Stubblebine. And he had a field officer whose job it was to look for talented psychic people. And when he saw what was going on, he reported what he thought to Stubblebine.

A couple days later, I ran into Stubblebine in the hall. And he got in my face and said, "Did you kill my computer with your mind?"

In my head, I saw my grandchildren still paying off the costs of the damage in the future. But I knew he wouldn't ask that question if he didn't know the answer. So I answered him, "Yes, sir."

"Far fucking out," he said. "Have I got a job for you!"

And that's when they recruited you to join the remote-viewing project?
BUCHANAN: Yes. My reaction was, "We're on *Candid Camera*, right? The army doesn't do this stuff." But they brought me out to Fort Meade and I became one of the viewers in the unit. When my skills got better, I became the trainer.

What's the most amazing experience you've had?
BUCHANAN: Everybody thinks that we had the most amazing job in the military, and really we did. But after you do it eight hours a day for five days a week, you realize that you're just going to work. It's a job. We would do some of the most far-out espionage and mentally travel to all these sites, but at the end of the day we just wanted to go home.

But tell me something really interesting that happened.
BUCHANAN: Ten times in seventeen years, I've had a PSI experience.

What's that?
BUCHANAN: A perfect site immersion. You see what you're viewing so completely that you can't tell that you're not there. I live for it. In that, though, if you try to walk through a wall, it will really hurt you. The first time it happened, the Russians had developed a death ray—an extremely powerful particle beam weapon. They wanted to see how the particles moved to figure out how it worked and what it was. But they couldn't get anyone in there, so they decided to put a remote viewer in. They said, "We need someone to volunteer to step inside a death ray."

And you volunteered?
BUCHANAN: They moved me to the site and sent me back in time to when the beam was fired. I was describing it to them. And then they said, "Step into the beam." I stepped in, and all this sandlike stuff was peppering me. I looked, and there were thousands of images of me in the beam. And my awareness was coming from all the points at once.* [. . .]

Now that the program is declassified, can you teach anyone how to remote view?
BUCHANAN: Definitely. When the information first came out, we got eight to twenty applicants a day. I turned down ninety-five percent of them—flaming kooks, really bad. Now I'd say that ninety-five percent of the people who call us are very levelheaded. What we teach is the real thing. This is not a toy. If someone has mental problems, you don't teach them this stuff.

Do corporations ever call you because they want to spy on competitors?
BUCHANAN: Yes, a significant number of corporations have been getting training lately.

---

* Note that Buchanan was verifiably a sergeant in the army and part of a remote-viewing espionage unit. As for the rest of his story, that's for you to decide.

How many?
BUCHANAN: I can't say, but enough to make the other companies worry about it.

[JANE'S ADDICTION]

In 1991, Perry Farrell, the singer in Jane's Addiction, started what became the pre-eminent touring alternative rock festival, Lollapalooza. But success is a mixed blessing. By Lollapalooza's third year, he complained, "I felt like it had come out of my hands. The tug was that hard. People just saw like a money Ferris wheel there with every bucket full of cash."

For a while, Farrell considered selling his stake in Lollapalooza. To prevent this from happening, music executives involved in the festival gave him more control for its fourth season.

Everyone tells me you have all these great ideas for Lollapalooza, but the corporate side of the festival always blocks them. So I thought that instead of doing a regular interview, we could discuss your dream Lollapalooza.
PERRY FARRELL: If we do that, what'll happen is somebody else will do it. Or they'll borrow one great idea and I'll get real bugged about it. It happens sometimes because I'm always blabbing around about ideas and stuff.

So let's just discuss a few of the ideas.
FARRELL: Okay. I guess one of my main ideas would be to have a place called Perry's Space and (*hesitates*) . . . It's like you get shuttled out to space—you know, to a place that could hold a few thousand people. There would be three stages out there, because (*pauses*)—I'm thinking to myself—you'd have a few thousand people on the main stage, yeah. That would work. The drive is always nice for clearing your head.

Would there be music on each stage?
FARRELL: You could also have other things. We could have maybe alien bands playing. And who knows what kind of techno stuff they would have to present. I mean right now we've got computers, right? But who knows what they've got. They might have like plutonium rides, where you'd really be like shot up in space and get a quick rush or something. And then instead of parachuting down, you would float down.

Imagine the insurance the festival would have to pay.
FARRELL: Actually, it would be nothing. You couldn't get hurt. There might be strays that were shot into space and something happened, like current from a black hole that was like ten zillion miles away was starting to sort of gravitate toward us and people are getting sucked out. So there might be one casualty per show. But there always is anyway at the regular Lollapalooza shows, so . . .

So what would be on the main stage?
FARRELL: There's a good question. God, all the alien music probably wouldn't make sense. But they would produce things like certain kilohertz or megahertz because they would know how to physically manipulate your body through sound to make you cry and fall in love and actually have orgasms.

How about for the art and technology portion of the festival?
FARRELL: For their technology, they might show you crafts of flight like we have out in Nevada at Area 51. Maybe you would have virtual simulations of flying saucers and how they were made. They would probably give us classes on how to clean up the environment and how to repair the ozone. I think they could turn us on to everything that we had questions about, including robot training and how to have your own human slave, you know. Zombie slaves.

Why do people always assume aliens are more advanced than us? Maybe they're not.
FARRELL: I think they are. They're way more advanced. Wouldn't that be nice, to have your own zombie for a minute? You just go behind a curtain.

And then what?
FARRELL: And you could program your own zombie.

Is there something else you're thinking of for Lollapalooza in the less-distant future?
FARRELL: Yeah, this year I'm trying to get like autopsies going on the third stage.

Literally?
FARRELL: I have a doctor friend of mine who wants to perform autopsies. I'm gonna try to get it for the West Coast. See if he can do it.

Lollapalooza staff confirmed that Farrell was planning to show autopsies at the festival, though, not surprisingly, the idea never came to fruition. Instead, in 2005, Farrell helped start Kidzapalooza, a rock festival for children.

[LUCIA PAMELA]

Lucia Pamela may be best known as the mother of Georgia Frontiere, who inherited the Los Angeles Rams (when her sixth husband drowned) and moved them to her hometown of St. Louis. But to music aficionados, Pamela is a celebrity in her own right. Voted Miss St. Louis in 1926, Pamela started what many believe to be the first all-female orchestra, Lucia Pamela and the Musical Pirates. She also started a singing duo with Georgia, the Pamela Sisters, and was cited by Ripley's Believe It or Not! for having memorized some ten thousand songs.

But if you ask Pamela what accomplishment she's proudest of, she'll tell you it was building a rocket, touring the Milky Way, and beating Neil Armstrong to the moon, where she recorded her album *Into Outer Space with Lucia Pamela*. Clearly, the line between fact and fiction doesn't exist for Pamela, which is what eventually made the album an enduring cult classic.

Where did you record your album?
LUCIA PAMELA: It was recorded on Moontown. I was the only one from Earth there.

Is that where you saw the roosters and the blue wind you sing about?
PAMELA: All of the music is true. And most of it is from experience. I also made a coloring book about the trip.

For children?
PAMELA: It's for people of all ages. Children aren't the only ones that like to color books (*pauses*). Have you ever been to the moon?

No, but I'd like to go.
PAMELA: The moon was quite surprising. Besides the moon, we found other areas outside the earth. I can't remember whether we named any of them or not. We went to Venus, Mars, Neptune. . . . I was quite surprised to find that there was an awful lot of Oriental people there.

What was Nutland like?*
PAMELA: Oh, it was a beautiful place, and everybody there was wonderful. But they couldn't speak English. Most of them spoke different languages, mostly Chinese, Japanese, and French . . . and Almond.

When was the last time you visited the moon?
PAMELA: This time last year, we flew up to the moon, yes. Me and some friends of mine. I've got it written down who flew us there. I can teach people how to travel to the moon and Mars and Venus. I also teach music and ice-skating. It doesn't take a long time if they really want to learn. I'll help anybody who wants to be helped.

Do you have any predictions for the future?
PAMELA: I want everything good to happen, but I want the weather to be good. If the weather is good, then everything is good.

In 2002, Lucia Pamela died in a Los Angeles hospital at the age of ninety-eight.

[CHRISTINA AGUILERA]
SCENE 3

After a press conference, Christina Aguilera walked into a back room, sat on the floor next to a fireplace, and zoned out again. Suddenly, she turned her face up to me and, in a girlish pout, asked . . .

CHRISTINA AGUILERA: What did that woman [reporter] say about Britney?

She said that a Baptist organization had named her role model of the year or something.
AGUILERA: But what did she say Britney did to get it?

She promised to keep her virginity until marriage.
AGUILERA: Oh? (*Rolls her eyes and looks into the fire, then turns back again, perturbed.*) I can't believe that.

That bothers you?
AGUILERA (*scrunches her face, disgusted*): She's not a virgin!

---

* One of the moon villages Pamela sings about visiting, where she meets citizens like Messieurs Walnut, Pecan, Cashew, and Filbert.

Aguilera's publicist rushes in to prevent her from saying too much in front of a reporter.

PUBLICIST: Maybe it's Jessica Simpson. She's like that.

The publicist whisks Aguilera away. When night falls, the interview continues in Aguilera's Toronto hotel room as she snacks on pizza, Coke, and Chips Ahoy cookies.

AGUILERA: The secret to eating junk food is to only eat a little at a time.

I've heard you talk about spirituality a few times. What are your beliefs?
AGUILERA: I'm Christian, and I believe in God. I wish I could go to church more often on Sunday. I really do. That's also a reason why it's so important to stay grounded, because it could all be taken away tomorrow. All of this [success] isn't something that I did. I don't view it like that. It's something that is totally there for a purpose. He wants me to do what I'm doing for good, do you know what I mean. But I think my personality fights with that sometimes. (*She switches on all the lamps in the room.*) I'm afraid of the dark. I have nightmares.

That makes sense for you.
AGUILERA: Really? I'm afraid of spirits and things. Especially with living in hotel rooms. You never know who was in there before you, or what happened exactly in this room. I hear these stories. It freaks me out.

Did you see spirits when you were a kid?
AGUILERA: I used to see my guardian angel when I was very young. My mom and I were playing hide-and-go-seek one time. I ran up the stairs and my mom was saying, "I'm going to get you, I'm going to get you." And all of a sudden, I looked up and stopped dead in my tracks. There was this guy and he was in an all-white outfit, just kinda glowing. He was looking down at me. He had a white beard.

Was he looking over you benevolently?
AGUILERA: Yeah, he was looking down at me calmly and very peacefully.*

---

* Shelly Kearns on her daughter's visions: "We did everything we could to catch her and make sure this was something she actually was seeing. I thought maybe it was my dad, because my father died when I was twelve. But this was a particular person who looked very different. I asked what kind of clothes he had on and she said, 'No, covers.' Then she pulled the sheet out from under the covers to show me. It makes you wonder who that was or what it was about."
   So what does she think it was? "The way things happen in her life, the pattern was so obvious, we thought there must be some divine intervention. Early on, I realized I don't have to be nervous about anything, because God has plans for her."

So that should help you sleep at night, knowing someone's watching over you.
AGUILERA: It should. But usually I can't, so I end up just writing in my journals. I've been on my own, and it's kind of lonely and crazy when so much stuff is thrown at you. Sometimes you feel like the whole world is waiting for you to mess up *(pauses)*. I kind of wrote a song about what I've been going through this year. Want to hear it?

Sure.

She rolls off the couch, staggers sleepily into the bedroom, and returns with a small, lined notebook.

AGUILERA: I wrote this song, and it has kind of a gospel feel. Have you heard Mariah's first album? It's kind of like "Vanishing," but it's more personal. I wrote it with Heather Holley, who wrote "Obvious." I wish I had a tape with the piano part. It would mean so much more with the music, but maybe you can just imagine it.

(*She turns her head away, so that she's gazing out of the picture window, and sings:*) "The world seems so cold / When I face so much all alone / A little scared to move on / And knowing how fast I have grown." The piano gets really soft here. (*Singing again, her voice crescendoing:*) "And I wonder just where I fit in / Oh, the vision of life in my head / Oh yes, I will be strong . . ." Then there's this whole belting thing in the chorus.

She finishes the song and sinks into the sofa exhausted. Minutes later, she is under the covers in bed, curled on her left side in a crescent shape.

True to her word, years later, Aguilera spoke at several women's shelters, donating $200,000 to one of them.

[BRITNEY SPEARS]
SCENE 2

More than most other musicians, you're under a microscope all the time. Why is it that other entertainers can discuss doing drugs, but—
BRITNEY SPEARS: But if I go out and have a drink, it's like, "Oh my gosh, Britney went and had a drink. What's going on?" I don't understand it. I don't understand why. It's really bizarre.

Maybe the reason is because early on you set up an image for yourself that people are holding you to?

SPEARS: See, that's such an irony. People are like, "You were so innocent, da da da da," and all that. And I'm like, "No, I wasn't. You guys said I was too sexual when I first came out with '. . . Baby One More Time.'" You can't win, man. You know what I mean?

Well, we can probably figure out why everyone held you up to that standard.

SPEARS: I don't know why.

Maybe it's because—

SPEARS: I don't know. I have no idea.

Maybe it's because you did play a part in making your virginity an issue and telling teen magazines that you wouldn't drink or—

SPEARS: I'm growing up. I'm twenty-one. I can't play with dolls forever. I mean, I love my dolls and I still collect them. But you understand what I'm trying to say.

So how do you keep people's expectations and criticisms from getting in the way of just living your own life?

SPEARS: Well, I try not to read anything, because it's all bull at the end of the day. It's really silly. I mean the stuff about me, personally. Trust me, I'm such a victim of going and sitting there and buying Us Weekly. I find it so interesting. I do, I do. But I choose not to read stuff about me. It's just weird. I try to make it basically about my music and that's it.

It's interesting how every record you make, people always say it's your "grown-up record."

SPEARS: I think you never grow up. If anyone says that they're completely full-grown, what's the fun in that? It's like every day you want to learn something new. Every day you want to challenge yourself and get better. It's not like this one's the grown-up record: This was just a moment in my life that I'm going through. I'm not grown up and I'm not a little girl. I just am.

[JORDY]

With his catchy single "Dur Dur D'Etre Bébé!" ("It's Tough to Be a Baby") at number one in multiple countries—and sales of one record for every minute he'd been alive—Jordy, France's five-year-old dance music sensation, seemed to be succumbing to the decadence of stardom. When *Details* magazine assigned me to meet him, the first thing he did was ask the translator to take him to the toilet, where he peeped under occupied stalls in the women's bathroom. When he returned, he demanded that a young girl be brought into the room.

What do you want a young girl for?
JORDY: *Pour jouer au docteur.*
TRANSLATOR: To play doctor.

What about Alison [his girlfriend]?
JORDY: *Oui, j'ai baissé ses pantalons et j'ai dessiné des fleurs sur ses fesses.*
TRANSLATOR: Yes, I lowered her pants and drew flowers on her butt.

Do you ever play with boys?
JORDY: *Je n'aime pas les garçons. Ils se battent.*
TRANSLATOR: I don't like boys. They fight.

When Jordy's parents enter the room, we discuss his fame as he sketches a picture of a fire engine on a piece of paper. Oddly, beneath the fire engine, he begins drawing a row of lines dangling to the ground.

What are those lines there?
JORDY: *Des zizis.*
TRANSLATOR: Penises.

Ten minutes later . . .

Do you think all this attention is affecting his development?
PATRICIA CLERGET [Jordy's mother]: He's a very normal child. All the attention hasn't affected him at all.

CLAUDE LEMOINE [Jordy's father]: He still wants to be a policeman or a fireman when he grows up.

As his parents speak, Jordy jumps on the table, grabs his crotch, and proclaims . . .

JORDY: *Je suis Michael Jackson!*
TRANSLATOR: I am Michael Jackson.

Less than a year after this interview, the French government banned Jordy from television and radio due to concerns that he was being exploited by his parents. Jordy later legally emancipated himself from his parents and formed his own rock band.

[PJ HARVEY]

Artist is an overused term when it comes to musicians. Most are primarily entertainers, giving the public what it wants. Their motivation is not self-expression but attention and acclaim. If no one were watching, they wouldn't be making any noise. When I met PJ Harvey—one of the most important rock musicians of her generation—at a London hotel, I pretty quickly discovered she was not an entertainer.

Do interviews serve any purpose for you?
PJ HARVEY: Well, I don't enjoy them.

Oh yeah?
HARVEY: I hate interviews. I don't particularly want to sit here and talk about myself. I'm not thinking about my fans. I do them because I feel like I have to do them.

Why do you have to?
HARVEY: Because it's good for people to know that I'm here and because maybe someone that hasn't heard the music before will pick the article up and will want to buy the record.

But the interviews don't serve any purpose for you, even as far as getting to talk out ideas or thoughts?
HARVEY: No.

Because you—
HARVEY: They mean nothing to me.

I had heard that you were very open in your first interviews but then regretted it.
HARVEY: I think to begin with, I was. I tried to answer every question as best as I possibly could, and then you learn slowly not to trust anyone. And you learn you have to put barriers up and give only what you want to give.

I think people do that because they're worried they're going to be judged for communicating what they really think.
HARVEY: You know, I'm not sitting here talking to you being myself at all. It's very guarded, and I'm just giving you exactly as much as I want to give and what I'm comfortable with today. Maybe if you'd interviewed me tomorrow, it might be different.

I actually am interviewing you tomorrow, too. But I get what you're saying. For me, the point of an interview is not necessarily to promote someone's music, but to let people know who someone is beyond their music and maybe enable others to learn from their experiences or outlook or creative process.
HARVEY: Yet people who write these things form their own kind of opinion. And none of it is right. I mean, I hope one day I get to the point where I have to do very, very few interviews, because I do feel it's an intrusion of my privacy.

Yesterday, when you were talking to those two Japanese girls, they were saying that they had sent you a couple of letters. Do you read your fan mail?
HARVEY: No. Some people have managed to find my home address and they send it there. But I find it a bit intrusive, so I tend to not read those out of principle.

So you've never corresponded with your fans at all?
HARVEY: No.

Not even—
HARVEY: No.

What's written on your hand, by the way?
HARVEY: Serum. I'm not going to explain that for you.

Maybe I don't want to know.

HARVEY: It's my personal notepad. Everything I have to remember goes there. And when I see this person, I have to talk about serum. [. . .]

Could you record what you felt was the greatest album you've ever made, and then bury it in the ground somewhere afterward—knowing no one else will ever hear it—and still be satisfied?

HARVEY: I don't know. That's a very interesting question. It's very much a need I have, to write music and to make things. Not just music things, but little pieces of artwork that mean nothing to anyone else, that I never show to anybody else. I keep sketch pads I'll never show to anyone. I write loads of words I'll never show to anybody. It's for me—and I need to do it. It's part of my learning process and part of my life, of being here and experiencing as much as I can. So, yes, I think I could make an album and never play it to anyone, and it wouldn't really make much difference.

$$\left[\begin{array}{c} \textbf{LADY GAGA} \\ \textit{SCENE 4} \end{array} \right]$$

Midway through the interview, Lady Gaga asked me to stop recording. She sang a new song, "Born This Way," a cappella, then opened her MacBook and played demos of half a dozen other tracks she was working on. Wendi Morris, her tour manager, shook her head in disapproval, since the album wasn't supposed to be released for at least nine months. "He's going to write about other stuff," Gaga protested. "I just want him to know who I am."

I'm going to ask you a question I've asked a few other artists: If you finish this album and you feel it's the greatest album you've ever made, could you then go bury it somewhere and know that no one is ever going to hear it, but still feel artistically satisfied for having completed it?

LADY GAGA: No! No way!

So far, only one person has said they could do that and feel satisfied.

LADY GAGA: Whatever artist said that is lying to you.

I'll tell you the one person who said yes. It was PJ Harvey, and I think I believe her.

LADY GAGA: I would believe PJ Harvey. But you know, to be totally honest—and I don't like to say anything bad about other artists at all—but I will say hypothetically, any artist that's on a record label that's putting out music that tells you they don't care about fame is lying to you. Because you can always just make music in your room at home by yourself for no money.

Right, and she *was* doing an interview.
LADY GAGA: And you're doing an interview, so why? Even if they don't really believe they're lying, they're lying. I think it was John Lennon that used to say anyone who says they don't make music for people to hear it, they're full of shit. Go make music in your room. It's so dumb to me. Are you thirsty?

I'm fine. Your fans seem to really like what you stand for, because some people need to be reminded that it's okay to be different.
LADY GAGA: I love what they stand for. I love who they are. They inspire me to be more confident every day. When I wake up in the morning, I feel just like any other insecure twenty-four-year-old girl. But I say, "Bitch, you're Lady Gaga, you better fucking get up and walk the walk today," because they need that from me. And they inspire me to keep going.

On her tour bus that night, she discusses finding a mentor in the writer Deepak Chopra, and crying hysterically to him before a recent show about a dream in which the devil was trying to take her to hell.

Do you have any recurring dreams?
LADY GAGA: I have this recurring dream sometimes where there's a phantom in my home. And he takes me into a room and there's a blond girl with ropes tied to all four of her limbs. And she's got my shoes on from the Grammys. Go figure—psycho. And the ropes are pulling her apart.

I never see her get pulled apart, but I just watch her whimper and then the phantom says to me, "If you want me to stop hurting her and if you want your family to be okay, you will cut your wrist." And I think that he has his own like crazy wrist-cutting device. And he has this honey in like Tupperware, and it looks like sweet-and-sour sauce with a lot of MSG from New York. Just bizarre. And he wants me to pour the honey into the wound, and then put the cream over it and a gauze. So I looked up the dream and I couldn't find anything about it anywhere. And my mother goes, "Isn't that an Illuminati ritual?" And I was like, "Oh my God!"

You definitely have a martyr thing going on in that dream. Instead of bleeding openly, you take it all inside and cover it up.
LADY GAGA: You know what's so funny is that's what Deepak said to me. He said that I was recognizing my own cultural death and resurrection. I wrote that song I played for you right after I had that dream. So my dreams do induce my creativity.

They have to come from somewhere.
LADY GAGA: And they gotta go somewhere. I can't leave them in my brain or I'll go crazy!

Her tour manager serves her white wine and chicken strips, which she dips copiously in ketchup. She discusses her recent diagnosis as "borderline lupetic," which means that she is at risk of developing lupus, the autoimmune disease her aunt Joanne died from before Lady Gaga was born.

So what changes did you make in your life once you found out?
LADY GAGA: I make much more of an effort now to minimize the drama or the stress in my life. I take care of myself. I drink and I still live my life, but I could never let my fans down. That would kill me to have to face that extra obstacle every day to get onstage. It's completely terrifying, so I'm just really focused on mind, body, and soul. And also, Joanne—I believe that her spirit is inside of me. So, you know, my closest friends have told me that it was just her way of peeking in to say hello.

That's an interesting way to think about it.
LADY GAGA: And I've got her death date on my arm.

Next to the Rilke quote?
LADY GAGA: Yeah. She was a poet and a writer, and I guess I truly believe that she had unfinished work to do and she works through me. She was like a total saint. So maybe she's living vicariously through a sinner (*laughs*).

Minutes later, the bus stops in front of a hotel to pick up Lady Gaga's assistant and continue to Manchester for the next concert.

I'll let you get to Manchester. Let me see if I missed anything.
LADY GAGA: What are you saying? You got way more than anyone. And you saw two shows. I feel raped (*laughs*)!

You *have* given me a lot of good stuff . . .
LADY GAGA: Use the stuff that's going to make me a legend. (*To her tour manager:*) I want to be a legend. Is that wrong?

[**CURTAIN**]

ACT THREE

OR

MEAN GUYS WITH LONG HAIR

SYNOPSIS

Enter Robert Plant and Jimmy Page, who say the only person they're scared to meet is Jerry Lee Lewis, whose wife says he is misunderstood, unlike Brian Wilson's wife, who makes sure he's not misunderstood by talking for him, while Judd Apatow understands and lets his best friend go down on his wife, &c.

[LED ZEPPELIN]
SCENE 1

It was the opportunity of a lifetime. I'd just started working at the *New York Times*, and my editor asked me to interview Robert Plant and Jimmy Page of Led Zeppelin. According to their publicist, it would be the pair's first in-depth interview together since the band broke up fourteen years earlier.

As I timidly entered Plant's hotel room two weeks later, he lit a stick of White Light Pentacles incense as Page took a seat on the couch next to him, both flaunting leather pants and long billowing manes. I sat across from them and asked my naïve questions about their lives and career, and they responded flippantly but honestly. I knew the story was going to turn out great. But then, forty minutes into the interview, I looked down at my tape deck and noticed I'd accidentally plugged the microphone into the headphone jack, which meant that all I had was forty minutes of blank tape. I reached for the microphone and surreptitiously tried to rectify the problem—and was instantly caught.

ROBERT PLANT: Gosh, what's that you have on top of the microphone?

Oh, it just had a protective covering, which was scraping off.
JIMMY PAGE: Microphones have protective coverings these days?
PLANT: Have you been getting any of this?

I think it's fine.
PAGE: Where were we?
PLANT: God knows. It doesn't really matter, because it's gone.

We were talking about, if John Bonham hadn't died, would you have continued making music as Led Zeppelin into the eighties?
PLANT: I don't know. Was when John died the right time to stop? Maybe 1980 was already a bit late to stop. Maybe we should have stopped before.
PAGE: But anyway, we couldn't have carried on without John. We had been working as a four-piece in such an integral, combined unit for so long that to get somebody in to learn those areas of improvisation just wouldn't have been honest to any of us, and certainly not to his name.
PLANT: That's where the Who went wrong, really. And they went wrong with a hell of a thump, because they got a drummer who was so inanimate.

There have been a lot of books written about your backstage antics, but is there one story that's your favorite?

PLANT: Oh, who knows? You can't be specific about anything so far back. You should ask maybe some of the cast who aren't in this room. Maybe some of the housewives from Des Moines. Why don't you go to Schenectady and see if you can find the girl who stood by the Coke machine when [Jeff] Beck stuck his Telecaster through it?* I mean, there's loads of people who've got stories to tell just waiting to be on the *Letterman* show.

Does it bother you that your crew has divulged so many of these stories?

PLANT: I don't think we really ever saw the crew. In fact, I don't even know whether we had one. Who knows? Maybe whatever was in those books was written about somebody else completely. If you're not there to refute it, it just rolls on and becomes some kind of legend, and I don't know whether that's good or bad.

PAGE: (*Groans.*)

PLANT: I really spent a lot of time personally, while Jimmy was doing all this damage, reading books on Celtic literature and the Welsh Triads. I was the youngest guy in the group. I was a Catholic.

PAGE: Any other excuse?

PLANT: My arms are folded because I'm insecure.

I'm sure a lot of the carnage started just due to the newness of the situation of being on the road.

PLANT: The carnage?

PAGE: Rape and pillage?

PLANT: No, it started, I think, in Norway and Sweden in about the year 620. The only thing we did was we didn't bring the same hats. And also you got really shitty record deals in 600 AD.

PAGE: That's why there were horns on their hats then.

PLANT: That's right. Well, they never got any fucking royalties. But I think the thing is that Ahmet Ertegun† was still telling lies back then. As the horde came ashore in Northumbria, cutting the throats of the holy men of the cloth, Ahmet was going, "I'm going to give you twelve percent." (*Refills his tea.*) You want a cup of tea?

I'm good.

PLANT: So who have you interviewed lately that made you go, "Wow!"

---

* According to legend, in 1969, the guitarist broke open a vending machine backstage with his guitar to obtain some cola to mix with his Jack Daniels.

† The head of Atlantic Records, the label Led Zeppelin was signed to.

Tape it _ANYWHERE_

Most recently, it was probably Carl Perkins. He's in his sixties and the coolest guy I've ever met. He doesn't even have to try.

PLANT: I think that's another thing you learn as you get older. Sometimes people try so fucking hard to be somebody else in an attempt to be cool and be loved. But there's not an original shape for any of us, really. Not you as a journalist nor me as a singer nor him as a guitar player.

Did you ever meet Elvis?

PLANT: We met Elvis in LA. I suppose we were with him for about three hours, weren't we?

PAGE: Something like that.

PLANT: We were there longer than anybody had been known to in living history. He wanted to know who these people were who sold more tickets than he did quicker. He'd met Elton John and he thought all English people were like him, so we got around it. We had a good time, didn't we?

PAGE: He was very funny.

PLANT: He was very sharp, too. Forget the legends and all that crap. He was as bright as you like. Although I loathed that period when he came out of the army. I felt he'd betrayed us, like when your heroes get old and you don't like them anymore because they're not hip.

Is there anyone you've ever been scared to meet?

PLANT: Jerry Lee Lewis, and maybe—what's that bloke that sings in Guns N' Roses?

PAGE: (*Laughs.*)

There's a knock at the door.

PLANT: Who's that at the door? Is it the fifty-year-old middle-aged hooker I ordered?

[*Continued . . .*]

==== **[JERRY LEE LEWIS]** ====

After much hemming, hawing, and postponing, Jerry Lee Lewis—not just one of the originators of rock and roll but perhaps its first real punk—agreed to get on the phone just before traveling to New York for his first show there in a decade. It was an odd interview, however, either because he was wary of the press (which had bashed him after his 1957 marriage to his thirteen-year-old cousin, the deaths of two of his wives and two children, and his arrest for being drunk and brandishing a pistol outside Graceland) or because he had a hearing problem—or, most likely, for both reasons.

When I read your interviews, you seem to talk as if rock and Christianity are opposed to each other. Do you feel that way?
JERRY LEE LEWIS: I don't quite understand what you mean.

Often, you talk about rock as if it's a darker side to your persona.
LEWIS: Oh yeah, well I understand where you're coming from. That still remains to be seen. I don't want to lead kids in the wrong direction. I'm just trying to get it straightened out the best way I can. I believe that God will show me the way when the time is right. If he don't, I'm a loser. And I don't like losing.

Did you ever think of becoming a minister like Al Green or Little Richard?
LEWIS: Yes, I have. I think about it quite often.

And what do you think about it?
LEWIS: Well, I think that I either should do it or shut up about it.

So I guess you're shutting up about it?
LEWIS: It's something you don't play around with. If I go in that direction, I'll stay in that direction.

When you hear modern rock bands, do you feel you have a connection to the music?
LEWIS: These kids and these people are so hungry for the truth.

But when you listen to it, do you still hear your sound in it or do you feel like it's gone off on its own tangent?
LEWIS: I started it. You know, it was Elvis Presley, Jerry Lee Lewis, Chuck Berry, Fats Domino, Little Richard. We kinda kicked it off. And I would imagine we'd be held responsible for how it sounds today.

Did your *Killer!* book come out in the United States?
LEWIS: I think God gives us enough sense to work our own problems out (*laughs*).

JERRY LEE
MINISTRIES

ALL ARE WELCOME!

TONIGHT'S SERMON

*"Writing About
Good Things."*

Did your *Killer!* book come out in the United States?
LEWIS: Pardon?

You did an autobiography, right?
LEWIS: Yeah.

Did that come out in the United States?
LEWIS: It was written in Ireland. I went over to Ireland. The biography, is that what you're talking about? It's a good book and it will be released in the United States here in the next couple of months.

What publisher?
LEWIS: It's the only book that's the truth. I finally got the truth down for the first time. All these other books just distorted everything and wrote things that ain't even true at all. Not even true at all.

Do you know who published it?
LEWIS: No, I really don't. People in England.

The so-called scandal that people say hurt your career when you announced your marriage in England . . .
LEWIS: Yeah.

Do you think that same thing would hurt a musician's career today?
LEWIS: No. Well, it's just one of those things. I really don't know how to explain that. That would be hard to explain. It did happen.

I don't know if you've heard of R. Kelly—the big R&B star. He married his fifteen-year-old protégée and his career keeps going fine.
LEWIS: Yeah, well, I'll tell ya. It would be . . . Excuse me, my wife's trying to get me off the phone. Come to the show. We'll finish the discussion then. They're coming in the door on me. Would you like to say a word to her? *

Sure.

---

* Not his cousin, who was his third wife, but his sixth wife, Kerrie.

LEWIS: Well, it was nice talking with ya, and I'll turn you over to her. God bless ya! See you in New York.
KERRIE LEWIS: Hello?

So are you coming to New York with Jerry?
KERRIE: Oh yeah, I'll be there. What did you ask? He's making faces and things. I'm fixing to knock him out. That's what I'm fixing to do. (*To Jerry:*) You're not bothering me. Sit down! . . . I'm not going over there. . . . Okay, I love you too. I'm coming to the house in a minute. . . . I'm still mad at you, and you're gonna get it. (*To me:*) Sorry.

Are there any new things going on in Jerry Lee's career that I should mention in the article?
KERRIE: Well, there's hundreds of things. But do y'all really write about good things?

We write about good things.
KERRIE: Nobody cares that I'm sixty years old, that I work out on a HealthRider every day, that I'm the best I've ever been. But, you know, they taped a video at the Ryman [Auditorium] in Nashville where he did four encores and he probably moved from his head to his toes every limb and muscle, so they knew he didn't have arthritis—or whatever the disease is with the hands or the shaking. He was perfect! The kids are taking music lessons. We got Lee learning on his daddy's piano and Derek learning on a James Burton signature guitar, so the kids are rolling right along.

I think at this point it would be more of a surprise to read all these good things.
KERRIE: Jerry, number one, does not grant interviews. Okay, he doesn't do them. Unless they want to pay him some stupid ridiculous amount of money. Only because he says they all start the same: "You were born in 1930.* You started playing piano at nine. Your daddy sold thirty-nine dozen eggs to get you to Memphis. Uh-huh. And they bought you a piano by mortgaging the house. Uh-huh. They lost their house so you could keep the piano. Uh-huh." He's basically kind of gotten an interview written. It's about a hundred pages. "Here it is. You write it. It's the only thing you're gonna ask me. You're not gonna ask me anything good and if you do, you're not gonna print it." So he just doesn't do them.

---

* He was born in 1935.

The fans probably wonder what he's been doing now anyway. They know the past.

KERRIE: Exactly. His manager, Jerry Schilling, you can thank for this. He said, "It's the *New York Times*. They've been around for a hundred years." Jerry basically says to me, "You know, I would do interviews every day all day long if people would treat me nice and write good things rather than going back to when my son died or a wife OD'd or I married my third cousin." I mean, that was thirty years ago. Here he is with a family of twelve years, a brand new career, not a thing wrong with his health. He's got life insurance for the first time in his career. He's paid off his debt to the IRS. I mean, you know, things are going his way more than you could possibly ever imagine.

I'm glad I talked to you to get all this.

KERRIE: Jerry probably wouldn't even offer it. He says, "Well, they don't want to know anyway. They should be asking me if they want to know."

Jerry Lee and Kerrie Lewis divorced in 2005. According to the Memphis Commercial Appeal *newspaper, he accused her of sleeping with a bodyguard and a Pentecostal minister, and she accused him of being an abusive "washed-up rock and roll singer who was past his prime."*

[BRIAN WILSON]
SCENE 1

Every time I've interviewed Brian Wilson of the Beach Boys, he's grown a little more coherent. This, heartbreakingly, was him at his best. It took place in Chicago, where the notoriously reclusive Wilson had moved with his wife of three years, Melinda, in order to record a new album, continue recovering from his lost years of drug abuse and mental illness, and escape the control of his former therapist, Eugene Landy. The previous day, Wilson had performed a show billed as the first solo concert of his life.

Are you used to working as hard as you did yesterday?

BRIAN WILSON: Yeah, I was a little bit shook up.

MELINDA WILSON: No. You're not used to it.

BRIAN: I mean, what am I talking about? It was pretty scary.

Were you happy with the new documentary about you?

BRIAN: Yeah. I thought once in a while my face will have a twist of emotional pain coming out of it, but not too obvious. It's not like I'm really suffering.

MELINDA: But that was still partially a painful time. It was getting out of those really horrible [Eugene Landy] years. It was just on the tail end of that, you know.

BRIAN: Actually—

MELINDA: I think sometimes it's easier to talk about it once you've been through it and you see the light at the end of the tunnel. But when you're going through it, it's kind of rough.

What do you attribute your recent productivity to?

BRIAN: I long to make music. I love music. That's what it really is. I love music (*laughs*). I like making it, too. I like making music.

MELINDA: With Brian, it's totally in his soul. It's part of his existence.

Several people told me they communicate best with you not in speech but musically. Why do you think that is?

BRIAN: I think I put it off. I put off the vibration, and people can pick it up.

MELINDA: And basically—don't you think, too, Bri?—in life he's kind of shy. With music, he can write a song and get the point across and not have to deal with the actual conversation.

BRIAN: Yeah, she's right, you know. She knows me.

[*Continued . . .*]

[JUDD APATOW]

When people watch a film, questions often come to mind that they'd be curious to ask the director if given the opportunity. After watching director Judd Apatow's *Funny People*, which stars his wife, Leslie Mann, and his best friend, Adam Sandler, as lovers, that opportunity arose.

What was it like directing your wife in a sex scene with your best friend?

JUDD APATOW: You know, oddly enough, I was giddy that whole afternoon. I don't know why, but it just cracked me up.

So it didn't feel weird to watch that?

APATOW: It didn't feel weird at all. I loved the idea that their sex went straight to cunnilingus.

Hmm.

APATOW: Really, I found it funny. It made me laugh. I've watched Leslie have kissing scenes with other people where I wanted to kill myself or vomit. But maybe I have so much affection for both of them that I was happy to watch them play a really intimate, funny scene.

I guess if it was awkward for anybody, it would be Adam.

APATOW: They were both okay, mainly because I was amused. If you notice, though, I didn't write a full ten-minute scene of lovemaking. And (*smiles*) I didn't do a ton of takes.

[LED ZEPPELIN]
SCENE 2

Jimmy Page answered the door. Standing there was the band's publicist, who had been walking the hallway for the last hour to break in Page's new shoes for him. Page then sent him on his next mission: to buy CDs of new bands.

JIMMY PAGE: We want to stay in touch with the underground, but we don't have time to go to record stores.

ROBERT PLANT: I don't know. I don't trust them to buy music for me. These record labels are useless. If I want to have Technicolor sex in an underground club, they won't know where to take me.

So how has your playing changed since you last performed with Robert?

PAGE: I used chords in the past and tunings, but now I just put my fingers anywhere. So whatever technique I used to have, I try to destroy. The more atonal it is, the better.

What's a good example of that?

PAGE: The triple-neck guitar? That's a mandolin, a twelve-string, and a six-string. But I need two pairs of arms for it really. Now I have to make a decision as to what neck to play at what point in time. It gets rather confusing for an old man.

PLANT: Making decisions and playing music is tough, especially when you've got a very small pyramid descending over you as you're playing. Get it?* I think you can put it down to a sense of humor, actually, the whole thing.

---

* A reference either to the laser pyramid that Page used to perform in or *This Is Spinal Tap,* which parodied, among other bands, Led Zeppelin—or probably both.

The whole thing?
PLANT: The triple neck! You should have a rubber hand come up and start playing it.
PAGE: If I get enough necks, I can put in a wheel and fit a rim around it, and literally just hold onto it and do cartwheels down the stage.
PLANT: In Emerson, Lake & Palmer—or was it Tower of Power?—they used to spin the drummer. The drummer used to go in a gyroscope and be spun around during his solo. That was the carefree seventies. Not a trick in sight.

Out of curiosity, how do you feel about "Stairway to Heaven" becoming this masterpiece that every aspiring rock guitarist must learn?
PLANT: I think we're in a disposable world, really, and "Stairway to Heaven" is one of the things that hasn't quite been thrown away yet. But it's been mistreated. I think all radio stations should be asked not to play it for ten years, just to leave it alone for a bit so we can tell whether it's any good or not.
PAGE (*laughing*): Maybe they don't play it anymore, I don't know.
PLANT: I can't believe we wrote so many words in that song.

I found it strange that you were an opening act for Lenny Kravitz.
PLANT: I will always do stuff like that. Opening for Lenny Kravitz was a huge facetious show of anti-ego because he was using so many shapes of ours anyway.
PAGE: Shapes is a nice way of putting it.
PLANT: And he knew that! And I knew that. And everybody in the crew, the band, and the audience knew that. He used to sit enthralled if I wanted to tell him a tale. Or he'd ask if I could get him a pair of my Landlubbers, which were these old jeans with the slit pockets and flares. He's playing the music he really likes to play and he does a great job, too, you know, but the originality is a little questionable.

Do you mind if I refer to my list of questions?
PLANT: You've been doing very well so far without them.

I've been using them, but I just don't like to ask random questions out of context.
PLANT: When they're out of context, are you embarrassed by them?

Well, the interviews are better when they're more conversational. But to be perfectly honest, I'm worried that the first half of the interview didn't record, so I want to make sure I didn't miss anything.
PLANT: I knew it!

[*Continued . . .*]

[LENNY KRAVITZ]

During a weekend with Lenny Kravitz in New Orleans for a *Rolling Stone* cover story, he seemed to constantly evade questions about his musical influences. Finally, as we sat in his living room after a concert at the House of Blues by the funk band Zapp, I decided to try one more time.

This might piss you off, but . . .
LENNY KRAVITZ: Go for it.

That song "Rock and Roll Is Dead" begins with this riff that sounds exactly like Led Zeppelin's "Living Loving Maid (She's Just a Woman)."
KRAVITZ: You mean the first line in the song?

No, the guitar part and then that Robert Plant yowl you do. I was wondering whether you were making a joke by singing, "Rock and roll is dead," in a song based on a Led Zeppelin riff that everybody still steals.
KRAVITZ: No, it's just a riff that I came up with.

You came up with it on your own?
KRAVITZ: Yeah. I mean, you know.

I suppose people are always thinking your riffs came from elsewhere.
KRAVITZ: That's all right. How many riffs are there? Every riff you could say sounds like something else.

I suppose, but some riffs sound more like past riffs than others.
KRAVITZ: It's just the blues, really.

So you don't think the introduction to that song sounds anything like "Living Loving Maid"?
KRAVITZ: No. I mean, I think it has a Zeppelin-type quality. Oh, I don't know. Let's not talk about it.

[FLEETWOOD MAC]

With over nineteen million copies sold, Fleetwood Mac's *Rumours* ranks among the top ten best-selling albums of all time. Yet despite this success, drummer Mick Fleetwood, the band's de facto leader since 1967, not only struggled with the usual drug and alcohol excesses, but also ended up declaring personal bankruptcy. Some thirty years after forming the band, however, he finally seemed to be getting his act together.

I heard that you were booked to play the Woodstock anniversary concert, which is strange because you weren't at the first one, were you?
MICK FLEETWOOD: The original Woodstock we turned down years and years ago. We didn't even know what it was. We were doing something in Detroit or somewhere. Of course, it turned out to be a wildly historic event that we didn't take part in. One often wonders what would have happened to the early incarnation of Fleetwood Mac had we done that. We might have been the new Led Zeppelin, who knows? *

So what made you decide to do the new one?
FLEETWOOD: Quite honestly, they were prepared to pay us very handsomely for doing it.

How does it feel to be touring sober?
FLEETWOOD: It's a whole new ball game. I'm clean and sober and enjoying life. I have a lot more energy. I would have still been up in the old days. I would have been raging. I would have been busy faking my way through this interview, praying that I wasn't going to start stuttering.

What do you think encouraged your excesses in the first place?
FLEETWOOD: I think touring is a perfect surrounding for this. What happens in any performance situation is that you get very professional at monitoring yourself, and you're able for the most part to perform very adequately under the influence.

But after the show, that's when it starts. Because you got such a high off the show, plus you're high anyhow. So where do you go from there? You don't want to

---

* Though Led Zeppelin also turned down Woodstock—for a better-paying gig in New Jersey.

go down, so that's when you start your socializing. You go to the bar and you have a hotel suite, so you invite people back to the room. And you get your women in there, and wouldn't it be fun to do this or that? Before you know it, you're looking at eight in the morning and you're supposed to be getting on a plane and going to the next show and you feel like shit.

So what was the low point that made you realize you needed help?
FLEETWOOD: I took my abuse to the bottom of the ladder. I was in bad, bad shape two and a half years ago, and not many people knew it because I was able to function. People said, "Well, Mick's okay. He drinks and he does a certain amount of cocaine, but he's not that bad."

The fact of the matter is that it *was* that bad, and no one knew it. I would have to go walk on a stage or do an interview, and I'd literally be dying inside, sweating and twitching. So I bottomed out and simply said, "I've had enough. I'm forty-five years old, end of that chapter." And it's been that way ever since, and with no inkling to relapse.

Does it feel strange to be touring without [singer and keyboardist] Christine McVie?
FLEETWOOD: After the amount of time we've all been doing this, she's earned the right to do what she wants to do. And she doesn't want to leave the band, but she doesn't want to go on the road. When we first looked at it, it was a little scary and disappointing. But Brian Wilson does a similar sort of thing with the Beach Boys.

[BRIAN WILSON
SCENE 2]

How much of your past do you remember? Are there periods that are clear and periods that are darker?
BRIAN WILSON: My darkest memories are from Malibu. I was in a program, a doctor's program.
MELINDA WILSON: Honey, that's something we don't need to go into. And I'll tell you why: We've got a lot of legal issues.
BRIAN: Forget it. Skip the question and go to another question.
MELINDA: Just skip the Landy time, Brian.
BRIAN: Okay.

Are there other parts of your background you remember very well?
BRIAN: When the Beach Boys and I used to record in my house in Bel Air, that was a good vibe. I had a good time then.
MELINDA: I'm curious, what do you mean by dark periods or cloudy periods?

Of memory.
MELINDA: You mean because of the drug thing? Why not address it? Yeah, Brian did drugs, but I don't think he did anywhere near the amount of drugs that people think he did. We know people in the music industry who did far more than he ever did. The parts that you're talking about are probably the medical problems that he had instead of drug or alcohol problems.
BRIAN: Yeah, drug-related problems. Yeah, I think she's right. Yeah.
MELINDA (*sighing*): But people kind of get all that mixed together.

Everybody experiments. Especially in LA.
BRIAN: Do you live in LA?

I just moved out there—to West Hollywood.
BRIAN: What street do you live on in West Hollywood?

I actually live off Gardner.
BRIAN: You live on Gardner. What address?

Right around Beverly.
BRIAN: I lived down toward Santa Monica. I'll be darned. I used to live on that same street. In an apartment?

A Spanish-style apartment.
MELINDA: Knowing him, I can't even imagine him living there. I can't imagine him in that Hollywood scene.
BRIAN: What's your address?

It's 366 North Sierra Bonita, actually.
BRIAN: I was on 1047 North Gardner. Near—not Clinton, Santa Monica.

It's amazing you remember that. That was over thirty years ago.
MELINDA: See, now do you think he remembers the past? We've had so many lawsuits, and he's constantly going through depositions and these attorneys come

in thinking he probably won't remember anything, and he just blows them away. What was your batting average in high school, Brian?

BRIAN: About .169.

MELINDA: How do you remember some of that stuff? It's amazing.

[*Continued . . .*]

[THE WHO]
SCENE 1

A marriage between two people is difficult enough, but a band, where four or five people are in a relationship, can be a minefield of ego, miscommunication, resentment, and control issues—especially when the artistic, financial, and personal stakes are so high. Though time supposedly heals all wounds, in the case of the Who, that didn't seem to be the case when singer Roger Daltrey, unable to get a Who reunion going, tried another approach—and paid the price for it.

In a rehearsal studio a week before his sold-out Daltrey Sings Townshend concerts at Carnegie Hall, Daltrey had put together a sixty-five-piece orchestra from Juilliard and a hundred-person crew to help him pay tribute to the songs he'd sung by Who guitarist and songwriter Pete Townshend. But his tributee didn't appear to be as honored and grateful as he'd hoped. Shaking his curly blond hair in disbelief, Daltrey complained about Townshend to orchestra conductor Michael Kamen.

ROGER DALTREY: Has Pete decided what he's doing yet? I think he may be a very big down point in the show.

MICHAEL KAMEN: He's giving me another song called "The Shout." Do you know that song?

DALTREY: What do you mean he's decided to perform "The Shout"? I don't even know that song. I just think that to do something that obscure at that point in the show is suicide.

KAMEN: I tried very hard to get him to do something else.

DALTREY: I should show you the letter he wrote: "I'll do anything you want." He doesn't even want to play with the orchestra now. He changes his mind every day.

KAMEN: It'll be all right on the night of the show.

DALTREY: Yeah, I know, but you just don't do that to friends, do you? He's mad, isn't he? The man's obscene. I'm really up to here in it. (*Flushed, Daltrey walks with his manager to a dressing room, where there's a couch with a large white sheet over it, and says to him:*) Was she that bad you had to put a sheet over her?

He sits on the sheet.

So what made you decide to do this tribute?
DALTREY: Quite simply, I wanted to do it for my fiftieth birthday. I know this is going to sound clichéd, but it is the truth: I was the guy who sang, "I hope I die before I get old." And I've survived, much to my surprise—with a lot of luck, too, I should add. I wanted to celebrate my fiftieth birthday in a grand way with music, because without rock and roll in particular, I would have been a factory worker. I was an uneducated yob. Still am in some ways.

Was it hard to get Pete to agree to do the show?
DALTREY: Initially, no (*laughs heartily*). He's still changing his mind as usual. But Pete's Pete and he'll never change.

How do you feel now when you perform material from over thirty years ago?
DALTREY: I can't sing the early songs like "Pictures of Lily" and "I Can't Explain." I mean, I can sing them, but I can't get the sound right. There was something about the way I used to sing them because I was squeezing myself into them—putting a suit on if you like—that I can't re-create now. I've worn the suit for too long.

Do you find it funny to be paying tribute to someone who has frustrated you in so many ways on this project?
DALTREY: I used to get incredibly angry because I didn't know you can't out-articulate Pete. Pete by his own admission is a compulsive liar, and a lot of those lies have been aimed at me in the past and they still are. But to answer those lies would be just joining the same camp. I try to do it sarcastically sometimes, but I try not to be bitchy because I don't feel bitchy about it. I get incredibly angry sometimes because it makes me feel like everybody . . . But take Pete's interviews and look at what he says about everybody, because he changes his mind so many times it really is like Peter and the Wolf.* Unfortunately, that's where our relationship is at the moment. I don't know where I stand (*laughs*). I think that's being really honest.

Are you planning to do anything for the thirtieth anniversary of the Who this year?
DALTREY: I refer all Who questions now to Pete.

[*Continued . . .*]

---

* By which he means the Aesop fable "The Boy Who Cried Wolf," not the Prokofiev children's composition *Peter and the Wolf.*

[OASIS]
SCENE 1

Oasis guitarist and songwriter Noel Gallagher sat in a hotel bar in Manhattan, wearing a loud paisley shirt and drinking a beer. From a side door, his manager appeared. "I just got off the phone from England," he announced. "Your album's sold more in one week than Blur's did in a month."

"Pigs!" Noel yelled triumphantly, pumping his fist into the air.

You guys are the top British band right now. If you were playing back in the sixties, do you think you could compete with the Beatles?
NOEL GALLAGHER: In the sixties? What year is it now, 1995? If it was 1965, and we'd just put out our second album, we'd be absolutely the pop kings of the world. It would've been the Beatles, the Rolling Stones, Oasis, and then the Who. No one else. I firmly believe that. If we were out in 1975, it would have been the Sex Pistols and Oasis. And if it were 1985, it would have been the Smiths and Oasis. I feel we could chance it in any decade. I could say to any band member from any era, "Pick your best song. Give me the best song you think you've written, and I'll pick mine." And I think the best of ours would be above the best of theirs.

[*Continued . . .*]

[THE WHO]
SCENE 2

In which Pete Townshend very thoughtfully undermines the fiftieth birthday celebration Roger Daltrey has been working so hard on . . .

What made you decide to take part in Roger Daltrey's show, since you had the option of saying no?
PETE TOWNSHEND: Do you think so?

I would think so. Maybe I'm wrong.
TOWNSHEND: Maybe you're wrong.

When I asked Roger about a Who reunion, he said, "Ask Pete." So do you have the power to just snap your fingers and make that happen?

TOWNSHEND: I really don't think that's accurate. I think it's not about when to perform, it's about the need to perform. I don't think people expose themselves to all the rigors of performing for fun. They do it because they really, really have a need to do that. And I just feel that if the Who thing needs to happen, it will happen. And if it doesn't, it doesn't.

That's probably the attitude that perplexes Roger.
TOWNSHEND: I think Roger likes to think this is all about my intransigence, but I don't think that's right. I just won't initiate anything and I won't say yes to anything without thinking about it very, very hard. I've always been very conservative in that respect.

That makes sense, but when everyone else wants to play and you don't—
TOWNSHEND: I did for many, many years honor the Who democracy. We would sit around and vote before deciding to do something, and I went along with that. But in the end, I started to lobby the other members of the band to get the kind of results that I wanted. So I effectively took the Who off the road between '75 and '76 because I just felt that I had had enough and Moon seemed to have had enough, even though he didn't know he'd had enough.* And eventually when I left the group, one of the senses of relief I had was not so much that I didn't have to work with the guys in the band again, but I didn't have to lobby them all the time and fight the democratic functioning of a group.

But what's the point of having a democracy if you can't accept the majority decision?
TOWNSHEND: That's one of the things that makes all groups time limited: Democracy itself requires a change of government every now and again. And what happens in groups is that you end up with many dictatorships, which are not very creative. And if not dictatorships, terrible collusive relationships in which everybody does what everybody else wants in order to get a quiet life. It just doesn't work for the creative life at all, sadly. And it does mean that we're all very nostalgic for those early days of relationships when it did seem to work.

I suppose it's like a marriage where people grow apart.
TOWNSHEND: And we lament that. But it's like saying, "What a pity George Burns and Gracie Allen had to die at different times. They should have just lived forever." And I think that's what I feel about the future of the Who: It is just an attendance

---

* Drummer Keith Moon died of a sedative overdose two years later.

to its history. That's it. People talk about what we can do in the future, and all that we can do in the future is look back.

That's a good answer.
TOWNSHEND: It's not an answer Roger would accept because . . . I shouldn't really speak for him, but I think that he has a dream or a vision that he could do it again. He could get me out of bed again. He thinks this is about me lying in bed (*laughs*). But, you know, I'm not lying in bed.

So he got you to do this birthday thing instead?
TOWNSHEND: Looking back at the Who's career, as wonderful as I'm sure this concert is going to be, all it's really gonna do is make us remember, those of us that were there, the better concerts that we did.

When was the last time you actually sang with an orchestra?
TOWNSHEND: In public, I don't know. I think the last time I attempted to do it was an orchestral version of *Tommy* where I was the narrator. I hated it. Absolutely hated it. I got drunk, and about halfway through I stopped and walked off.

What made you hate it so much?
TOWNSHEND: It just seemed like I'd spent my whole life trying to evolve rock and roll—in a way, advance it within its own terms—and somehow it was being co-opted and swamped by a much greater tradition, which was the tradition of the orchestra, classical music, and traditional opera. We had our own version of pomp and circumstance, and that was smashing a few guitars.

How did the band react when you first decided to start writing songs instead of doing covers?
TOWNSHEND: Well it was actually a reaction of relief. We went to Fontana [Records] with a very, very good version of a Slim Harpo song called "Got Love if You Want It" and a really good Bo Diddley song called "Here 'Tis," both of which I think would have been ballroom hits for the R&B crowd. And we were told that they wouldn't do. We had to have original material. This was kind of the Beatles fad era when everybody was expected to write their own material.

I'd written a couple of fairly sophomoric songs for the band to play really just for fun, and everybody was very encouraging about that, Roger included. But by the time it was released a bit later, Roger really felt that his power base in the band was being threatened somewhat by me writing, so we co-wrote "Anyway, Anyhow, Anywhere" together. And he remembers contributing quite a lot and I remember him contributing very little. But we did it together in a sense to find out whether we could co-write, and I actually felt that we couldn't. So I just stuck to my guns and proceeded to be the writer and the power base did shift.

What are some of the qualities you liked about Roger back then?
TOWNSHEND: When I look back to the very early years, a lot of the things that I used to regard as Roger's negative points, I now view them in a kind of very positive way. Like he used to be quite dominating and threatening. I used to drink a bottle of whiskey and smoke forty joints at night listening to Jimmy Reed, and if he hadn't come around and gotten me out of bed, I wouldn't have done a gig or done anything. I think that in the early days, we needed that kind of discipline. He was a working man. He used to get up at 6:30 in the morning and go and do a job every day, and then at the end of the day, he'd come around and pick me up, pick Keith up, pick John [Entwistle, bassist] up and take us to the show.

When I talked to Roger, he said, "I don't know where I stand with Pete," which seemed like a strange comment.
TOWNSHEND: You know, I just hope nobody knows where they stand with me. That's the way I like it.

Undiscouraged, Daltrey toured later that year playing Who songs with Simon Townshend—Pete's brother—on guitar instead. After two more years, Pete Townshend relented and began touring with Daltrey again, eventually releasing the first new Who studio album in twenty-four years.

I asked your brother this same question: If your band was playing in the sixties, do you think you could compete with the Beatles?
LIAM GALLAGHER: I think we'd be the Beatles.

Then what would the Beatles be?
GALLAGHER: They'd be the Beatles, too. And if the Beatles were here now, they'd be Oasis.

[*Continued . . .*]

[RINGO STARR]

In the Los Angeles studio of producer Don Was, Ringo Starr didn't sit down for an interview; he braced himself for one. Though he was affable and open, he also seemed tense, like a dog expecting at any minute to get hit by a stick. That stick is the Beatles. Everywhere Starr had gone that day, people treated him more like a museum piece in a Beatles exhibit than like a person. Modest by nature, he tended to brush off the attention and avoid the word *Beatles*, referring to the group simply as "we" whenever possible.

Add to this Starr's desire to be taken as seriously as John Lennon but his inability to articulate and conceptualize as well, and you have an interview that, at every turn, grew increasingly awkward—especially when Starr was asked about his habit of flashing peace signs on both hands and saying, "Peace and love," repeatedly.

What made you start using the "peace and love" catchphrase you always say?
RINGO STARR: Every record has some peace and love song on it.

I'm talking more about the way you say it.
STARR: Yeah, I say, "Peace and love. Hey, peace and love." Well, I think it certainly came from the sixties and, you know, we* were peace and love. You'll find photos of us and it just became more and more, and I had this dream that one day everyone on the planet will go, "Peace and love," and there will be a psychic shift.

For my birthday last year in Chicago, I had the twelve noon peace-and-love second. I told people, "Just stop wherever you are at noon and say, 'Peace and love.'" And, you know, that's a great vibe to put out. Really.

Do you know what a meme is? It's an idea that spreads virally. Is that the point?
STARR: Well, I didn't invent it, but I'm trying to spread it, like Maharishi and TM [transcendental meditation]. But I've been put down so badly for peace and loving. (*Harshly:*) "Oh, he's peace and loving, you know what I mean." Hey, I'm only saying "peace and love." What's there to be angry about?

You've gotten shit for it?
STARR: Yeah! People are like, "That's all he does now."

---

* The Beatles.

Well, you do say it a lot.

STARR: Yeah, some people can't take it.

It's better than saying "war and hate" all the time.

STARR: There's a lot of that out there. And we have a track about that. Let's get back to the record.

Okay. The last thing I was going to ask about, and this is such an asshole journalist question . . .

STARR: I hope you write it like that (*laughs*).

I will, because I wouldn't know how to answer it. But what is love and how does one attain it?

STARR: Well, for me, love is to try and be kind and understanding. I mean, I am loved by many people and I love many people, but, you know . . .

In the case of fans, they say love, but they probably mean respect.*

STARR: Well, you cannot help but respect someone if you love them. But you can't say, "Oh, there—that's what it is." It's an emotion. It's a feeling. It's a state of being. Not a state of mind, because I don't know about you, but there's many states in my mind (*laughs*).

It's easy for people to talk about love, but when it's so vague like that, I think it's hard for people to practice it because they don't have the tools or know how to let go of ego and get there.

STARR: I think we all have the tools. I'd like to say I've looked at peace and love since I was born, but that's not true. However, I've become more conscious of it and it's become more and more part of my life. My grandchildren, as soon as they see me, they go, "Peace and love," you know what I mean. It's how they are.

Okay, let's get back to the music. Your song "Peace Dream" has a lot of similarities to [John Lennon's] "Imagine." Was that something you were thinking consciously?

STARR: Well, I brought John into it, is that what you're talking about? I brought John into it because, you know, you always try as a songwriter to express a moment, and I can always talk about John, Paul, and George. And just like John Lennon said in Amsterdam from his bed, and that was the first time he did that

* Ref. Strauss and Gorelick, *Love and Respect*.

peace thing, so he was trying to move peace and love along, too. So it was a peace dream, you know. It was a natural thing to do. It would have been awkward if you'd have done it, you know what I'm saying. But it was easier for me because I knew the man and, you know, I did know that moment that he and Yoko were in Amsterdam.

And then you had Paul McCartney play bass on it?
STARR: Well, he was in for the Grammys, and we always hook up if we're around. Of course I had to play him the track because of the John Lennon line, and he said "fine" and so he played bass on that.

When you say you had to play it for him, why is that?
STARR: Well, because it says "John." Let's not be silly.

You mention a lot of other people by name on the album that you probably didn't check with anyone about.
STARR: I mean, you know, John was in the band, Paul and I were in the band. I just didn't want it to be like we were Beatle-ing out, you know. So I played it to him for that reason. With respect.

[PAUL McCARTNEY]

One would think that when someone has been not just a Beatle but also knighted by the Queen of England, they wouldn't worry so much about what other people think of them. But perhaps it just makes them worry more.

It's been a while since you've released one of your own albums.
PAUL McCARTNEY: The record company said to me, "We don't really need an album this year." So I've just been making music for my own fun. It took the pressure off. It's just a song album, a regular album, which is cool because there's been so much *Anthology* [documentary and CD] stuff around the Beatles.

So you're in just the early stages of recording?
McCARTNEY: Not even. My album probably won't be out until next spring. There's probably going to be another *Anthology* thing around Christmas, so I don't want to go out in competition with that. It's a dumb move, and also it doesn't look right. It looks like I'm trying to upstage the Beatles. It looks like I'm trying to say, "Hey, I'm better than the Beatles." No, it's just not the thing to do.

You've also turned Linda's photographs* into a short movie about the Grateful Dead. Did you do that before Jerry Garcia died?

McCARTNEY: Yeah, the sad thing was that I was in touch with a couple of the guys. I spoke to Bob [Weir, Grateful Dead guitarist] and we had a good phone conversation. I said, "Hey, I'm putting this thing together, and I want to show it to you guys when it's finished." I finished it and I was just getting back in touch with them, then I went on holiday. When I reached America, I heard on the news that Jerry had died and I thought, "Oh shit, you know, I was just about to show the film to him."

Were you both friends?

McCARTNEY: I'd been in correspondence with him, because he was a painter and I thought he'd like this. Unfortunately, I missed him and the bad thing then was I thought, "Oh shit, there's going to be a lot of people out there who will think, oh, I'm cashing in on the fact that Jerry's died." So I immediately got out a press release and said, "Look, I've had this movie for a year now and it's nothing to do with . . . What's more than that, I'm not gonna release it now. You know, I'm going to wait for a little while." So I suppose it has become a little bit of a tribute to Jerry because he's died.

I noticed there was a big gap in the years between its showings.

McCARTNEY: I just didn't want to look like I was cashing in on his death, you know.

[THE GRATEFUL DEAD]

Less than two months before he died in his sleep at a drug treatment center, Jerry Garcia was performing with the Grateful Dead on its seemingly endless thirty-year tour. This stop was at Giants Stadium in New Jersey, with Bob Dylan opening. Some 51,000 people rippled with nearly every note as the band stood practically still, speaking scarcely a single word to an audience that worshipped not necessarily the band members, but the ritual of their improvisatory performances.

In the years after Garcia died, I did a number of interviews with members of the band (including drummer Mickey Hart and bassist Phil Lesh) and its extended family as they wrung their hands, trying to find a way to keep the ritual going without him.

---

* His wife Linda McCartney, a former rock photographer, was being treated for breast cancer at the time. She died eighteen months later at the age of fifty-six.

MICKEY HART: There really is life after the Grateful Dead. We didn't think there was going to be life after the Beatles at one time, and John died, but there was still life. We miss the Grateful Dead. Everybody who's been touched by it will miss it.

PHIL LESH: This is a period of transition. Everything has changed. You'll see us again, but I'll never see Jerry, I'll tell you that.

HART: This morning, I was looking at NBC. My eyes are not like they used to be, and the sunny weather symbol over Florida, it had glasses on and it looked just like him. I said, "There's Jerry over Florida."

LESH: I'm looking for a live tape that we can release from the band that just came to a close, the last incarnation of the Grateful Dead (*pauses, then corrects himself*). Not the final incarnation, but the last up to now.

Two years after Garcia's death, with the band still frozen by indecision, Grateful Dead lyricist Robert Hunter, who'd hung up his guitar because he said he felt "redundant," decided to tour playing the songs he'd written for the band.

ROBERT HUNTER: There's no one else out there carrying the torch of the music. If I didn't do it, I'd just be getting older and fatter.

After another year passed, the band decided to build a 65,000-square-foot Grateful Dead museum called Terrapin Station as a mecca and meeting place for Deadheads.

LESH: With Jerry's death, everything changed. We were no longer a viable touring operation. We couldn't even support our entire staff. To make a smooth transition, we had to fall back on merchandising our archives, and that became the cash cow for the whole organization. But it couldn't stay that way, just putting out our old live concerts until the material and interest dwindled away. [. . .] So with Terrapin Station, we want to keep that relationship and have Deadheads keep the same kind of community they had with the band.

The museum, however, never got off the ground. In the meantime, Lesh, Hart, and guitarist Bob Weir couldn't take it any longer and reunited for a tour as the Other Ones.

DENNIS McNALLY [longtime Dead publicist]: Please don't call it a reunion. A reunion suggests picking up where you left off. They will play the same material, they may even get to the same places, but they'll get there different ways. This is an evolution. It's going to be very different.

Five more years passed until the band decided to finally just let go and do it. The surviving members renamed themselves the Dead and began touring, playing their old songs. But they chose an unlikely replacement for Jerry Garcia: a woman, Joan Osborne, famous for her hit, "One of Us."

JOAN OSBORNE: I knew of course about the band and loved some of their songs, but I was not a Deadhead. I didn't follow these guys around living in a VW mini-bus selling grilled cheese sandwiches in the parking lot of their shows. I sometimes get the feeling like I'm living out somebody else's fantasy, like the wish sort of landed on earth in the wrong spot. It should have hit that guy three seats over who's been wishing for it every moment since his first Dead show.

A year later, Osborne was replaced as singer of the Dead by Warren Haynes of Govt. Mule so the band could sound even more like it did during its heyday with Garcia.

[GROUPIES]

When I wrote a book with Dave Navarro, I asked him why he regularly called two-thousand-dollar prostitutes to his house when there were countless girls willing to sleep with him for free. "I'm not into hurting little girls' feelings anymore," he explained. "A hooker is not going to show up on your doorstep at four in the morning, saying she just moved from Michigan so she can spend her life with you."

From the outside, rockers may seem to live a dream lifestyle when it comes to sexual decadence. But in many cases, the women they sleep with are not just looking for sex. They're looking for something more than that. And a one-night stand can end in theft, a paternity suit, a statutory rape charge, or years of being stalked. At a Grateful Dead show, I interviewed Marta, a petite blond hippie, who shared her experience.

MARTA: I sort of have a boyfriend in the Grateful Dead.

Which member are you dating?
MARTA: I shouldn't be telling you this, but it's Bob Weir. Well, I don't know if it's right to call him a boyfriend. After our last meeting, I went totally crazy.

What happened?

MARTA: Well, I first met him after a Dead show. I got all dressed up. I mean, super-tight pants that just showed off my ass and this really white blousy revealing top. And I danced in the center of the rows on the floor, so the band was checking me out and singing songs at me.

How did you know that?

MARTA: I just knew. I could feel the energy.

How did you end up meeting Bob?

MARTA: After the show, I waited for a little while in my chair because I knew they were going to send someone out to take me backstage. But security made me move, so I ended up going to the parking lot. By the time I got out there, someone told me that I'd just missed Bob.

So you got all dressed up for nothing?

MARTA: Well, it was meant to happen, because I met one of their roadies, who took me to a party they were having after the show. I was outside singing, and Bob went out to take a piss, so we started talking. And we went back to Bob's place and had fantastic sex: four times in the night.

When I woke up, Bob wasn't there. So I lit up a cigarette and walked outside, and Bob was sitting there with all these business types. They all saw me standing there naked and Bob gave me this smile like he was really getting off on it.

Then what happened?

MARTA: I put on my clothes and came back out. And Bob said, really cold, "Anyone want to give um, um"—he was struggling for my name and then he got it—"Marta a ride home." I could tell he was really relieved that he remembered my name.

I just looked at him and said, "You got a light?" I said it really tough. I'm sure he didn't expect it. Anyway, no one was going my way. He eventually said to one guy something like, "Marta's got a place in Costa Rica. Maybe you can talk to her about that." And I'm like, "Fuck you." So I started to leave and said something cold again. He said, "I'll call you at the hotel." I asked him if he wanted the number, and he said he'd look it up.

Obviously he didn't call you.

MARTA: No, but I saw him again a few months later. It was at this party after a Dead show. He was there with all these girls and I was talking to Jerry and getting along. We were really flying, and he asked what I was doing. And I said, "Waiting for Bob over there." He thought I said "Bozo," and we started laughing for the longest time because we were so fucked up.

So then I go to the bathroom and Bob comes around the corner with like five girls hanging onto him, and the second he sees me I just get this wave of bad energy. Like a literal tidal wave pouring at me, and I'm stunned. I go to the bathroom and I look at myself in the mirror, and I look horrible, terrible.

Did you speak to Bob at all that night?
MARTA: No, we didn't talk. After that, I basically stayed at my parents' house for the next six years. I went crazy. Every time I looked in the mirror, I saw the devil. I thought I had the possibility to save the world and I blew it. Bob was the devil, Jerry was God, and I was the angel.

[MONSTER MAGNET]

For every Woodstock, there's an Altamont; for every Timothy Leary, there's a Charles Manson; and for every Strawberry Alarm Clock, there's a Monster Magnet. Monster Magnet is the downside of psychedelia. Its members have long, dirty hair and inhale reams of drugs, but they're not hippies. They're not metalheads, either. They're something much, much worse. So when their first album was released, before they became as popular as the people they hate, I talked to Monster Magnet frontman Dave Wyndorf about the revenge of the suburbs.

Where are you from in New Jersey?
DAVE WYNDORF: The Red Bank area, twenty miles north of Asbury Park. It's an old suburb with farmland on the outskirts, then new suburbs and big malls and kids hanging out in parking lots. All the stuff on our record is just like the culture we grew up with, what a lot of kids in the suburbs grew up with—the same old shit.

Like that movie *Over the Edge?* *
WYNDORF: That's definitely the scene I came out of. We wore a lot of unfashionable hairstyles and rock shirts. We made all our money selling bags of weed and handing out pills and stuff like that. And we went to parties and played Stooges and punk rock records to outrage everyone. We chose to be misfits. We hated all the jocks and figured we'd go the other way and do the punk rock thing.

---

* Starring a young Matt Dillon as a teenage suburban burnout who's shot by a police officer.

You use a lot of heavy metal devil imagery on your album though . . .

WYNDORF: Satan and all that is just like an evil thing. It basically stands for everything but the kitchen sink, because you're so doped up nothing else will do. (*Shouts:*) *Satan, this, that, tits, everything!* You've gotta go like totally overboard, you know. Nothing else will cut through that haze of being drugged out.

What kind of fan mail do you get?

WYNDORF: A guy sent me a videotape from somewhere in like Texas or something and it said: "Dear Monster Magnet, you're my favorite band. Me and my friends did a lot of acid and went out and killed dogs with shotguns." They had a videotape of it and I was like, "Holy shit, what did I fucking do?" I wrote them back: "Cool out on killing the dogs, man. Kill each other. I'm sure both of you guys have done something that makes you eligible for getting killed and I'm sure the dogs haven't."

Music's always been good for inspiring kids to do stupid things.

WYNDORF: Yeah, there was an article in a paper here about a supposed devil cult who were just capturing people's pets and sacrificing them. Everybody went nuts and it was like a big fucking scary thing. And what it turned out to be, which is even scarier than devil worship, was that there was no religion at all. It was just a bunch of really stupid metalheads who thought it was cool to cut up dogs. I don't know about you, but an idiot in a Slayer shirt going, "Duh, I'll kill a dog"—that's fucking scary.

In the sixties movements, drugs were seen as an enlightening, happy, free thing, but on your record, they're an entryway into a dark world.

WYNDORF: We were so behind here that the sixties didn't come until the seventies. So when I was a kid, I used to watch all the movies on TV like *Psych-Out* and *Woodstock.* And I thought that everybody was all together. Then when I finally got old enough to do that stuff, I realized that there's really no brotherhood involved here at all. There's just a bunch of freaks trying to rip me off for some bad speed.

So what drug scene were you into?

WYNDORF: Acid. Everyone should take acid at least once in their life. Looking back on when I was in high school, I can't imagine not having done that stuff. I would have been like a jerk if I hadn't done it—a bigger jerk than I am now.

What about that idea that if you take acid more than three times, you're certifiably insane?

WYNDORF: Yeah, that's me. When we were doing all this acid—when you're really young and really stupid—we would just do tons of it, like three blotters at a time, and try to live out *Fear and Loathing in Las Vegas*. That was our idea of a good time, just quoting Hunter S. Thompson, riding around in cars, and like breaking things and setting things on fire. There was no like lovey-dovey shit around here at all. It was in the seventies and everybody still looked like hippies, but they weren't. They were just mean guys with long hair.

But then there's the flip side of things today, like a Grateful Dead concert.

WYNDORF: They're just like a bad country and western band. They seem to represent the new generation's idea of the sixties, and they have enough ticket sales behind them to stay alive. So now this Grateful Dead thing is just an excuse for kids to go on the road. When you're that young, you don't realize the scam that's about to envelop you. Deadheads are the people out there who want to go to a concert and don't want to mosh. On one side, you could call them peaceful folks; on the other side, you could call them pussies.

In 2006, Wyndorf impulsively swallowed a bottle of sleeping pills on an airplane in an apparent attempt to kill himself. He was unsuccessful.

[SLAYER]

The following interview is from the only article I wrote for the *New York Times* that was removed from the newspaper. Fifteen minutes before the paper closed, the story was pulled because of Slayer bassist and singer Tom Araya's quotes about his fascination with murder. Not surprisingly, the front page of the paper the next day featured a story about a mass murder and mass suicide in Switzerland.

When you sing about suicide—

TOM ARAYA: There aren't any suicide songs on *this* album.

What about "Killing Fields"?

ARAYA: If you look at each verse, they're different mannerisms of why people kill.

Such as?
ARAYA: There's demons in us that make us kill sometimes that we can't control. Passion makes us kill sometimes. Emotional pain can cause someone to go out and kill. When it comes to murder, man has a free will, a choice to kill.

But there's also a lyric about "the suicidal hold."
ARAYA: The suicidal hold means that when someone snaps, they don't realize what they've done. And that's the suicidal hold. "Can't beat the rush that leaves a suicidal hold"—meaning that it's suicide to commit murder because you're going to get yours in the end.

It's interesting that a band that writes so much about violence and murder also advocates strong punishment for those things?
ARAYA: That's how I feel. No, there isn't a contradiction. We make the ugly side of life very visible, and I feel that people who commit such crimes should suffer and pay the consequences for their crimes.

So do you think by getting the violence out in song lyrics, it keeps you from acting on those impulses?
ARAYA: Sometimes writing lyrics purges some of my anxieties, some of my violent side. With the band, I'm able to channel those feelings.

What would you do if you didn't have the music as an outlet?
ARAYA: If I wasn't in the band, I'm sure I'd be doing something.

Something meaning?
ARAYA: Meaning murder.

I laugh. He doesn't.

[OASIS]
SCENE 3

As the drinks continued, Oasis singer Liam Gallagher grew a little more cerebral . . . or something.

LIAM GALLAGHER: Everyone goes around saying, "God, God, God, God." What the fuck did he leave us? The Beatles left us loads of songs that I could believe in and helped me understand why I felt sad, and helped me get up off my bum and do something about it.

Do you believe in God?
GALLAGHER: When I was fourteen, I used to believe in God. I grew up a Catholic. I'm not a Catholic no more. I don't believe in God. There's no one upstairs. There's no one downstairs. And if there is someone upstairs and there's someone downstairs, who's on the left and who's on the right? 'Cause no one knows what way they're facing, do they?

What made you lose your faith?
GALLAGHER: It's 'cause if you get married, you can't even get divorced. So my ma gets married to this geezer, has three kids. The old boy starts playing around. She don't like it, but she has to stay with him because her religion don't permit her to divorce. She grew up all her life on religion, believing in God, going to the church every Sunday, taking the body of Christ and all. When she finally gets divorced, she's not allowed in the church anymore, so she's getting a whack on the head. So she thinks religion's bollocks. And she's right. She got divorced because he was caning her, so what's that all about? Bollocks. If anything, God's a bad man. But there ain't no God. There ain't no man upstairs.

Do you believe in any kind of spirituality?
GALLAGHER: God's within yourself. You're your own God and you're your own devil. You do your fucking thing, you get in your own little vibe, you settle your own shit, be nice to everyone, and if anyone gives you shit, you don't ever speak to them ever again.

Do you think you have a soulmate?
GALLAGHER: One day I'm going to meet myself. I've already met him, I think. But one day I'm going to meet the equivalent, a woman who's myself. A person who looks like me and thinks like me, but is a woman. I'm going to fall in love and, like, sail away. (Metallica drummer Lars Ulrich enters the hotel to hang out with the band. Liam glances at him and snorts.) He's off his head.

What do you think happens when you die?
GALLAGHER: Everything's going to be sweet once you go. Death is a cool thing. People go, "Death is bad." Fuck off, death is life. Life is death.

What do you mean?

GALLAGHER: It's simple. Death is a beginning. Of course life goes on. You can't just go in a box and go underground. Your body goes. But we've all got the same bodies—legs, cheekbones. Everyone's got them. But, fuck all, they're useless. What makes you think, what makes your views, love, and all those things—that's from your spirit.

So do you think there's reincarnation?

GALLAGHER: I believe in soul or spirit, though I don't know what it is. Maybe your soul and your spirit is yourself. You do your thing, and this world and this life here is the equivalent of hell. You are living in hell with loads of madheads who give you shit all the time. And I think you do come back. Reincarnation is cool as fuck, yeah. But I don't want to come back here, to this shit. I don't wanna do that.

Where would you go instead?

GALLAGHER: Well, I want to go to heaven, where you won't get touched by this shit that goes on. And you'll have to guide someone else who's living here, who's like fourteen years of age and has to go through this shit for the first time.

Do you think you have a guide?

GALLAGHER: I think someone's guiding me. But wherever they are, they don't know what to do with my life. They're just going, "Fucking hell, heavy shit." But as I'm speaking, my head's going off, speaking to him, "Keep on doing what you're doing, guiding me not to lose my plot."

[ERIC CLAPTON]

"With Eric, we don't create publicity; we try to eliminate it," Clapton's publicist explained on the way to his tour rehearsal in the outskirts of London, attempting to convey just how rare the opportunity to talk to him was. I didn't fully understand why Clapton was so cagey about talking to the press until the interview began: He was brutally, self-deprecatingly honest, to a degree that was the exact opposite of his contemporaries in Led Zeppelin.

Dressed in a T-shirt and jeans, and dining on lamb hotpot, he spent two hours politely opening new and old wounds, most movingly the death of his four-year-old son, Conor, who'd accidentally fallen from the fifty-third-floor window of a New York City apartment three years earlier.

COCAINE

DROPS

— prepared by the —

CLAPTON MANUFACTURING CO.

FOR FATIGUE OF MIND OR BODY.

What kept you from returning to drinking and drugs after losing your son?
ERIC CLAPTON: My experience of that was that it showed me that I know nothing. Up until that point, I probably still hadn't accepted that I was powerless, really. I didn't know the true nature of life until that day. And then it was shown to me that everything can be taken away at any moment and I have to look for the positive. And I was able to do that by continuing to abstain and saying, "Look, anything can happen and you don't have to resort to drugs." So it became a gift in a way, a gift for me to show other people that I'm not being callous about this. It fucking did me in to lose him, but it doesn't honor his memory for me to do myself in as a result. It does nothing for the memory of my son if I then indulge in self-pity or self-destructiveness.

At what point in the grieving process did you come to that realization?
CLAPTON: I was told and advised almost instantly after his death to live my life from that point on in honor of his memory, to do things that he would be proud of. And that immediately gave me somewhere to go. In times of stress and trouble like that, you need something to hang onto and focus on quickly, and that was a very positive direction for me to go in.

Are you recording?

Yeah.
CLAPTON (*picks up tape deck*): Oh, interesting.

So are you in any sort of therapy?
CLAPTON: I'm in a one-to-one sort of family counseling once a week, and I talk to this person a lot on the phone. I really don't know that I trust my own judgment in terms of relationships, be it with my business partners or with the band. I have to talk about everything. I have such a strange, deluded idea of what the world is about that if I'm left to my own resources, I would go insane. I would, because my head tells me all kinds of things that just aren't true. And if I'm left with that, or if I believe it, I don't know what I would do.

Go insane in what way?
CLAPTON: Like the other people out there who end up being reclusive and un-happy and desperate and finding ways to kill themselves—slowly or quickly or whatever it is. And I was in that gang for a while. Quite a while. I just wish I'd found a means of communicating with kindred spirits sooner. All this therapy keeps me in the land of the living and reasonably sane.

When you heard about Kurt Cobain, did you think that could have been you at one point in your life?

CLAPTON: Oh yeah, he was quoted as saying things that I totally identified with. Like being backstage and hearing the crowd out there and thinking, "I'm not worth it. I'm a piece of shit. And they're mad—they're fools—if they like me. This is a sick situation. If they knew what the truth was about me, they wouldn't like me."

I've identified with that a million times. I just don't know why that couldn't have been stopped. I don't know why no one couldn't have gotten through to him. It was a powerful self-destructive situation that . . . I heard he tried treatment. I don't know what happened there. It's just a fucking shame, because he was very, very talented and a lovely man. I mean, to my eye. I did this MTV show. And for the most part, it was hype and Hollywood packaging and bullshit. And then Nirvana came on, and they blew my mind. I thought he was beautiful. You know, it broke my heart.

Was there anyone who could have helped you when you were at that point?

CLAPTON: No, no. Good point. No, it had to come from inside me. When I did this Rainbow show—it was quite a well-known thing that happened in the mid-seventies. Pete Townshend, Steve Winwood, Ronnie Wood, and a whole host of people—friends—were trying to save me from this shit by having me play a concert. I was doing a lot of heroin. They got me to rehearsals. They did everything for me. All I had to do was show up, and I didn't give a fuck. And it didn't make any difference.

But you made it to the show . . .

CLAPTON: I did the show, but I don't remember being there. We tried to make a live album of it. I don't remember anything about it. And I carried on using heroin. It had no effect on me whatsoever.

Though—

CLAPTON: Maybe that's a bit harsh actually. Maybe something filtered through, because I didn't die. Maybe I was going to die and maybe that stopped me from dying. And maybe that had something to do with my recovery in the long run. But, in actual fact, it's pretty well impossible to force someone to look at themselves if they don't want to.

When's the last time you went back to that dark side?

CLAPTON: I do it every day. I've been in a relationship with someone for quite a while, and it's on and off a lot. It's quite a volatile thing. And often it's my fault. If I hear someone's criticism, I get on their side. I quickly buy into their way of thinking. And it's not real at all. It's a sickness that I've had all my life and will probably have until the day I die. It needs constant attention (*laughs diabolically*). It makes life a very, very funny, interesting journey for me, because I don't see anything the way other people do. Well, a few people do. Some people understand (*laughs wickedly again*).

[BRIAN WILSON]
SCENE 3

Does your music help you deal with personal issues, like in "Lay Down Burden"?
BRIAN WILSON: You like that song? That's one of our best.
MELINDA WILSON: Brian and I, we had a tough year last year. In four months, I lost my dad, and he lost his mother and his brother. So I think "Lay Down Burden" was the way he dealt with his losses.

It must be a difficult thing with no immediate family left anymore.
BRIAN: That's true. I've got just me left. The last of the Wilsons.

Were they an important support system to you more recently?
BRIAN: Oh yeah, are you kidding? Carl and Dennis were great, great singers. They were good singers.
MELINDA: He means personally, honey. He's talking about emotional security. Did it give you emotional security to have your family alive?
BRIAN: Yeah, it did. It was. But it's gone now.

The press release for the album advertises that it's a return to *Pet Sounds*. Did you want to revisit *Pet Sounds*?
BRIAN: I wanted to touch upon the love in *Pet Sounds*. I could never do another *Pet Sounds*. But the love I put into it, I used that same love and put it into my album now. It came right out of my heart.
MELINDA: I think it's other people that make those comparisons. I've never seen him say, "I'm going to do this song or that song because it's like that." I guess people will always compare everything he does to *Pet Sounds*.
BRIAN: This new one, I hope they like it better than *Pet Sounds* even. I have a feeling they're gonna like it.
MELINDA: But you have to remember, honey, when you first made *Pet Sounds*, nobody really liked it.

BRIAN: Yeah.

MELINDA: It's really funny because all we hear is "*Pet Sounds, Pet Sounds*," but if he had to depend on the income from *Pet Sounds* to live the type of life he lives, it wouldn't have happened. The songs that were really successful for him were the surf songs, the car songs. *Pet Sounds*—

BRIAN: Revisited.

MELINDA: Whatever. But commercially it was a flop in the sixties.

Will you still do a few dates with the Beach Boys?

BRIAN: No, I don't think so. I've had my times. Now that [my brother] Carl's gone, I don't want to go onstage. It's not the same without Carl and it never will be. Even recording, it makes me feel bad to think that we don't have him as our main singer anymore. It's just one of those things.

It's interesting because the Beach Boys now play to the nostalgia crowd, while you've still retained a reputation as an artist making new, important music.

BRIAN: I know. I love rock and roll. I always have liked it. I really want to try for a rock album that I think people will like and will buy, and will really like a lot. And buy. Because we need . . . We don't need the money so much, but it does help. Money's not the object. With me, money isn't the object. Art is the object.

MELINDA: We had talked to the guys about doing something with [producer] Don Was. But there were too many different directions. And it didn't seem like anybody was willing to just do what he wanted again. So that's why we decided to can that until he got his own stuff out of his system. I think they may have lost some confidence in Brian. I don't know exactly. It's really weird.

BRIAN: I'm going to get something to drink. I'll be right back.

[*Continued . . .*]

[PINK FLOYD]
SCENE 1

Lounging poolside at a Houston hotel, Pink Floyd vocalist and guitarist David Gilmour explained that he would like to design his own version of the Sex Pistols's infamous "I Hate Pink Floyd" T-shirt. His would be just like theirs: a savagely defaced Pink Floyd *Dark Side of the Moon* tour shirt with the words "I Hate" scrawled on top. Except on the back, he continued, "Mine would read, 'Well, most of them, anyway.'"

He was referring, particularly, to fellow Pink Floyd singer and songwriter

Roger Waters. After Waters left the band in 1985, he discovered that the remaining members planned to continue as Pink Floyd without him. So he sued Gilmour and drummer Nick Mason for using the name Pink Floyd. The case was eventually settled unamically, and Gilmour and Mason continued on as Pink Floyd, rehiring keyboardist Rick Wright, who had been forced out of the band by Waters.

In Houston, Gilmour, Wright, and Mason were in the midst of their second tour as Pink Floyd without Waters. Between games of Marco Polo with Gilmour's children, I tried to prod them—as well as their childhood friend and touring Floyd guitarist Tim Renwick—to talk about their former bandmate.

Have you spoken with Roger at all?
RICK WRIGHT: There's been a total noncommunication. I last spoke to Roger about ten years ago. I think Dave and Nick last spoke to him via their lawyers. No one has spoken to him, I don't think at all.

A lot of the new album is about miscommunication. Do you think that's a reference to Roger?
WRIGHT: I wouldn't say the album's about Roger at all. I wouldn't say the breakup of the band was about a lack of communication, either. I think there was a big violent disagreement over what the band should be and also a whole ego thing, which I have to say mainly came from Roger, who began to believe he was the band. We all acknowledge his contributions a lot—to the writing particularly. But it wouldn't have worked without Dave and myself and Nick. I think his solo career is proving that.

What about the song "Poles Apart"—that could be about Roger?
WRIGHT: I'm not sure if "Poles Apart" is about Roger. Did you ask Dave if it was about Roger?

Yes.
WRIGHT: What did he say?

<hr />

I know much of the album is about your divorce, but is "Poles Apart" also about the band's differences with Roger?
DAVID GILMOUR: The minute someone says to you, "That lyric could be construed as being about Roger," you go, "Fuck." And then you've either got to steer

yourself away from it or just sort of let it happen. But none of the things on the album started off having anything to do with him.

So they may have ended up being about him?
GILMOUR: Did they? You'll just have to work it out for yourself. There are two songs that appear to be, but aren't necessarily. What do they say, "Never explain, never complain"? (*Sticks a finger in his ear and picks at something.*)

How's your hearing from all the shows?
GILMOUR: My hearing's a little bit down, but not so bad. *Rolling Stone*'s terrible stupid book, which never checked its facts when it printed its terrible stupid whatever-it-is guide to rock and roll, got my date of birth wrong by two years. It makes me the oldest in the band when I've always been the youngest. Whereas everybody else is fifty or fifty-one, I'm forty-eight. But never mind. They never ring up and check the facts, there you go.

<hr />

When's the last time you spoke with Roger?
NICK MASON: I think the last time I talked with Roger was '87. There was plenty of bad feeling then. Now one is less desperate to retrieve friendships. There's so much else going on, particularly family, so you tend not to worry so much if you fall out with people. Maybe women are more forgiving. I only say that because my wife seems to have retained friends longer than I have. Or maybe I'm just a really horrible person.

<hr />

Out of everyone, you're closest to Roger now since you used to play in his solo band. So why do you think he and the rest of [Pink Floyd] split ways in the first place?
TIM RENWICK: There was a lot of tension between them all along. Gradually over the years, Roger considered that he was really the main force behind everything. Certainly, I remember when he sat me down and played me the demos of *The Wall* to prove how much of it was his. In a way it sort of disproved it because the form the songs came in was so raw, you could hardly listen to them. They were really nasty. It was Dave and [producer] Bob Ezrin who came in and made things palatable musically and sweeter.

Have you talked to Roger recently?
RENWICK: Strangely enough, we haven't heard a peep out of him on this tour: not a word, no response whatsoever. I'm glad really because it just soured the atmosphere on the last tour because it would come up all the time. Whenever anyone puts Roger down, that's the end of it. He takes it very personally.

[*Continued . . .*]

Though Roger Waters wouldn't talk to me for the *Rolling Stone* article I was writing on his former bandmates, I waited a while longer, until he had something to promote and was more inclined to do press, then tried him again. Unfortunately, he wasn't very happy about the story that had run in *Rolling Stone*.

ROGER WATERS: I'd be interested to know why you wrote, "This one's Pink," in the caption under Dave's picture in the article.

That was strange. I have nothing to do with the captions.
WATERS: Right.

But my editor, David Fricke, was telling me he wished the article he'd written on you guys when you originally split had the headline, "Which One's Pink?"
WATERS: It was a strange judgment call.

I don't think he was trying to say that David Gilmour was Pink Floyd and you weren't. I think he just liked the reference.*
WATERS: I don't know. David Fricke was just such a chicken in '87. I gave him the whole deal and he didn't print a fucking *word* of it.

You're kidding.
WATERS: I sat with him for a whole afternoon in a hotel in Berkeley and I gave him the whole story. He had *everything*. He had all that stuff about how they delivered the album to the record company and the record company said, "This doesn't

---

* To the Pink Floyd song "Have a Cigar," sung from the point of view of a clueless record executive, who asks the band, "Oh, by the way, which one's Pink?"

sound enough like Pink Floyd. Go back and start again." And so they did and all of that, and what a complete travesty it was.

I'm surprised, because that's the kind of thing I was looking for.
WATERS: I gave him the whole fucking story and he didn't print a word of it. He just went, "Well, they both seem like nice guys to me." It was a pitiful piece of . . . nonsense. I really . . . I thought it was pathetic.

Why do you think he would do that?
WATERS: Who knows why, whether it was for personal reasons, whether he thought it was too controversial, or whether it was something else. It was an absolute cop-out. When I read it, I just thought, "You wanker!"

Do you mean—
WATERS: I was really disappointed. Pissed off. Because, you know, this is *Rolling Stone*, the hard edge, the cutting edge of rock and roll journalism. Here was a proper story. Here were two people who were prepared to rip each other's throats out in public, and he wouldn't print a fucking word of it.

I wonder—
WATERS: It was a real snow job. I mean, if it were me in that situation, why not print both versions? Let people make their minds up. If you've got two people who are prepared to stand up in public and slug it out, what good fun!*

So what made you stay silent when Pink Floyd toured this time without you?
WATERS: Stayed silent about what?

You didn't speak out about them touring as Pink Floyd, like last time.
WATERS: Because I understood that maybe only fifteen or ten or five percent of the audience was there because they were interested in the work and got it, and the rest were just interested in a day out. And so, you know, people are going to make their own decisions about the work and whether it's good or not, or Pink Floyd or not. You know, it's none of my business, really.

In a way, but Pink Floyd was a lot of your life.
WATERS: I know what *I* think, but that's my business.

---

* David Fricke responds: "I guess he didn't like that story because it gave both sides. I didn't pull any punches in it. I didn't slug anybody, either. It was the proper story, told from the middle, which was not a comfortable place to be. But it was the only right journalistic one."

Would you like to eventually get to a place where you're no longer seen as a former member of Pink Floyd, but just as yourself?
WATERS: You know, there's pros and cons to all these things. If one was being truly grown up about it, I would say, "No, I would prefer at this point in my life not to be burdened with that kind of celebrity." However, the infant in me still wants to go, "Look at me, look at me, I did it!" After all, we're only ordinary men.

Eleven years after this interview, Waters and the rest of the band performed together as Pink Floyd for the first time in nearly a quarter century, setting aside their differences for a benefit to fight global poverty. Three years later, Rick Wright died of cancer at the age of sixty-five.

[LED ZEPPELIN]
SCENE 3

One portion of the Page and Plant interview that wasn't recorded was when they commented on why the only other surviving member of Led Zeppelin, bassist John Paul Jones, wasn't invited to join them for their reunion concert on MTV, *Unledded*—or for the album and tour scheduled to follow. So after the interview, I called Jones to get his thoughts on it.

Did you see the *Unledded* broadcast?
JOHN PAUL JONES: I saw a bit of it last night actually for the first time. Poof, it's just doing all that old stuff again, isn't it? It didn't really grab my attention for very long. I thought we did it really well before. It's time to move on, really.

Would you have participated if you were asked?
JONES: I thought maybe I might have, but maybe I wouldn't. It depends on what I was doing, I suppose. But as I wasn't invited, it's an academic question. I don't know what they say about it, but I haven't heard from them for months and months. Eighteen months ago was the last time I saw Robert, I think. For whatever reason, they decided not to ask me. Did you ask them?

Yes, I did.
JONES: I'm just kind of interested. Because I read about it in the papers and then I called a friend just to say, "Oh, by the way, did you see the latest rumor?" And he replied, "Didn't they tell you?" I went, "Oh, great." Maybe I might have joined them and maybe I wouldn't. But I think it was a bit discourteous of them not to say anything at all.

When I asked them why they didn't invite you, first they made a stupid joke about how you were downstairs getting their bags or something.
JONES: Yeah, that sounds like them.

Then they said that it wasn't right for the material, because it would have made the material too complicated.
JONES: Hmm, one slightly naughty thing I was thinking as I was watching the MTV thing (*giggles nervously*) is how many people it took to replace me, and how few people it's taken me to replace them.

Fifty-one additional musicians played with Page and Plant on Unledded; *John Paul Jones, at the time, was performing in a trio. The following year, Page and Plant finally performed with Jones again at Led Zeppelin's induction into the Rock and Roll Hall of Fame. "Thank you, my friends," Jones said in his acceptance speech, "for finally remembering my phone number."*

[BRUCE BROWN]

When the genre of independent film is mentioned, cleverly scripted and artfully filmed features come to mind. But Bruce Brown has come to define an even more independent aesthetic. Long before extreme sports was an industry, let alone a catchphrase, he became a one-man film production company and traveled the world with his wind-up Bolex camera, making surfing movies—until one day, in the mid-sixties, *The Endless Summer* broke through and made him one of the most famous documentary filmmakers of his time.

BRUCE BROWN: We did it that way because we didn't know any better. Like when we got on the plane to Hawaii to make the first movie, I had a little book, *How to Make Movies* or something.

Did you ever wish you'd gone to film school?
BROWN: Fortunately I didn't have any training, because then I would have learned I couldn't do what I had been doing. After several years, I got a call to go speak at a college film school, and it was like a comedy routine. Every time I told them how I did something, they'd laugh. They'd ask, "What about a work print?" And I'd tell them, "We didn't have a work print. We showed the original film."

Weren't you worried about it getting damaged or lost?
BROWN: You know, I'd carry it with me everywhere. I wouldn't ship it. We really couldn't afford another print. They would say, "Well, how'd you edit it if you didn't have a work print?" And I told them, "I'd just crank it through the viewer and close my eyes where I thought a cut should be. And then I'd crank it four turns or so to where the next shot was, try and visualize the cut, and then cut it. Once it was cut, that was it."

So you'd play the film with all the splices at theaters?
BROWN: Yeah, a splice would always come apart when we were showing it. My wife was running the projector, and she had a bunch of tape and would fix it while it was still running.

The music was played on a reel-to-reel tape recorder. If it fell out of sync, I'd stick my finger on the reel to crank it up or slow it down. When a scene would fade out, I'd pause the tape recorder, then start it up again. And somehow it just worked.

And for the voice-overs, were they just on the film itself?
BROWN: No, I did all those live.

You mean just talking along with the movie?
BROWN: Yeah, I just stood up on the stage with my little tape recorder and microphone and narrated the thing. And I'd get better through sort of trial and error. If I said something and it was kind of like, "Boy, that was lame," then I wouldn't ever do that again. So over the years, after showing these old films fifty or sixty or seventy times, I'd get a narration that worked. And if I had a certain kind of audience, I could change it.

Which is why your narrations have this stand-up comedy element . . .
BROWN: It's kind of funny, because somebody in New York or LA would want to show one of the films on television and they'd go, "Well, that's not funny." And I'd go, "I've showed it to like fifty thousand people and they all laughed. It's funny. Don't tell me if it's funny or not funny!"

Would you ever change the movie itself between showings?
BROWN: We would do that, too. There'd be a sequence that wasn't working very well. So we'd just go re-edit it before the next screening. We had an old Volkswagen van, and I would sometimes edit the thing on the way to the showing.

So was surfing kind of a bad-boy thing when you started filming it?

BROWN: Oh yeah! *Real* bad. Everybody's parents when you surfed in those days were like, "God, you gotta stop doing that and get a job." You know, we didn't like to work any more than we had to to get by, so it wasn't like we were trying to get ahead in the world. We were trying to get a hundred bucks to go to Hawaii. When I was in high school in California, there was nobody that surfed and there were about three thousand kids in the school.

But didn't things like the Beach Boys and the *Beach Blanket Bingo* movies eventually make it more mainstream?

BROWN: With the Beach Boys and all that, it was like, we *hated* that music to begin with. In fact, at the time, we thought jazz was the cool music. A friend of mine was one of the original managers of the Beach Boys and he begged us to let them play at the intermission of a movie in San Diego. So they got up and played, and the audience was booing them. I felt sorry for them. At the time I thought, "God, these poor guys, they're never gonna amount to anything!"

[BRIAN WILSON]
SCENE 4

Were you always a nervous person?

MELINDA: You should talk to his high school buddies.

BRIAN: My nerves went through a lot of damage because of the amphetamines I took. It took my brain up, it really did. I'm really sorry for taking uppers like that. Then I took a lot of cocaine—a very, very lot of cocaine. Wait a minute, wait a minute. Scrap that. What am I talking about? I just . . . I forgot this was an interview. Do not mention anything about the drugs.

MELINDA: Everybody knows it, Brian. It's the amounts that people get screwed up about. Everyone knows that he took drugs, but it's as I said before: It's just easier to blame every fuckup on drugs.

I actually asked that question because having a very domineering, critical father can make someone nervous and hesitant later in life.

MELINDA: If you talk to kids who went to high school with Brian, he was always a nervous kid. Don't you think it's because of your dad, Bri?

BRIAN: Yeah.

MELINDA: Because you had to tiptoe and walk on eggshells.

BRIAN: That's perfect. Perfectly put. He fouled my brain up. He fouled me right up, man. I went out in life scared as hell. Everybody that I looked at was my dad

looking back at me. He beat me up, you know. It was as traumatic as hell. I really went through a bad, (*raises his voice*) bad, bad childhood.

MELINDA: He could do something one day and his dad would be totally cool with it, and he could do the same thing the next day and his dad would go bonkers.

BRIAN: He was all fouled up. He had a bad childhood himself.

So how did that affect you as a parent?

MELINDA: That's what I think is amazing about Brian. Generally speaking, kids that come from abusive families turn out to be abusers. His dad did. But he didn't. He turned out to be the exact opposite. Even when we decided to adopt babies, he said, "No spankings ever." I think you spanked Carnie, what, once in your whole life?

BRIAN: I slapped her on her butt (*slaps his hands together*). One time. She cried a little bit and I said, "I'm sorry, Carnie. I didn't mean it." But just the one time.

What did she do?

BRIAN: She made a peanut butter and jelly sandwich. She made two. I said, "Only one," and I caught her in there making a second one. But it was no big deal.

How has it felt to be a father again? *

BRIAN: This time it's a much more deeper feeling, because I get to spend much more time with my daughter. I didn't get to spend a lot of time with my original daughters.

MELINDA: He was kind of busy being a Beach Boy.

BRIAN: And it was being over at friends' houses and goofing around and staying out all night.

MELINDA: But mostly it was being a Beach Boy.

BRIAN: I'm going to have to say good-bye. I feel a little bit light-headed. I'm going to go upstairs. I appreciate it very much. It was one of the longest and greatest interviews I've ever had. It was a long one and a great one both. You guys can carry on. I'll see you all later.

MELINDA: Okay (*laughs*). That was really unusual for him.

I really appreciate it.

MELINDA: I may have come off kind of defensive. I'm always trying to protect him. Not that he can't protect himself, but he's the most naïve, forgiving, wonderful guy I've ever met in my life. In the past, it's had a tendency to get him in some trouble—legal trouble.

---

* At the time, Brian and Melinda had adopted two children. In the following twelve years, they adopted three more.

Out of curiosity, how did you meet Brian?

MELINDA: I was selling cars in LA in 1986, during the Landy years for Brian. Dr. Landy had been in threatening to buy a car from me for a month and finally decided not to. But he called and said he wanted to bring a friend of his in, and he brought Brian in. And that's how I met him: I sold him a car. The first one he looked at, he said, "I'll take it." It was the ugliest brown ugly car. Later Dr. Landy asked me on a date for Brian. Now that I look back on it, that whole thing was choreographed by Landy. But what he didn't count on was that Brian and I were going to like each other. It was really bizarre, but I had really liked Brian in the short period of selling him the car. I thought he was really . . . different.

[CURTAIN]

ACT FOUR

— OR —

SOMETIMES YOU JUST WANT A GIRL WHO WILL SIT ON A BOTTLE

[SYNOPSIS]

ENTER DAVE PIRNER, WHO PISSES IN A FLOWERPOT, **AN ACT OUTDONE BY INCUBUS, WHO PISS ON EACH OTHER** AND DEBATE THEIR HOMOEROTICISM, WHILE KATEY RED DODGES BRICKS **BECAUSE HE WANTS TO BE A GIRL,** SOMETHING TWIGGY RAMIREZ OF MARILYN MANSON DOES FOR TWO WEEKS **BEFORE RESOLVING TO GET BREAST IMPLANTS AND ROBBING A GRAVE, &C.**

[SOUL ASYLUM]
SCENE 1

The scene: A hotel lounge in Austin, Texas. Dave Pirner, singer in the Minne-apolis rock band Soul Asylum, perches on the edge of a sofa. Drummer Sterling Campbell sits on an adjacent chair, leaning in closely. It is my first cover story for *Rolling Stone*. It is also the band's. We are both excited about this. The time is two a.m.

DAVE PIRNER: But look, Socrates was fucking Greek, man. I mean, what influence has that culture had on us as people now? Those wrapped-up leaves with rice in them . . .

Soul Asylum's publicist arrives.

PIRNER: . . . I mean, that shit doesn't taste *that* good, but it tastes pretty good. And you kind of sit there and you eat it and you go, "All right, these motherfuckers, they ate this shit and they made a bunch of motherfuckers drag fucking rocks up a hill to build some big old colossal thing. And they tried to create this whole society. And what was the food left over from that? These fucking grape leaves wrapped around rice."

PUBLICIST: I have a recommendation to make, as a publicist. You guys could stay up all night talking, but the on-the-record portion of the interview should be over at this point.

STERLING CAMPBELL: No, no, no, no.

PIRNER: I think I can be held accountable for anything that I should say. I'll tell you what I want to know, though. What's *Rolling Stone*'s angle here? Do they think we're rock stars and suck or what? What do they want to know about us, just be-tween me and you?

PUBLICIST (*coughs*): What would be the most natural, obvious question to an-swer that: The new record? Coming off the tremendous success of *Grave Dancers Union*?

PIRNER: I mean, what the fuck could possibly be interesting about us?

PUBLICIST: (*Silence.*)

PIRNER: Exactly. That's the right answer.

PUBLICIST (*flustered*): Is the tape recorder running? Could you turn it off?

100%
Natural
ENERGY
BOOST

"I got the JUICE."

PURE
JUICE

The tape recorder is shut off. The publicist sidles over to have a word with Pirner in private, then departs for his hotel. Pirner stands up, walks to a large vase, unzips his pants, and pisses in it.

[Continued . . .]

[INCUBUS]

Since Incubus's first top ten single, the band has been known as one of the nicest groups in rock. During a decadent week that involved ordering strippers and getting kicked out of clubs in Las Vegas, band members were doing their best to destroy that myth. And they were succeeding, until one of their girlfriends stepped in.

DIRK LANCE [bassist]: Some bands like Kid Rock get the girls who just want to sleep with the band, but we get the girls who want to talk intensely about the music. And then you feel bad if you want to sleep with them, because they're there for the band and the music.

You should feel lucky that they're actually into the music and the art of what you're doing.
LANCE: Yes, that's true. But sometimes you just want a girl who will sit on a bottle. [. . .] We went to an in-store* once and this kid asked, "What's it like being in the most homoerotic band around?"

I don't really think of you guys as homoerotic.
LANCE: Well, we are pretty homoerotic, but I don't think that we're *that* homoerotic.

Drummer José Pasillas walks in the room, asks to have his handwriting analyzed, and writes on a piece of paper: "My name is José Pasillas, the second. I love women and all else about women. I may be gay but not sure." Singer Brandon Boyd blurts in response . . .

---

* Industry jargon for a promotional performance at a record store.

BRANDON BOYD: José peed on my hand yesterday.

JOSÉ PASILLAS: Yes, it was great. Our relationship is thriving right now. It's at an all-time high.

BOYD: We've known each other all our lives, and it's gone beyond that brother thing. After one show, the showers were like locker-room showers, and José just fucking pisses on me. And so I did it back. And then everyone's all like, "You guys are fucked up." But him and I are like, "It's just pee. We're in a shower."

I've noticed there's a split in the band as far as rock star behavior goes.

BOYD: Totally. Mike [Einziger, guitarist] and I keep it like on a more boring level. We dull up the band a little. No, for real—like, if some of the other guys were in a different band, I guarantee there'd be like pyrotechnics and chicks dancing onstage. You know, full on.

MIKE EINZIGER: Yeah, I have no desire to see that sort of thing. But I know we have that option if we wanted.

CAMERON [his girlfriend]: No, you don't. You're dorks.

[KATEY RED]

Outside the Factory, a club in East New Orleans, a small crowd was raving about a performance by rapper Katey Red. "A lot of things wouldn't be going on in this town without her," said Mankind, a producer. "She's hot right now."

Katey Red, however, is not a she at all. Born Kenyon Carter, Katey Red may be one of the first openly homosexual rappers and transvestites to have earned respect in this notoriously homophobic world. Add to that a chronic stutter, and you have an unlikely regional success story, even in a city with a rich culture of cross-dressing.

"She's six foot two and wears a size fourteen shoe," said Earl Mackie, who signed Katey Red to his label, Take Fo' Records. "I always tell her, 'Man, you could have been a basketball star.'"

Are you surprised to see so many straight guys in the audience?

KATEY RED: N-n-n-n-o. See, the reason why the guys come by is 'cause they want to see the girls bend over and shake their behinds. And the girls come by just so they can shake their behinds (*laughs*). [. . .] I don't mean no harm to nobody who don't like homosexuals, but I have to do my thing. I'm getting somewhere with it.

Earl told me you had a lot of fears when you first started.
RED: I was a punk under pressure. When I first started rapping, I was s-s-s-scared. I was worried somebody might come on the stage and stab me up. I was scared my whole life was gonna change. But I'm not scared no more. My whole life did change—but for the better, not for the worse. I'm the first homosexual rapper.

The rap community can be homophobic. Has anyone ever threatened you?
RED: Sometimes, but it was no hard threat. Just the other day I had to fight another homosexual. She had a bottle in my face, but I took care of her (*laughs*). I took care of her, baby (*snaps fingers and laughs again*).

So it's the homosexual community that gives you a harder time?
RED: Yeah, but I'm trying to still endorse for the homosexuals. All of us just try to stick together. She got jealous 'cause I'm a rapper, so I'm popular and all the boys like playing with me. I don't want that type of reputation b-b-b-because I have an old man. And these boys don't want nothing but sex, you see what I'm saying. I got love for my old man. I gotta stress that point.

At what point did you realize you wanted to be a girl?
RED: I realized when I was five years old. I started p-p-putting on fingernail polish and my mom, she gave me a whupping and told me I don't supposed to do that. Then my cousins played football and they told me to come play with them, but I started playing with baby dolls and all that. So I made thirteen and had sex with a girl. And you know I enjoyed it, but I didn't get nothing out of it. I was always thinking about boys. So I had sex with a man when I was fifteen. Then, when I made sixteen, I had sex with a girl again to make sure I really didn't want it.

Was it tough for you growing up?
RED: Yeah, usually kids saying like, "You sissy bitch," and trying to pitch bricks at me. But every time they pushed at me, I was fighting back.

When I was in Earl's office, he was calling your mom and—
RED: Where are you from again?

I'm from the *New York Times* in New York.
RED: You hear my music in New York?

I heard about you in New York and I came down here to interview you.
RED: So you're from a record company?

A daily newspaper. It's called the *New York Times*. When it comes out, you'll get some attention for sure. Anyway, it didn't seem like your mom accepted what you were doing.
RED: She won't accept the name Katey. She named me Kenyon. So when people call the house and ask for Katey, she corrects them and says, "His name is not Katey. I named him Kenyon." She's strict. She's not satisfied that I am like I am. But I'm taking care of myself and I'm taking care of her, too.

What do you want to happen when the record comes out?
RED: I'm trying to make it big.

How big?
RED: To the top. Way up. As far as I can go.

Eventually, other gay rappers like Sissy Nobby, Big Freedia, and SWA (Sissies With Attitude) began to emerge in New Orleans. Red teamed up with them to start the "sissy bounce" scene, which, almost a decade after this interview, began receiving international acclaim.

[MARILYN MANSON]
SCENE 1

Lying in bed at a Holiday Inn in Florida, Twiggy Ramirez, longtime bassist in the group Marilyn Manson, was staring at the ceiling. His eyebrows were shaved, and he was wearing purple lipstick and pink and blue eye shadow. He was, as his band-mates put it, *twigging out*, having snorted too much coke earlier that night—and most likely every night before it.

TWIGGY RAMIREZ: I think I've managed to fool most of the kids in America into thinking that I'm a woman.

Are you sure about that?
RAMIREZ: My mother was telling me that she mentioned that her son was in Marilyn Manson. And this woman goes, "Yeah, well my son is in love with the girl in the band who plays bass." And my mom said, "That's my son, you know."

I think you're pretty unmistakably a guy.
RAMIREZ: Well, I have thought of possibly maybe taking female hormone pills and growing breasts, just to have them. And I took some female hormone pills. Actually, they were basically birth control pills.

How long did you take them for?
RAMIREZ: I took two a day, and ended up doing a whole month within two weeks. And then ended up getting sick. So I'd have to get implants, I guess (*pauses, looks at tape recorder*). I'm getting nervous: The tape is getting smaller.

That's okay.
RAMIREZ: Yeah, so is there anything you really, seriously want to ask me?

Yeah, who is Tony Wiggins?
RAMIREZ: Tony Wiggins is a close friend of ours. And I've been keeping in touch with him lately. He was our bus driver. And he tried to kill us on the *Portrait* tour.

In what way did he try to do that?
RAMIREZ: Just with, uh . . . Well, he didn't chase after us with a knife. I mean, he chased after someone in [our record label] Interscope and knifed him because he was all fucked up. But he just tried to kill us through horror experiences. You have to know Tony Wiggins. He's a Southern gentleman, with ideals from the South. And he tried to kill us a bunch of times through sex and drugs, and pain as well.

So what happened with the Interscope guy?
RAMIREZ: When they wouldn't let him put these tracks on our record, he went after one of the representatives at Interscope that had nothing to do with it to begin with. So he's not allowed to hang out with us anymore.

What tracks wouldn't they put on the album?
RAMIREZ: There were documents of stuff that happened when we were with him.

Drug things?
RAMIREZ: All kinds of things.* Looking back on the stuff we did with him, some of it was just so ridiculous. I just wonder what I was thinking.

---

* Marilyn Manson explains the following day: "On the original version of our album, there were tracks that were taken from videotapes we'd made in real-life situations. One of them was someone confessing to me about having sex with someone in their family when they were younger. The other recording was a woman asking us to kill her. It was very intense because at one point [Tony Wiggins] is beating her and she's saying, 'My life doesn't matter anyway. Just kill me.'"

Like what?
RAMIREZ: This is going to open up a whole myth probably, but we went grave-robbing. Once you pull someone's bones out of the ground, it stays with you forever.

Because of the guilt?
RAMIREZ: Because it made me look at death just a whole different way. After you pull the pieces of someone's bones out of the dirt, it makes you realize how totally useless everyone is. I had them lying around a hotel room for a while, and there were all sorts of pieces. There was a skull cap and ribs and finger bones. And I used to wear the bones in my hair. It was a very bizarre part of my life. We were in the hotel room and someone had a pot pipe, and I don't smoke pot. So I put a piece of the human bone inside the pipe and began to pass it around, and I told them what it was. They didn't believe me, but they all began to smoke this bowl of human bones. The room smelled like burnt hair. And they just kept on doing it, with this bad taste and all the bones going up in smoke.

I wasn't going to ask this, because it's a corny question, but in fifteen or twenty years, what do you see yourself doing?
RAMIREZ: Probably dead. I think everyone is going to be dead.

[*Continued* . . .]

[COURTNEY LOVE
SCENE 1]

The place was Courtney Love's house in Los Angeles. The time was very late. The moment was when she leaped off her bed and suddenly said . . .

COURTNEY LOVE: Say hi to Kurt.

She walks to a dresser, pulls open a drawer, and removes a square-shaped tin. She removes the lid, revealing a plastic bag full of white ashes. A faint smell of jasmine emanates from the tin.

LOVE: Too bad you don't do coke. Otherwise I'd suggest taking a metal straw to it.

Yeah, I don't think that would be the right thing to do.
LOVE: I'd like to though.

She pulls a round tin from the drawer and opens it. Inside are very soft blond tufts.

LOVE: His hair. (*She opens another round tin.*) More hair.

[*Continued . . .*]

Looking back on the heyday of disco, few songs have remained timeless, and most of those had something to do with the members of a band called Chic, whose many hits and productions (among them "Good Times" and "Le Freak") went on to be sampled in dozens of rap singles. As Chic bassist and producer Bernard Edwards described the band's philosophy, "It's about a good vibe, it's about a good groove, and it's about good clothes." In a poignant interview, his bandmate, guitarist and producer Nile Rodgers, recalled their last show together on the final night of a concert series in Japan . . .

NILE RODGERS: Bernard wasn't feeling well. And being the kind of musician he is, there's no way he's just going to leave the stage or cancel the show. We never cancel shows.

So midway through the concert, we were doing "Let's Dance." And all of a sudden, the bass dropped out at the beginning of the verse. I thought, "Damn, that's clever."

I went, "Good job, 'Nard!" And I turned around and didn't see him. He had passed out, and the roadies had picked him up and placed him behind the stage. And he was just sitting there playing.

When we took a break in the middle of the show to change clothes, I realized how incredibly sick he was. This is a person I love closer than any family member, a person I know better than anyone who has ever walked this earth. And I knew there was no way he was leaving that stage before the show was over. That's how we were brought up.

In the second half, he got it together and was in front of the drum riser. But he wasn't doing all the choreography we had rehearsed. I'll never forget his last speech to the people from Japan. He told them, "I'm a little sick with the Tokyo flu, but I'm still here." He told me how much he loved me and how we've been together a long time and he would do anything for me. It was so poignant. Then we went into "Good Times" and everybody in the house started singing it with us.

Ten thousand people who didn't even speak English singing "Good Times" at the top of their lungs was so powerful.

At the end of the show, Bernard was crying in my arms, and he just said, "You know, man, we did it. This music is bigger than us."

Then at the hotel, I went to check on him, but he didn't answer the door. I got a maid to let me in, and there he was, lying on the sofa, dead.*

The way that the Japanese people dealt with Bernard's death totally changed my outlook on life. The police brought me to the station. And after I'd been interrogated, the chief took me downstairs to the parking lot and he gestured to me, "Come over here." I didn't know where he was taking me. I thought it was the bathroom or something. I went into this little room, and they had taken out all of their stuff and set up a shrine. And Bernard's body was there dressed in a white kimono. He was in a coffin with a glass front, and they had put up Buddhist candles and everything. And they just said, "Here, go be with your friend."

I went in there and I told Bernard how much I loved him and how I never could have done any of this stuff without him. It was the most beautiful, spiritual, peaceful closure that I could ever have wished or prayed for.

[PATTI SMITH]

At the *New York Times*, there's a rule when writing obituaries: A reporter must attempt to talk to a relative or close friend of the deceased (or occasionally the coroner's office or another first-hand source) in order to establish the cause of death. Often, this means being put in the uncomfortable position of phoning a crying mother to ask how her son died or a grieving wife to ask how her husband passed away. So when Fred (Sonic) Smith, the guitarist in the influential pre-punk band the MC5, died, I ended up on the phone with his wife, Patti Smith, the equally influential punk singer and poet, who had disappeared from the music scene some fifteen years earlier to be a wife and mother.

But rather than being upset that a nervous reporter was calling to question her about the death of the man she loved, she was grateful that her husband was receiving recognition in the paper of record. After the obituary ran, she began calling on holidays just to leave messages wishing me well. The following year, shortly after her brother died of a stroke, she emerged from retirement to go on the road with Bob Dylan and agreed to a rare interview.

---

* Edwards died of a rare strain of pneumonia less than twelve hours after first experiencing the symptoms.

What made you decide to start performing again?
PATTI SMITH: It was because of my brother. He passed away on December fourth, but the last day I saw him was the weekend after Thanksgiving. He took me for a drive, and he had the soundtrack to *Natural Born Killers*. [My song] "Rock N Roll Nigger" is on it—and he put it on really loud, and we drove around. I was really totally just desolate.

And he said, "I'm gonna get you back on your feet, babe. You're gonna go back to work. Working will help you get your stride again. I'm going to be right there with you." And that's the last time I saw him alive.

What's more important to you right now: your music itself or making the memories of others live on through the music?
SMITH: Well, I think the latter. I don't have any particular message right now. I just want to sort of make sure that the people I've loved and lost aren't forgotten. Last week, we visited my brother's grave and we left cigarettes at his grave. With all the work that I'm doing, I feel like he sort of got me in that frame of mind. The other thing is that Fred always told me he didn't really play live anymore, but there would be two people he would come out for if they ever called upon him, and that was Bob Dylan and Keith Richards. So I kind of feel like I'm doing some stuff for Fred, too.

People always write that you disappeared to become a housewife. If you could rewrite that sentence, what words would you put in the place of housewife?
SMITH: I don't mind being called a housewife, but I didn't disappear to be a housewife. I disappeared to be by the side of the man that I loved. It was a sometimes difficult but an always honorable position, and I think nothing greater could have happened to me at that time. I learned a lot of things in the process: some humility, for starters, and respect for others. We had two beautiful children. And I developed my skills and hopefully developed into the clean human being that I was as a child.

Is it strange to have to defend that decision?
SMITH: People like to think you went and stopped working. There's no job harder than being a wife and a mother. It is the most difficult task any woman, I think, could ever embark on. It requires infinite patience, humility, empathy, and dignity—or lack of dignity. It's a position that should be respected and honored, not looked upon as some sappy alternative. It was much more demanding and required much more nobility than the other work that I did.

Are you worried that your return to the public eye will affect your children at all?

SMITH: I'm always constantly aware or learning how it affects them. That's my primary concern. Nothing is more difficult for them than to have to see their father misrepresented. I try to do everything that I can to make sure that he's represented respectfully, which is so much why that was really beautiful what you did. I will always be grateful for that. The record could come out and you could hate it, and I would still respect you.

[COURTNEY LOVE]
SCENE 2

The following is a transcript of Courtney Love talking to her then–eleven-year-old daughter, Frances Bean, on the phone in the middle of her *Rolling Stone* interview.

COURTNEY LOVE: I was in jail, do you know that? Some guy got hurt at a show. It happens at every show every time. He says he got hurt with a microphone stand.

. . .

LOVE: Yeah, though my show was okay. I lost my voice, so it should have been better. But the police are after me.

. . .

LOVE: We're going to move the hell out of California. That's what we're going to do.

. . .

LOVE: They put me in a cell. It was so scary.

. . .

LOVE: Stay away from the tabloids. The things they're writing are the worst. I'm reading things saying I'm going to die.

. . .

LOVE: Are people saying anything to you at school?

. . .

LOVE: No? There's no whispering feeling or bad vibe there?

. . .

LOVE: No? Good, good.

[*Continued . . .*]

[ORLANDO BLOOM]
SCENE 1

Sometimes interviews are just awkward.

Let's say you're about to meet an actor. He's an extremely nice guy and he's just starred in what he thinks will be the biggest movie of his career, but he hasn't seen the actual film yet. You, however, have recently seen an advance screening. The problem: It's not very good.

Our story begins in a dingy rooming house on the island of St. Vincent, where a phone call is made to Orlando Bloom to discuss his upcoming movie, *Kingdom of Heaven*, a Ridley Scott-directed epic featuring Bloom as a crusader hero named Balian. Bloom is staying in a ritzy hotel nearby to film a *Pirates of the Caribbean* movie. Unfortunately, he has to cancel the interview.

ORLANDO BLOOM: I thought we'd get a cocktail, but I have a five a.m. call time tomorrow.

I understand. It's just good to be in the Caribbean.
BLOOM: Did you manage to see any bits of *Kingdom*?

I saw an early screening of the whole film.
BLOOM: No way! You saw the whole thing? I haven't even seen it yet. I'm dying to know what bits they put in and what bits they left out (*pauses*). Well, maybe you should come by. I have to eat dinner anyway. And I was going to do it alone.

Fifteen minutes later, over dinner at the Young Island Resort . . .

BLOOM: What did you think?

I thought it was gorgeous. Epic.
BLOOM: Did you think it was great?

I think it could be great, but there are a few things about the story and the character that threw me off.
BLOOM: Actually, what kind of movies do you usually like?

I like these kinds of movies.
BLOOM: Does it open with my character in jail?

No, there's no scene like that. It opens with your wife's body on the road.
BLOOM: How about the swordfight at the end? What did you think of that?

Um, I don't think that was in there, either.
BLOOM: You don't get that? The last time I spoke with Ridley, he said it was in. But maybe he took it out. What happens is he approaches me in the street and we end up having this swordfight. It ends with him on his knees and me about to deliver the fatal blow. Then I say, "I'm leaving," like he doesn't deserve it.

That's cool.
BLOOM: It would have been cool, but it's not in there. How was the Knights Templar scene?

That was actually in there. It looked great.
BLOOM: How does it compare to *Gladiator*?

It's a completely different movie.
BLOOM: But *Gladiator* pulls you in more?

I guess it did, for me.
BLOOM: Because of Russell Crowe?

No, because of the tension between him and the Caesar. There's no obstacle between Balian and what he wants. He just sort of floats through it all, and the action just happens to him, until the end.
BLOOM: That's what's fascinating about it. He's a man who's lost his wife and child, and has no concept of how to cope with that situation and what to do next and so is in turmoil, in that nihilistic state. So he's sort of dragged through the movie by different people.

He's like a passive hero, I guess.
BLOOM: I really felt the character was me. I've never read a script like that one— not like that means a lot in my few years of working. Do you think Ridley Scott will get recognition for it?

Doesn't he already have recognition? He directed *Blade Runner* and *Alien*.
BLOOM: But real recognition?

Like what?
BLOOM: Do you think he'll finally get an Oscar or some award for it?

I don't know if this is his film for that. But I'm sure it's going to be number one at the box office.
BLOOM: It's . . . it's . . . you know what I mean. Hopefully. Knock on wood (*raps on the table*). Oh, that wasn't wood. But that is (*raps on a salt shaker*).

Kingdom of Heaven *was number one at the box office on its opening weekend, though it wasn't ultimately nominated for any Oscars. It received a rating of thirty-nine percent on the website Rotten Tomatoes.*

[*Continued . . .*]

$$\begin{bmatrix} \textbf{SOUL ASYLUM} \\ \textit{SCENE 2} \end{bmatrix}$$

The scene: Another hotel room in another city. On a glass tabletop sit two wine bottles, one of which is empty.

DAVE PIRNER: The preconceived notions that I have about you are pretty fucking right on.

Thank you.
PIRNER: I mean, they are. Okay, like seventy percent of this *Rolling Stone* article is going to be bullshit, man, about what you think this band is about. And you're going to pick out some quotes to support what you think is going to fit your take on the band. And what pisses me off is that I have no fucking idea what your take on this band is. Dude, you're twenty-six.

I should never have told you I was younger than you.
PIRNER: I know you shouldn't have. But let's talk about it. It's exciting to me because I think you're a hotshot. And I think you have some sort of angle on me. You're going to pit me against Courtney Love and Mike D. But I've met Yanni. I probably know more about Yanni than you do.

You probably do.
PIRNER: I probably do. And I know he's got kudos with all the dudes that have never even been interviewed for this magazine, right? So me and you are going to try to conduct a good interview and you're going to write an article telling me something I don't know about the band.

I'm not writing this article for you. I'm writing it for the people who listen to your music.
PIRNER: Honestly, what do people fucking care about musicians and the music they make? I don't think they fucking care. And I don't need this article. I don't need this interview. But, to tell you the truth, I'd like it if you could make me into someone other than my material. But you've got a project on your hands. And you've got a bunch of pretty dysfunctional guys to talk to.

So maybe it will be an article about dysfunction. The point is, let's stop discussing the article and start discussing the music.
PIRNER: But come on, Neil. Let's be serious, man. I'm not going to say, "I think this material that I've just written is the best material I've ever written and everybody should buy my album." But it's true.

If that's how you feel . . .
PIRNER: It is. What's better than that? There's nothing. Put my face on the cover of *Rolling Stone* magazine and give them my record, and I'm fulfilling my responsibility as a human being on this planet. Maybe somebody will buy the record because my face is on the magazine. Hey man, that's pretty happening. The system is working with me and I'm working with the system. And I'll lose so many things because of this. I'll lose the chance to have a normal life. I've already lost it.

I know.
PIRNER (*panicked*): You know? I've already lost it?

You just said that. But this is not a normal life. If you want a normal life, though, you can always have one.
PIRNER: Yeah, you know, I'd like to settle down and have kids some day. But it ain't going to happen, and I'm okay with that. And I have to . . . Wait, I'm talking myself into it right now. I would like that in my life. I would like to settle down and have kids and have a reasonable life. But it ain't going to happen, man, because music is my first love and I've given everything up for it. But off the record . . .

Pirner says something about his new album off the record. Don't worry, it's not that interesting.

Did someone teach you how to say "off the record" since our last interview?
PIRNER: Yes, my publicist did. It's totally . . . I hate the word *totally*. Don't ever use the word totally. Every time I say the word totally, that's off the record, too.

[*Continued . . .*]

[ANDY PRIEBOY]

Some musicians come so close to fame: They have the looks, the talent, and the personality, yet they never quite get there. Andy Prieboy, a songwriter and composer whose closest brush was as a former member of the band Wall of Voodoo (though not when the band had its one and only hit, "Mexican Radio"), is one such artist. With little provocation, he will tell anyone about his seven close calls and failures. And anyone listening will hear the sound of someone who once felt destined to be a rock star struggling to let go of that dream.

Four years before this interview, he was scoring porn films to survive. But then he decided to give success one more swing, with a very promising musical he had written about Axl Rose featuring his girlfriend, Rita D'Albert, former guitarist in the all-female rock band the Pandoras.

Did you ever think that you wanted to be famous?
ANDY PRIEBOY: Was it ever my goal to be famous? Is that what you're saying?

Yeah, exactly.
PRIEBOY: Sure, when you're like sixteen or seventeen. At my age at this point, the idea of being a rock star is almost like asking if I believe in Santa Claus. Talking about Wall of Voodoo is like talking about Chubby Checker. Nobody cares. You know, being a rock star is like a great dream for pimply teens, for fucking megalomaniacs who, you know, if they can't get a hit record will go on *Jerry Springer*, you know what I mean.
RITA D'ALBERT: And having lived so close to it in Los Angeles, you really start to question, "Oh, do I really want that?" You see the drawbacks.
PRIEBOY: It's like what I said to you [Rita] the other day. The thing that you and I lack is star fuckability. Nobody wants to fuck us. Seriously. A lot of the A-listers that I know are big garbage bags full of pus and vomit that just sort of roll around. And there is this whole crowd of people who feel that they are insignificant, and once they pick this big vomit bag up, they get to hang out with them and become

significant. "Oh, let's go pick up the vomit bag because everybody will know that we are really important too." And Rita and I aren't like that.

D'ALBERT: We don't kiss up to famous people. There have been people at our shows, and we don't pursue it or even acknowledge it (*pauses*). Except for now, as we're talking about it.

PRIEBOY: A lot of them are genius self-promoters who fall apart so that everybody can come pick them up and fuss over them and that whole thing. Rita and I, we're not the types that people want to come and take care of. And I don't think we could literally become major celebrity stars, because we aren't really—

D'ALBERT: We don't like the drama.

PRIEBOY: Yeah, the drama thing. I mean, I don't think I'm that dysfunctional. I do my self-destruction very slowly, one cigarette at a time. But we are not little pus-filled vomit bags.

D'ALBERT: In the beginning, we were reading all the *Enquirers* and the *Stars* that were coming in the mail, and I got really disgusted with the things that came out of these people's mouths that become so self-important. And I guess having a baby really helped me realize that I have issues with men, and all these people are so self-centered and think they're so important. I forgot where I was going with it, but I guess I'm too old . . . Sorry to get on a high horse.

PRIEBOY: Well, how does Marilyn [Manson] feel about all this? Because he seems to be pretty . . .

D'ALBERT: He seems very intelligent.

You mean about the sycophants?
D'ALBERT: All the trappings of celebrity.

He embraces it. His philosophy before he got famous was, "If you act like a rock star, people will treat you like one."
PRIEBOY: He has to come to our show.
D'ALBERT: Yeah, do you think you could invite him?

Prieboy's Axl Rose musical received rave reviews. After a long run in Los Angeles and performances in New York, it captured the interest of Broadway producers. But the negotiations fell apart, the musical was abandoned, and Prieboy and D'Albert broke up—though they did end up performing a medley from the musical on Late Night with Conan O'Brien.

[MARILYN MANSON]
SCENE 2

Waking up late one afternoon, Marilyn Manson called my hotel room and said to meet him in his suite. I walked in to find Radiohead and Monster Magnet CDs on the dresser, a jewel-encrusted skull on the bedside table, and a shirtless Manson apologizing for the stink. There was also a CD with Smashing Pumpkins leader Billy Corgan's phone number on it. "That was a stupid thing to do," Manson said. "Now he's going to get a lot of crank calls."

The two had met for the first time the previous night, during which time Manson had talked Corgan into snorting Sea-Monkey eggs and tried to stuff the end of a glow-in-the-dark bracelet down Twiggy's penis hole.

He suggested adjourning to the hotel Jacuzzi. However, it was difficult for him to get into the water: He tried once and backed down because someone was already in the tub. He tried a second time and changed his mind because one of the garter-clad fans scouring the hotel for him had just walked by. The third time, he got lucky, and the following conversation took place about the article, which would be his first cover story in *Rolling Stone*.

MARILYN MANSON: Did Twiggy tell you at all about our Dr. Hook rituals that we had in the past?

No, he didn't tell me.

MANSON: Well, when we were heavy into our couldn't-care-less, let's-drink-and-do-all-the-drugs-we-could-ever-want-in-one-night era . . . And by the way, this comes and goes: There will be another one in the future, I'm sure. But this one was in the past, and we would always listen to the album *Sloppy Seconds* by Dr. Hook, which, if it were released today, would probably be banned because it talks about blatant drug use and sex with minors and necrophilia and bestiality. And of course it has the song "Cover of the *Rolling Stone*," which we always used to sing and listen to when we were doing drugs because it has that line in it, "But our minds won't really be blown like the blow that'll get you when you get your picture on the cover of the *Rolling Stone*." So that was always a longtime goal of ours, because I don't think Dr. Hook ever got on the cover.

I think they were, actually, but after the song.
MANSON: Right. So we vowed in honor of our love for Dr. Hook to someday be on the cover of *Rolling Stone*. If I'm not mistaken, that guy, I think he has like a wooden leg and an eye patch, which he may have done himself just for the look.*

Don't you collect wooden legs or something?
MANSON: Yeah, I collect prosthetic limbs and keep them with me on tour and around the bus. I have about fifteen total, like legs and arms of all different shapes and sizes. I've always had just a weird fetish for those. The other day that guy came up and he wanted to give me the prosthetic leg he was wearing.

What did he say?
MANSON: He didn't say anything. He was just like hopping around, trying to give it to us.

And did you take it?
MANSON: No, I didn't end up getting it, which disappoints me.

I'm sure he had more at home.
MANSON: Yeah, we should have taken it. I'm just used to saying no.

After a little while, he leaves the hot tub because he feels sick. We return to his room, where he discusses the many spurious rumors about him: that he had a rib removed so he could fellate himself, that he was a child actor on The Wonder Years, *and that he's into S&M.*

MANSON: I have people come up to me and ask if they can cut me while I cut them or if I can put out a cigarette on their face. I can understand that people are trying to make a first impression, but I think that a lot of people think that because in the past I've cut myself that I'm into sadomasochism and I like to do that to other people. They don't understand it was just an expression of what I was doing onstage. It was a piece of time. They can't comprehend that it's not what Marilyn Manson is about (*pauses, reflects*). It has to be the right circumstance.

---

* The eyepatch was real. Singer Ray Sawyer lost an eye in a near-fatal car accident, though his legs work just fine and he's never used a wooden limb.

I noticed that one of the guys on your crew has a bandage on his finger, but it looks like a fake finger.
MANSON: I think he broke his finger. But I could talk him into cutting it off, you know. I could. I'm into taking everything to the extreme. My motto is that a lot of people have gone most of the way, so you really have to go all the way if you want to make anything of your life.

The phone rings, and Manson makes plans with Twiggy to see a movie with Billy Corgan that night, then apologizes again for the stink in his room.

You were talking about going all the way . . .
MANSON: I think I'm starting to understand myself in my own way. As far as people go, I'd like to be able to say no or be able to turn women down. Or just be in a position where I don't need other people. I've felt for so many years that I was the person who always wanted to fit in. Now I'm in a position where I can be as misanthropic as I'd like to be. I don't know if it's my way of paying everyone back or if I'm just bitter.

He walks to his suitcase and starts pulling out things to show me, from photographs of himself to a concert T-shirt of the metal band W.A.S.P.

Now that you've accomplished your goals, maybe even overshot them, where do you go from here?
MANSON: Every once in a while, I'll step out on the balcony and think about jumping. I'll think, "Is this the final thrill, because I'm numb to everything else?" (*Stops rifling through his belongings and reconsiders.*) But I feel I have more to accomplish. I think I have a lot more in store that people really won't expect. I mean, besides [bringing about] the end of the world.

[*Continued . . .*]

[DAVE NAVARRO]

Very late one Thursday night, Marilyn Manson was at the home of guitarist Dave Navarro, who sat shirtless at his computer. On Navarro's left side, a cigarette lay burning on the edge of a table next to a syringe filled with cocaine. On his right, there was a photo of Courtney Love that Manson had brought over. It depicted Love sprawled on the floor outside Trent Reznor's hotel room. They scanned the photo into Navarro's computer, then blew it up so they could read a message she'd

written in lipstick on Reznor's door. Then they continued to enlarge the image, until Love's vagina could be seen under her hiked-up dress. Altogether, this art project lasted some two hours. After Manson left at sunrise, Navarro posed the following dilemma.

DAVE NAVARRO: Someone asked me today, "If Courtney Love, Marilyn Manson, and Billy Corgan were drowning in water, who would you save first?"

Who asked you that?
NAVARRO: I don't remember. Who would you choose?

You can't choose Courtney, because she'd pull you down too and you'd both drown.
NAVARRO: And Manson would make me want to drown.

Or he'd talk you into drowning just to entertain himself.
NAVARRO: And Billy would just watch, and talk about how he could have saved us better than everyone else.

═══ [THE SMASHING PUMPKINS] ═══

At one point, the Smashing Pumpkins were the biggest rock band in the world. Two years later, when the band released an album called *Adore*, which was more electronic and experimental than its predecessors, they weren't. In an interview so candid that afterward the president of his record label called and chewed me out for printing it, Billy Corgan grappled with the album's failure to live up to his expectations.

BILLY CORGAN: You know what, I have to . . . I have to tell you in all candor that I've been really surprised by how quick the world turns on you.

What do you mean?
CORGAN: It's . . . it's staggering. I can't get into the specific politics, but all I can tell you is that the moment that your shit doesn't keep rolling, the wind blows cold real fast.

Like the way the press builds you up to knock you down?
CORGAN: I'm not just talking about the media. I'm talking about the inner work-

ings of my world. I think that the band has been a little surprised because we thought we could push the artistic envelope a little and not necessarily work the machine. And I think we've been really surprised at this attitude of, "Oh, what have you done for me lately?"

Who's been saying that?
CORGAN: I'm talking on every level of the music business. And for us that's a little hard to believe. I mean, we're back to where we started. When you find out you're too strange for alternative radio and you're not heavy enough for rock radio, you're left going, "Well, where *do* we fit?" And you suddenly find yourself without an anchor. It's been a really eye-opening experience.

Ultimately you have to decide whether you're making pop or you're making art.
CORGAN: Yeah, I like to think both.

And do you think this is happening because of the way this record is doing or because you're not playing the game like they want you to?
CORGAN: I think that when the record came out and didn't explode right off the block, all those people that had been proven wrong by the band commercially in the past went, "Oh well, another one down the tubes." It kind of let us know, "You will always be on the fringe of it. No matter what you do, no matter how you do it, you're never gonna be in that one circle."

The circle where you're established and accepted and don't have to prove yourself anymore?
CORGAN: It's more . . . It kicked us in the head. There's that sick thing sometimes where you feel like you can reach for that one last brass ring, but you've got to realize that you're just not of that DNA and there are some people that are. And do you really want it anyway?

So what is that brass ring for you?
CORGAN: We've had huge, huge alternative songs. I mean, we've made it into the greatest hits of the grunge era. But if you look at us in a completely crass, objective way, the one thing we have not achieved is we have not had top ten records.* So we've reached that fork in the road where you're either going to go in that [downward] direction or you're going to continue to build as a band like U2 and R.E.M.

---

* By records, he means singles. His previous two albums were both in the top ten on *Billboard*'s pop chart.

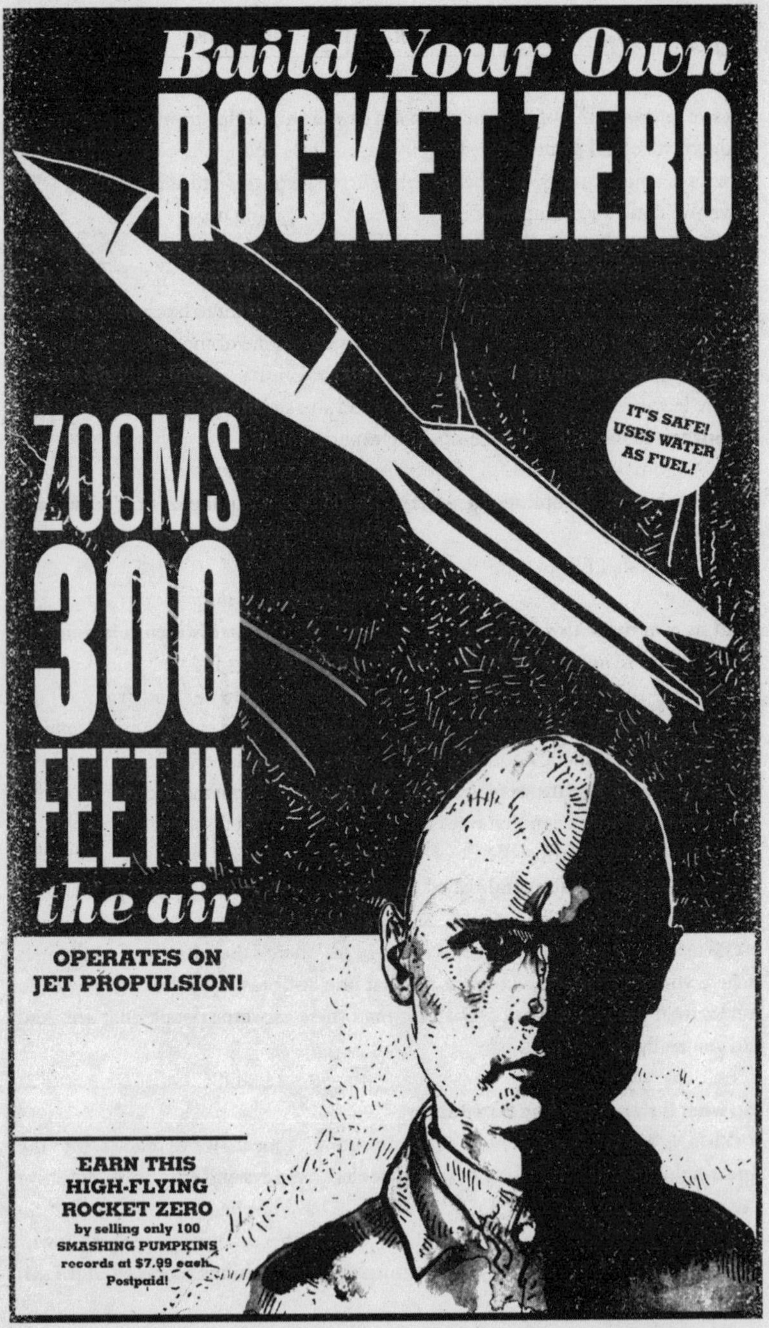
Build Your Own
ROCKET ZERO
IT'S SAFE! USES WATER AS FUEL!
ZOOMS 300 FEET IN the air
OPERATES ON JET PROPULSION!
EARN THIS HIGH-FLYING ROCKET ZERO
by selling only 100 SMASHING PUMPKINS records at $7.99 each Postpaid!

did. We've taken kind of a funny swing at it and realized that maybe that world is so shitty, you don't want it anyway.

But now, instead of being rebellious, it seems like giving up.
CORGAN: Well, for me, I think the only thing I fear is that it's like a missile or a satellite or something. If it slows down too much, you start to fall out of orbit. And I think I don't want to exist falling out of orbit. I either want to burn out or I want to be a cult kind of band. I mean, I either want to be one of the biggest rock stars in the world or I'd rather be Alex Chilton.

I'm surprised to hear you say that.
CORGAN: I'm not interested in the middle at all. I mean, give me glory or give me a packed club with people who appreciate the nuances. But the middle? Not at all interested.

Despite the grim picture Corgan painted, Adore *still entered the pop chart at number two, was nominated for a Grammy Award, and sold more than a million copies.*

[ALEX CHILTON]

During an hour-long interview from his home in New Orleans, the reclusive singer, songwriter, and guitarist Alex Chilton talked about being a sixteen-year-old pop singer in the sixties group the Box Tops, with whom he cut the number one hit "The Letter"; the burden of being in one of the most influential but obscure rock bands of the seventies, Big Star; self-destructing afterward as an alcoholic; and the previously unpublished experience below.

A mutual friend said to ask you about the time you were staying with Dennis Wilson [of the Beach Boys] and met Charles Manson.
ALEX CHILTON: Well, I was staying at Dennis's house, and Charlie came after I had been there a few days and stayed, too.

And that was all? You just stuck around a few more days and left?
CHILTON: Uh, yeah.

Could you tell at that point that he was capable of the things he ended up causing to happen?

CHILTON: No, I didn't really have any inkling that . . . I mean, there were a couple of things in retrospect that were kind of weird, but at the time I wasn't thinking, "This guy's a homicidal maniac." Although, you know, the vibes were kind of weird.

What were the weird things in retrospect?
CHILTON: Well, I remember once I went to the grocery . . . Uh, are you planning to write about this in the *New York Times*?

I don't have to write about it in the story if you don't want.
CHILTON: Yeah, I don't think it's a good idea (*laughs nervously*).

I guess I'm curious.
CHILTON: One time I was going to the grocery store, and one of his girls got wind of that. And so she brought me a big, long shopping list of things that they wanted me to get—and no money to get it with. So I said, "Well, it's all right." It being the sixties and California, I thought I could spring for some groceries. So this is out in Malibu, and we were staying up on the hillside looking down over the ocean. So I had to go all the way down the hill to the Pacific Coast Highway on foot and then carry all these groceries back up the hill. So that was kind of tough. And when I got back, some of the girls, like, met me in the driveway before I ever got to the house. And they looked at the grocery bag and they said, "Well, you forgot the milk." And I said, "Aw, gee, I'm really sorry I forgot the milk. Too bad."

Right, and then—
CHILTON: And then they went on in the house and I sort of ambled on behind them. And by the time I got to the front door, they were standing in the doorway, blocking the door. And they said, "Charlie says go get the milk."

So what did you do?
CHILTON: I don't know exactly what I said, but I think I said I wasn't gonna go down to the bottom of the hill and bring the milk back up the hill.

And so that's the big story?
CHILTON: Yeah.*

---

* Afterword, I interviewed Phil Kaufman, the road manager famous for stealing his friend Gram Parsons's corpse and burning it. Kaufman also happened to have produced Manson's album *Lie* when they were in jail together, and had this to say about him: "He's an asshole. When I got out of prison and stayed with Charlie for a while, I was impressed at first: Here's this guy having sex on demand—and with young pretty girls. I said, 'You got a good game going here. Don't blow it.' But he did."

This seems like a good place to end for now.
CHILTON: Okay, well, good luck trying to write anything good out of what I know.

In March 2010, Alex Chilton complained to his wife, who he'd married seven months earlier, that he was experiencing shortness of breath and chills. Because he didn't have health insurance, he didn't seek medical attention at the time. The following week, he died of a heart attack.

= [**DAVID KORESH'S GIRLFRIEND**] =

One thing modern-day pathological cult leaders seem to have in common is that they're frustrated rock and roll stars. Charles Manson, whose musical supporters included Neil Young and Dennis Wilson, sent his followers to murder the residents of a house formerly occupied by a producer who refused to sign him. And when Branch Davidian sect leader David Koresh (born Vernon Wayne Howell) and some eighty followers perished—some shot each other, others killed themselves, and others died in a fire in the compound—after a fifty-one-day standoff with the FBI in Waco, Texas, many believed that the only known recordings of his rock music perished as well. That is, until his ex-girlfriend Sandy Berlin entered the picture.

How did you know David Koresh?
SANDY BERLIN: I first met him when I lived in Tyler, Texas. He was twenty and I was barely fifteen. My dad ran a Seventh-day Adventist Church, and he was my dad's protégé. We ended up taking him on a trip with us to Minnesota. Vern and me sat in the backseat the whole way. It was kind of another world back there. He was quoting me Bible verses from the Song of Solomon. Then he asked me to marry him in a tree once we got up to Minnesota.

Did you say yes?
BERLIN: Well, he insisted on telling my dad. And of course my dad blew up and wanted to send him back on a bus. So that's when they started falling out.

Was he playing music at the time?
BERLIN: When I first met him, he refused to pick up the guitar because he said Satan would come through his fingers and he'd play rock and roll. I was a member of the church band, but he thought it was too pop-ish. So when he picked up his

guitar again, he started listening to rock and roll. He would take the meanings in the songs as a message from either God or Satan.

Where would he perform?
BERLIN: He would go down to bars sometimes and bring his guitar, and he'd stand up and start playing. Other times he would go to a parking lot and start playing. He would hit the Seventh-day Adventist camp meetings. A lot of the preachers in camp meetings knew about him. But his style of playing was getting more and more like rock and roll, and they don't have rock and roll in the Adventist churches. So they would reprimand him and tell him, "Vernon, you can't do this."

Did you notice anything else strange about him at the time?
BERLIN: He started having dreams, and every dream he said was a message from God. His soul was in turmoil all the time, and I guess that's when he started getting strange. He was kind of a baby Christian, because he had only been off drugs for a year. Once he tried to humble himself by cutting his hair.

Because he felt bad about his sins?
BERLIN: He almost literally beat himself over the back about his sins. But he couldn't seem to quit sinning. And the more he couldn't quit, the more he needed to find an excuse for them. He had a terrible guilt problem. My dad couldn't reason with him.

And then . . .
BERLIN: I guess he started preaching to everyone. One time he pushed my dad aside in church and kept saying "God told me I'm supposed to marry your daughter." My dad sent me away a couple weeks after that and expelled him from the congregation.*

Did you continue dating him after that?
BERLIN: We stayed in touch. Vernon and me had little codes: He'd give me one ring over the phone to call him back, then half a ring to let me know that he loved me. I ended up going with him for about two years. During the second year, I saw him on and off. Over those two years, he started getting more and more fanatical. It got weird.

---

* Which is what led Koresh down the path to Waco to join the Branch Davidians instead.

In what way?

BERLIN: I'd ask him if he thought he was a prophet, but he was evasive. After the tenth time, he said, "Yes, I am." I told him, "I don't think you're a true prophet." He would sew scriptures together to come up with his doctrine: He'd just close Bibles, open them up, and point to a verse at random and say that's what God wanted him to put together.

So how did you end up with his music?

BERLIN: I told him I needed a tape to study what he was trying to tell me. I told him, "Please put some music on there." I was in love with him and I always will love him, but I don't agree with what he did.

Did he ever try to get you to go to Waco?

BERLIN: He wanted me to go to Waco and sing with his band. I think that music was one of his recruiting tactics. I had a drum set and a keyboard, and he went nuts trying to get me there. He taught me his style of playing guitar, though my mom didn't like it. The last straw for me was when he wanted to take me away in his trunk.

Was that the last time you saw him?

BERLIN: No. He always considered me his wife. He'd look me up once a year or try to call me. Once he spent three days looking for me here in Fort Dodge. He had Steve Schneider* with him and his son, Cyrus, and he showed up in the driveway. He was [also] calling himself Cyrus then, which is the same thing as Koresh. I was going with somebody else at the time. So he played for a few hours and preached. He was weaving all this strange stuff together. When he got done, we were like, "What did you say?"

What were his plans for the music?

BERLIN: He started what he called Cyrus Productions. If he was to release an album, he was going to release it on his own and start his own label.

How did you feel when you heard about what happened at Waco?

BERLIN: It felt awful when the fire was going on. He made everything so spiritual and cosmic. To a fifteen-year-old girl, I was enraptured with him. I called his mom up while the fire was happening. She started bawling. We both knew he was dead. Of course, he believed that him and all his children would be saved.

---

* Koresh's right-hand man, who the FBI believe shot Koresh and himself in Waco.

What made you decide to finally come forward with the recordings?
BERLIN: At first I didn't want to tell anyone I even knew him. I was afraid: People were disappearing who said they knew him. So I didn't talk to any reporters at the time. My brother made me put the tapes in a locked box because he knew the FBI would want them. Some people said I should release them, but I was afraid of the publicity, of anger, of what the other families might feel.

So what changed?
BERLIN: His mother asked for a copy of one of them. She said, "Well, Sandy, I think it's okay. There's nothing too bad that's said on there. A lot of people want to know what he was like in his own words. It could benefit psychologists and people who study cults."

And how do people feel now that it's out?
BERLIN: Davidians are glad, and his mother is glad.* You can hear the heart behind him. He was sincere. Part of the proceeds go to his oldest daughter, who's fourteen. Most of his other children were killed, so I picked her.

$$\left[\begin{array}{c} \textbf{SOUL ASYLUM} \\ \textit{SCENE 3} \end{array} \right]$$

The scene: The Corner Bistro, a bar in New York's Greenwich Village, closing time.

DAVE PIRNER: Someone told me I'm supposed to be the voice of a generation, the big crappy voice of a generation. But how could that be? No one can be that pure. Like Bill Clinton: He doesn't really encourage people to be different. He doesn't encourage anybody to do anything.

I don't know if that's totally true.
PIRNER: Does he encourage people to do evil shit?

No.
PIRNER: Has he ever?

He might have at some point.
PIRNER: Do you encourage people to do evil shit? Would you just tell somebody to do something dirty and lowdown and fucking awful? Am I going to tell my friends to go out and do something that I wouldn't do? I don't think so.

---

* In 2009, Koresh's mother was stabbed to death. Her sister was charged with the murder.

But you might have once.
PIRNER: No, not once. Not ever.

Not even encouraged someone to pull the fire alarm at school or, like, jump over something dangerous on their skateboard?
PIRNER: I did do it one time. I told a girl to touch the fire in a cigarette lighter in a car, and she burned her finger. The guilt that I felt just overwhelmed any importance that I felt about anything. But I think there's a better way, and I think that my band is delivering the quality in a way that has never been delivered before. My ideals are better. Do you think they're better?

Better than what?
PIRNER: Better than the president's. I met Bill Clinton. And I do think my aspirations are fucking higher than his, man. And I met fucking all these dudes, man, and I don't know who they fucking are, but they're in this fucking country and my ideals are higher. But I'm an idealist. There's this guy who wrote this book called *The Lucifer Principle*. He keeps trying to identify evil. But it's not that complicated, man. I think whether you're talking about Charlie Manson or Henry Rollins or fucking Neil Strauss, there's this unharnessable rage and anger and this terrible beast that exists inside everybody. Basically, I think that some people suppress it better than others.

So how good are you at repressing it?
PIRNER: I'm a pacifist. But I still have the ability to fucking kill somebody with my bare hands. I can do it. I have the potential. Today, I woke up early and was ready, for the first time in my life, to leave for the airport on schedule. But I couldn't find my pants, and I had all my shit in the pockets. So I got real angry and started punching my duffel bag. I mean, I have it in me. I don't want anybody to doubt my potential to wreak negative energy upon the entire universe, because I could kick ass pretty badly. But I would never use that negative energy (*long pause*). Destruction is good, I guess, as long as you're destroying the right shit. And, I don't know, bring the questions on, man.

[*Continued . . .*]

[MARILYN MANSON]
SCENE 3

Shortly after the *Rolling Stone* article was published, Manson's star grew even larger. Soon he was the favorite bogeyman of conservative watchdog organizations, most notably the American Family Association, which began claiming that Manson concerts included bestiality, Satanic altar calls, ritual rapes, and the distribution of free drugs.

Though none of this was true, some politicians, parents' groups, and religious organizations believed it. As a result, nearly every town Manson passed through on tour tried to prevent his concerts from taking place. Some threatened to pass legislation banning him from performing on State property; others actually offered him money to go away—as the state of South Carolina did to the tune of $40,000.

According to Manson's manager, the band's ticket sales shrank by twenty percent as a result of parents telling their kids not to see the shows because of the rumors. After a new and threatening letter from People for the Ethical Treatment of Animals came through the fax machine, Manson decided to comment on the allegations for the first time.

"I have to put an end to it," he explained. "If people are going to hate me, I want them to hate me for the right reasons."

So we took a look at the sworn testimonies posted on the American Family Association's website and, one by one, Manson responded to them.

THE ALLEGATION: I have witnessed Manson pull out small chickens, several puppies, and kittens out of the bag and throw them in the audience. [. . .] Manson will then [. . .] not start the show until all the animals are dead.
THE RESPONSE: I like dogs. I have a dog. There is no reason why I would want to kill animals. Not only is it just pointless and ridiculous, but if I were doing things like that, I wouldn't be onstage. I'd be in prison.

THE ALLEGATION: I witnessed Manson call for the virgin sacrifice in which all the children in the concert arena are pushed forward by the crowd to be dedicated to Satan.
THE RESPONSE: I've never worshipped the devil. I consider myself as much a member of the Church of Satan as where I was baptized as a kid, St. Paul's Episcopal Church in Canton, Ohio, or as much as I'm a member of Blockbuster Video

or the library. If I had to describe my beliefs, God and Satan are like your left and your right hand, just like Marilyn and Manson. It's two words to describe the two sides of what you are.

THE ALLEGATION: I have witnessed rapes at most concerts. The crowd get[s] into a frenzy and females are held down against their will and raped many times as Manson prods them on.
THE RESPONSE: Now how can someone actually believe that I could be involved in something like that and I wouldn't be in prison? The guy who runs Meadowlands tried to cancel my concert. If he had come to me and he was crying and he said, "I think your music is hurting the youth of America; I don't want you to play," I'd sit down and talk to him. But that's not the case. You know what the guy said? He said, "If Marilyn Manson thinks they're gonna play here, they can sue me." So I did—and I won.

THE ALLEGATION: Manson has a team he calls his private Santa Clauses. They come at the crowd from the sides and throw out bags of pot and cocaine throughout the entire audience front to back.
THE RESPONSE: That is ridiculous. If I had a giant bag of drugs, I would not be passing them out, especially for free. I would be backstage doing them, as I have in the past.

[MIKE TYSON]

Imagine: It's less than a year after Mike Tyson bit off part of Evander Holyfield's ear in the ring, and Tyson has barely talked to the press since. You're interviewing a rapper named Canibus, and suddenly he tells you that he's in Mike Tyson's hotel room and asks if you'd like to speak to him. You give your assent, and a gentle, girlish voice soon answers.

MIKE TYSON: Hi.

Hey, thanks for doing this. I was sitting with Marilyn Manson at the Ivy the other night and you pulled up in some crazy scooter or something.
TYSON: We seen him, too. My assistant wanted to go over and give him a kiss, but I said, "You go over. I'm riding this bike and gone" (*laughs*).

Give him a kiss?

TYSON: She loves him. She said, "Man, you ain't never hear the song, (*sings*) 'It's good people, baby, good people. Good people, the good people.' " Dude, that's the song he made?

"Beautiful People"? Yeah.

TYSON: I never heard that shit, man (*laughs*).

So how did you meet Canibus?

TYSON: I'm into the music scene so intensely and when I heard him, I said, "Yo, man, Canibus is hot." [. . .] We talk about rappers the way we talk about fighters. For twenty years I've known about all these rappers: Grandmaster Flash and everyone when they first came on the scene, Grand Wizard Theodore, and the L Brothers. People a lot of rappers now aren't even aware of. I was down with those guys, the founders.

How did you first hear about them?

TYSON: I must have been ten or eleven when I was put away [in a juvenile detention home for purse-snatching]. And all we had was music. We battled with people and entertained ourselves. We built an industry that way (*pauses*). Are you a critic?

Yeah, I write about music.

TYSON: We'll have a showcase one day and we'll get in touch with you, and you can . . . What's your name again, my friend?

Neil.

TYSON: Well, Neil, you can come and give your opinion on what you think of the new industry that's going on.

Is this for your new record label?

TYSON: Yeah, Tyson Records. Big business took rap away from us. We made the industry, but we have no control over the destiny of the music. There's no control over it. Definitely. Hip-hop and rap. Nothing.

So are these some of the things you've been doing to stay busy since losing your boxing license?

TYSON: Yeah, well, it was nice talking to you.

[PUFFY COMBS]

The party at Puffy Combs's white, cliffside Hamptons mansion was a crowded affair, with black-suited security guards and three giant television sets showing the Mike Tyson-Evander Holyfield fight. All eyes were on Puffy Combs as he stepped up to a microphone on the lawn. At the time, he was one of rap's most powerful and feared men: In the last few months, he'd released two number one singles, been accused of four murders, and witnessed his close friend and collaborator, the Notorious B.I.G., gunned down in Los Angeles. Combs clasped the top of the mic stand with a wiry hand and fingered the gold chain that peeked out of his pink silk shirt.

"We've got apple pie, cherry pie, chocolate ribbon cake, and cookies," he announced. "And the ice cream truck is still outside if anyone wants Popsicles or candy or beach balls. Thank you."

There are probably four murders you've been accused of over the last year—
PUFFY COMBS: Unless I'm sleepwalking, I don't know how I have the time to be running around doing that gangsta stuff. When the *New York Post* or the *Daily News* or the *Times* paints a picture of me like I'm on the level of John Gotti, but on a black tip, people think that I can possess that power or possess that emotion and heartlessness and coldness to take somebody's life, you know what I'm saying. I never punched—no, not never, but I haven't punched anybody in the face in the last couple of years, let alone all this stuff!

If you punched somebody in the face now, you'd get a multi-million-dollar lawsuit.
COMBS: I just want to one day get judged for what somebody sees. And it's wrong to do that to my life, because I'm too important to young black people. They should be bringing somebody down who's living wrong, who's a bad influence. I'm a good influence if you all give me a chance, if you all write what you all see.

That's why I'm here.
COMBS: I'm definitely tired of it. I'm not going to be talking about it anymore. We're talking about it now just to get it out of the way. It's crazy. It's like saying you're a rapist. You're not a rapist, are you? Have you ever raped anybody?

No, no.
COMBS: How ludicrous does that sound, if I said you're a rapist?

Definitely. But every time shit happens now, somebody's always saying, "Puffy did it."
COMBS: I ain't done shit. I want to live a good life. I want to have a positive influence on people. I want to enter a room and have people feel good and say, "Oh, the party's started."

A week after the party, the interview continues at Combs's Manhattan studio, where he's working on a Boyz II Men song. "I want strings in the break and more percussion all over it," he tells the engineer, who scoffs at these vague instructions as soon as Combs leaves the room.

Elsewhere in the studio, an employee tells his girlfriend that he had to buy a Rolex because everyone else he works with has one, while in a back room another employee asks about a gun permit. Combs sits down on a couch with some takeout food. He stretches out his right arm, which has a brutal-looking scar on the wrist.

What's that from?
COMBS: A broken champagne glass. Another part of the cross I be talking about I got to bear.

Because people are saying that you tried to kill yourself?
COMBS: There's no way I could have done that. If I did it with a knife, it wouldn't be uneven like that. Also, I'm right-handed, so if I had a knife, I would have cut my left wrist. And I just think I would have made sure I really killed myself. Also, I'm a little bit too smart, so I know if you really want to kill yourself, you go this way (*gestures up the wrist along the vein*).

Is that how you'd kill yourself?
COMBS: I think if I killed myself, I would probably want to go to sleep. I don't think I would want to sit there and bleed to death (*pauses*). I don't even want to kill myself, so I don't even think about it. Shit, if I had to, give me some sleeping pills, man. Let me go to sleep and wake up in heaven.

I think I'd jump off a building because I want to know what it feels like.
COMBS: Oh, you crazy. I ain't crazy. I just want to go to sleep. I don't want to know how long it takes: I be asleep.

DIDDY CREAM
ICE CREAM TREATS

WE GIVE EXCELLENT
SERVICE

WHEN YOU TASTE THE
COLDNESS ... YOU'LL KNOW
A PARTY HAS STARTED
IN YOUR MOUTH.

DIDDY CREAM COMPANY
NEW YORK, NEW YORK

Aren't you suing Wendy Williams or someone for posting a pornographic photo of you on the Internet?

COMBS: No, I wasn't suing her. I was going to sue the *New York Post*. The *New York Post* had a picture of me mooning a crowd on my yacht. I can take my pants down and sling my dick* all over that yacht, you know what I'm saying. It's my motherfucking yacht.

[ORLANDO BLOOM]
SCENE 2

Orlando Bloom and his entourage, all tan men in their late twenties with close-cropped dark hair—a tattooed personal assistant, an Israeli bodyguard, and an Australian physical trainer—decided to rent a yacht and spend an afternoon exploring the nearby island of Bequia.

As we approached the island, Bloom stood shirtless in the front of the boat, facing the water with his arms outstretched as the waves broke against the bow of the ship and sprayed him in the face.

Do people often ask you why you have so little dialogue in your movies?

ORLANDO BLOOM: *Elizabethtown* has more dialogue. I have a huge voice-over. But, I don't know . . . I couldn't tell you why that is. No one's really asked me before.

But have you noticed it?

BLOOM: I have noticed it. Somebody told me Steve McQueen used to say, "Cut the line; give me the close-up." And I always thought that was kind of interesting. Look at Clint Eastwood. He's a master at that.

But when Eastwood does speak, what he says has a lot of poignancy and weight.

BLOOM: Exactly. You know what? Maybe the precedent was set with *Lord of the Rings*, because Legolas didn't say very much at all. But what he did say was really important. He'd say, like, "Orcs" or something. Actually, he didn't say anything really very important. I don't know (*trails off and starts thinking*) . . .

---

* Combs, speaking backstage at the Grammys about Janet Jackson's indecent exposure during a Super Bowl halftime show: "I have three sons. I don't mind. I'm very happy for them that they were able to see one of Janet Jackson's breasts in their lifetime. If I had known about that, I would have tried to steal the show in my own right, and I would have exposed to America something that you still would have been talking about."

Off-camera, are you talkative in a group?
BLOOM: No, not that much. I was more like that when I was a kid. I, uh . . . At least, I think I was . . . No, maybe not. I don't know. It's hard to say. I can remember points where I was like . . . I was never so much talkative. But if I had something to say, then I would say it. I don't know . . .

You seem like you think a lot—maybe too much.
BLOOM: Yeah, that is true. Definitely!

And because you can be critical of yourself, you'd rather err on the side of underacting than overacting. You'd rather give them more Paul Newman and less Jim Carrey.
BLOOM: Yeah, yeah, exactly. It's funny because I have noticed the way different people perform. And I'm still twenty-eight. I'm still defining what sort of actor I'm going to be, and it probably won't be for a while yet until I really find my niche. And I'm not in any hurry. I'm still figuring it out—and I hope I always am.

[SOUL ASYLUM]
SCENE 4

The scene: Hotel room, New York City, 4:30 a.m.

The context: I got Pirner into a sold-out concert by the high-principled Washington, DC, post-hardcore band Fugazi at New York's Irving Plaza earlier that night. When he asked how I did it, I jokingly told him, "I got the juice."* Hours later, I was still paying the price for my words.

DAVE PIRNER: Say, "I got the juice," man!

Uh, I got the juice?
PIRNER: I can't believe that you said that!

You mean earlier today? It was a joke.
PIRNER: Yeah, well, you thought it was a joke, but there's not a lot of people who have the nerve to say, "I got the juice."

No one has the nerve to say it seriously, maybe.
PIRNER: But you had the juice to get into Irving Plaza.

---

* The meaning of juice in this context would be pull or influence, not heroin, steroids, or GHB.

It doesn't take much.
PIRNER: I didn't need my manager, man.

Cut it out.
PIRNER: Do I have the juice? You know, I don't try to present myself as the voice of a generation. I'm presenting myself as a thirty-one-year-old man who has been writing songs for fifteen years, half a life. And fucking A, I've got the juice, man. You started this juice thing.

I know. And now I've got to follow through with it.
PIRNER: I never started it.

That's true.
PIRNER: I didn't.

Right.
PIRNER: I look at you and you look at me. And I figure that, like, our shit is pretty readable.

Um . . .
PIRNER: You got the juice, man. This is quite frankly a piss, because I don't even have the juice around you, man. You're like the hottest cat.

Oh, give me a break.
PIRNER: Mark E. Smith of the Fall, has he got the juice?

I think Mark E. Smith is the seed for a lot of people who have the juice now.
PIRNER: Yeah, you're right. All these people are talking about the juice. And what you really want is the seed. And I aspire to have the seed.

    You know, man? Sometimes I do have the seed. And I follow through with the juice.

[*Continued . . .*]

[JIMMY MARTIN]

Some interview subjects are so excited to be in a big newspaper that they do stupid things in front of the person who's about to put them in that big newspaper. This was the case at the World of Bluegrass convention in Louisville, Kentucky, when seventy-two-year-old guitarist and singer Jimmy Martin stood at the entrance to the hotel, wearing black boots with rhinestone crosses and a cowboy hat almost as red as his face.

So how did you get to be the king of bluegrass?
JIMMY MARTIN: More people are recognizing me and accepting me as the king of bluegrass. They walk up to me and say that Bill Monroe is the father, and you're not his son, so you're the king. They told me I was the bluegrass equivalent of Hank Williams and George Jones. But it didn't give me a big head.

A fourteen-year-old boy carrying a fiddle walks up.

BOY: Can you autograph your CD for me?
MARTIN: I'm getting in the *New York Times* right now, and you're bothering me.

Boy starts to walk away, dejected.

It's okay. We can take a break while you sign it.
MARTIN (*to boy*): Okay, I'll write it. (*Scribbles his signature, then to me:*) Can you print that I shook hands with Ricky Skaggs at the Grand Ole Opry and said, "You are the biggest motherfucker in country music"?

I don't think I can use that word in a family newspaper.
MARTIN: I did call Ricky an asshole. You can say that, can't you?

I don't think so.
MARTIN: At least can you say that my record still made a lot of money?

Jimmy Martin died in 2005 of bladder cancer. He was seventy-seven.

[SOUL ASYLUM]
SCENE 5

The scene: Same hotel room, same city, later.

DAVE PIRNER: Were we just talking about Salt-N-Pepa?

No, we weren't. But we can.
PIRNER: Have they got some kind of juice?

Not the juice again.
PIRNER: Yeah, one of those girls has got the juice. Do you know which one it is?

I'm going to go with Salt.
PIRNER: Or is it Pepa? Which one has the juice?

The short one.
PIRNER: You like the little one?

I don't like her. She just seems like more of a leader.
PIRNER: You think she's got the juice?

Oh, I don't know.
PIRNER: She's the one who can't carry a tune. She just raps. Same with TLC. I like
the girl who can't sing.

I don't think any of them can sing, except maybe Chilli sometimes.
PIRNER: See?

See what?
PIRNER: That's why you're the music critic, man. You guys can put people to the
test and you know who can't carry a tune. Who else has the juice?

I don't know. Elvis? John Lennon?
PIRNER: That's kinda tough, Neil. You're kind of busting my balls here.

I'm not busting your balls. It's just—
PIRNER: You are kinda busting my balls.

It's an easy answer.
PIRNER: It's not an easy answer. It's not. Because . . . they're dead. I mean, they don't have the juice, man. Dead people don't have the juice.

[*Continued . . .*]

[COURTNEY LOVE]
SCENE 3

Courtney Love walked to the unmade bed in her Manhattan loft and collapsed on top of the sheets. *Boogie Nights* played on a small television set nearby. "I could never shoot myself up," she sighed. "The one time I tried, I still have bumps on my arm from it."

She rolled up a sleeve of her pink cotton shirt to show the damage. "Here's my imitation of my heroin addiction," she said as she sat upright. She rapped on the wall and yelled, "Kurt? Kurt? Are you in there?"

Then, in a gruff voice, she answered for him, "Get some hot water."

She slapped her arm to imitate the injection, then spoke to his imaginary presence: "I didn't feel anything."

She slumped back against her pillows. "He hardly gave me anything: just [the residue from] the cotton. Prick! That was the extent of my heroin addiction."

Our interview was supposed to have been just a single controlled hour at the offices of Love's record label, Virgin. But instead it had moved and metamorphosed into a three-day interview, the entirety of which was spent imprisoned in her loft near Chinatown.

The following is an accounting of the money Love borrowed during that time . . .

- $100 for books on fraud-busting, though a portion of it appears to have been spent on a small baggie of white powder, which turns out to contain baby powder or crushed aspirin or something. Love explains: "I can't believe I just did drugs in front of a journalist for the first time, and I don't even know what they were."

- $20 for a cab ride to have the "books" delivered.

- $20 for pound cake and Rice Krispies Treats from a nearby deli. She keeps the change.

- $20 for takeout food from Rice.

- $18 for cigarettes, root beer, and pastries.

• $20 for acupuncture needles, which she proceeds to stick in my legs and chest, and attempts to insert in my head. "I've been doing this since I was young," she explains as she wiggles the needle in my right leg. Her authority is accepted until she starts trying to stick me with used needles off the floor.

[PEARL JAM]

At the end of my interview with Pearl Jam in Seattle for *Blender* magazine, singer Eddie Vedder pulled out a Polaroid camera, snapped a photo of me, and then wrote my name in marker on it and added it to a stack of Polaroids he'd taken of other journalists that day.

Did you take that Polaroid so you can remember who the writer is when the story comes out?
EDDIE VEDDER: Well, I guess so. But by the end of the night, I get to show a friend of mine, "Look at all these people I talked to. It's, like, pretty unusual, huh?"

But what made you decide to take the photographs in the first place?
VEDDER: What? Uh, well, in particular, there was one guy from Germany who, two years ago, wrote some stuff that absolutely was fabricated. I mean, it would have never come out of my mouth, and that was very interesting. So I always wanted to remember what he looked like, in case I ever saw him again.

What would you do if you saw him again?
VEDDER: Um, I don't know. But that was one reason.

You could also record all your interviews to make sure nothing is fabricated later.
VEDDER: Yeah, I remember having that idea, but that was back when I was really new at this. Now I'm ready for people to just twist it around. I mean, I don't know. I respect you as a writer. But I think Jeff [Ament, Pearl Jam bassist] did something for your magazine that he felt betrayed about because he felt he was represented the wrong way.

I'm not sure what story that would be, but I've had articles edited that changed how I was trying to represent someone.

VEDDER: The week before I began doing interviews, I started thinking about, well, having speaking points. But it just seemed too conscious. I've got a bunch of shit in my brain, and you are kind of extracting some of it. But I don't know how it's going to sound. That's up to you. You can take any slant and make me sound like an egotist. I don't know. It's out of my control.

It would be hard to make you sound like an egotist.
VEDDER: That's one nice thing about regaining underdog status after a couple of records, because people are less likely to tear you down. And, to be honest, I didn't like that process. Whether it was something as trivial as Bon Jovi making fun of where we were coming from in a video or Liz Smith wearing grunge-wear, it all felt really strange. And I was trying not to take it personally, but it felt weird, because we were only being honest. Here I go talking again. But I think that people might be ready for, I don't know, real information.

In the sense of . . . ?
VEDDER: What is going to happen is we are going to finish talking and I'm going to think, "Oh, I didn't talk about this or these other things that are just much more important." Like to support third-party [presidential] candidates. Understand that there is something wrong if we can't get a third candidate to be a part of the debates. We should legalize non-THC hemp. There is no reason not to do that. Throw that in the hat when they're talking about cutting down more trees. And I've been hearing that everyone is wearing fur again. Those are the things I think about.

[BON JOVI]

Jon Bon Jovi, the golden-haired leader of eighties pop-metal superstars Bon Jovi, might be one of the only singers who gets stumped when asked the following question.

Can you name a current rock star who's a bigger sex symbol than you are?
JON BON JOVI: Rock music?

Current rock music.
BON JOVI: Currently? Luh luh luh luh luh, let me think about it for half a minute. Sheryl Crow?

I was kind of thinking male sex symbols.

BON JOVI: Oh, well, let me think. I don't really think about guys like that. Hmm. Man, oh man, man. I don't know. Eddie Vedder or something? I don't really know.

Hmm, I don't know if he's a sex symbol.

BON JOVI: Michael Bolton has all those women . . .

Yeah, that might be.

BON JOVI: Oh my goodness, who is one? I have to think. I . . . I don't know.

I think you've answered my question.

BON JOVI: So it's me . . .*

Or maybe different kinds of people have their own sex symbol. To some people, it's Michael Bolton. And maybe to other people, it's Trent Reznor. And to other people, it's you.

BON JOVI: Yeah, right. Right, right, right. That's probably the spectrum right there.

But you must be aware of it?

BON JOVI: It's very strange, because when people react to you like they do, you think, "Oh, right, I'm supposed to be special." And then you go, "Calm down, you're not," and you get over it. Personally, I don't pay attention to that nonsense. There's probably five kids in the audience at any given concert that are going to be on that stage themselves some day. And every night you just have to be better than you were the night before if you want to keep doing what you're doing.

You've resisted the temptation to make songs for shock value or about darker themes that might have paid off in the metal days. Was that ever a direction you thought of going in to escape the ballads?

BON JOVI: I couldn't do that, for one reason: It wouldn't be real. I dislike it. I've been real honest that my heroes were, you know, Southside Johnny & the Asbury Jukes. And people go, "Well, weren't you supposed to like Led Zeppelin?" And I go, "Well, I *didn't*, so I'm not fashionable." And when Seattle was happening, I didn't grow a goatee and get work boots. I just didn't do it. And like it or not, damn the

* Shortly after this interview, Bon Jovi was voted "sexiest rock star" by *People* magazine.

torpedoes, at least I didn't jump on someone's bandwagon. At least I can go to sleep at night and know I wasn't being a whore.

So what *have* you been listening to these days that you're liking?
BON JOVI: Joan Osborne, she's great. And the new Soul Asylum.

The scene: Same hotel room, same city, 7:30 a.m. Pirner and I have been in his room with no one else present for more than three hours, and the only mind-altering substance he has taken (to my knowledge) is alcohol.

DAVE PIRNER: Who were we just talking to?

No one.
PIRNER: We were just hanging out with someone else. Someone else was here.

I don't think so.
PIRNER: Are you sure about that? There was, like, a third dude here. Or maybe we left his room and came here (*pauses, thinks*). All right, just for you, I'm going to remember where we were ten minutes ago or twenty minutes ago.

We were here. The only other people we've talked to in the last twelve hours were Tommy the bartender and the cab driver.
PIRNER: Okay, we were in somebody else's room. It was somebody that was totally busting my balls for the past three hours. It wasn't even you, man. I think it was somebody that I know.

You got me.
PIRNER: Well, I remember watching you actually explaining to the other dude how you had to leave. And I was totally uninvolved in the whole thing. That's why I expected you to remember it. [. . .]

Listen, I really gotta go because I have to work tomorrow.
PIRNER: You can't leave. There are a couple things we have to talk about. I know you're going to write that we suck because all we do is sit in hotel rooms and drink beer.

If I wrote that, I'd be a hypocrite. That's all I've done.
PIRNER: Oh yeah, I hadn't thought of that. I'll tell you something: I think I'm the most important single songwriter you could be talking to.

Let's discuss that tomorrow. I really have to go to sleep.
PIRNER: Challenge me (*hits my knee*). I dare you to challenge me on anything. I'm so fucking credible. Name one way in which I'm not credible.

(Silence.)
PIRNER: You never challenge me on this shit, and you never will. And you don't really give a shit.

I care as much as you do. This is the first *Rolling Stone* cover story for both of us.
PIRNER: Then please bust my chops.

A housekeeper knocks on the door. Pirner sends her away.

Okay, tomorrow I will bust your chops.
PIRNER: Fire any question at me, man (*hits my knee again*). I can answer any question. Ask me anything. Go ahead. Right now. Ask me anything you want and I'll give you the best answer I could ever give you.

Good night. You need to get some sleep, too.
PIRNER: Come on, man, we were just getting warmed up.*

The next night, I join Soul Asylum manager Danny Heaps and guitarist Dan Murphy at a diner to discuss the marathon interviews with Pirner.

DAN MURPHY: I had to leave the other day because the conversation was getting weird, with Dave talking about killing himself and all.

Last night was even stranger.
DANNY HEAPS: I went to wake up Dave at one o'clock today. It took me an hour.

---

* After a Soul Asylum concert in New York that week, during which Bruce Springsteen jumped onstage to join the band, the Boss tried to explain Pirner's behavior thusly: "Dave and I sort of talk on the phone a little. It was a pretty confusing experience when I was that age. Being worried about [being a rock star] is good, in my opinion. I was always worried about it. I don't know if it helped, but I know that it was good to worry about it."

But when he finally opened his eyes, the first thing he said was, "I think Neil beat me, man."

At the end of the night, Dave said to ask any question. And I really wanted to ask him, "Are you afraid of being alone?"
MURPHY: That would have been a good question to ask. Dave is incredibly insecure about some things. He just needs a pat on the back once in a while.

[CURTAIN]

ACT
FIVE

OR

THE ROCK AND ROLL CLICHÉ

CAN GO

FUCK ITSELF

SYNOPSIS

Mötley Crüe is arrested for assault, Ernie K-Doe calls the police for help, and Rick James is released from prison, while Taylor Lautner claims he's never even gotten a speeding ticket before asking about Zac Efron, who is hiding from paparazzi and impressed by Tom Cruise, who hits a clock, &c.

[MÖTLEY CRÜE]
SCENE 1

The moment I decided to do a book with Mötley Crüe was the moment I first met them: backstage after a concert in Phoenix, during which bassist Nikki Sixx kicked a security guard, drummer Tommy Lee spit on another guard, and singer Vince Neil told the crowd to seize the stage, which it did, tumbling over barricades and causing thousands of dollars in damage. As I walked to the dressing room to introduce myself as the writer who'd be profiling them in *Spin* magazine, I heard concert security guards talking on stage left.

SECURITY GUARD: Get the guy who kicked Jim! The one with a beard. We're fucking pressing charges.

I run back to the dressing room to warn the band.

Hey, I just heard security talking. They're getting the police to arrest you.
NIKKI SIXX (*laughs*): Are you the guy from *Spin*?

Yeah, but I'm serious.
SIXX: Did Nick [Cua, Mötley tour manager] put you up to this?

No, they're really coming back. I would leave if I were you.
SIXX: Did you ever interview Johnny Thunders?*

No, but I've interviewed Kenny G.
SIXX: Oh, just wondering.

I attempt to convince Sixx to leave before he's arrested, but he thinks it's a birthday prank, because in half an hour he will be thirty-nine. Suddenly, six police officers burst into the dressing room.

POLICE OFFICER ONE: Is this the guy who attacked the security officer?
POLICE OFFICER TWO: I don't know. They both have facial hair.

---

* Pioneering punk guitarist who died of an apparent methadone overdose in 1991, though some suspect foul play.

MÖTLEY CRÜE
SOAP FLAKES

THE
NATURAL
GOLDEN
FLAKES
with the lasting lather

POLICE OFFICER ONE (*to Sixx*): Put your hands behind your back.

POLICE OFFICER TWO (*to Tommy Lee*): You too.

TOMMY LEE: Why me? I didn't do anything.

POLICE OFFICER ONE: We'll check the videotape to see which one of you it is.

POLICE OFFICER TWO: We're also placing you under arrest for inciting a riot. And for inciting girls to expose their breasts.*

NEARBY ROADIE: Is that a bad thing?

LEE: Can't I put something on? I'm in my shorts.

POLICE OFFICER TWO: No, just come with us.

The police lead Sixx and Lee, who is wearing nothing but tight rubber shorts, into the corridor and toward the backstage exit. Two teenage Mötley Crüe fans tentatively approach them, each clutching a copy of Shout at the Devil *on vinyl.*

FAN: Can you sign these for us?

Tommy Lee nods his head back toward his handcuffs.† As they're led out of the arena, I return to the dressing room, where Cua is arguing with police. Meanwhile, Vince Neil blow dries his hair nonchalantly, as he has throughout the incident, while guitarist Mick Mars lounges in a chair nearby.

MICK MARS: Well, what did you think of the show?

[*Continued . . .*]

ERNIE K-DOE
SCENE 1

In history books, Ernie K-Doe is best known for recording the 1961 number one rhythm and blues hit "Mother-in-Law," a song he found discarded in a studio trash can. But to the denizens of New Orleans decades later, he was known as a bona fide character, brimming with unpredictable energy and an unchecked ego. At an awards ceremony I once covered, for example, he told the crowd, "There have only been five [*sic*] great artists in the history of rhythm and blues: Ernie K-Doe, James Brown, and Ernie K-Doe."

---

* A staple of the Mötley Crüe show, during which Tommy Lee walks to the edge of the stage with a video camera and encourages girls to flash for him. In the end, Sixx lamented after he was released, "We didn't get charged for any of that. We didn't get charged for any good stuff—only assault."

† "I think that topped the time some guy asked Ozzy to sign an autograph while he was taking a shit," Sixx says proudly the next day.

On the edge of the Tremé neighborhood, at the Mother-in-Law Lounge, a bar he'd opened with his wife Antoinette, K-Doe could be found almost nightly, performing impromptu concerts and talking about himself nonstop.

"I'm cocky, but I'm good," he responded when I arrived with a *New York Times* photographer and asked to do a story on him.

Later that evening, he led us outside to his small touring van, and we huddled together on the seats as he gave one of his last interviews. Afterward, we returned to the bar to take photographs and watch him perform.

The trouble began when K-Doe suddenly stopped belting the song "White Boy / Black Boy" and looked directly at me . . .

ERNIE K-DOE: We had a good interview, didn't we?

Are you talking to me?
ERNIE: I was good to you, wasn't I?

You sure were.
ERNIE: Then why are you trying to record my show?

Everyone in the bar turns to look at me.

I'm not recording it! It's not even on.

As I hold up the tape recorder to show him, his wife, Antoinette, runs at me from behind the bar.

ANTOINETTE K-DOE: Give me the tape!

I wasn't recording the music. It was just in my lap because I don't have a bag and it's too bulky to fit in my pocket.
ANTOINETTE: I saw you recording. We aren't playing any more music till you give us the tape.

I'd give you the tape, but I have other interviews on here and I need them.
ANTOINETTE: We let you interview us. We let you take pictures of us. We waived our fee and didn't charge you anything.* And now we want the tape. Give it to us.

---

* To the best of my knowledge, Ernie K-Doe has never charged anyone for an interview, at least not successfully.

I can play the tape out loud to prove I wasn't recording the music, if that would settle this.

ANTOINETTE: Lock the door. Nobody's getting out of here until he hands over the tape. And I want the photographs, too.

A small, stocky man, either plainclothes security or a loyal patron, runs to the door and stands menacingly in front of it.

BAR REGULAR: Let's just hear some music. I'm sure he didn't tape it.

ANTOINETTE: This ain't your business. (*To me:*) Ernie K-Doe is a legend. I am sick of people coming in here and taking advantage of us. You ain't even from the newspaper. I saw what you were doing. You went into the back room to switch the tapes, then came out here and started recording.*

I went into the back room to make a phone call.

ANTOINETTE: If you won't give it back to us, then I'm calling the police. That's K-Doe's music on there. So it's his property.

I can play the tape. I swear I wasn't recording the music.

ANOTHER REGULAR: Give her what she wants. The police will probably throw you in jail because they support this bar.

Listen, I'd love to. But I've been doing interviews at Jazz Fest all week, and they're on this tape. And I'm not giving it to anyone.

ANTOINETTE (*on the phone*): This is Antoinette K-Doe at the Mother-in-Law Lounge on Fifteen Hundred North Claiborne. We got someone here who's stolen something of ours and won't give it back. I want him arrested.

Fifteen minutes of no music and dirty looks later, two policemen enter the bar.

ANTOINETTE: They were making tapes of us and taking photographs of us, and we want them. It's our right.

POLICE OFFICER ONE (*to the photographer and me*): Give me y'all's driver's licenses, and wait outside.

---

* As an R&B singer coming up in the fifties and sixties, K-Doe was no doubt cheated out of his fair share of profits from his music, which may help explain why they thought I was trying to make a bootleg of the show to somehow sell for personal gain.

Ten minutes later, the police come out and talk to us. I explain what happened. One of the officers goes back inside and returns with Ernie and Antoinette.

POLICE OFFICER ONE: If y'all don't come to a resolution right here, we're going to have to take you in to the station and take depositions for a civil case. And I don't think y'all want to go through that.

If you'll just let me play you the tape to prove there's no music on it—
ANTOINETTE: No, he's lying.

Listen, I was just trying to help a musician I admired get some attention. I have no interest in even writing the piece at this point. I'll erase the interview right now if that will settle things.

I partially rewind the cassette and start recording over a small portion of the interview.

ANTOINETTE: I want to hear the part you erase. I'm not going to let you leave here with anything.

I'm recording over it now as we speak.
ANTOINETTE: Man, that is no good.

What do you want? I just want to get this settled in a peaceful way and go back to my hotel.
ANTOINETTE: I know. I really want to get inside and get to my business, too.
POLICE OFFICER ONE: I understand, but now you got yourself in a situation. Just make sure that they know the interview is all erased from the tape. You can't just leave and tell her, "I'm gonna promise you that by the time I get home, it's erased." You stay here till they're sure that he's not on that tape anymore and then y'all are even.
POLICE OFFICER TWO: Why don't you just give me the tape?

I have other interviews on here that I need.
ANTOINETTE: Right, but you see what it is: You want everything *you* want, but you ain't willing to give nothing back this way.

I'm erasing it as we're speaking. It's recording right now.
ANTOINETTE: You didn't say that!

I said I was recording it. It's recording us arguing right now.

POLICE OFFICER ONE: All you want to do is undo what they did. If they say they don't want you to use it and y'all are not going to use it, that should be the end of it. Now y'all agree.

ANTOINETTE: And we want her film.

POLICE OFFICER ONE: I'd like to do this in a peaceful way. I'll tell y'all, I'm not used to this type of stuff. I won't lie. All I know is y'all entered into an agreement: maybe not a contractual agreement, but at least a verbal agreement to do something. That verbal agreement has been breached, even if it's in her mind. Even if it's her perception for whatever reason. But I can tell you that if you don't give her the film, we're going to have to take all y'all in.

The photographer hands Antoinette a blank roll of film, and keeps the film with the actual photos in her pocket.

ANTOINETTE: I saw you use other rolls of film.

PHOTOGRAPHER: That's all I took.

ANTOINETTE: I'm going to a one-hour place to get this developed so I can make sure it's all the pictures. If this is the wrong film, I need to get in touch with you. And I know you don't even work at the newspaper.

Here's my card. You can call whenever you want.

ANTOINETTE (*taking the card*): I can have that business card printed up anywhere. Really, you need an identification.

Fifteen minutes of arguing later, including giving the police the name and phone number of my editor at the newspaper and emptying the photographer's bag for them, the tape reaches the end of the side.

The interview is erased now.

ANTOINETTE: Wind it back to make sure it's just us talking outside.

I rewind it partially and play the tape.

I'm sorry this misunderstanding happened. I was only trying to help so that people outside New Orleans could know about the bar and what you're doing here.

ANTOINETTE: This man is a legend. He doesn't need any publicity. Nobody can publish no article or picture unless we give them permission. I'll sue them.

POLICE OFFICER TWO: Why don't you go back inside? We'll handle it from here.

Ernie and Antoinette return to the bar, and the police give the photographer and me a lift back to our hotel.

POLICE OFFICER TWO: This is what happens when you have a woman like that running a man. K-Doe, he didn't say anything the whole time he was out there. But in his wife's head, that was her perception of what happened. And in the mind of a woman like that, perception becomes reality.

Thanks for dealing with this.
POLICE OFFICER TWO: Well, I always wanted to know what went on in that bar anyway.*

[*Continued* . . .]

$$\boxed{\begin{matrix} \textbf{RICK JAMES} \\ \textit{SCENE 1} \end{matrix}}$$

In the late seventies and early eighties, Rick James was funk's crossover king—a gaudy performer with long braids, a pencil mustache, and a string of irrepressible hits, most notably "Super Freak." But by the early nineties, his star had fallen and burned itself out. He set himself on fire with a crack pipe; was charged with kidnapping a woman, burning her with a crack pipe, and pistol-whipping her (charges that he denies and that were later dropped); and was ultimately convicted along with his girlfriend, Tanya Hijazi, for cocaine possession and assaulting a woman who'd met with them about a record contract. A year after being released from prison, Rick James sat down on a leopard-skin couch in the sunken living room of his home near Los Angeles to discuss his three years behind bars.

Did you do much songwriting in prison?
RICK JAMES: I wrote a lot of music about me and what I was going through in prison. There's so much music in me. I write songs like I sit on the toilet and shit, you know: It just comes out of me. I don't never have to strain to write. Never. I wrote over three hundred songs when I was down. I was writing six, sometimes nine songs a day.

---

* I ended up writing the story on K-Doe and this incident in the newspaper that week, and with no hard feelings. The New Orleans newspaper, the *Times-Picayune*, reported on the episode afterward, concluding, "The K-Does said they were going to sue the *Times*, but the story was oddly flattering to them."

Was "So Soft So Wet" one of them?
JAMES: Yeah, "So Soft So Wet" was written in the pen.

It seems like something that would come from being shut away from women for so long.
JAMES: Yeah, exactly. It was strange because that's the first time I had been celibate for such a long period of time. But after a year or so, it was like second nature. And I didn't watch *Baywatch* or any of those things where I could be sexually aroused. I mean, I had enough problems with the female COs [corrections officers] who were always trying to get at me.

Get at you?
JAMES: You know, a lot of the correction officers were female and they would always come to my cell and stuff like that. So if I wanted to really have sex, I probably could have on a bunch of occasions. There's also a lot of homosexuality going on in prison, and I can understand it. I mean, guys are there ten or twenty years. But I was, like, thinking of my old lady the whole time and wanting to do the right thing. And she would send me very erotic letters sometimes. So, yeah, that's how "So Soft So Wet" came about (*laughs*).

There's a line in one song where you talk about the COs. Is that about the females or the males?
JAMES: No, no, it wasn't really anything about female COs. It was like a lot of those guy correction officers, they come to a prison governing men, but they come with attitudes like they're on their period, you know. Like when women get to be real bitches when it's PMS time, well that's how they come. And a lot of them were never the same every day. Some would say hello to you one day and the next day they'd cuss you out and call you a bunch of niggers or something. And it was like whatever happened to them during the day with their wives or their relationships, they would bring to the job. So to me they were like a bunch of bitches in drag.

What kind of prisoner were you?
JAMES: When I first got locked up four years ago, I was totally bitter and totally angry. I was angry at the system and I was angry at myself. I felt like my life was on hold. That's probably the simplest way to put it.

In what ways were you angry at yourself?
JAMES: I was angry at my own stupidity because I indulged myself all these years and acted out in such a way that I would end up there. I had always been a free

spirit and always gotten what I wanted. Then, when I started adjusting, when I realized I only had a year and a half more to go of this, I started to settle down. I started to work out. I worked in the library. I started to read. I read my whole time, five and a half months in LA County before I went to Folsom.

Do you think maybe you needed that time in prison to just get off drugs and calm down?
JAMES: I think any time longer than three years would have been too much. If I would have gotten out in eight months, I probably would have gone right back to drugs because it would have just been too easy. So three years was really enough time. I mean, that's three Christmases, you know.

And you also weren't there for your mother—
JAMES: Actually, I was out on a million dollar bail from the case when I went to my mother's funeral. But I should have spent more time with her and tried to understand a little more about what she was going through raising all those kids and being a black woman alone. I was very devastated by her death. All she ever wanted for me was to be free of drugs and be happy.

Do you feel like what you did in your wild days was wrong or do you miss it at all?
JAMES: I'm very religious and spiritual. I know the things that I shouldn't be doing. As a human being on this planet, I mean, I know it's wrong for me to go smack the shit (*gesturing to my photographer*) and take this camera and throw it out the fucking window. I know that's wrong, okay. I know it's wrong to be snorting cocaine and smoking freebase all the time and all that kind of shit and just freaking out with a bunch of bitches. I know that shit is wrong. And I've always known. Other than being numbed by drugs, the bottom line is I did some shit that was very harmful and I owe it to God to still be alive today.

The door opens and Tanya Hijazi enters the house, followed by the couple's five-year-old son and her mother, who took care of the boy while his parents were in prison. James takes a short break to talk to them.

[*Continued . . .*]

[TAYLOR LAUTNER]

It was the first in-depth interview Taylor Lautner, the then–seventeen-year-old poster boy who plays Jacob the werewolf in the *Twilight* movies, had done in his career. And after this round of questions, he probably wished it were his last. Sitting on a gym mat at a martial arts studio owned by the coach who trained Lautner to become a world karate champion, we decided to see just how well-deserved his squeaky-clean reputation was.

Have you ever snorted a line of cocaine before?
TAYLOR LAUTNER: A line of cocaine?! No.

How about heroin or pot, or any drug?
LAUTNER: I've never done any drug before.

Not even pot once?
LAUTNER: No.

How about cigarettes. Have you ever smoked a cigarette?
LAUTNER: No.

What about a pipe or a cigar or a clove cigarette?
LAUTNER: No.

Have you ever been arrested?
LAUTNER: No.

How about traffic tickets. What's the worst moving violation you've ever gotten?
LAUTNER: I've never gotten one. Wow, this is interesting.

You've never even been pulled over?
LAUTNER: No speeding ticket, no red light, no reckless driving.

You're kidding. Um, how about urinating on public property? Have you ever done that?
LAUTNER: On public property?

Like an alley or a park bench.
LAUTNER: I guess, like, forests or in the woods if it's an emergency.

That doesn't count. What about drinking: Have you ever been drunk?
LAUTNER: No.

Come on, I don't believe that.
LAUTNER: I could just be answering no to everything.

Okay, here's my analysis. You've never done drugs, you've never been arrested, you've never gotten a traffic ticket. But you've probably been drunk before and maybe watched some porn.
LAUTNER: Okay, okay. Yeah, it is up to you for interpretation.

So if you've been drunk, what's the harm in saying it? There's nothing wrong with it.
LAUTNER: Can I ask you something?

Sure.
LAUTNER: What did you do with Zac Efron when you interviewed him?

[ZAC EFRON]

At the time of this interview, Zac Efron ruled the world—or at least the prepubescent world, thanks to his heartthrob role in Disney's *High School Musical.* Yet he was surprisingly unaffected. "I have never done interviews like this before," he confessed when we met at a North Hollywood diner. "I'm still so new to this."

The nineteen-year-old actor was living by himself in a small, cluttered apartment nearby and sleeping on a mattress on the floor. Although this seems like a recipe for disaster—a teen star living on his own just a few miles from dozens of Hollywood clubs—Efron showed no signs of following in the footsteps of Lindsay Lohan and Britney Spears. But that didn't mean he was an angel, either, as I learned the following day over a golf game at a small local course.

ZAC EFRON: There's people, by the way, all over the golf course, on the edges, probably taking pictures of us right now.

Paparazzi?
EFRON: I think so. They were following me from my house. I just drove straight down Riverside, so I don't think I lost them. Normally I make a few laps, but I thought I was late.

Thanks for making the sacrifice.
EFRON: They find you anyway, because they work in teams.

Some people say that the secret to avoiding scandal is not to be hypocritical. If you have nothing to hide, you have nothing to lose.
EFRON: Which puts me in a funny place at night.

So how have you managed to avoid being scandalized then?
EFRON: You know, I'm nineteen. It's not my aspiration to be the next rock star. I'm not going to be partying on tour buses with Poison. I'm the same age as some other people who are dealing with scandals and stuff, but it's easy to have fun at our age. I just don't think you have to do it at three a.m. in the Viper Room. What's the point?

See, you've just proven that you never go there, because the Viper Room closes at two a.m.
EFRON: Literally, I've never been. Actually, you know what's funny is: I have not been in a Hollywood club. I don't even have a fake ID. But I've got friends out here and we do what kids our age are doing. We just don't need people taking photos of us and spreading it everywhere.

Other people need the validation of the public, and they don't care whether it comes from appreciation of their creative work or a photo in a gossip magazine.
EFRON: Exactly. A lot of problems you see people having in this business is that it becomes about their personal lives and not about their work. I never want to contribute to those magazines. Matthew McConaughey has single-handedly funded the tabloid magazines for the past two years now. Single-handedly. If he would put on a shirt and just get away from the beach, maybe there would be a few less paparazzi around.

If you think about it, McConaughey's parents had a volatile relationship and Paris Hilton's parents were never really around for her. Perhaps because you come from a stable family that you know will always be there for you, you don't need the outside validation as much.

EFRON: That's huge. Some people don't have that. And when you've got a dad and a mom and a little brother who are constantly poking fun at your imperfections and laughing with you and joking with you and doing things that a family should do, it's impossible to get a big head. There's nothing better than being able to go home and escape and literally not speak of Los Angeles for two days.

One day you're going to have to research a role about a guy who's a party animal, and then have to—
EFRON: And then I would party. That would be a chance for me to break the rules. When that moment comes, and I'm playing the high school kid at a party, believe me, I'm going to know what to do—(*emphatically*) believe me, I'll know what to do. (*Looks up at the sun.*) I'm probably getting too much sun right now. It starts to look fake. I don't like to be super-tan. (*Moves into the shade.*)

Who are some of the actors you admire?
EFRON: Tom Cruise is huge. He's worked with everyone. And they praise Tom Cruise because of his work ethic, because he, you know, gives 110 percent everywhere he goes. He's constantly growing as an actor, and every project that he does he's learning new things. *Mission: Impossible* and all those movies that he does, a lot of the stunts are really done by him.

That's true. I did an article on him and he took me to motorcycle wheelie school because he was practicing to jump a trailer for *Mission: Impossible*.
EFRON: Are you serious?

[TOM CRUISE]
SCENE 1

While I was interviewing Tom Cruise in his trailer at motorcycle wheelie school, he did something interesting. He tilted a picture of his children on the table closer to him. And it made me wonder: Everything about him has the appearance of being so perfectly in order that it raises the question . . .

Are you obsessive-compulsive?
TOM CRUISE: No.

Little things don't bother you if they're out of place?
CRUISE: No, things don't bother me if they're out of place. But I want to be prepared in an airplane. Because if I take someone up in an airplane, what's the worst-case scenario? Death.

Well, that's obvious.
CRUISE: No, I'm very responsible. I'm one of those people that if I say I'm going to do it, I don't need a contract. I will do everything I can to get it done.

So maybe you're obsessive but not compulsive.
CRUISE: No, I just show up on time. If I'm not there, people are concerned because something went wrong. Something major went wrong. (*He erupts in a long laugh, then suddenly stands up, looks at a clock on the microwave that reads 2:04 p.m., and smashes his fist into the clock.*) I have a production meeting at three p.m. I have to go right *now*.

[*Continued . . .*]

[SLIPKNOT]
SCENE 1

In a successful band, there's often one person with fire in his eyes, who's going to make it to the top even if he has to drag the rest of the group kicking and screaming over hot coals to do it. In Slipknot, the mask-wearing new-metal band with numbers instead of names, that role is filled by clown-costumed percussionist Shawn Crahan (aka No. 6). Backstage before a concert just outside San Antonio, Texas, Crahan whipped open a cabinet and gazed at a stack of yellow plastic drinking cups. He carefully set aside the top cup, then selected the one below it and emptied a can of Mountain Dew into it.

Why didn't you use the top cup?
SHAWN CRAHAN: Because someone could have come in and put something in the cup and just put it on top. I always take the second or third one down. And next time I'm going to take the sixth one down because I've just told you what I do. That's the way I work. People think I'm crazy. Maybe I am. But I know what's going on.

Is now good to talk—
CRAHAN: You know, I didn't know we were going to do an interview right this second. I told my wife I'd call right back when I saw you. She'll yell at me, but guess what? She'll get over it because she knows I'm on a mission, and nothing's going to get in my way.

What's the mission?
CRAHAN: I am on a world-domination mission. Slipknot is not just an average band. It's not just music. It's a way of life and it's the real way of life. When I go

MISSION
Incense

USED FOR INDUCING A POWERFUL STATE OF WORLD DOMINATION.
DIFFUSES A DREAMY FRAGRANCE THAT SUSPENDS TIME.
APPROVED FOR INVOCATIONS AND COMMUNICATIONS WITH OTHER BEINGS.

MISSION INCENSE IS ONLY SOLD IN PACKAGES OF NINE. READ LABEL FOR WARNINGS.

out onstage, the rock and roll cliché can go *fuck* itself. I would like to meet the gentleman or the lady who invented the rock and roll cliché, and I would like to go back in time and systematically remove them from even being born by removing their parents, taking it all the way back, because there's no place for that anymore.

What *is* the cliché exactly?
CRAHAN: You know, fucking sex, fucking drugs, just the fucking idea of *I need to be a rock star, I need to treat my fans like shit, I need to fucking be broke, I need to overdose on heroin.* Bullshit, dude. In two months, I'll have been married for seven years. I have three healthy children. I don't cheat on my wife. I will never cheat on my wife. She's my best friend. She saved my life and she enabled me to start this band. I owe her everything, and when I'm done with this, I will spend the rest of my life doing what *she* wants to do. As far as the drugs and alcohol go, people do what people do. We drink, we do whatever, but we're under control.

When I did the Marilyn Manson book, he put it this way: It's the abusers who make the users look bad.
CRAHAN: Exactly, enough said. We keep each other in check. And at the end of the night when I'm back in that dressing room and I take that mask off, man, I feel good about what I'm living. And you have to understand, at the end of the night my mask usually consists of no less than vomit, spit, and some sort of blood. Other nights it's other things. Maybe some urine made its way on there somehow. Whatever, you know.

Slipknot singer Corey Taylor—aka No. 8—enters the room.

COREY TAYLOR: What are you doing?
CRAHAN: Hey, Corey, come here! I need a light (*grabs a stick of incense from a pack on the table*). What is this, vanilla? Doesn't anybody know what Nag Champa is?
TAYLOR: No.
CRAHAN: Let me smell it. Get a little spirit in here (*smells the incense*). All that fucking vanilla . . .
TAYLOR: It smells good to me.
CRAHAN: No, it's negative.

[*Continued . . .*]

[TOM CRUISE
SCENE 2]

Cruise's parting gesture stuck with me. He hit the clock. The guy actually punched a clock. Now, it may have been just a solid gesture of resolution from an actor who does everything with a strong physical presence and intensity. Or it may have been evidence of a darker, more temperamental side rearing its head.

When I met Cruise for a meal a few days later, I asked him about it. Several times, however, he'd start to answer a question, then pause for several seconds and suddenly start talking about something else. In public relations, this avoidance tactic is known as spinning.

Do you ever lose your cool?
TOM CRUISE: Yeah, I lose my cool. But I'm not a hothead. I'm not someone who screams at people. It takes a lot.

Do you ever take it out on yourself, then, instead of others?
CRUISE: It depends on the situation, know what I mean (*long pause*). You look at something and you think, "How much is it going to take to get it done?" Because nothing keeps me from doing something.

But what if something does? Like you really need to get something done, but you're not prepared and running late and stuck in bumper-to-bumper traffic?
CRUISE: You gotta know me. If it really needs to get done, I'm going to get it done. If I decide I'm going to do something—ha ha, you gotta know, Neil, heh heh, you got to know, ha ha—it's gonna get done.

So you've never hit a wall?
CRUISE: Oh man, I hit a lot of walls. I hit a *lot* of walls. But there are moments where you just say, "Okay, I'm going to climb over the wall."

I meant that literally.
CRUISE: Literally, have I hit a wall? Like literally?

Yes, you're upset, you lash out in anger. It happens.
CRUISE: Gosh, it's been a long time since I've hit a wall. Probably not since I was a teenager. When things start to get chaotic, I get calmer. If I get upset or freak out,

it's not going to help a situation. If something happens with the kids or whatever, I don't panic. I just kind of listen and try to watch. I make myself kind of go, "Okay, what's really going on here? What's happening?"

But I noticed the way you hit the clock yesterday. And in *Rain Man* and *Jerry Maguire*, there are scenes where you lose your temper so well that you must have some experience of the emotion.
CRUISE: I mean, there's a lot of times where I can get intense. Sometimes it depends on the situation and what it calls for (*long pause*). You know, you can't control everything. You do what you can to make things go well, and especially when you have so much stuff going on, you have to prioritize.

It can't be that easy.
CRUISE: It's not that it's necessarily easy. But I don't want easy (*long pause*). That's why you're out there riding a motorcycle. The second you stop learning stuff, man, you're dead. I remember starting out when I was seventeen or eighteen years old and wanting to be an actor. And I said, "You know, I want to learn about this." I look at you. You have an adventurous spirit. That's cool, because you aren't going to be that guy who is seventy years old and won't venture out.

No, I'll be calling you, creaking with arthritis, saying, "Hey, man, I've got a hang glider on the roof. Want to come over?"
CRUISE: And I'll say, "Let's fire it up, man. We might not live through it, but it will be a hell of a ride."

[*Continued . . .*]

[HUGH HEFNER]

In the Playboy Mansion in Los Angeles, Hugh Hefner, age seventy-two, sat in the library in his second skin: a red smoking jacket and black silk pajamas. On the table in front of him were a bottle of Diet Pepsi and a plate of cookies, accessories that replaced his pipe after his 1985 stroke. He spent most of the interview discussing a lifestyle concept he had recently come up with, thanks in part to his introduction to Viagra: having multiple live-in girlfriends simultaneously, an idea that would later get him a reality show. His first batch consisted of former *Baywatch* actress Brande Roderick and twins from Chicago named Sandy and Mandy—while, at the same time, his wife Kimberley Conrad, who he'd separated from a year earlier, was living in an adjacent house.

Would you feel jealous if Kimberley started dating?

HUGH HEFNER: I probably would. I probably would. She does some dating. I still care about her and vice versa. We still love each other.

How would you feel if Kimberley started dating twin brothers?

HEFNER: We'll cross that bridge when we get there. But, actually, I think the fact that I am seeing three ladies rather than one probably does make it easier for her. If I were seeing only one person continually, then it would be a much closer comparison to the marriage and that would be, by its nature, more difficult.

Would any of this be possible without Viagra?

HEFNER: Well, I think it would be very difficult without Viagra. I think they're underselling Viagra, because it's more than an impotence drug. It's a recreational drug. It eliminates the boundaries between expectation and reality. It permits a level of pleasure that is otherwise just something you hope for. I think it's as important in its own way as the birth control pill. It's being tested now on women, because there is some indication that with them it may have some similar effects. [. . .]

What would you do if your photo editor came up to you and said he had just found out that the woman you were planning to shoot as your next centerfold was HIV-positive?

HEFNER: I don't know. Rebekka Armstrong was a centerfold and is HIV-positive— and may have been at the time she was a centerfold. I'm not sure. She thinks she acquired it in her teens. But I don't know about that question. I'm not sure.

What about plastic surgery? Do you think people have taken it too far?

HEFNER: I think it's like medicine. Anything that makes you feel better about yourself is perfectly appropriate. Why should one be required to stay in a box that was handed to them by either nature or by their parents or peers? Why not create yourself? Why not be the person you want to be?

A lot of people in our culture today are self-invented celebrities, but you were one of the first to do that.

HEFNER: I don't know if I was the first, but it's certainly very dramatic in my case. I think that, you know, there is a light that is handed to you by your parents and society, and then there is a light that if you are smart, you can create for yourself. In other words, Bernie Schwartz reinvented himself as Tony Curtis. Archie Leach reinvented himself as Cary Grant. They had obviously made films, and the films were enough to help them, but I think that in another way, we all try to do that if we're smart. And I certainly did.

When did that process begin for you?
HEFNER: My first reinvention was when I was in high school. Having been rejected by a girl I had a crush on, I literally changed the way I dressed and went for what I perceived then as being cooler clothes: yellow cords and saddle shoes. And I changed my name: I started referring to myself as Hef for the first time.

I wonder how much rejection drives people to become stars.
HEFNER: Or repression. I think that without question, you know, rejection may be a part of it, but primarily it comes even earlier than that.

So for you, it came from being raised in a home without affection?
HEFNER: Yes, although there was a point in time that my mom said she was really sorry and that she herself had been raised in a very oppressive home, so she had been unable to show that affection. And I said to her, "Mom, anything that you may have done that was less than ideal was a blessing. It motivated me to create the world that I have created and accomplish what I have accomplished."

So sometimes it's the sand in the oyster that creates the pearl. You need some irritation. You need some repression or some conflict. And my life would have been much less satisfying if I didn't have that.

Do you think you've reinvented yourself again now?
HEFNER: Well, to some extent. But what I'm doing is I am revisiting, you know, the guy I was before. And with a vengeance.

[OTHA TURNER]

Slouched in overalls and a cap in his trailer home in Gravel Springs, Mississippi, Otha Turner, at age ninety-one, was a living argument against health fads. He smoked like a chimney, drank as much hard alcohol as he pleased, and ate red meat (sometimes scooped raw out of the animal). Yet he was as fit as a racehorse, performing backbreaking work on his farm all day long and marching tirelessly in concerts with his fife and drum band. After the interview, Turner gave me a fife he'd made. When I asked him to sign it, he sheepishly scrawled an "X" on it. In his nine-plus decades, he'd never learned to read or write.

Fife and drum is a rare form of American roots music, which predates the blues. It is, some believe, the most solid link between American and West African music. When the musicologist Alan Lomax first recorded Turner and his peers, he considered it to be one of the greatest finds of his life, writing, "I never expected to see this African behavior in the hills of Mississippi."

At the time of this follow-up interview almost two years later, Turner was believed to be the last surviving fife and drum musician of his generation, laboriously hand-making fifes from bamboo cane on his property and playing improvisatory pieces that mix traditional military music with traces of West African polyrhythms, woodwind music, and dancing.

Who did you originally learn this music from?
OTHA TURNER: I was sixteen and I saw this old man, R. E. Williams. He was a hog farmer. And he was blowing the fife. I said, "Will you make me one of them?" And he said, "If you're a good boy and you listen to your mama, I'll make you one." And he made me one.

How did you start performing?
TURNER: I tried and I tried, just learning, then I stopped. Then the neighbors found out I played. And once a person finds you can do something, they worry you, just like you.*

How did you know Mississippi Fred McDowell?†
TURNER: Fred McDowell was the first friend I met that played music. We used to ride in a buggy to perform at the suppers and picnics. Then he arranged for us to play away in Tennessee. And that started it all.

Are you teaching others to play so the tradition doesn't disappear?
TURNER: Mm-hmm. You can't write no music for a fife. You can't print it. You got to do it. And some of my kids and grandkids, they done it.

---

* Meaning that, like his neighbors, I badgered him into these interviews, which took place thanks to his daughter Bernice and Luther Dickinson of the North Mississippi Allstars. Dickinson had first heard of Turner when he saw him performing on, surprisingly, an episode of *Mister Rogers' Neighborhood*.
† Legendary bottleneck-guitar bluesman. As Turner tells it, Alan Lomax drove by one day and asked Turner if there were any blues musicians in the area. Turner led him to the home of McDowell, who Lomax was soon after credited with discovering. It wasn't until years later that Lomax heard about Turner and his music, and returned to record him.

How do you feel about coming to New York to perform next week?
TURNER: I'm thinking about quitting.

Why is that?
TURNER: Because I'm an old fella and I done got tired. And I don't like those elevators going up as high as a tree. I'm an old fella. I like to stay on the ground.

A year after this interview, Otha Turner passed away at the age of ninety-four. His Rising Star Fife and Drum Band, however, continued to perform, led by his granddaughter Sharde Thomas.

[KRAFTWERK]

If the blues led to the start of the rock and roll era, then the German group Kraftwerk was the beginning of the end. In the early seventies, while its contemporaries were playing psychedelic rock, Kraftwerk was not just inventing electronic dance music but creating robots and mannequins to perform instead of the band itself. The innovators of disco, electro-funk, rap, new wave, industrial, and techno were all influenced by Kraftwerk's electronic rhythms and processed vocals. After trying for a year to interview the band's founding member Ralf Hütter, I flew to Japan to see Kraftwerk perform and he finally consented to his first interview with an American journalist in over fifteen years.

Do you have trouble getting all your equipment past customs?
RALF HÜTTER: We have to have long lists of inventory with numbers for every instrument or device. People fear we're bringing in some kind of weapon. In some countries, we're not even allowed to take in our mainframes because they could be misused to program missiles. But they're only there to make music.

When you first started, what were some of your influences?
HÜTTER: We didn't really have any. We consider our music as ethnic music in a way. It is from postwar Germany. Being the first postwar generation, we were without any line of historical continuity. We just started from zero. Culturally speaking, we didn't have our own musical language. At first, we had to find some kind of sound, create some kind of industrial sound, and then we added voices.

ELECTRIC
Remote Control Battery Operated

ROBOT

EYES LIGHT UP ⚡ **ARMS SWING IN RHYTHM**

⚡ **WALKS FORWARD & BACKWARD** ⚡

EASY TO BUILD
PLANS ONLY $1⁰⁰

ANOTHER LABOR-SAVING DEVICE FROM YOUR FRIENDS AT
POCKET CALCULATOR MFG. CO. DÜSSELDORF, GERMANY

So you turned to electronics because there was no popular tradition attached to them?

HÜTTER: It just seemed quite normal to create music in today's technological society with new instruments. Why play an instrument with nineteenth-century technology and a limited sound range when today's instruments have so many more variations? When you go to your doctor or your dentist, you don't want him to use a wooden hammer. You should expect from music the same as what you expect from science or medicine—to be working with up-to-date technology.

Back then, you had to invent your own instruments. Now anybody can walk into a store and buy a synthesizer for forty dollars. Has this changed the way you make music?

HÜTTER: This is what we predicted. A very long time ago we were outsiders, but always we had this vision of electronic music as the new Volkswagen. It's transportable—you can do it in your home, you can do it anywhere—and therefore we always had this vision of this techno music. And with the robots, before we had the mannequins, we always had the idea that one day they could do our work for us.

A lot of your albums have also been about transportation—bicycles, cars, trains, automobiles. So is your next album about air travel?

HÜTTER: No, we are not very positive about air travel. We're afraid of flying.

[ERNIE K-DOE
SCENE 2]

Eight months after the K-Does tried to have me arrested, a journalist friend in New Orleans said that Antoinette wanted to speak to me. I called her with some trepidation.

"You have to start the New Year off right," she said, and went on to explain that the "misunderstanding" had been cleared up. Not only was I welcome back, she announced, but I was "invited to come and do an article" on them as well.

That summer, however, Ernie K-Doe died from cancer of the esophagus.

In his absence, the Mother-in-Law Lounge became even stranger. The shows continued, with regulars performing, at Antoinette's request, her husband's hits (and even appearing in blackface as K-Doe to escort her to public functions). Photos of K-Doe adorned the walls and artifacts from his life were sealed in glass display cases. In addition, there were souvenirs for sale: plates, glasses, mugs, and candles emblazoned with photographs of K-Doe. On closer inspection, it became evident that these images had simply been glued to the items.

But most unsettling of all was the lifelike mannequin of K-Doe that sat regally in the corner of the bar, with long black hair and glistening fingernails. Occasionally, Antoinette, accompanied by a bodyguard to protect the statue, would take it to make public appearances, charging people to pose for photos with it.

How did you end up getting that mannequin?
ANTOINETTE K-DOE: One of Ernie's fans, Jason, felt that it was too soon for Ernie to pass, and he said that he would do a bust for me. I said, "If you can do a bust, why not do a whole statue for me?"

I notice you keep it very well-groomed.
ANTOINETTE: The hands come off so I can take them across the street for a manicure. It's the same place Ernie used to go. I always said the only time Ernie left home was to go across the street and get his nails manicured (*pauses*). I like to keep him looking good now like he did in life.

What else do you do to take care of the statue?
ANTOINETTE: A lady named Geannie Thomas keeps the makeup on it, keeps the hair fixed, and changes the clothes. He's fully dressed, from underwear to socks to everything that he used to wear. A lot of times when I bring the statue out, people want to talk to me about an interview or touch it, so I have to have somebody there to keep it presentable. Do you want to talk to Geannie?

She gets Thomas.

How did you start helping out with the statue?
GEANNIE THOMAS: She gave me the opportunity to be part of the legacy. I used to be a dancer in his show, but now I have a commercial cleaning business. I miss him, but with all the things in the lounge and the statue, it's like he's right here with us. People say, "That looks spooky. Aren't you scared?" I say, "Scared? I love the man."

Is it a lot of work to keep him in such good condition?
THOMAS: It's a job, because we want to make sure Ernie goes out there right. Everything that Antoinette designed for Ernie to wear when he was alive, from the crown down to the boxer shorts, that statue wears. Even the watch keeps time. We do a little powder to keep the shine off the skin, and make sure the hair is right

and the tie is sitting right and the sleeve is pulled down, so that when fans go to hug him and take photos, he looks as good as he did in life. It's like he's right here with us.

(*To Antoinette:*) **Has it been hard on you to run the lounge without him?**
ANTOINETTE: In the beginning, it was hard. You lost a legend, but I lost a husband. I had to reach down and find my inner strength, because if you close the Mother-in-Law Lounge, you disappoint millions of people around the world. If he'd gotten murdered, I'd look at fans and say, "Are you the guy who killed him?" But he died in God's hands. And I didn't do anything wrong to him while he was living (*long pause*). I have my weak points, but just when I feel like I'm going to fall to my knees, a fan will come in the door and say, "We remember Ernie." And that'll lift me back up.

What are your plans for the statue now?
ANTOINETTE: His legacy is too big. I don't want to have it all to myself. My desire that I pray for every day is to be able to travel with his statue, because he was a traveling person. I want to get in touch with Smokey Robinson, so maybe we can bring it up to New York and do a show there.

During Hurricane Katrina, Antoinette K-Doe brought the statue and the liquor upstairs and stayed there for a week with a shotgun, firing it at looters who tried to approach the bar, until she was airlifted out. The damaged building was repaired through donations. Four years later, during Mardi Gras, Antoinette, age sixty-six, died of a heart attack in the lounge. Her daughter ran the bar for a year, but was hospitalized after a car smashed into the front door.

[WAX FIGURES]
SCENE 1

Where do wax figures go when they die?

For more than a quarter century, the Country Music Wax Museum was one of Nashville's most colorful tourist magnets. One in every nine visitors to Nashville walked through its doors, gawking at life-size replicas of Hank Williams, Loretta Lynn, and Dolly Parton.

But this was no ordinary wax museum: Not only did country legends donate their clothes and instruments to their wax figures, but many even came into the museum and personally tended to their characters.

But one day, the Country Music Wax Museum quietly shut its doors, a casualty of Nashville's rush toward modernization and its focus on its booming health-care industry over its music legacy. In place of the homespun country tourist mall where the museum stood along with quaint oddities like the Hank Williams Jr. Museum and the George Jones Gift Shop, the city decided to build a traffic circle, offices, and a luxury hotel.

In the midst of all this change, the wax figures disappeared—along with their vintage finery and original instruments. So I decided to track them down, not just because of the probable monetary worth of the collection but as an analogy for Nashville and country music's lost traditions.

Most of the other shops and museums in the area had already gone out of business or been torn down, but three stores remained open, including the Hat Closet.

JIM COOK [Hat Closet owner]: I really don't know what happened to the figures. I know the car museum here had a big auction for its cars. Maybe they sold them. We've been here for eleven years in March, but now we're selling everything off. The city decided that they want the convention business, but they can't create that new image of Nashville without killing the old one.

Inquiries at the prestigious Country Music Hall of Fame and Museum across the street from the former wax museum reveal little. Administrators say they were never offered the collection and believe the figures were melted down. An employee named Chris Dickinson, however, suggests that perhaps the figures were sold to the Music Valley Wax Museum on the city's outskirts, where the recently demolished Opryland theme park lured the tourists who once kept the mall's shops in business.

DORIS HARVEY [Music Valley Wax Museum assistant manager]: They did offer their collection to us. But they didn't want to break the set, and we already had many of the same figures.

Harvey can't find any information on who made the offer, so I begin looking into the history of the Country Music Wax Museum, trying to locate former employees and owners.

Years ago, the museum was tied to the most powerful people in the city. One of its first chiefs was Paul Corbin, a political operative who worked on campaigns for John F. Kennedy and Robert F. Kennedy. After their assassinations, Corbin found respite from politics in wax figures, often borrowing their boots to wear around town.

The museum was eventually taken over by Dominic DeLorenzo, described by former employees as a good-looking, slick-talking charmer who persuaded Nashville luminaries like guitarist Chet Atkins to invest in the museum. But DeLorenzo left Nashville for New York and disappeared, leaving behind a pile of creditors, some of whom believe that he faked his death. Using the New York Times *research department, I track down DeLorenzo's son, Dominick.*

Are you familiar with the Country Music Wax Museum?
DOMINICK DELORENZO: Of course. My father was one of the founders of Aurora Publishing, and I think they started the museum in maybe 1971 because they wanted to get into entertainment. I worked at the museum when I was in college in the seventies. They eventually put glass up because people kept reaching in and breaking off fingers and taking them as souvenirs. For a while, I had one of the original heads of Johnny Cash.

What made your father leave the museum?
DELORENZO: He moved to New York to start another publishing company. And before he left, he was eating at a Peking restaurant and sold the museum to the owner of the restaurant.

Some people I talked to said they believed your father was still alive.
DELORENZO: I've heard that. But he died of cancer. We buried him in Massachusetts.

Do you have any idea where the wax figures are now?
DELORENZO: I have no idea. But the restaurant owner my father sold the museum to was Daniel Hsu. I don't know where he is, but you can try his old office manager. Her name is Michelle Honick.

I call Honick, who fills me in on her former boss. Under Hsu, the wax museum thrived and the area around it blossomed into a tourist mecca of odd novelty stores and shrines to musicians. It was Hsu's close contact to country stars through his restaurant that enabled the museum to continue to amass its impressive collection of clothing and artifacts.

Was all the clothing in the museum donated by the stars themselves?
MICHELLE HONICK: Every outfit was original, except Hank Snow's. Some fan had stolen the clothes off his figure. He said he'd give a new outfit only if they redid the wax figure so it was better looking.

I remember Jim Reeves's wife came in after he died to get his figure to look better, and she redid the whole thing and set up the whole display. I always thought it was funny, because when she left she set a picture of herself up on the mantel.

Which stars do you remember taking care of their own figures?
HONICK: Minnie Pearl came in and put the dress on her wax figure herself. Barbara Mandrell designed the hair for her wax figure. And Reba McEntire brought in new outfits for hers. One of the reasons why some stars aren't in the museum is because they were asked to supply costumes and they didn't supply them.

Do you know where Daniel Hsu is now or if he still owns the figures?
HONICK: I don't know. Daniel left town because his parents were ill, and eventually he started selling medicinal herbs. I don't know if they did a written deal of who would get the stuff. I think when he left, he assumed it would keep going and didn't know they'd turn part of the building into a Shoe Warehouse. I hope they're okay. They're kind of fragile. I remember sometimes a hand would fall off. It was a little spooky.

Any idea how to track down Daniel or the wax figures?
HONICK: You may want to call Phyllis Shoemake. I think she was the last museum director.

I call Shoemake . . .

PHYLLIS SHOEMAKE: Daniel was an extremely colorful person to work for. He used to have a Chinese art museum: You came out of the wax museum into this Chinese art museum. And it had some of the most beautiful things you've ever laid your eyes on: a pair of cloisonné ponies worth over forty-five thousand dollars, and beautiful urns and vases. It was the best put-together museum I'd ever seen.

Were there other valuables in either of the museums?
SHOEMAKE: I think Uncle Dave Macon's teeth were made of real gold.

Do you have any idea where the wax figures may be now?
SHOEMAKE: John Berry [former building manager] might remember, but he's dead. Daniel may know, but he's difficult to reach. He went to work at a company in California called Brion Herbs. I sell his medicine for a living. He used to say that anyone who ever worked for him always came back.

I call Hsu's office at Brion Herbs repeatedly, but he doesn't phone back. It seems as if the search has hit a dead end. Until luck intervenes . . .

[*Continued . . .*]

[CHET ATKINS]

When I moved to Nashville to write about the roots of American music, one of the people I most wanted to interview was Chet Atkins. He was one of the best guitarists of his generation, credited with producing and performing on more records than any other guitarist, from Hank Williams's "Your Cheatin' Heart" to Elvis Presley's first number one, "Heartbreak Hotel." As a producer, he discovered country music's first African-American superstar, Charley Pride, and was one of the chief architects of what became the Nashville sound. There are few honors Atkins hasn't received in Nashville: There is a street, a festival, and a day named after him, and two days before this interview, there was an unveiling ceremony for a statue of him in the center of town.

It took a long time to get Atkins, who was seventy-five, to agree to this interview. When I finally met him in his office in Music Row in Nashville, I found out why.

I looked at the newspaper archives before I came down, and they only went back to the seventies, but I noticed they'd never done a feature on you. Do you remember if the *New York Times* ever interviewed you before?
CHET ATKINS: I don't know and don't care.

I caught a little bit of the ceremony for the unveiling of your statue the other day. What did you think of it?
ATKINS: Uh, I got real sick. I had three strokes in the past year and I think they thought I was going to be gone, so the city wanted to build a statue.

Do you really think that's why you've been getting so many awards in the past few years?
ATKINS: Yeah, they thought I was going to bite the dust.

So do all these honors make you uncomfortable in that respect?
ATKINS: It doesn't mean anything to me, really. I don't pay much attention.

When you were coming up, they referred to country music as hillbilly music. Do you remember when country first came about?
ATKINS: That all started back in the late twenties when a talent scout from RCA Records would come here and audition people and say, "What have you got that's

new?" And they'd sing some old standard. He'd say, "That's not new. You know that's old. I want something new!" His name was Ralph Peer.*

So he would talk those guys into writing their own material. And those hillbillies down there—I don't like that word—they'd try to do their own thing when they auditioned for him. So he was always bragging, "I started the nigger business and I started the hillbilly business." And he's right, because they were singing them same old damn songs over and over. And that's the answer to that question.

You'll have to forgive my memory. I don't remember too well since my last stroke, but I can converse fairly well.

I saw you at Carnegie Hall a few years ago. Do you plan on doing any other performances?
ATKINS: I have not in quite a while. I just hang around.

Are there things you want to get done or accomplish now?
ATKINS: My record company is after me all the time to make an album, but I haven't done it. I probably will. But I don't want to bore the people too much.

Do people come to you a lot for advice on their own records?
ATKINS: Yeah, they do. But I don't honor those requests.

You don't?
ATKINS: No, because the business is changing constantly and my advice to them is, "I'm an old hand now. I don't play what people want to hear, and you should go to some younger people and make that request."

I don't know about that.
ATKINS: It's true. They should. [. . .]

I appreciate you taking the time to do this interview. And I think that statue down there looks beautiful.
ATKINS: Yeah, it does. When did you see it?

I drove by to take another look yesterday.
ATKINS: Was it raining?

---

* Through his auditions, collected and available as *The Bristol Sessions*, Peer discovered the Carter Family, Jimmie Rodgers, and other artists who became the founding figures of country.

No, it wasn't raining.
ATKINS: I went by to see the statue a few days ago. It was dark, and rain was falling all over it. And the lights were all on it and it was just shining and . . . I don't know what I was going to say.

You were just saying that you went to see it in the rain and the rain was glistening off it.
ATKINS: Yeah.

And what did you think?
ATKINS: What did I think of it?

Yeah, when you saw it.
ATKINS: I thought the guy is very, very good that did that. There are a lot of statues in town, but I've never seen one that had the likeness that his does. I hope it lasts a very long time.

A year and a half later, Atkins died in his home of complications from cancer at the age of seventy-seven. His statue still stands today in downtown Nashville.

[WAX FIGURES
SCENE 2]

Though some journalists like to keep the stories they're researching top secret in case the competition finds out, another method is for writers to tell everyone they encounter about a story in the hope that eventually someone will know something that can help. And this is what happened during dinner with a press agent at Virgin Records, Lorie Lytle, and a new signing to the label named Tom Mabe, a comedian famous for pulling pranks on telemarketers.

Do you remember the Country Music Wax Museum?
LORIE LYTLE: Of course, right there at the head of Music Row.

I've been doing a story trying to track down the wax figures, because they went missing when it closed. Do you by any chance know anyone who might know what happened to them?
LYTLE: I think I saw them.

What? Really?
LYTLE: *Country Weekly* moved its offices into the building where the museum used to be, and six months ago they had an open-house party. And they had Hank Williams in the reception area, wearing his original suit with the music notes on it.

Do you know where they found him?
LYTLE: I don't know. You should call someone at the magazine.
TOM MABE: You're still gonna do the article on *me*, right, buddy?

Lytle gives me the number for Bob Cannon, a reporter for Country Weekly.

So do you know where all the wax figures went?
BOB CANNON: That's easy. They're all in the basement of the old building, which is where *Country Weekly* is. There are forty of them melting in the basement. They're locked up, because at one point some vandals were breaking in and knocking pieces off.

Do you have the landlord's number by any chance?
CANNON: I don't, but I can try to find it for you or get you in touch with the maintenance guy.

Rather than waiting, I visit the Off Broadway Shoe Warehouse, which also opened in the former wax museum building, and ask the manager for the landlord's information. He puts me in touch with Jim Caden, who, after several calls, reluctantly agrees to open the storage room.

A week later, I meet Caden and Michael Horton, the building's maintenance man, in an alley behind the shoe store, where they unlock a thick door.

JIM CADEN: I don't want you to write anything too silly.

Like what?
CADEN: You know, anything making fun of the South or some of the positions these figures are in.

I understand his warning as soon as Horton flips on the lights. The pieces look more as if they belong to a country music chamber of horrors than a wax museum. Horton gestures to a wax face that's been smashed by vandals.

MICHAEL HORTON: That was Ronnie Milsap's head.

Elsewhere, Barbara Mandrell's head, with the hairpiece she had designed, is impaled on a stick. George Strait's figure lies on the ground with its head cracked, and its eye poked out and resting on its neck. Johnny Cash, all in black, stands against the wall, one arm hanging below his knee. Pop Stoneman's autoharp rests on a bench, covered with detached fingers. And Uncle Dave Macon's gold teeth are gone.

So who actually owns these?
CADEN: Daniel was the guy who owned the building and a lot of stuff that was in the building, and those wax figures are somewhere between his, the publishing company's, and mine.

Despite the damage and theft, vandals haven't touched the most important items in the collection: the costumes. Not only are they valuable because of the stars who wore them, but many were designed by Nudie the Rodeo Tailor, the famous country-music-clothing designer whose rhinestone-encrusted and heavily embroidered outfits hang not just in the Country Music Hall of Fame but in art museums. To determine the worth of the collection, I call Mark Medley, the archivist for the Country Music Hall of Fame, and ask him to come across the street.

As soon as he walks into the basement, his jaw drops. He stops at a figure of country music pioneer Jimmie Rodgers and examines his famous outfit.

That can't be real.
MARK MEDLEY: It's not a replica. There's a Sears logo on it. It's one of his real singing-brakeman suits.

I've seen photos of Buck Owens wearing that [other] suit over there. And the clothing on the Carter Family is real.

What about Minnie Pearl's hat?
MEDLEY: That hat looks real to me. And Minnie Pearl hats are hard to find. . . . And look at the label in that Johnny Cash suit. It says, "Made for Johnny Cash."

After authenticating Cash's Gretsch guitar, handwritten lyrics by the Stoneman Family, and more than a dozen Nudie suits, he stops at a figure of Kenny Rogers lying on the ground with its face smashed apart, left hand missing, and legs amputated below the knee.

MEDLEY: Kenny would not be happy with this.

All together, there are sixty-two wax figures, not counting various busts and body parts, and almost all with authentic stage outfits, instruments, or other items.

What do you think all this is worth?
MEDLEY: They're intrinsically valuable as collector's pieces, but the fact that they also belonged to stars like Hank Snow and Hank Williams kicks it into high gear. This collection of suits is really the most complete I've ever seen. Their historical and monetary worth is considerable.

Are you going to buy them for the museum?
MEDLEY: I'd like to. It's much more complete than the museum's collection. Some of the objects we have representing these people may just be a cigar or a hat (*pauses*). I think when these people gave all these items, they thought they'd just give them to the museum instead of donating them to the Salvation Army. Now, to be honest, I don't know if we could afford them.

(*To Caden:*) So what are you going to do with them?
CADEN: I don't have a clue what I'm going to do with them. I'm just sitting on them, but I don't even know where Daniel Hsu is, to be quite honest. I thought some bolt of lightning would strike us and we would figure it out. But we really have no plans.

For years afterward, the figures remained in limbo, decaying untended while Nashville raced after its cosmopolitan dream. Eventually, Caden began auctioning items individually, until the whole collection, like Nashville's past, was scattered to the winds. Whatever wax parts remained were destroyed.

[MOBY]

Hail pounded brutally on the skylight of Moby's New York apartment, threatening to break the glass. His bookshelf, containing everything from Flannery O'Connor to *The Machiavellian's Guide to Womanizing*, rattled from the storm. Moby stopped speaking every now and then to look worriedly around the room. His apartment was bare and sparsely furnished. It was the same place he'd lived when he recorded his breakthrough techno single, "Go," almost a decade earlier. Though his standard of living didn't seem to have changed, a lot had happened since then. For example, outside the window, an eighty-foot-tall jeans advertisement emblazoned with Moby's hairless head was staring right at him.

The first time I interviewed you, when your first album came out, you were living in this same house and it was just as empty. Has your life changed much?
MOBY: I was talking about this with a friend of mine. I have been making records for ten years, and this record has been the most successful of my albums. But the material circumstances of my life haven't changed at all. I live in the same home. I wear the same clothes. I have for the most part the same friends. And when I travel, I stay in the same hotels and travel with the same people on the same tour bus. The only real difference in my life is I get to meet more people. And I get to look at a picture of myself eighty feet tall every time I walk out of my house.

What did you think when they put that ad outside your house?
MOBY: I was so excited. The first ad that went up in that space was Foxy Brown, and I remember walking up Broadway and just being like, "Oh fuck, that's huge." At the time, it was the biggest photo of a human being I had ever seen. I remember just for a split second thinking, "Wow, that would be so cool." And it happened. Maybe I shouldn't say this, but I love it.

Do people recognize you whenever you walk past it?
MOBY: I still never get recognized. Small bald white guys like myself, we all kind of look the same. I went out to dinner the other night and this woman asked me, "Have you ever met your doppelganger?" And my answer was, "I see my doppelganger twenty times a day."

A friend of mine spent about five or ten minutes taking my picture in front of my billboard on a Sunday afternoon with thousands of people walking by, and no one recognized me. Really, white guys with shaved heads, we all look the same.

Have you ever had one of those moments where you catch a glimpse of your reflection in a mirror or see yourself on television, and for a moment you see yourself as a stranger would?
MOBY: I have had that happen and I never, ever like what I see. My reaction is usually like, "Who's that guy with the bad posture?" or "Who's that inbred coal miner over there?"

I was dating someone and we were sitting on a couch watching me talk on television and I was just sitting there thinking, "Why does she like me?" I was looking at myself, and for the life of me I couldn't see why anyone would find me attractive. My first instinct was to cover up the TV or something so maybe she wouldn't see what I'm seeing.

Have you heard of Alexander Technique?
MOBY: What's that?

It's a discipline that basically puts your body into alignment, and helps with everything from your posture to your voice.
MOBY: Maybe I should do that for my posture. In the mid-eighties, I dated a woman and her father had just unbelievably bad posture and I know that I'm going to end up like that, like this stooped guy with a terrible slouch like skulking around.

Then you should fix it now.
MOBY: My grandmother used to do it all the time. She would dig her knuckles into my spine and say, "Stand up straight!" But it never worked. In my case, it's from playing music: In order to see the guitar, you have to hunch over. Maybe I should get a back brace or hire someone to follow me around and tell me to stand up straight. [. . .]
    By the way, I think your tape is about to run out.

How do you know? You didn't even look at it.
MOBY: I know. It's strange. But half the time when I'm doing an interview, all of a sudden I get this feeling that something's weird, and then . . . (*click*).

Tape ends.

[PRINCE]

The problem with interviewing Prince is that he doesn't let journalists record his voice. So it either takes fast penmanship or a really good memory to capture the moment. In one encounter, he played new music and then performed a private concert at his house in Los Angeles. In another, he talked about being a Jehovah's Witness for forty-five minutes. But the most memorable Prince encounter was my initial one at a press conference I attended shortly after being put on staff at the *New York Times*. At the door, security guards checked to make sure no reporters were bringing in tape recorders.

RANDOM JOURNALIST: Are you concerned that releasing an album only on the Internet will hurt it on the pop charts?

PRINCE: When you're taking all the proceeds, I don't worry about how well it does on the charts and I don't need a number one. I'm number one at the bank.
RANDOM JOURNALIST: When did you decide to do this tour?
PRINCE: I think when I was seven.

If journalists aren't allowed to record you speaking, why are there TV cameras in the room? Aren't they recording you speaking also?
PRINCE: You and I can discuss that later.

I assume Prince is just blowing off the question. But as soon as the press conference ends, he walks off the podium and straight up to me. He then waggles his finger, indicating that I'm supposed to follow him.

I trail him past rows of snickering reporters and into a back room. He leans against a wall and a large bodyguard thrusts his arm in front of Prince's chest like a barrier fence, as if worried I'll stand too close to the diminutive pop star.

PRINCE: Why did you ask me that?

Because it doesn't make sense. If people can't record your voice with tape recorders, why can they record them on videotape?
PRINCE: That's a good question. I don't let people record my interviews because sometimes they release bootleg recordings afterward.

But can't they do the same with a videotape?
PRINCE: We know the placement of each camera, so if they do that, we'll know who did it.

What if they release only the audio as a bootleg?
PRINCE: (*Silence.*)*
BODYGUARD: He has to go now.

= [**THE FAKE BOOTSY COLLINS**] =

Long before creepy people were pretending to be celebrities on social-networking sites, they were posing as celebrities in real life. One of the most persistent impos-

---

* My theory: Not being recorded also gives Prince plausible deniability if a reporter quotes him as saying something that gets him in trouble. However, he was willing to bend his rules during the press conference because he wanted national television exposure.

ters was a gentleman claiming to be Bootsy Collins, the flamboyant bassist best known for playing with Parliament-Funkadelic.

Here are a few highlights from his seventeen-year-career as a funk grifter: Johnny Carson had him scheduled to appear on his talk show; the promoter Bill Graham not only booked him for a benefit, but gave him a few thousand dollars to find more acts; pop rapper Gerardo put him in his backup band on *The Arsenio Hall Show*, after which the bad Bootsy stole hundreds of dollars in equipment; and one woman even married him, thinking he was the real Bootsy and hoping he'd get her a record contract.

"He came in the day after we opened and the security guard said he was Bootsy," one New York club owner remembered. "I gave him drinks, and we started talking. That day, I lent him fifty dollars. I got him booked for January, and gave him six hundred dollars for a four-thousand-dollar booking. Then he kept coming back to borrow a little money, saying things like, 'My mother's sick.' So I started getting concerned. I talked to Bootsy's manager and found out I'd been dealing with the wrong Bootsy."

Bootsy's road manager, Dana Davis, added, "He has seventeen aliases, but we've had the FBI out after him." Evidently the FBI didn't take the case too seriously: The fake Bootsy had recently made the mistake of leaving his phone number on Meters drummer Ziggy Modeliste's answering machine.

Hi, is Bootsy there?
FAKE BOOTSY COLLINS: No, he's not here right now.

Do you know when he'll be coming back?
FAKE BOOTSY: He's taping a special in Washington right now. I'm not sure when he'll be back.

Who am I speaking to?
FAKE BOOTSY: Leroy, Bootsy's bodyguard.*

You know there's been a fake Bootsy running around?
FAKE BOOTSY: Yeah, we know. You have to be careful. We've got the police after him, though.

---

* When a promoter named Maurice Bernstein tried to track him down, the fake Bootsy also identified himself on the phone as Leroy the bodyguard. Called for comment, the real Bootsy responded, "I once had a Leroy who worked for me, but I don't know anything about this guy. [. . .] I'm flattered someone would go to the extremes to be like me, but when he starts to make my name look bad, that's another thing."

I saw Bootsy at the Public Enemy show and he promised to produce my demo tape. I was wondering how I could get it to him.

FAKE BOOTSY: He's real busy right now. He's leaving for Detroit next week to cut an album with George Clinton and then going to London to talk with Phil Collins about playing with Brand X. You know, they're putting Brand X back together? But if he said so, I'm sure he wouldn't go back on his word. I can't make any promises about when he'll get it back to you, though.

Is there any way I can get the demo to him?

FAKE BOOTSY: Why don't you drop it off here? I'll make sure Bootsy gets it. You know he's starring in a movie about the Mothership? Listen, maybe we can put one of your songs in it. Drop it off here.

Where are you at?

FAKE BOOTSY: 138th Street and Edgecombe Avenue [in Harlem]. You know where that is? We're in building eighty. Leave it downstairs for apartment twenty-six. Got that?

I thought Bootsy lived in Cincinnati.

FAKE BOOTSY: Yeah, but he spends a lot of his time here. You know, I've got a beautiful girl here and she's started taking her clothes off. I better go now, okay.

Should I follow up with Dana Davis?

FAKE BOOTSY: No, you don't want to do that. Dana doesn't like it when Bootsy works on the side.

[JACKIE CHAN]

When Jackie Chan was born, his parents were so poor, they considered selling him for food money to the doctor who delivered him. Eventually, they found another way to get rid of Chan: by sending him to a notoriously brutal Peking opera school, where he was beaten into becoming a stuntman.

Years before Chan's eventual breakthrough as a household name in America, I spent a month trying to find him for an interview. At the time, his latest Hong Kong movie was opening in a small Asian-run theater in Chinatown because it had no American distributor. He finally called me from Bangkok.

JACKIE CHAN: Hi, this is Jackie Chan speaking.

Hi.
CHAN: I think the phone has a problem.

Let me . . .
CHAN: Yeah, it's okay now.

Hi, Jackie?
CHAN: Yeah. Sorry about the—

Confusion? I wasn't told you'd be calling, but I'm ready.
CHAN: Willie?* Is Willie here?
WILLIE: Yes, yes. This is Willie here. Sorry for all the mistakes. When we're on promotion tour, because of the time difference, it's very hard to arrange. You don't
mind me listening in, do you, Neil?

That's fine.
WILLIE: Okay, go ahead then.

I wanted to start off by asking about the new film, *Rumble in the Bronx*?
CHAN: Did you see the movie?

I haven't seen it because it opens in Chinatown here in one week.
CHAN: Oh, okay. Have you seen any other of my movies?

Oh, yeah, I've seen almost everything for the past eight years.
CHAN: Okay.

Has anyone ever gotten seriously hurt while filming one of your movies?
CHAN: Oh, yes, many people get hurt.

Really?
CHAN: Some people almost die, yeah. I still have a lot of outtakes I cannot show
because it's too violent. So I just show the piece very quick.† But when you really
see the blood come from the mouth and nose, we send them to the hospital

---

* Willie Chan, his manager (no relation).
† At the end of Chan's movies, he shows the bloopers, several of which usually involve him or stuntmen
  falling, getting hit, or being taken away in stretchers.

Are You Taking a Journey Abroad?

I CAN FURNISH

LIFE *and* ACCIDENT INSURANCE

The JACKIE CHAN COMBINATION ACCIDENT & LIFE
INSURANCE POLICY protects you NO MATTER
WHEN, WHERE, or HOW.

CHAN'S, HONG KONG — "ALL 206 BONES COVERED."

(*chuckles*). At that time, my manager has nothing to do but go to the hospital every day.

Do you ever work with American stuntmen?
CHAN: They have very good stuntmen. They really calculate everything. When I want them to do something, they check the load, put some string here, or put an airbag. Do a lot of things. It's really safe. But for us, we just do it now! Go away— just do it!

So is it hard to find stuntmen to work with you?
CHAN: Yes, quite hard. Quite a few people who work with me get hurt. But I have my own group of stuntmen. It doesn't matter.

I read somewhere that it's impossible for you to get insurance.
CHAN: Yes, because in Asia, where we're famous, all the people go and see my movies. They know it's very dangerous. So when I buy insurance, nobody there accepts me. And I know . . . (*speaks in Cantonese to his manager*).
WILLIE: In the insurance companies, when it comes to the movie department, he's blacklisted.
CHAN: I'm first on the blacklist.

(*Laughs.*)
CHAN: I speak the truth. But I really don't care. Right now, if I was really dying, whatever money they give me, I don't care. I can't use it anyway.

At the end of *Supercop*, you get hit by the helicopter when you're hanging from the train—
CHAN: Yeah.

And in *Armour of God 2*, you fall off the chains and get knocked out. Do you have any permanent damage from all the injuries?
CHAN: Oh, many. Like my right ear cannot hear properly because of Yugoslavia.

What happened?
WILLIE: He had a skull injury while filming in Yugoslavia.
CHAN: Did you see *Armour of God* part one?

Yes.
CHAN: Yeah, the ending scene, you can't see it, but blood was coming out from my right ear. I almost died at that time.

I didn't know that.

CHAN: It's very big news in Asia. Every day, thousand phone calls, all the fans crying in the telephone. The news was covered almost one week. And then my head, my brain, my shoulder—so many injuries, oh, I can't tell you. From the head to the toes from all those years doing the stunts.

Do you ever think about—

CHAN: But don't worry, I'm very happy.

[SLIPKNOT] SCENE 2

You know that the more popular you become, the harder it's going to get to stay focused on your mission?

SHAWN CRAHAN: I can go do anything. I proved it to the maggots* and to everyone. We're from Des Moines, Iowa, man, and look at where we are now. I wake up every morning and think, "Jesus, I was just on *Conan O'Brien* and I lit myself on fire with no protection." Two days ago, my DJ lit himself up so bad. He had a back draft, and the fire went up two little holes in his pants and filled his coveralls up. He was a hot air balloon.

Was he badly hurt?

CRAHAN: He seriously burned himself. And did he do it the next night? What do you think?

I'm sure he did.

CRAHAN: He absolutely did. And he loved every minute of it. See, man, I'm really big into like time travel and all that shit. I always trip out thinking about, you know, if you and I went back in time right now and we went back to your mom when she was four and we took the lollipop away from her, it would affect her whole life.

Like chaos theory?

CRAHAN: I'll be honest with you: The nine of us onstage is a very magical thing. It cannot be duplicated. It cannot be replaced. It is an energy ball that at almost any given time, there's nothing more powerful going on in the entire world. I'm talking about manmade. (*Enter Chad Gray, Mudvayne singer.*) What's up, Chad?

---

* I.e., his fans.

CHAD GRAY: We put a little tree of life together out in the dirt with some rocks and stuff. Man, we need to get some ham and some honey and shit like that so we can conjure some insects.

CRAHAN: Let's do it.

GRAY: And take some pictures.

CRAHAN: All right, I'll get my digital camera. I'll be right there. (*Exit Chad Gray.*) That's the lead singer for Mudvayne. One of the best bands that's going to come out.

So what are you guys doing with the tree?

CRAHAN: I'm fascinated with the bug world. I believe the bug world is like Slipknot. Every day you walk outside your front door. . . . Maybe you don't because you live in New York, right?

There's a bug world there, believe me.

CRAHAN: So every day you walk outside to a world that you ignore. But the bug world is fascinating and true. It is very, very violent and surreal. Imagine living in that world, and doing one thing one second and being eaten another. Imagine being trapped in a web. Imagine being flown off by a bird. If you were going to be a bug doctor, you would spend ten of your lifetimes learning how to do surgery on wings, ten eyeballs, things that make webs. What the fuck is a web? How's it fucking made? How many more fluids do they have than humans?

And so you're saying—

CRAHAN: Basically what I'm getting at is, Slipknot is a world you've been ignoring. And I'm going to make you fucking deal with it. You don't have a choice: Here I am. How you doing? I'm the fucking camel spider that you don't lay on the floor on, because if you do I'm going to come up and I'm going to bite your face so fast that I'm going to inject the fucking numbing thing that you'll just think was a little scratch. Then you'll itch it real quick, and I'll come back and eat your fucking face while you're sleeping and you won't feel it. And when you wake up, I'll eat it down to the fucking bare bone, and I'll leave all the arteries and everything alone, and you won't have a fucking face and you'll be forced to deal with me. And that's what Slipknot is.

What happens if the band becomes mainstream and it's no longer subversive?

CRAHAN: I won't need to be in the band anymore. But I'll still be involved in everything. I'm involved with you right now. You're going to write an article.

And you're going to get involved with that?
CRAHAN: Well, it depends on you. It depends if you're going to follow the mold, if you're going to ask the same questions you ask everyone else, if you're going to write stylistically like you always write. It's up to you. Or if you're going to go back and break your mold and fucking set it on fire. I can give you the stick, I can give you the cloth, I can even fucking douse it in gasoline. But it's up to you to fucking tell it like the way it is. And if you do, then you're going to set it on fire.

I think I know what you're saying.
CRAHAN: It's the truth, man. I don't know how you feel talking to me, but let's say you're positively charged and you're glad you came here. It's a momentous day that you're going to see a show tonight. You're going to be on fire. But what's going to happen from the minute you leave and you get back to *it*?

That's a good point. Writers have an experience out here covering something, then they return to reality and being truthful to that experience becomes secondary to keeping their bosses happy.
CRAHAN: It's up to you. Let's see what happens to you. Because I'll tell you what, bud, I'm going to be watching. I'm going to get this and I'm going to read it and I'm going to decide whether you and I can ever talk again.

[*Continued . . .*]

[MÖTLEY CRÜE]
SCENE 2

When writing music books, occasionally the rock and corporate worlds butt heads. Especially when it comes time for publishing lawyers to read the manuscript. The following are a few of my e-mails with Nikki Sixx and Tommy Lee of Mötley Crüe during the final stages of production on the band's autobiography *The Dirt*. Obviously, the writing in capital letters is theirs.

Nikki,
A few more questions from the lawyers. We're getting there.

1. Lovey: She is definitely dead, right?
SHES DEAD . . .

2. That scene where [name removed] says that you're Satan. Is that all completely true?
YES

3. The lawyer is worried about all the stuff we say about [name removed]. Do you think she'd ever sign a release?
SHE WOULD SUE . . . SHES A MONEY WHORE . . .

4. This is a silly one, but you can confirm that Lita did drugs, specifically Quaaludes?
CAN I CONFIRM IT??? WELL I WATCHED HER . . .

5. Can anyone else confirm that you fucked [name removed]'s wife? They want me to e-mail [name removed] and see if he's cool with it.
GOOD LUCK

6. They're worried about some of the [name removed] stuff, mainly where we mention the story about him giving Freddie Mercury a blow job. Can we confirm?
DUDE I DONT KNOW . . . HAHHHAHAHHAA

7. Would you be so kind as to confirm that it is true that Ozzy licked your pee and that he shit on Tommy's bathroom and wiped it on the walls.
I WATCHED HIM SNORT ANTS AND LICK PEE . . . ASK TOMMY ABOUT THE OTHER

8. On another note, we need a caption for the photo of you guys in the bathtub.
YA, VINCE WAS COKED OUT OF HIS MIND, TOMMY AND NIKKI JUST SHOT UP 10CC OF HEROIN AND MICK WAS SO DRUNK WE HAD TO PROP HIM UP SO HE DIDNT DROWN

MISS YOU, MY FRIEND . . . IM BACK ON THE AA WAGON FOR NOW . . . I ALMOST KILLED MY DUMB ASS . . .

———◆———

Tommy,
Here are the questions from the lawyers. They're pretty stupid, but please answer them all for me so I can get them off my back.

1. Can you confirm that Ozzy shit in your bathroom and wiped it on the walls?
. . . YES!!!!

2. Did you see him lick up Nikki's pee?
HELL YES!!!!!!

3. When you say you found a "gang of fucking speed," the lawyers want to know: How much exactly is a gang? And what kind of speed?
NONE OF THIS MATTERS AS LONG AS NO NAMES ARE GIVEN!!

4. And, finally, this is my favorite: Can you confirm that you had Polaroids of [name removed]'s rear end?
NO FUCKIN NAMES . . . I DON'T WANT ANYONE COMING BACK TO ME SUING ME!!! FUCK THAT!! I'VE BEEN SUED WAAAAAAAY TOO MANY TIMES AND HAVE LEARNED MY LESSON!!! NO NAMES!!! LETS HOOK UP!!!!

══════ **[HUGH LAURIE]** ══════

For fans of Hugh Laurie's roles on British television programs, where he generally plays bumbling, foppish, dim-witted characters, it was somewhat of a surprise when he became a star in America playing the exact opposite role: a smart, cynical misanthrope in *House, M.D.* So *Rolling Stone* sent me to the set of the show to talk to him about it.

HUGH LAURIE: You sound like you have a cold, maybe. Do you?

A little bit. I did a book with Mötley Crüe called *The Dirt,* so I went out on the tour bus with some of those guys for a concert last night.
LAURIE: You see, I feel like I'm such a disappointment to you. I mean, you're hanging out with Mötley Crüe and now you're talking to some middle-aged fucking actor on a TV show. This must be just so . . . I wish I could give you some Mötley Crüe stuff. I wish I had a tour bus. I wish I had—oh fuck, I wish I had something. What can I give you?

Well, for starters, what's up with that picture of a bucket of antidepressants [in your trailer]?
LAURIE: Oh, oh, yes. Yes, that was from a friend. A friend from England. Yeah, should I leave it there? I think I probably should leave it there. Well spotted. You don't miss a trick. Now I'm terrified of what else you've seen.

Actually, I don't know if I told you this, but I've always followed your career and—
LAURIE: No!

Oh, yeah, I have from—
LAURIE: Oh my God.

From, you know—
LAURIE: That's slightly unsettling.

I'm not crazy obsessed or anything.
LAURIE: No, no, no. But I feel like you're going to say, "I notice your career and find it reprehensible in so many ways."

That's exactly what I was going to say.
LAURIE: And then, "What the hell were you thinking?"

That was on my list of questions, too.
LAURIE: I knew it.

Actually, I always thought that you were going to get bigger roles in America earlier. When Hugh Grant started getting popular here, I thought, "This is an opportunity for"—
LAURIE: Anyone called Hugh.

Exactly. I was actually thinking that where he was a sort of likeable, bumbling romantic character and you were—
LAURIE: A dark machine with ruthless ambition, yes? [. . .]

With *House*, you became a completely opposite sort of sex symbol than the bumbling type you played in movies around that time.
LAURIE: It's . . . I don't accept it at all. I don't see that character as sexy, but he has a sort of Byronic charm. He's damaged and he's sort of a loner.

Maybe, but two different people at the photo shoot said that they thought *you* were sexy.
LAURIE: Those people who said that are barking up the wrong tree *(pauses)*. Who said it?

I think it was the—
LAURIE: I shouldn't even ask that. Never mind.

It's okay. It was one of the female producers of the show. And the gay male manager of the studio. So you got both sides.
LAURIE: What was his name?

I don't remember his name.
LAURIE: Oh, was he the guy in a white sweater?

I thought you didn't want to know.
LAURIE: Right, yes. I don't. No, don't tell me. [. . .]

Have you found that playing House has affected your personality and made you more cynical or misanthropic?
LAURIE: No, though I suppose being on television has changed my life. I feel very self-conscious and I feel like I can't go out. I hate being looked at. I hate being photographed. There was this awful woman last night taking photographs and I wanted to scream, "I just want . . . Stop taking, you know . . . I hate this!"

In what way?
LAURIE: I have this weird superstition about the camera stealing part of your soul. I sort of believe in that, actually.

Are you serious?
LAURIE: It does. Well, obviously in terms of my molecular structure, I haven't lost anything by being photographed. I understand the laws of physics. But I suppose an understanding of physics leads you to believe that if the photographer has something, you must have lost something.

[RICK JAMES
SCENE 2]

When you got out of prison, what was it like making music sober?
RICK JAMES: Oh man, when I first got out of prison, I wondered if I would be able to tour, because I didn't know if I could perform coherent as opposed to fucked up. But even in the old days, at the highest point of my cocaine abuse, when I was spending five thousand or six thousand dollars a week freebasing—smoking

cocaine—one thing I never did was smoke cocaine before a show. But I would snort a little—very little, because it would fuck up my voice if I did too much. I would also throw down some drinks, some cognac or something.

When was the last time you played in New York?
JAMES: The last time I performed in New York City was in like 1991. I had an album out called *Wonderful*, which didn't do that wonderful in the charts. And I wanted to play the Apollo because I didn't think I was going to be on the earth long. I thought I was going to die—I was going to overdose—so I wanted to do a lot of the shit that I hadn't done. And one of the things I had never done was play the Apollo.

What are some of the things you want to do now that you're sober?
JAMES: I want to go to Russia. I was offered to go to Russia on an Arm & Hammer deal and play, and that didn't interest me then because I knew I couldn't find any cocaine over there. And I'd like to go to Africa. And I never went to Japan only because I didn't want to be on a plane that long and still not have drugs when I got there. So now I want to go to Japan.

You know, it's like, I used to think of my life in terms of, "Well, will there be any cocaine when I get there?" Or, "What's the charge if they find me with it? Will they lock me up in a jail forever like *Midnight Express*?" So everything was predicated around how much coke is there and how much will they have for me when I get there, which is a really stupid, insane way of thinking.

What about this interview—
JAMES: We would never have done this interview years ago. Back then, I'd be in my room for an hour. Then I'd come out, spend a couple minutes with you, and go back to my room and smoke cocaine again. You'd be here the whole night and your whole interview would say, "We didn't talk much, but we saw the smoke and the redness in his eyes and the freaks running around butt naked" (*laughs*). No, you would have never seen kids running around and Christmas trees all lit up like you do now (*pauses*). Nobody knows in the whole world, but I just got married.

Congratulations. Shouldn't you have married her while you were in prison though, so you could get conjugal visits?
JAMES: Well, I thought about doing it before, but every time we tried to do it, believe it or not, something would happen. Because she was my crime partner also,

Hotel
Royal Palm

SWAKOPMUND,
NAMIBIA

*The Perfect Hideaway, Romantically
Lit and Ventilated, Room Service
Available for All Your Needs,*
WRITE FOR FOLDER AND RATES

they didn't want her on the prison grounds, no matter what. So even if we would have gotten married, they wouldn't allow her conjugal visits.

Ever thought of writing a book about your experiences?
JAMES: I'm finishing a book. This is a chronological, no-punches-pulled, tell-all book. Sex, drugs, and funk and roll. Not rock and roll, funk and roll! Plus serious freaks.

You know, the secret to writing a book is to be totally honest, even if you feel it's going to make you look bad sometimes.
JAMES: Exactly. I have to be, man. All through my career, I've tried to be as honest as I can. I always felt when I made it, I wouldn't be afraid to say, "I shit, fart, and jack off every now and then. I like pussy." I was never gonna be one of those motherfuckers who's gonna say, (*whines*) "I don't do drugs. I don't smoke marijuana." Fuck that. I do it all. Yeah, and it brought me down, but so fucking what? I'll tell you, man, a lot of motherfucking celebrities and a lot of people are gonna be up in motherfucking arms when I write this. There's gonna be some shit flowing. Well, I don't give a fuck. It's therapy for me, plus it's the truth.

Any other plans for the new year?
JAMES: My basic thing for the year is just to stay positive, centered, and focused. And leave that motherfucking cocaine alone.

In 2004, Rick James was found dead in his home of a heart attack. Traces of cocaine—in addition to Valium, Xanax, Vicodin, and meth—were found in his bloodstream. He was fifty-six. His autobiography, The Confessions of Rick James: Memoirs of a Super Freak, *was released posthumously.*

[**SLIPKNOT**]
SCENE 3

Evidently, Slipknot clown Shawn Crahan approved of the article I wrote about the band. Because when he released an unexpectedly melodic pop-rock album with his side project To My Surprise three and a half years later, he agreed to talk again.

Thanks for doing this.
SHAWN CRAHAN: I remember you, man. I have a plaque of your interview up on my wall. For what it's worth, man, I've learned so much since we talked last time.

It's been a while: three or four years. I'm not doing any interviews, but of course I remember you and we hit it off and things are cool. You have an art form, I have an art form, and today's special because two people get to talk.

You sound like a completely different person.
CRAHAN: I'm not very good at talking to the press, I found out. I'm not afraid to say that I'm a little embarrassed by some of my behavior. There's been all kinds of things that have happened in the last two years, especially here in the States, that have changed the human thought process. There's not one person today who doesn't understand that we're living in a different world. And I'm not ashamed to say that I've been a boy. And I'm getting better in my mind and I'm getting healthier. I'm shutting up and I'm listening.

Is there something else that made you change?
CRAHAN: I've lived the other road. I've been in the forest. I've lost a lot of friends, and I've had to grow up. I went out in front of sixty thousand people and I felt isolated from them. I had mass quantities of power to make a difference, yet not a moment of speaking to make a difference. I'm now only concerned with making songs and speaking to people. I want to speak to Wall Street people. I want to speak to businessmen who push insurance. I want to talk to the teachers. I want to go to colleges and give seminars. I want to sit down with kids in classrooms and have them challenge me. I want to communicate, because I'm thirty-four and I've been shutting out communication.

This is something I meant to ask when we last met, but what was your relationship like with your parents when you were younger?
CRAHAN: I've been alone my whole life. I was an only child. My parents built me a small apartment in the basement, not because they wanted to get rid of me, but because they trusted me to have my own shower, phone line, cable. They let me grow up like a little boy should, but I grew up very alone. So now I'm trying to break the only-child, spoiled-rotten crap and trying to get to reality. I am understanding how to take this word *I* out, and I'm telling you, Neil, it's so beautiful. [. . .]

It's hard to tell if this is another phase or if it's real growth, but either way, I'm impressed by how much more at peace you seem to be with yourself and the world.
CRAHAN: You don't know what it means to me, man. I didn't think I could change. I still haven't gotten out everything. I'm going to go deeper and deeper. But you

don't know how much I appreciate that you took the time to say those kind words. You made my day. I'm going to share that vibe with people around me, and that vibe will become their vibe. In all honesty, thank you. Have a great day, man. If you need anything else, you can call. And if we're ever around and you want to pop in, feel free. Let me show you the ropes.

[TOM CRUISE]
SCENE 3

While interviewing Tom Cruise in a back room at the Scientology Celebrity Centre, I asked his mother, who'd joined the church at her son's behest a year earlier, whether Scientology conflicted with her Catholicism. Not at all, she replied. "I think Jesus wants me to be here right now. My church may not agree, but I personally know that."

For some reason, the notoriously press-phobic Tom Cruise had spent a week taking me around various Scientology buildings in Los Angeles and introducing me to some of the higher-ups. It was the first time he had let a journalist into this world, and just about the last.

I don't know if you are allowed to say, but what OT* number are you?
TOM CRUISE: Well, I can't say. Do you know what OT is? Do you know?

I know what it stands for and what it means, but probably not like you do.
CRUISE: Yeah, I mean, it's . . . I don't have anything not to discuss with you, but I'd rather you understood it more.

Actually, one of the things I wanted to ask was, okay, a lot of smart people are Scientologists and I want to know what—
CRUISE: Just ask it.

How much has Scientology helped your career?
CRUISE: It's helped tremendously. I would not have had the success that I've had without it.

So in what ways has it made your success possible?
CRUISE: There are things that I can apply to my life that have helped me grow as an artist, in ways that I wanted to and in ways that were beyond my wildest dreams.

---

* OT stands for Operating Thetan, supposedly the highest state of spiritual being. By passing church courses, Scientologists advance through levels, each one bringing them closer to this state and then ultimately beyond.

I'm asking more about concrete ways it has helped.
CRUISE: What do you mean?

For example, are there people you've met in the church—lawyers or contacts or other resources—who have had a direct impact on your career?
CRUISE: I'm trying to understand.

Let me try another way of asking this: People always say that there are ways in which becoming a Scientologist helps actors get parts in movies.
CRUISE: No, not for me. It was the tools that they had that I used. No other way *(pauses)*. That doesn't make sense to me. I really don't know *(long pause)*. If you really want to know, get *What Is Scientology?*, the book, and look at it, because that's what Scientology is. It's a very large body of knowledge with tools that are available. It's ah . . . It really is the shit, man.

So what about it appealed to you?
CRUISE: I mean, Scientology, the very word means knowing how to know. It's an applied religious philosophy. It's not dogma. It's not about belief. It's not someone telling you, "You must believe this. You must believe that. You must live your life this way." You learn things for yourself, and you go out and apply it and see if it works for you. And it's about improving conditions in your life. That's what I wanted. And Scientology has given me that and more.

But what do you think of its reputation? As soon as someone mentions Scientology, most people think negative things about it.
CRUISE: No, not really. No. What I get is a lot of interest. People want to know what is going on. Ah, and then there are the other people that just don't know. It's just like anything: It's ignorance. People that just basically hate. There are racists and bigots in all fields and all walks of life.

Okay, there are those kind of people out there. But separate from them, most people really are scared when they hear the word Scientology. They feel like it's a cult and it's hard to get out of.
CRUISE: Who are those people that say those things? Because I promise you, it isn't everybody. When you get down to it as a percentage of the populace, it's a very small percentage. Believe me, I've been through it. But I look at those people and I say, "Bring it. What do you know about it? I'm a Scientologist, man—what do you know? *(Louder:)* What do you know?" I don't mind answering questions.

So what should they know?

CRUISE: I have to tell you, Narconon is the only successful drug rehab program in the world. Period. It is the only one that rids the body of the toxins and helps these guys. And when you talk about Criminon, when you talk about Study Tech* . . . What is [society's current] solution? Drugging people, putting labels on people, and junk science. And these Scientology programs are available to anybody and everybody. Some people, well, if they don't like Scientology, well, then fuck you (*rises from the table*). Really. (*Louder, pointing a finger at the imaginary enemy:*) Fuck you. Period (*sits down again, face reddened*).

Okay, I get that. And I agree with a lot of the things you've said. But why not just pick and choose from all the great bodies of knowledge, instead of taking one thing and saying, "This is it"?

CRUISE: When I started out, I was like, "Whoa, this works." And then I got interested in how the hell does it work? Why does it work? That's why I became a Scientologist.

I also feel that it's not good enough for me to be doing well. I want to help my kids, my movies, people. I get great pleasure out of seeing people do well in life. I don't take any pleasure in seeing people fail.

I agree. I like learning from others and I like helping them. But—

CRUISE: I know. We need people like you. We really do.

$$\left[\ \textbf{CURTAIN}\ \right]$$

---

* These are all Scientology programs. Narconon is a drug rehabilitation program; Criminon is a prisoner rehabilitation program; and Study Tech is a system of learning developed by Scientology founder L. Ron Hubbard.

ACT SIX

OR

A HUNDRED MILLION DOLLAR PAYCHECK

SYNOPSIS

ENTER THE NEPTUNES,

WHO BLOW OFF AN INTERVIEW,

WHILE KORN TRIES TO PAY THE JOURNALIST NOT TO DO IT,

BECAUSE CHER SAYS THE MUSIC INDUSTRY

CAN KILL YOU,

WHICH IT DOES TO JOSH CLAYTON-FELT

and tries to do to the Backstreet Boys,

though Billy Joel has learned

TO BE A PROSTITUTE,

WHICH INSPIRES THE RZA
TO CONDUCT HIS OWN INVESTIGATION, &C.

$$\begin{bmatrix} \textbf{THE NEPTUNES} \\ \textit{SCENE 1} \end{bmatrix}$$

When *Esquire* ran a special issue featuring the best and brightest ideas and minds in the country, the editorial board named the Neptunes—the production team of Pharrell Williams and Chad Hugo, responsible for hits by Britney Spears, Justin Timberlake, and Snoop Dogg—as the most promising musicians of the moment. With Bill Clinton penning the introduction to the issue, the producers were in high-caliber company. So I called their publicist to schedule time with Pharrell. Below is the first of five interviews with him, all of which are included here in their entirety.

Hey, this is Neil Strauss from *Esquire*. Thanks for doing this.
PHARRELL: Hey, I'm having a house party. Can we reschedule this?

Sure, when do you want to—
PHARRELL: (*Click.*)

[*Continued . . .*]

$$\begin{bmatrix} \textbf{KORN} \\ \textit{SCENE 1} \end{bmatrix}$$

It was supposed to be the biggest, most mainstream press exposure the hard rock band Korn had gotten to date: the cover of *Spin* magazine. Yet two weeks after the interview, the band's management company, the Firm, called and offered me ten thousand dollars not to write the article.

Evidently Fieldy, the band's bassist, had gotten into a fistfight with *Spin*'s creative director during the photo shoot and the band didn't want to be on the cover anymore.

An hour later, an editor at *Spin* called and said the magazine was thinking of killing the story because the band had called another staffer at the photo shoot "a cunt."

"That's part of their charm," I explained.

By that point, I'd spent enough time with these five misfits from Bakersfield, California, to see them piss off just about everybody they crossed paths with. At the Fuji Rock Festival in Tokyo, Fieldy picked a fight with a member of Primal Scream by repeatedly insisting, "You look like my uncle Bob." An hour later, he was an-

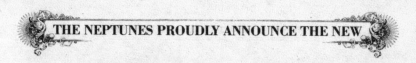

noying Garbage singer Shirley Manson by repeatedly sticking a toy keychain in her face and setting off various sounds without a word of explanation. Meanwhile, Korn singer Jonathan Davis was yelling at drum-and-bass star Goldie, "Fuck you, dick!" And Junkie XL, a dance musician from Amsterdam, turned down dinner with Korn because he thought the band members were assholes.

But he was wrong: The guys in Korn aren't assholes. They just want some love—and when they don't get it, they act out. In his hotel room, raving drunk the night before the band's Tokyo performance, Davis stood on a chair and explained.

JONATHAN DAVIS: We go to these goddamn festivals, and no fucking goddamn band will love us. We get no fucking love at all. It's like we're in our own little world. We're not that goddamn scary. What the goddamn fuck? For once in my life, please love me: I'm in Korn.

Well, you guys weren't out there making friends today.
DAVIS: We're nothing like that, man.

Leaps off chair.

Like what?
DAVIS: Any of that shit!

Any of what shit?
DAVIS: Any shit that's out there. There's so much rehashed shit. You see it around us at the festival: Musicians fucking hate us. *Fucking* hate us!

Why is that so important?
DAVIS: I don't know. What can you call it?

Call what?
DAVIS: [Our] music. What can you call it? It's like the Clash: What the fuck can you call the Clash? Fucking punk, pop, reggae? That's a great band.

People call you heavy.
DAVIS: They do?

I'm talking about your music.
DAVIS: Yeah, we just want to be heavy. That's what it is. All we want to do is bring heavy back into rock and roll, because goddamned Ben Folds Five sucks. It's fuck-

ing *Cheers* music. With us, it's fucking special. We're all completely different.* I'm a sissy, basically. Fieldy's hip-hop, Head and Munky are Head and Munky, and David [Silveria]'s got tits† but he's a great drummer. All we have in common is that we're all freaks, we're all fucked up, and we're all on drugs.

Later that night, Davis plays a track from his new album, then explains . . .

DAVIS: That song's about how I thought I'd become a rock star and not get picked on anymore, but my band still calls me a fag.

I've noticed that.
DAVIS: Everyone thinks I'm queer (*sighs*). And I kind of am—except for the dick part.

At two a.m. the phone rings in my hotel room.

Hello.
DAVIS: Know what I said about us being outsiders? Forget it.

Why's that?
DAVIS: Prodigy walked up to us.

Great.
DAVIS: We were downstairs drinking, and all of them were there. And there was skinny model ass everywhere.

Were the models coming up to you?
DAVIS: No, not at all.

But Prodigy were.
DAVIS: They were like, "What's up, guys?"

Good for you.
DAVIS: I think it's coming around, man. Wanna come upstairs and cuddle?

---

* Korn fun facts learned in Tokyo: Guitarist Munky wet his pants onstage once, Fieldy won't touch stairway handrails because he's afraid of germs, second guitarist Head drinks six-packs of beer alone in his bathtub, and Davis refuses to touch or lick female genitalia.
† Most people would call them pecs.

I'm wiped. Let's talk after the show tomorrow.
DAVIS: Yeah, you're probably right. [My bodyguard] Loc told me I can't do coke tonight because I have to work tomorrow.

[*Continued . . .*]

[THE NEPTUNES]
SCENE 2

Three days later . . .

Thanks for rescheduling this.
PHARRELL: Sure, man.

One thing that sets you apart from other producers is that you don't differentiate between genres—
PHARRELL: Dude, can I tell you something? I really don't give a fuck about different styles. Music is music. In the eighties, that's the way it was. On the big black station here in Virginia—we would listen to 103 Jamz, which I would love for you to print, and that station would play all kinds of shit.

What artists have you been working with lately?
PHARRELL: First, there's Mystikal. I would love to just go to the dustiest part of Georgia—even though he's from St. Louis.* I would love to go to a desperate area, with no people almost, very country, and just record his album in a shack. And then . . . Actually, I'm about to go out now and get some chicken. So can I just call you from the road?

Okay, but make sure you call this time.
PHARRELL: Promise.

[*Continued . . .*]

---

* Actually the rapper is from New Orleans, though the collaboration was postponed when Mystikal was imprisoned the following year for sexual battery of his hairdresser.

CHER
SCENE 1

Sometimes stories collide. For example, you're on the phone with Cher for the *New York Times* while you're at guitarist Dave Navarro's house writing a book with him.

Do you mind talking to Dave Navarro? He's with me right now and wants to say hi before I let you go.

CHER: Sure, I'd love to.

DAVE NAVARRO: How are you?

CHER: I'm good.

NAVARRO: I just couldn't allow this phone call to be made from my house and not get in and say hello.

CHER: Oh, I'm so happy that you did. My son has been a huge fan of yours for such a long time.

NAVARRO: Is that right? I've met him several times.

CHER: Yeah, he was little when you first met him. I mean, well, he's twenty-three now, but he's been a fan of yours from the get-go. He's struggling, but that's good. You need to struggle if you're going to be in music because you're going to struggle sometime one way or another.

NAVARRO: Oh God, yeah, ain't that the truth. But he seems to be doing well.

CHER: Yeah, I think he needs to stay on the straight path. But he's a good boy inside. It comes easy to him because he's really talented, but he doesn't know that it's not enough.

NAVARRO: I know. That was a mistake of mine.

CHER: I hope he gets through it.

NAVARRO: I do, too. I didn't know he was having that hard of a time.

CHER: Yeah, he is, kind of. He's really trying to address it and yet he doesn't. You know how to get anything done, you have to say, "Yeah, it's a fucking problem." He's at that place where he wishes that it wasn't a problem.

NAVARRO: To run to a self-help group at that age can be really traumatic. It's almost worse than what any drug can do to you.

CHER: Yeah, you know, it's in this place where I just don't know which way to turn.

NAVARRO: You can't force him. He's got to do it himself.

CHER: So I'm just laying back but, boy, I'm not a good layer-backer when it comes to my kids, and especially to him.

NAVARRO: I don't think any parent would be. My father wasn't. I lost my mom when I was very young and I was a heroin addict for a lot of years. And my dad, as much as he knew he had to sit still and wait, couldn't stand keeping quiet.

CHER: I just don't want to see my son turn out like his father, because his father was a really great, fabulous, wonderful, funny, special man. And finally the drugs just became him. He wasn't himself. He's been taking them for so long that there's just nothing left of him.

NAVARRO: I've met him a few times, too, when I was trying out those rooms for a while and . . .

CHER: Board those guys up and just move on.

NAVARRO: I know, you kind of have to, huh? There's only so much you can do and—well, I tell you, I appreciate it so much to say hello, and I'm just a great admirer myself so . . .

CHER: Thank you. Have a really good time with your life and your music.

NAVARRO: Thanks very much. I'm really excited. I'm just now doing something by myself and it's the first time I've really been able to do anything like that.

CHER: Great. You know what, maybe when I come home we'll get together.

NAVARRO: I would love that so much.

CHER: Okay, great. Am I going to talk to the boy again that I was just talking to?

NAVARRO: Would you like to? It's up to you.

CHER: Sure, I want to say good-bye.

Hi.

CHER: Hi. He sounds so sweet, doesn't he?

He's very nice.

CHER: Well, I really wish him well, because he sounds really, really good. Boy, you know, I gotta tell you something: If this business doesn't fucking kill you, then you can just come back and hopefully be the best person you're ever going to be, because it's the only business that eats its young.

[*Continued . . .*]

[JOSH CLAYTON-FELT]

The following is a cautionary story that shows just how heartless record labels can be.

It begins in 1996, when Josh Clayton-Felt, who had a couple minor hits with his band School of Fish, submitted his second solo album to A&M Records. The label sent him back to the studio to record more songs, and then sat on the album for eight months, promising to release it soon.

Then, in a surprise announcement, A&M was bought as part of a corporate merger and collapsed into the Universal Music Group. Clayton-Felt was one of some 250 artists dropped in the downsizing afterward. This would have been a relief for him, but the label refused to give Clayton-Felt his music back.

Any progress in getting the rights to your music?
JOSH CLAYTON-FELT: I've spent the last four months saying to them, "I know I was dropped, but can I have the record back? Or can I release it independently myself and give you a percentage of the sales?" But they said that basically the only way they'll release it is if I'm on a major label and the label pays a lot of money to Universal for the record. But I don't want to do that: I just feel like it puts me in a bad place creatively.

What about just re-recording the songs and putting them out yourself?
CLAYTON-FELT: I can't do that, either. What I didn't know is that they own the songs I turned in. So not only are they not willing to give the record back, but they won't let me re-record the songs. According to them, I can't re-record them for five years.

Why do you think they're doing this? It's not like they're making money off the music.
CLAYTON-FELT: I tried to figure out why they want to do this. I think they know the power of the Internet and the artist, and maybe by taking 250 artists and shelving them, they're eliminating the competition.*

So what are you going to do?
CLAYTON-FELT: It's tough. I even went to the point of thinking: What if I changed my name, or had a band instead, or wore a dress and played the songs? But from what I understand, there are probably a hundred artists who have albums shelved because of the merger. My idea is to find these artists and do an album where I can't record my song but Joe or whoever can, and Joe can't record his song but Paul can. We'd each put in our best song and give it to someone else. It would be making a statement about the whole being more important than our individual needs. If this can be turned into something positive, I'd be happy.

---

* Speaking on condition of anonymity, an executive at Universal offered a different reason: "Money's money. We aren't big enough to handle settlements for all these acts." Meaning, presumably, that the label didn't want to pay the attorney fees involved in returning the music to the artists.

I think a lot of artists would just give up and record new songs in your situation.
CLAYTON-FELT: I'm not giving up on these songs. I love them. Maybe the record company will see the article and it will put them more in a place of their heart than their wallet.

Unfortunately, the story didn't sway Universal Music Group. So Clayton-Felt decided to go into the studio and re-record the music anyway. He explained in an e-mail that at least this way he could make the album he always wanted without executive meddling, and maybe Universal would allow him to release it before the five years were up.

He finished recording on December tenth, 1999—almost four years after he turned the original album in—and told friends that it was now, finally, perfect. But then something unexpected happened: The following day, he developed severe back pain, which he thought was due to stress. When he went to a hospital to have it looked into, he was told he had testicular cancer.

When Universal heard about his illness in early January, the label finally gave him and his family control of the record. But it was too late: By then, Clayton-Felt was in a coma. At 4:45 in the morning of January nineteenth, he passed away at the age of thirty-two.

But death was not the end of the story of Clayton-Felt's music.

LAURA CLAYTON BAKER [his sister]: We worked on getting the record out for two years. There were just constantly frustrations: waiting for the paperwork, waiting for photographs, getting the artwork done, scheduling. Everything seemed to take so long because he wasn't there to help make the decisions.

STEVEN BAKER [his brother-in-law and president of DreamWorks Records]: A lot of people at DreamWorks came through and listened to the songs and liked them, and have had a great love and respect for the record. So I was able to get the label to put it out. The deal with DreamWorks is that they're pressing and distributing the record, and our family is paying for marketing and publicity.

Several former employees of A&M who used to work with Clayton-Felt volunteered to do the marketing and publicity for free. In the meantime, his mother coordinated a network of fans in different cities to help with local promotion.

MARILYN CLAYTON-FELT [his mother]: He said that his work wasn't finished here, so I tried to finish it. Well, finish is too final. I tried to bring it to the world.

BACKSTREET BOYS
SCENE 1

The Backstreet Boys have sold more than seventy-five million albums around the world, a number that few pop acts have surpassed. In their prime, they were a pop juggernaut, breathing new life into MTV, the record business, children's radio, and teen magazines.

But along the way, a very similar band with the same management company and the same songwriting and production team surpassed them in popularity: 'N Sync. As 'N Sync's star rose, the Backstreet Boys seemed to disappear. After much coaxing, Kevin Richardson, the oldest member of the band, agreed to sit down and discuss life behind the scenes as a pop phenomenon—and what happens when five young men put to work as pop puppets grow up and develop minds of their own.

There's a lot of pressure on you for this next record. Do you feel it's a make-it-or-break-it moment?

KEVIN RICHARDSON: Yeah, I feel like it's a very crucial record in our career. In April, we just had our nine-year anniversary. In nine years, we've had five albums, including the greatest hits album. So I just want to put out something I'm proud of, and happy and excited about. The last record, and I'm not whining or complaining or blaming anyone because it sold a lot of copies, but for me personally, creatively, I wasn't happy with it.

Why not?

RICHARDSON: I wanted to experiment more. I felt like we should have.

Experiment in what way?

RICHARDSON: Just working with different people—exploring, taking chances, taking control, and trusting in *our* gut. But, you know, it's not always easy. There was all this pressure and fear from our label and our management company at the time. And I'm like, "Guys, we've got millions of fans all over the world. If we make great music, that's all that matters."

So tell me one of your ideas they wouldn't use.

RICHARDSON: You know, we've thrown all kinds of ideas around. We thought about having an album that was about different styles and flavors of pop. Like almost a compilation, but it would be all us doing the music and a picture of like a lollipop on the front with the words, "Suck on this."

[*Continued . . .*]

[BILLY JOEL]

Backstage at a Person of the Year dinner produced by the organization that runs the Grammys, Billy Joel sat in a large armchair, sweating after his speech under the hot lights of the stage. His acceptance speech began with him saying that Sting, who was trying to save the "fricking rainforests," was probably more worthy of the award. He spent the remainder of the speech addressing an important issue pertaining to artists of his caliber: asking industry members in the audience to set him up on a date with Nicole Kidman.

Is your record company upset that you haven't recorded anything new in so long?

BILLY JOEL: I'm an artist who hasn't handed in an album since 1993, and my record contract says I'm supposed to hand in albums. Now you can't get blood from a stone, and the record company understands that. I think people have all these assumptions about what kind of power a record company has over an artist. I never had a bad relationship with Columbia Records. I was fortunate enough to have come up in the early seventies, when there was freeform radio and I had album cuts played and I wore whatever dopey clothes I wore and I had bad hair and the whole thing.

But you were taken advantage of a lot back then, too.

JOEL: I have to audit my record companies all the time. I've had managers who've taken me to the cleaners. I've been fleeced numerous times. There are certain promoters who were less than aboveboard. I was with a guy named Artie Ripp who was taking a piece of the action from me for twenty years, and that's not right. I think it's time for artists to climb out of the ivory tower, to stop living in a dream world, and to come buy groceries with everybody else and find out how the rest of the world lives.

In the sense of getting involved with the business side of things?

JOEL: It's a job. And if you don't see it as a job, then you're kidding yourself. There's a lot of work that goes on underneath the surface of this tip of the iceberg called the star. Most of it is promotion, marketing, politics, business, legal, and accounting. It's the music business. It's a business, not the Boy Scouts.

Some people would respond that artists should just focus on making music.
JOEL: I, for a long time, did not want to face up to the fact that there was capitalism involved in music. I thought that prostituted the art. "Oh my God, there's money. I'm not doing this for money. I'm doing this for the art." Well, I found out there are a lot of other people perfectly willing to take that money.

[WU-TANG CLAN
SCENE 1]

I first met the Wu-Tang Clan in a loft in the Meatpacking District of Manhattan, where the rappers were watching a rough cut of a new video and reading books like *The Mind* and *The Prophet*. The RZA, the group's producer and mastermind, pulled me into a garbage-strewn stairwell so we could talk in private—and so he could smoke a hand-rolled cigarette. Maybe it was laced with hash; maybe it was laced with PCP; maybe it was laced with both; or maybe it was just tobacco. We will never know.

The conversation began with an in-depth analysis of his cryptic lyrics . . .

How about the [lyric], "I stand close to walls, like number four the lizard"?
RZA: That's only for the hardcore fan, right there. There's a movie called the *Five Deadly Venoms*. You ever heard of it?

Is Woody Allen in it?
RZA: No.

Then I haven't heard of it.
RZA: It's phat. You should see it. So there's five deadly venoms in it, and number four is the lizard. And they talk about how he climbs walls. That's my style, staying close to walls.

In "Bells of War," you say, "Illegible, every egg ain't edible." And then later, "Got to catch this paper to buy Shaquasia a glacier / Melchizedek a skyscraper."
RZA: You can take every egg ain't edible in a lot of different ways: from the female, from the biblical, from the idea that everything that you see ain't good for you. That's like universal knowledge. The other lyrics are about my children. See, I got to make this money to buy her a whole glacier. I want to buy my son a whole skyscraper. I gotta make a buck.

You have two kids?
RZA: I don't even know how many babies I got.

You must know. Wouldn't all their mothers be hitting you up for money?
RZA: That's what the money I make is for anyway. I don't like to talk about babies. Say if I've got five babies with five women, I'm working for them. I'm not working for me. [. . .]

Did you make any money by adding America Online software to the interactive CD that comes with *Wu-Tang Forever*?
RZA: I didn't make no money from that. I don't know who did, but I didn't.

So what is—
RZA: Hold on, do you think there's money to be made from that?

I think if America Online is going to be making money by getting new subscribers from people who bought the Wu-Tang CD, then you should get something.
RZA: I didn't go that deep into it. That's good information. I'll investigate that.

So what's your ultimate plan? Where are you trying to get to with your music now?
RZA: I might be backing out of it. My little brother's making tracks now. And there's about twenty-one mothers trying to make my beats, so I don't got to make beats no more.

What would you do?
RZA: When I complete this, I'm going to be a doctor. That's my love right there, my lifetime goal. I've got a few stumbling blocks I've got to overcome. But I'm going to make something special for the planet. It's going to be something that's going to remain. There are 109 elements—everything you see is composed of them. I'm going to put some of that shit together. I'm studying it all—mental, physical, chemical. I'm studying the body, circulation, tai chi, all that.

What's your specialty going to be?
RZA: My specialty's going to be peace. I'm going to do it, man.

[*Continued . . .*]

[CURTIS MAYFIELD]

Curtis Mayfield is responsible for some of the most seminal soul, funk, and inspirational music of all time, from his anthem with the Impressions "People Get Ready" to the theme from *Superfly* to the samples that have fueled over a hundred R&B and hip-hop songs. But in 1990, while preparing for a concert in Brooklyn, Mayfield was struck by a falling lighting scaffold that paralyzed him from the neck down.

In your music, you sing about peace and how there are better years coming. Now, when you hear those songs twenty-five years later, do you feel peace and better years have come?
CURTIS MAYFIELD: Well, I believe never lose hope. Never lose faith in your dreams. In spite of this world, there is still a whole lotta good people in it—and I must believe that. So I'll never give up and just lose total hope for mankind itself. And I'm a rather pessimistic fellow (*laughs*). But I'm optimistic about people and I must be. I mean, especially in my shape today. If it weren't for a lot of good, good people about, I'd be in *bad* shape. So just keep the faith. That's what [congressman] Adam Clayton Powell used to say.

I suppose some things have gotten better and other things have gotten worse. I guess that's how it always works.
MAYFIELD: Ain't that life? But somehow we still manage and somehow, if you look for it, you can still live for happiness. It might be a little harder trying to achieve, but you don't give up, you know. Can't give up to these losers, man. In spite of these people that drag you down and create crime and hardship, you gotta believe that people are better than that.

Has the accident changed any of your ideas about life or what we're supposed to do with the time we're given?
MAYFIELD: Well, no, nothing's changed too much. I'm the same person. I just happen to be paralyzed. Of course, you have to deal with the complications of being in this particular order, but I still carry my spirits as high as I can. If anything, after the accident and seeing beautiful people of all colors, races, and creeds come to my aid and having their love, respect, and especially prayers, I must believe in mankind even more.

Are you still able to perform?
MAYFIELD: Oh, I have no plans of performing again. Being a quadriplegic, it will be just a little too testy. It's really always a life-and-death situation—almost every minute of the day. Then there's the cost of just getting me around. You know, when I get up and go anywhere, it can cost me from ten to twenty thousand dollars between making travel arrangements, taking along a nurse, getting baths, and all the other stuff I need just to survive. So performing is out of the question.

On one hand, it's been great to see your music celebrated with three new compilations and two tribute records, but on the other hand, do you kind of wish that people were doing it anyway before the accident?
MAYFIELD: A lot of people say that I didn't get the credit I deserved in my day, but I was never overly saturated with success either. I may not have been making music in these times where they're making twenty million dollars a year, but somehow I managed to survive. I raised all my children and I'm living a decent life. I'm a great believer in the saying, "It may not come when you want it to, but it's right on time."

What do you think is the most important thing you've taught your children?
MAYFIELD: Live by example.

Shortly after this interview, Mayfield's right leg was amputated because of complications from diabetes, which developed due to the injury. He died a year later at the North Fulton Regional Hospital in Roswell, Georgia. He was fifty-seven years old.

[BACKSTREET BOYS
SCENE 2]

Tell me if you agree with this: You're human beings who some people just see as cash cows, right?
KEVIN RICHARDSON: Mm-hmm.

And because of that, the corporations that release your music are so worried about their bottom line that they're not always going to do what's best for the group.
RICHARDSON: I mean, when you have the level of success that we've had, there are a lot of expectations and responsibilities that are put on you. And with all of the business coming in, it blocks the artistry.

So maybe [your second management company] the Firm was the right place when you started there, but—

RICHARDSON: When *Millennium* came out, they were the right place. We were all so depressed and so sad and so tired of fighting everybody. We were dealing with lawsuits and fighting our original management company—and the managers locking our production equipment up, our stage, everything.

They locked up your equipment?

RICHARDSON: Yeah, our past manager. We were trying to get out of management contracts. We gave them an ultimatum and we had attorneys give them notice. And they locked our production equipment and stage and everything up and said, "You guys are supposed to do a tour, but you're not getting your equipment."

And you wanted to leave the contract because—

RICHARDSON: Our contracts were just exploiting us. We were being taken advantage of. And there's the fact that they were managing us and then they signed 'N Sync, and we thought it was a conflict of interest.* Again, we have nothing against the guys in 'N Sync. They're talented and we respect them, but they were directing them to work with all the writers and producers that we worked with. And they were using them against us, saying, "Oh, if you guys don't do this gig, we'll just book 'N Sync."

I talked to your former manager, and he said that Disney had wanted to broadcast a Backstreet Boys concert special, but you guys turned it down and so he gave it to 'N Sync instead. And that special is what really started their career. Is that valid?

RICHARDSON: Yeah, we passed on that show because we wanted to spend time with our families at Christmas. It was either Thanksgiving or Christmas and we just came off the road in Europe, and that opened the door for them. But they worked hard. They deserved it. Everybody wants to pit us against each other. Everybody wants to say that—not everybody, but a lot of people say, "Oh, they took the crown," or whatever. Like there was a crown.

So how did you get your equipment and stage back from your old manager?

RICHARDSON: We basically settled. We left them and the Firm rescued us. I'm grateful for that. At that time, they had Korn and Limp Bizkit, and they were a

---

* Lou Pearlman, the Florida aviation entrepreneur who created both bands, responded: "The Backstreet Boys got so big, they got tired. And after a while, it became not about managing them but reasoning with them."

smaller company. But now they've built a huge powerful company and they're good people. Please make sure you reflect that in the interview. I don't want to bag on them, but this past year, some bad decisions were made and some bad advice was given.

Like when your tour was sold to Clear Channel* for a hundred million dollars—
RICHARDSON: Big mistake.

Big mistake?
RICHARDSON: We lost control of our ticket prices. Big mistake. We alienated some of our fans who couldn't afford to come to the show. Big mistake.

So why did you do it?
RICHARDSON: When people were throwing that big number on the table, it was tempting. But we asked questions. We asked about ticket sales. We asked about the control aspect. And we were told not to worry. And it hurt us. We lost control— and we were advised to do that.

So what were the pros of doing that?
RICHARDSON: The pros of doing that was a hundred million dollar paycheck.

That's a good pro.
RICHARDSON: I'm gonna tell you what happened. We made a deal with Clear Channel for a hundred million, right? We put a production together to play in arenas and then expand to go into stadiums. We spent that money—a *lot* of money. Well, then the economy dipped. And also, to be honest, when our managers and we saw the 'N Sync ticket sales not doing very well in stadiums—which, by the way, 'N Sync put their tickets on sale purposely right before ours, which is—

Which is capitalism.
RICHARDSON: Well, the thing about this I want to make clear is that we have nothing against those guys. We respect them. They're very talented and they work their asses off.

I'm sure it wasn't the band's decision.
RICHARDSON: I mean, they hadn't even put out a single yet. And the purpose was to beat us to the punch, which is fair game. It's tactical. But once we saw their

---

* Clear Channel Entertainment was a concert promotion company that bought the rights to the entire Backstreet Boys tour.

tickets weren't selling very well and then the economy took a big hit, we were like, "You know what? We shouldn't play stadiums." I'd rather not play a sixty-thousand-seat stadium with thirty thousand people in it. So we all took a hit there. When the tickets don't sell, somebody's gonna have to cough it up.

Do you know who coughed it up? The House of Blues did, because the Firm talked them into giving the Mary J. Blige tour to Clear Channel to compensate for the money they lost on your tour.* Did you know that?
RICHARDSON: No, I didn't. That's . . . that's . . . wow.

But in the end, you were the third top grossing tour of last year, so I still think it was—
RICHARDSON: No, it wasn't safe. It wasn't safe. And that's one of the reasons we're not with the Firm now.

Hang on, I got to go to the restroom.

[*Continued . . .*]

===== **[JOHNNY STAATS]** =====

In order to interview one of country music's greatest mandolinists, Johnny Staats, I needed to get permission from his manager—not his music manager, but the manager of the UPS shipping facility where he worked as a driver. Even though Staats had recently signed a major-label record deal through Time Warner—an extremely rare feat for a bluegrass picker—he decided not to give up his day job in West Virginia. So his boss gave me permission to ride along in uniform with Staats as he ran his UPS rounds on a cold, snowy afternoon.

"I'd sure hate to lose him as a driver," said Doug Adams, Staats's supervisor. "But I don't know why a man with those talents continues working here. I guess it's the security."

So what are you going to do if your record company wants you to tour?
JOHNNY STAATS: I've saved up all my vacation days for concerts, but I reckon I can't tour. I have a wife and two kids, so I'm kind of stuck between a rock and a hard place. This job is real good money and the music business is shaky. One minute you're living on steak; the next minute you're living on beans.

---

* Mary J. Blige was one of the Firm's other management clients. And the House of Blues and Clear Channel Entertainment were rival concert promoters.

Have you ever thought of moving to Nashville to help your career?
STAATS: If I moved to Nashville, I'd have to leave the country life. I'm just an old country boy: I love to pick and hunt coons. (*He pulls up to a dilapidated red house and inspects it.*) These kind of calls right here are where you have to watch out for Fido. If there's pee on the porch, that's a warning sign for me.

He leaves a package behind a shovel on the porch, then walks briskly along the icy path back to his truck.

How long do you work each day?
STAATS: On a normal day, I work ten to eleven hours. I worked part-time at first for UPS, and the way I made extra money was in music contests. I learned to play everything I could find: mandolin, fiddle, guitar. At Vandalia, I came in first on guitar, first in mandolin, and third in fiddle.* That was a good payday. I made twelve hundred dollars just in contest money. I was the West Virginia mandolin champion three times. It would've been four consecutive years, but I had to work one year and couldn't get off.

How often do you practice?
STAATS: I used to practice a lot. In high school, the only thing I wanted to do was to play music. I'd practice seven to eight hours a day. I wasn't interested in football, basketball, nothing. I've played so long before I've seen blood come out from under my fingernails, seeping out the end of it (*sighs*). I miss having all that time to practice now.

Many a day, I'll take my mandolin with me, park the UPS truck in an old holler, and spend my lunch hour practicing. I've had people come up and knock on the door of the truck, wondering what that music was coming from inside.

He pulls up at an insurance office and walks inside to deliver a package.

Do you have any musical influences outside of bluegrass?
STAATS: Do you like classical? I listen to Mozart and Beethoven. Them's what I call geniuses. Mozart would play four songs in one composition. That's how I win the contests: I'll play a bunch of different songs and styles, just to show them I can do anything.

---

* The Vandalia Gathering, West Virginia's annual heritage festival, was where Staats was discovered by Ron Sowell, musical director for Mountain Stage, a live concert broadcast on National Public Radio. "I pride myself on knowing the West Virginia scene, and I'd never heard of Johnny Staats before," Sowell recalled. "It was like he materialized. He played as fast as any human can play mandolin, but every note was articulated and under control."

He flirts with the secretary, hands her a package, then returns to the truck.

What would you do if you made enough money off your new album to live on?
STAATS: I don't even know how I'd react if I ever made enough money as a musician to leave this job, because I'm so used to going to work. Boom! It would be a weird way of life when you're not told to be here or deliver this package. The music business isn't the real world.

(*He displays the palms of his hands. They are caked black with dirt.*) This right here is the real world. I've washed them three times today and the dirt still won't come off.

True to his word, Staats kept his job and didn't tour when his CD came out, though he did open a concert for the Dave Matthews Band. When I checked in with him a year later, he was working on his second CD during lunch breaks and after work, and preparing to perform with the West Virginia Symphony Orchestra. He was eventually dropped from the major label that signed him.

[JONI MITCHELL]

Joni Mitchell has been called the most influential female singer-songwriter of the twentieth century and has received just about every award a musician can, including at least nine Grammys and her face on a postage stamp. When the rest of the *New York Times* pop music critics and I selected the twenty-five most significant albums of the twentieth century, Mitchell's *Blue* was on that list. Those who saw her perform in the late sixties and early seventies were awestruck, describing her as unearthly and angelic. So while spending three days talking with her over games of pool in Hollywood and meals in Brentwood, I was surprised to discover that gratitude and humility were not among her strong points.

Here's what she had to say about . . .

. . . her songwriting.
I mean, there's layers and layers to this song. The lyrics have a lot of symbolic depth, like the Bible.

. . . producing.
I don't like the title producer. Mozart didn't have one.

"For those with the highest standards."

12-Pc.
Solo Dining Set

"HEJIRA" Design — Pressed glass, brilliant finish,
floral and medallion pattern, one set in carton, 30 lbs.

1 cup	1 sugar bowl
1 saucer	1 salt shaker
1 bread & butter plate	1 pepper shaker
1 dinner plate	1 vegetable dish, $9^{1/2}$ in.
1 footed tumbler	1 platter, $11^{3/4}$ in.
1 cream pitcher	1 covered casserole, 9 in.

34C-3577 - White . . . . } Set
34C-3579 - Blue. . . . . } $5.⁵⁰

. . . her most famous song, "Big Yellow Taxi."
It's a nursery rhyme. Of all the creations that are there, if you reduce it to this thing, it's a tragedy.

. . . her record company.
The record company has sat on this album, but sitting on me a little bit is not a bad idea, just to make it more timely. Because sometimes I'm too far ahead and people aren't ready for it yet.

. . . being an opening act.
Bob Dylan is the only artist I open to. Period. Or Miles [Davis]. But Miles is gone.

. . . gender.
One guy came up to me and said, "You're the best female singer-songwriter in the world." This was some years ago, and I laughed. He thought I was being modest. But I was thinking, "What do you mean *female*? That's like saying, 'You're the best Negro.' "

. . . astrology.
My daughter is a Pisces. She's the day of the explorer. I'm the day of the discoverer. She's a natural follower. I'm a natural leader. I can't help it. The stars put me there.

. . . her Grammy, *Billboard*, and Rock and Roll Hall of Fame awards.
Dubious honors. They knew that they had to do it, but they—at least the speechmakers—weren't quite sure what to illuminate in the work.

. . . charity.
After *Billboard* honored me, all of a sudden VH1, who wouldn't play my videos, decided to honor me, which means they get a free concert out of me. Then they hand me a check for my favorite charity, they take it away, and they get the tax write-off. So I refused to do it.

. . . a two-year-old article on her in the *New York Times*.
The guy was a bad observer, even down to what I was wearing. There were seven errors of observation in the piece.

. . . all of the above.
You think I got a trap mind or something? I guess I do. Yeah, I'm sensitive (*pauses*). I'm not a pitiable creature. It's just that I suffer very eloquently.

[JAY LENO]

Shortly before what was supposed to be his last performance on *The Tonight Show* before handing the reins to the younger Conan O'Brien, Jay Leno, wearing an over-washed blue button-down shirt and faded jeans, sat down in the show's green room to discuss leaving behind his legacy of 3,756 shows. Here are some choice excerpts.

Has there ever been a time where you showed up at the studio and you just didn't want to do the show?
JAY LENO: I would like to say yes, but I have to say no. I mean, that's what the job is. I'm a great believer in low self-esteem. The only people that have high self-esteem are criminals and actors.

I remember interviewing Joni Mitchell, and everyone was giving her all these awards and she was so ungrateful.
LENO: I love it when stars go, "Two hundred and fifty thousand dollars a week? I'm not working for that!" A million a month and you're insulted—really? You don't think you can be replaced?

I can't say I ever get like that. It always makes me laugh when people say, "Oh, Jay was exhausted." [Comedian] Alan King always used to say that exhaustion is a rich man's disease. You know, if a coal miner says to his boss, "I'm exhausted," the boss goes, "Get back to work!"

Do you ever have a distaste for someone you're talking to, and you have to keep it in check while interviewing that person?
LENO: Well, yeah, that happens a lot. You know, it's not a bully pulpit—I mean, with the exception of O.J. and those kinds of guests. But then there are guests who you don't agree with politically, but you figure, let's have them on. I remember I had Ann Coulter on the show. In my mind, because of the nature of what I do, I thought, "Well, she's a biting satirist. This is sharp commentary that I don't agree with, but I can see the wit in it." And then when she was here, I walked out to do the warm up and I saw this kind of white-shirt-red-tie brigade in the audience. And everything she said, they hooted and cheered to the point where it was distracting. I thought to

myself, "Well, maybe she really does believe all this crap." I didn't handle that one well.*

------◆◆◆------

A lot of people say that the secret to succeeding in show business is just showing up on time.
LENO: In show business, if you can physically make it to the stage for seven years, you'll always work. Most people can't do that. It's cocaine, you're too straight, you're too gay, you're too whatever. I see a lot of comics after five or six years honing an act, they begin to hate it and they resent the audience laughing at them. Nobody was funnier than Sam Kinison with that high-energy scream. But it got to the point where it's cocaine and guns, and now you're going 120 miles an hour in the street and—Boom! Boom!—he didn't make it to seven years. If you can make it through the seven, you're okay.

When it was decided five years ago that Conan O'Brien would take over the show, was it weird for you to know you were going to be replaced?
LENO: You know, taking over these shows is like tsarist Russia. There's too much bloodshed and anger. So I said, "Look, this is fine. Let's see what happens." Because back then, I thought, "Pssh, five years—that'll never come!" But when it happened, I still liked doing this. And ABC and Fox and everybody else seemed interested.

Why didn't you consider going elsewhere?
LENO: You know, showbiz is not that hard. People make it extremely difficult. The problem starts when you have to have all the money. I don't need all the money. It's just my wife and me. I don't have an agent. I don't have a manager. I've said this a million times and it's cliché, but I've never touched a dime of TV money. I put it in the bank and live off the money I make as a stand-up comedian.

If you had an agent, he would have told you, "Let's try to get a counter-offer and start a bidding war."
LENO: Yeah, it's stupid. My thing is, if I always make a couple bucks less than whoever the highest-paid guy is, then you're fine. You can't eat the whole pie. If you

---

* Branford Marsalis, who used to lead Leno's on-air band, felt even stronger about some of the musical acts he had to tolerate: "I haven't heard anything new that I've liked on the show. A lot of the bands we play with are just bad, especially those alternative rock bands. They can do it in the studio, but they can't play live . . . I see the audience applauding while they're playing, and I wonder if it's just because they're fans of the band and don't care, or out of spite. Because it certainly isn't because they sound good."

eat all the pie, you'll get fat, choke, and die. If you eat as much as you want and then give someone else some pie, then you have all these friends who are thrilled because you gave them a little piece of pie. It's not that hard.

———◆————

To what extent do you think your modesty and longevity are a result of the way you were raised?
LENO: My family was extremely stable. I had great parents. I wasn't one of those drunk-father or whore-mother deals. I had a wonderful childhood, and I never had any problems.

If I had anything, it was a sense that my mother came to this country when she was eleven. My grandmother had run off with a younger man, and my grandfather had too many kids and couldn't afford them. So my mother came to America to live with her sister, and always had a sadness that permeated her. Her natural inclination was not to be laughing. So when I was a child, I always felt I had to cheer my mom up somehow. To get even a laugh out of my mother was seen as a huge thing.

———◆————

What do you think you're going to miss most about *The Tonight Show*?
LENO: I don't know. I'm a creature of habit and I like doing the same thing every day. I won't really know until it's gone.

Is there anything you're wistful about? Like, "This is the last time I'll be on this stage" or—
LENO: No. I mean, I enjoy it and I love the people and it's fine. But what happens the day we leave? A truck comes through here and knocks all this down and it ceases to exist on any level anywhere. It's gone. So you can't grow that attached to it. The first thing about show business is, you don't fall in love with a hooker.

Evidently, Leno fell in love with the hooker: Nine months later, when both Leno's new program and The Tonight Show *failed to deliver strong ratings, Conan O'Brien was given thirty-three million dollars to step down and allow Leno to return to the show.*

[THE GAME]
SCENE 1

The Game didn't want to take his shirt off.

Though the rapper had no problem posing with his muscles flexed and tattooed torso exposed for the cover of his number one debut album, *The Documentary*, he didn't want to go shirtless for his *Rolling Stone* photo shoot. He refused to pose in a tank top as well.

After a few minutes of photos in a black beanie, faded blue jeans, and a baggy white T-shirt that bulged on the right side in the outline of a pistol grip—perhaps the quickest shoot in *Rolling Stone* history—Game jumped into his black Range Rover and pulled out of the West Hollywood studio, followed by the rest of his entourage in matching Range Rovers.

Why didn't you want to pose without a shirt?
GAME: I got the number one album in the country, so I can do what I want. I don't have to let myself get pushed around by anybody (*nods head and smiles*). I'm platinum, man. I'm already a millionaire, and I haven't even gotten a rap check yet. That's just off my mix tapes and my endorsements.

And soon you're going to get royalty checks.
GAME: Fuck those checks. I don't even need those checks, man. I'm not looking to make the bulk of my estate from rap. I'm looking at investments, endorsements, movies. Movies is really where I want to end up. The Ice Cube money has to be good.*

So do you see yourself as an artist or a businessman?
GAME: I'm a businessman. At the end of the day, I'm a young black entrepreneur, man. Rap is my tree stump. Then you got all these branches: You got the Nike deal, you got the Vitaminwater deal, you got the Boost Mobile deal, you got the movie shit. I mean, even my son's everywhere: He's about to do a Sean Jean deal and he's got Huggies calling.

He slams on his car brakes and screeches around the corner of Melrose and Spaulding.

---

* Ice Cube on directing: "The money restraints are the only thing that made me feel like I was over my head because we did not have enough money to shoot a lot of scenes I wanted in the picture. If I had two million more dollars, the movie would be shot better."

So where are we going now?
GAME: To the car wash. This is the best place in LA to get your car washed. And it's only seven bucks.

[*Continued...*]

THE NEPTUNES
SCENE 3

Two days later...

PHARRELL: Hey, it's Pharrell. Sorry it took me so long (*phone crackles*)... Yeah, go ahead, man.

So I'll make this quick. I just wanted to—
PHARRELL: Uh-huh (*crackling*). Hold on one second... Ben, dial 438-7897 and tell her I'm on my way over there... Okay, dude, can I call you right back? I promise I'll call you right back. I want to do this story.

[*Continued...*]

LOVE

Led by one of the few African-American psychedelic rock singers of the sixties, Los Angeles band Love released one of the genre's greatest albums, *Forever Changes*, a beautifully orchestrated masterpiece shot through with surreal lyrics. Plagued by drug abuse, arrests, and madness, the band just barely survived the era. The following is from a telephone interview with reclusive Love leader Arthur Lee.

What's your favorite backstage story?
ARTHUR LEE: I was backstage, having to listen to Janis Joplin sing. The Grateful Dead was opening for us. I was wearing triangular glasses, and Pigpen* came back to the dressing room saying, "You know what they say about people with triangular glasses? They have triangular minds." I sort of nodded, but then, when I was talking to the rest of the band, I realized what he meant. If I had realized it right away, I would have broken both of his legs.

---

* Former Grateful Dead member who died of a gastrointestinal hemorrhage at age twenty-seven.

What did he mean?
LEE: You know.

I don't think I do.
LEE: (*Silence.*)

So what are your plans for your new record?
LEE: When I wake up in the morning, I want to see me rise on the horizon. That's how big I want to be.

That's pretty big.
LEE: Yeah, pop music needs a king and I'm it.

One of my favorite lyrics of yours is, "Oh, the snot has caked against my pants / It has turned into crystal." A friend of mine heard it once and said, "Whatever drugs he's on, I want to be on."
LEE: What? There wasn't any drugs involved.

He was saying it metaphorically, as a compliment.
LEE: No drugs! (*Click.*)

Hangs up.

Shortly after this interview, Lee was imprisoned for firearm possession. He was released five-and-a-half years later. In 2006, he died at age sixty-one due to complications from leukemia.

$$\boxed{\begin{array}{c} \textbf{THE GAME} \\ SCENE\ 2 \end{array}}$$

The Game's arrival at the car wash caused something of a commotion. Teenagers pulled his CD cover out of their cars to get autographs; a friend of Game's showed off his new seventy-thousand-dollar Mercedes-Benz; and a music manager ushered Game into his SUV to hear unreleased tracks by a rapper named Smitty. As he got out of the SUV, Game boasted to the manager . . .

GAME: I met with [film producer] Joel Silver. He wants to sign me for like five movies. He wants to make me the next DMX (*pauses*), but without the crack.

Have you acted before?

GAME: I'm just multifaceted. I got a great personality, so I could do that. You can tell doing the interview that I can pretty much do whatever. If they tell me to act like I'm crying, I'll act like I'm crying. It's no big deal. I'm not shy at all. (*Waves at a friend walking past.*) That's Steve, one of my white homies. I got white homies, too.

I've noticed that with everything you do, you have this drive to be successful no matter what it takes.

GAME: Pretty much. I give a hundred percent to anything that I do, whether it be selling crack or fucking in the booth with Dr. Dre.

How did you start selling crack?

GAME: I didn't sell crack because I wanted to fuck anybody's life up. My mom will tell you that she doesn't regret the things I used to do for money, because I did what I had to do to feed my family. And as a man, we all should, no matter what it is.

But if you got busted, then you wouldn't have been able to feed anyone.

GAME: Yeah, that's one way of thinking about it. I mean, me selling crack on the corner in Compton didn't contribute to the crack epidemic in America. Take me off the corner and put me in college playing basketball, and there would be another guy on that corner selling crack. I had to do what I had to do to survive. Anybody would do it. And the people that don't are the people with no willpower, and we see them with signs when we're getting off the freeway.

What was the first money you ever made?

GAME: The first money I ever made was probably not made. It was probably stolen.

From who?

GAME: From my grandmother, man, or my mom or something. I was a real asshole to my parents and my mother and my grandmother, and I've spent the last three years making up for it. My mom is happy now. She's got a cameo in the new video.

Is there any parallel between the way you got to the top as a rapper and as a crack dealer?

GAME: I got successful dealing crack just by having the best supply, man. A lot of people, they don't know how to cook crack. You gotta do it right. And even though the financial reward isn't great in the beginning, it's about having longevity, you know what I'm saying. Everybody's going to come to where the good shit is. The good car wash is on Melrose: Everybody comes from far and near to the great car wash. The problems come when you're trying to make money fast and not making good product.

Did other dealers try to take you out?
GAME: Yeah, that happened. I got shot. Well, I don't know if that's why they shot me. I didn't get to ask them before they left. I really think that had a lot to do with it though, man. And it worked. They got me out of the building.* But, hey, I'm rich now, so who cares?

Is there anything you could have done differently that night to prevent it from happening?
GAME: Yeah, I could have not opened the door at all, which was my first instinct because when dealing drugs, you have to have an order of operations and you have to have rules. One of the rules was not to deal drugs after twelve a.m., and it was almost two in the morning. I was greedy, man. I opened the door, and in came the infiltrators. They were like the Decepticons.† It was like me against them and I was outnumbered. But I lived through it, man. I can honestly say that I wouldn't wish that on anybody, man. Bullets aren't the best feeling in your stomach.

Do you ever worry about getting shot like Billboard?‡
GAME: I'm not a pussy, man. I know that death is coming. It's not something I'm scared of or running from. It's gonna happen. So it's me against time right now. I'm fighting time to get all this shit done before my time is up.

How do you feel then about the times you've been on the other end of the gun?
GAME: I did drive-bys with my brother Fase. And we did gangbanging for a long time. But I also went to school and made straight As and got a scholarship to a legit top ten college. I don't have any regrets to this date about things that I have done, good or bad, because I never did anything to anybody who didn't impose threat or harm on my life or my family members. I kind of felt like the people I did things to deserved it, because I've never started any wars.

---

* In 2001, three men entered the apartment complex where Game sold drugs in Bellflower (near Compton), shot him five times, and left with his money and drugs. After he woke up from a three-day coma, Game decided to find a safer way to make money, so he started learning about rap—and real estate.
† The villainous alien robots in *The Transformers*.
‡ Game's best friend, sidekick, and rapper, who was shot by a rival gang member.

But you've finished them?
GAME: I've finished quite a few of them, man.

I noticed that you were strapped.
GAME: I'll be strapped for the rest of my life. It's just my comfort level. I'd rather spend money on lawyers and fight a case than be dead in a coffin fighting nothing.

[*Continued . . .*]

[MUSIC LAWYERS]

One of the more unpleasant duties of being a journalist is dealing with attorneys. To call them liars would be libelous, so it may be best to let one's words speak for themselves.

You were going to give me an accurate account of—
LAWYER: I was going to run through this with you.

Right.
LAWYER: The first accounts, particularly the ones on TV, had the following statements in it: One, she had overdosed on heroin and, two, she was rushed to the hospital and was under the influence of heroin. Both of those are absolutely false. First of all, she did not overdose on anything and was not treated in the hospital for an overdose.

So why was she in the hospital?
LAWYER: She had an allergic reaction.

To?
LAWYER: To, uh, er . . . I'll think of it in a minute, but . . . I'll think of it before we get through. But she had an allergic reaction . . .

So where did the overdose information come from?
LAWYER: I don't know. I can't, uh . . . I can't be responsible for inaccurate press reporting, you know, as to where or how . . .

I was just wondering if you had any idea who would have—
LAWYER: Yeah, irresponsible people in the media! Um, hold on one second. I'll get you the name of that thing or I'll keep thinking about it (*sounds of movement and*

rustling papers). Xanax. It's some kind of prescription drug. I shouldn't even say drug. It's a prescription *medication* that you take to deal with depression.

I don't think it's an antidepressant.
LAWYER: Well, that's a little harsh. That kind of sounds like Prozac or something. It's a medication a doctor gives to you. It's a mild version of Valium. Something like that. But it's hardly . . . It's not something that's abused.* It's not something that is some kind of drug, which you get high off of.

I guess it wasn't something she had been taking previously if she had an allergic reaction to it.
LAWYER: Whether she was or wasn't, I don't know, but, uh . . . In other words, I don't think this or anything else opens up her entire past medical history. She had an allergic reaction to it.

And what about the heroin?
LAWYER: She wasn't under the influence of heroin. She didn't overdose. I spent two hours with her at the police station and was with her for two hours afterward. I have been practicing criminal law for twenty-five years and have seen people under the influence of all kinds of substances, and she was absolutely sober. In fact, she was not booked for being under the influence.

What was she booked for?
LAWYER: She was booked for four things. One, felony possession of narcotics. Two, felony possession for receiving stolen property.

What was the stolen property?
LAWYER: The charge was about a prescription pad that was found in her hotel suite. The simple answer is that we've interviewed her doctor and the doctor left it there when he was visiting her. So it's not stolen property. There were no prescriptions written on it. It's the business of the police to investigate it, but I'm confident that's going no place.

And what were the other two charges?
LAWYER: Another charge was possession of drug paraphernalia. The fourth one involves possession of a hypodermic needle, which is a separate charge.

---

* According to H. Westley Clark of the U.S. Department of Health and Human Services, "Xanax can be and is abused. The effects should not be minimized." In 2008, thirteen million people were estimated to be abusing drugs in the Xanax family.

But none of those have any bearing on her admittance to the hospital?
LAWYER: No! Oh, she . . . no . . . None of them at all.

Right. So with the narcotics charge you mentioned, what was that?
LAWYER: It was not narcotics! It's some . . . it's . . . the police find white powder—or something that looks like white powder. So they arrest somebody for possession of drugs. But it's not drugs! I know what it is. I know where it came from.

Would you be able to tell me?
LAWYER: Sure! Absolutely. It's a Hindu . . . It's Hindu good luck ashes, which she received from her entertainment lawyer.

So that's not something one administers orally or shoots up?
LAWYER: Well, I don't know what you do with Hindu good luck ashes. I think you . . .

I don't know, either, so I was just asking.
LAWYER: Okay, I suppose you carry them around with you for good luck.

So it's not something you would ever ingest?
LAWYER: No, you don't ingest it! No. It's certainly nothing that you drink or eat. I mean it's . . . I certainly haven't decided to study the Hindu faith in order to properly represent her. I know it's not drugs. I know where it came from.*

So I guess what you're saying is the only charge that holds any weight is the hypodermic needle?
LAWYER: They did find a hypodermic needle. And we were able to explain what that was doing there and it was not there because of the administration of drugs.

Why else would it be there?
LAWYER: Well that's . . . I'll tell you what: Go to court and you'll find out.

---

* A Google search at the time of this book's publication produced no independent results for "Hindu good luck ashes."

[KORN]
SCENE 2

When a rock band is at its peak onstage, there are few spectacles more powerful and awe-inspiring. That's one of the reasons why women throw themselves at bands afterward. But what fans and groupies don't see is the mess that many bands are before going onstage. The day after Davis's rant about getting no respect, Korn was in a courtesy van on the way to the Fuji Rock Festival in Tokyo for its first live show in thirteen months.

FIELDY: I need a drink.

JONATHAN DAVIS: I've never seen you drink this early. You're fucking nervous.

FIELDY: I threw up this morning. Everyone else is so nervous, every time they think of the show they get ill. I took a whole bar of Xanax.

MUNKY: My heart's beating a hundred miles an hour. And I can't feel my hands. I'm not kidding.

DAVIS: I've done seven thousand shows before, and I'm still fucking scared. I woke up at five this morning and wrote out the lyrics to every song and sung them from top to bottom. I feel sick.

HEAD: Be strong, man, like Ozzy. He'd just get up in the morning, drink forty bottles of Jack, and be onstage.*

DAVIS: I'm not a man. I'm a bitch.

HEAD: Yeah, actually I've got anxiety for the first time. I had a dream that Caco [the guitar tech] fucked up my pedal board and there were only three on there. Then I had a dream that you guys switched the songs around on me and didn't tell me. I kept playing the wrong songs.

FIELDY (*tauntingly*): Head's gonna fuck up in front of fifty thousand people onstage. You could have major shit go wrong with your pedals. If one went out, you'd be fucked.

HEAD: No, I wouldn't . . . Then I had a dream that Rosie O'Donnell was our accountant. She called me and said, "I hate this fucking TV show crap. What I really want to do is get you your money."

MUNKY: Whose dick hurts from jacking off?

Backstage, the band's nerves haven't calmed any.

---

* Ozzy Osbourne actually suffers from severe stage fright.

IF YOU WANT YOUR
NERVES *TO BE* HEALTHY & STRONG

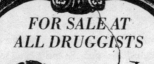

FOR SALE AT
ALL DRUGGISTS

TRY "EAR OF CORN" BITTERS

CURES SOURNESS OF THE STOMACH, WEAKNESS OF THE STOMACH,
BELCHING OF THE STOMACH, DYSPEPSIA, BILIOUSNESS, NERVOUS
HEADACHE, DEAFNESS, EFFECTS OF DISSIPATION AND LATE HOURS,
CHOLERA MORBUS, CONSTIPATION, DIARRHEA, STAGEFRIGHT, BRUISES,
TOOTHACHE, EARACHE, FROST FEET, AND DERANGEMENTS.

FIELDY: Let's all walk to the stage together, like a gang, know what I'm saying, brother. The whole posse. Everybody. (*The band begins to walk toward the stage.*) Walk slow. It will make you more confident.

DAVIS: I can't walk slow. I'm too scared.

HEAD (*to Loc*)**:** If I suck, will you tell me I was great anyway?

LOC [Korn's bodyguard and minder]: No, I'll tell you that you sucked and need to get in shape.

The show, as predicted, is a disaster. Head cracks himself in the head with his guitar, and the black stage is so sun-baked that the entire band seems to be on the verge of passing out. Nonetheless, tens of thousands of Japanese kids, never having seen Korn before, go wild, even opening up a mosh pit (a rarity at Japanese shows). As the band exits the stage . . .

FIELDY: We sucked. And you can print that.

DAVID SILVERIA: Are you going to write about how shitty we were?

Really, you weren't so bad, but the end got loose.

SILVERIA: I didn't get loose. I made it all the way through. The rest of the band fell apart.

Half an hour later, Davis approaches me.

DAVIS: What the fuck should I do?

About what?

DAVIS: I'm fucking through.

No you're not.

DAVIS: Yes I am.

No, you're psyched. You did your show and you got the props you wanted.

DAVIS: Yeah, I did good. What'd you say about the band? Loose?

Everyone has good days and bad days.

DAVIS: We're Korn. We're not ever loose. How the fuck do you think you got here?

You gotta have your off gigs?

DAVIS: Never. Never ever ever.

So are you pissed at the band?
DAVIS: It's not their fault. It's our first time in Japan. It's been a year since we last played. Fieldy's drunk off his ass and delirious. And Head thinks he's knocked himself half-conscious and goes to the hospital for stitches, and they give him a Band-Aid. Do you see what I'm stuck with here? It's four against one.

The following day, Davis breaks down. Literally. He has an anxiety attack, and spends the rest of the trip in bed with Loc babysitting. When I come up to visit, Munky is standing loyally outside his hotel room.

MUNKY: I feel so bad for Jonathan. I just massaged his back. But sometimes I just don't know what to do for him.

Inside the room . . .

How are you feeling?
DAVIS: A bit better.

Has this happened before?
DAVIS: My first anxiety attack was like five years ago: too many damn Mini Thins.* Drinking and that gave me anxiety. So they had to get Loc for me. With alcohol, I get too drunk and wake up, and it's like withdrawal. I get the shakes, I'm sweaty, I'm freaking the fuck out. And the stress: full-on stress. My stomach's just spitting out acid in my throat (*smiles feebly*). But I guess everything's got to be dramatic or it wouldn't be fucking good.

Or you could just stop drinking?
DAVIS: My psychiatrist says he should be helping me, but he's just looking for ways to get me high. But maybe I *should* start taking antidepressants—or go to AA. When the band's all joking around, the only way I feel comfortable with them—like I can join in—is when I'm drunk.

Let me know if there's anything you need tonight.
DAVIS: It's okay. I'm sorry I can't kick it in Tokyo with you tonight, dog. I'll make it up to you. I'll take you to Bakersfield.
LOC (*privately, to me*): I'm doctor, psychiatrist, brother, bodyguard, and father to these guys. Everyone's scared of them, but, really, they're just kids.

[Continued . . .]

---

* A diet pill containing ephedrine that truckers and others use to stay awake.

[THE NEPTUNES]
SCENE 4

Four hours later . . .

PHARRELL: Hey, I want to do this fucking interview. The fact that you guys chose us and the fact that you're even interested . . . I want to give you whatever you need. Ask whatever you want.

Okay. You were starting to tell me before about the projects you were working on right now.
PHARRELL: Right now? . . . Hold on . . . (*To someone else:*) See if we can get more money. . . . Can I call you right back?

[*Continued . . .*]

[BACKSTREET BOYS]
SCENE 3

Kevin Richardson returns from the bathroom and we head to his car, where he plays new recordings the Backstreet Boys have been working on.

With your *Greatest Hits* record, I felt like maybe your record company or managers needed money, so they rushed it out.
KEVIN RICHARDSON: Let me tell you what, the five of us wanted to put our greatest hits album out on our ten-year anniversary. That's what we wanted to do. We thought putting it out now was too early in our career. That's why we called it *Chapter One.**

Shouldn't your management company be fighting on your behalf?
RICHARDSON: Well our management company was supportive of the album and we weren't. And the record company was going to put it out anyway. So it's either promote or fight with your label, don't promote it, and risk it doing very badly. But ultimately, who is it that's going to get hurt? It's not going to hurt our label. It's going to hurt us. But it's just frustrating because the five of us are trying to do things for a long career and it's like our label sometimes, man, whatever. It's a necessary evil. I don't want to be bitching, but . . .

---

* Almost a decade later, there has yet to be a *Chapter Two* released.

But they're just going to work you until you die if you let them. Don't you feel like taking time off and just not being a Backstreet Boy?

RICHARDSON: That's true, and it was also our decision at first. We didn't stop for five or six years. But when Brian [Littrell, his cousin and bandmate] went in to have open heart surgery, it made me realize, like, "Wow, what are we doing? We need to maybe slow down and take care of ourselves." Because even I was like, "Let's go, let's go baby, let's do this."

Did Brian's illness have anything to do with how hard he was working?

RICHARDSON: Yeah. Brian was born with a congenital heart defect. He had a hole in his heart and he had to go every year to get checked up. And this one year, we had toured so much and he had been, you know, going, going, going, so this hole was getting bigger. The doctor said, "You need to get that taken care of." And I remember management at the time saying, "Well, can't you postpone it so we can finish this tour?" And this just hurt Brian so much, 'cause he's like, "Dude, this is my heart." *

Wow, that's cold.

RICHARDSON: Yeah, that opened all of our eyes. Though even at that point, to be honest, I was still cracking the whip—"aw, man, come on, you got to go"—until I saw him in the Mayo Clinic after his surgery. It really woke me up and I was like, "You know what, this is my cousin. He just had his chest split open and his heart out. And here I am worrying about getting back out on the road and selling records." It was a big wake-up call for me.

How did Brian feel about you cracking the whip at that point?

RICHARDSON: Brian felt hurt, you know. I hurt him. He felt like we all hurt him, because we didn't understand. But after that, I understood him even better. That brought us all closer.

What would you do if it all ended tomorrow?

RICHARDSON: Wow, wow. I mean, if it all ended tomorrow, meaning if nobody gave a damn about us and we didn't sell another record?

Yes, exactly.

RICHARDSON: I just got married and I want to start a family in a couple of years or whatever. If you can't enjoy your friends and family and your success, then what

---

* Asked to respond to the accusation, Pearlman said he supported the band taking time off for Littrell's operation immediately.

good is it? Because, you know, it's nice having fame and having some money in your pocket, but—it sounds so cliché—that ain't what it's all about. I didn't have no money before, and those were some of the happiest times in my life. You don't want to be wealthy and just worn out—grumpy and old and depressed because you have nobody to share it with.

After the Backstreet Boys released their next album, Never Gone, *Richardson left the band. A year later, he and his wife, Kristin, had their first son, Mason.*

$$\left[\begin{array}{c} \textbf{KORN} \\ SCENE\ 3 \end{array} \right]$$

A week later, Jonathan Davis came through on his promise. He and his minder Loc picked me up at my house and drove to Bakersfield, where "there's nothing to do but drugs and drink and fuck," as Davis's nineteen-year-old half-brother Mark explained when we arrived.

"We could go stop off and pick up a couple of hoochies if you want," Mark offered soon afterward. "And they're not bad looking, either—asses tighter than a motherfucker."

Davis passed on the hoochies. "I've been with the same bitch for seven years," he said. "My mack went bye-bye." *

After a tour of the town, including the high school where he was bullied and the mortuary where he used to work, Davis picked up his father, Rick, and drove to his dad's recording studio. The two were the spitting image of each other.

RICK DAVIS: When I was Jonathan's age, I had hair all down my back and was traveling around the country playing music. Who'd think I'd become old and fat, working at a government-funded TV station?

Did the [Korn] song "Dead Bodies Everywhere," about how you didn't want Jonathan to be a musician, ring true for you?
RICK: Initially there was a nervousness on my part. But [the song] forced us to sit down and go over all the issues and resolve them. And we did, didn't we?
JONATHAN DAVIS (*obediently*): Yeah.
RICK: I had lost everything in bankruptcy and I was going through a divorce, and at that moment I looked at my son and said, "Always have a day job to fall back

---

* Three years later, Davis and the "bitch"—his high-school sweetheart—divorced, and he married a porn star.

on." And fortunately he didn't listen to me. But everything's okay now. We never had bad blood?

JONATHAN: No, we were both fucked up.

RICK: I still remember when I drove back home after you moved to Long Beach. When I saw you were living in one corner of a garage, you have no idea how many buckets I cried driving home. But I thought, at least he's pursuing his dream. How would you feel if you saw [your son] Nathan living like that?

JONATHAN: Yeah, you're right. I wouldn't like it.

RICK: Now you know why I did what I did.

JONATHAN: I never realized how hard it is being a parent. We bought Maine lobsters once. I didn't want to kill them, so in the end, [my wife] Renee did. I was a little drunk, I think. And I told Nathan as a joke, "Your mommy just killed Sebastian [from *The Little Mermaid*]." I feel so bad about it now.

RICK: I'll be damned. Now you're a little drunk in front of your kid, making music and touring all the time, just like I was.

When his father leaves to go to the bathroom, Jonathan shakes his head in disbelief . . .

JONATHAN: Since I was thirteen, all we talked about was pussy. It wasn't until I started writing songs about him that we started talking about all that other stuff. He's not that bad now. But at that time, it felt horrible. When he asks me, "I wasn't a bad dad, was I?" what am I going to say, "You were an asshole"?

It does seem like he's trying to justify his behavior, but at least you can empathize with him a little more now.

JONATHAN: Ever since I've had a kid, I totally have new respect for my dad. He did fuck me over, but I can understand why. When he left to go on the road, he needed to put food on the table. He needed to pay hospital bills. I was asthmatic. I was in the hospital every fucking month from the age of three to the age of ten. When you're three years old, you don't think about that shit.

So do you think Nathan is going to grow up with hard feelings because you're gone all the time like your dad was?

JONATHAN: Probably definitely. It really freaked me out when I left to go to Japan and my son said, "You got to go to work? Bye daddy!" Then he rolled over like, "Don't talk to me." It hurt my feelings more than anything in the world. I don't give a flying fuck about this whole band. I just want to make my son happy.

That's one way of looking at it.
JONATHAN: It's a way that can keep me sane.

When Jonathan's father returns, the two spend some more time trying to connect, then we drive him home. As he leaves the car, Jonathan's dad smiles wanly and says . . .

RICK: I'd tell you that I'm proud of you, but you already wrote a song about it, so I don't know what to say.

Jonathan waves good-bye to his father from inside the car. As we drive away . . .

JONATHAN: So what'd you think of Bakersfield?

It's a shitty place to live and a shitty place to visit.
JONATHAN (*triumphantly*): You're pissed off. And you want to start a band called Korn, right? Now you understand—and you've only been here a few hours.

[TRICKY]

During our first interview, Tricky discussed his work with the dance-music collective Massive Attack and his skittish solo debut, both of which have come to define the genre known as trip-hop. For our second interview, he brought a photo album to a bar in Los Angeles and sat for an hour and a half telling tales about each person on the maternal side of his family, going back five generations. What follows are just a few stories from his family tree. All effort has been made to make sure that, in the jumble of information he manically regurgitated, the names and relationships have been reported accurately.

Great-great-grandparents
They were horse dealers and they had orchards. They brought horses from Ireland, and someone got hung.

Great-grandparents Arthur and Maggie
Arthur was a champion fistfighter of Knowle West [in Bristol, England]. He fought the king of the gypsies and won. All his children were boxers.

Great-uncle Martin
My auntie says he was born evil. I remember saying to her, "Why is everybody always so scared of Martin?" And she goes, "Because when he says he'll cut your throat, he'll cut your throat."

Martin used to get drunk and go smash everybody's house up. He stabbed someone fourteen times. Fourteen times! He went to Manchester and opened an illegal club, and what he used to do with opposition clubs is he'd walk in right past the security with a can of petrol, pour it on the floor, and fucking burn it down.

Great-aunts Maureen and Olive

They're both totally white, like Elizabeth Taylor white. But they looked like supermodels. I get them confused, but I think Olive married this posh guy who owned Morgan Motor Company. She didn't want Martin coming round smashing up the house. So Martin knocks on the door one day, and she opens it, throws pepper in his eyes, and stabs him in the stomach three times.

And I think it was Maureen that got her heart broken. She had two sons, and she gave one of them away. We used to walk up to school and I'd see my auntie passed out, like pissed up outside the telephone box, and we'd just leave her there. She actually got moved by the community because she'd piss on people's doorsteps and stuff.

Grandmother Violet

She used to be a chorus dancer, but she was also a fighter. She was wild. She once had an argument with Marlow and grabbed her arm and shut it in the back of the door and broke her arm.

Aunt Marlow

Violet is Marlow's mum, but no one ever told her. Violet had her when she was really young and not married, so she gave Marlow to her mum and Marlow grew up thinking she was the sister of my nan [grandmother]. And her head's *all* messed up, man.

Uncle Michael

When my uncle got murdered, I was in bed. I never slept when I was younger. I heard a knock on the door, and I heard my nan answer and it was a policewoman and a policeman. And they said, "Violet Godfrey?" She goes, "Yeah." And they go, "Your son has been murdered." Just straight away like that. I heard my nan start freaking out, but I pretended I was asleep because I didn't want to deal with it.

Uncle Tony

Uncle Tony became a gangster accidentally. On New Year's Eve one day when he was sixteen, he was at a bar and he went, "Happy New Year, mate," and this man who was about thirty head-butted him. And my uncle just went *bang, bang, bang* and knocked him out. It turned out this guy was the main gangster in Manchester. So my uncle accidentally became the man. Much later, a guy bit off his thumb in a fight over a club he was trying to take over. But he still won the fight and took over the club.

I remember one Christmas, someone mentioned his brother [Michael] and my uncle starts in, "I'm gonna kill that guy," talking about the guy who murdered him. And my nan, instead of saying, "Tony, don't do it," she says, "You're in court, Tony! Don't do him yet. Wait and do him after the court case!"

Mother Maxine
My mum was a really good fistfighter, really good. She and her sisters were all good-looking girls, and they used to go out and party and if any women said anything to them, they'd beat them up in the toilets.

She died when I was four, but no one told me anything. I didn't know she'd committed suicide until I was about twenty. I just knew she was dead and that was it. I think she killed herself in part because she had epilepsy and because of my dad. She didn't want to be looked after because of her epilepsy, and so she just ended it. She must have been really unhappy, but she did it like she wasn't unhappy. Like she went around visiting everybody in the family before she did it, acting very casually and wearing her best clothes.

Father Roy
I didn't meet my dad until I was twelve. He had a bad temper and used to carry a switchblade. He's a tall, dark, handsome Jamaican man—really handsome—and I think he was a philanderer. I'd say if he's a philanderer now, he was a philanderer then. He's lucky to be alive, I think.

When my mum committed suicide, my uncle wanted to do my dad. So my dad stayed away from there, because it was Martin who threatened him. And if Martin threatens you, you stay way clear.

Adrian (Tricky) Thaws
I got brought up all by women. When I was fourteen or fifteen I was sent to learn boxing, like all the men in my family. But I didn't stay there. I remember seeing this dress in a store window and I'm like, "That is a fucking wicked dress." It had short sleeves but was long, and I gave a girl twenty pounds to nick it for me. I wore it out the same night. I had dyed-blond hair and was into stuff like wearing dresses, and you can't be a gangster if you're doing that.

I got the name Tricky because my friends and I would all be in a squat together. There'd be about twenty of us all smoking. Then I would sneak off on my own and go to a club and hang out all night, and they wouldn't see me for a few weeks.

I decided to do music when I first heard Slick Rick. I'd never heard a human beatbox before.* We sat there and I'm smoking, right, and I heard this thing and it just fucking got me. I said, "Rewind it! Rewind it!" I listened to it again and again, and I said to my friend next to me, "This is what I'm going to do. I'm gonna be a rapper."

THE GAME
SCENE 3

At a video shoot three days later, the Game discusses his father, who was accused of molesting his sisters when the rapper was seven years old.

Do you still talk to your father?
GAME: No, my dad reaches out, but I've got a big grudge with him, man. My family's trying to encourage me to call him and talk to him, but I got this thing hanging over my head, man, and it won't let me. He's a hater. . . . I can't do it, man.

One day it'll be the right time to find your peace with him.
GAME: Now is definitely not the right time.

Did the whole thing mess up your sisters?
GAME: Everybody's pretty much good and nobody's devastated from the whole ordeal. But it's just hanging over my head. I just can't let it go. [. . .]

Why did you end up in a foster home instead of just living with your mom?
GAME: At that time, my mom wouldn't leave the home because that was our house and my dad wouldn't leave the home because he was kind of rebellious toward the whole thing. And so they just sent us away, man. Social workers were already on the case, and pretty much told me and my brothers and my sisters they'd split us all up rather than sending us to the same home. They totally fucked us up. I think I had it worst of all, man. They were with families; I was more institutionalized.

What was it like in the home?
GAME: I was pretty much the worst kid in the foster home. There were two Mexican brothers named Calvin and Chris, and I think about them from time to

---

* More likely, it was Doug E. Fresh and the Get Fresh Crew who he heard beatboxing, with a young Slick Rick rapping.

time. There was a white guy named Nathan and a black guy named Andre, who had a little brother named Willie. There was a guy named Herman in there, and another little kid named Chris, man. Then there was Ronald, who was the youngest. He looked up to me like a big brother. Kids would tease me in school, saying I had Mexican brothers and a white brother, because we all lived in the same house.

What were you like in school?
GAME: I was uncontrollable, but I was still smart. So I went to school and I got good grades, but I would bully and fuck the other kids up and do all kinds of weird shit, man. They tried to kick me out of elementary school because I brought Hennessy to school in fourth grade. I had kids drinking Capri Sun and Hennessy. I'm dead serious.

When did you start living with your mother again?
GAME: After all these attorneys and the social workers, the judge one day said, "Let these kids go home to their mom." That was almost eight years later, and when I came back, I was a young man now. Me and my mom's relationship was different than when I was seven. From seven to fifteen, I was alone. So when I come back, I've almost got facial hair. I rebelled against my mom, and I really didn't listen to her. I gave my mom a hard time, which is why these days I'm really taking care of her.

You had a brother who got signed to a label before you, right?
GAME: You mean Jevon? He had a deal with MCA. I was only twelve or thirteen and wasn't into rap then, but I thought it was crazy that he had a record deal on the table. But someone took his life before he was supposed to go.

Why did they shoot him?
GAME: It was jealousy over a girl. That's how it happened. I think he would have been great. I would rather him be alive and him rapping than me. I would give everything away if I could bring him back. That's just the bottom line.

[WU-TANG CLAN]
SCENE 2

What are some of your earliest memories of your family?
RZA: What kind, good ones or bad ones?

How about one of each?
RZA: I'll tell you what: I can remember my grandfather's birthday. That must have been 1971 or '72. A lot of poor people were there. And one motherfucking cake. I liked the cake. There were, like, flowers on it.

I guess that would be a good memory?
RZA: Heck yeah. When you're young, everything is good. I'll give you a bad one: When your father leaves your mother. That shit is bad. You still love everything, but the tear you feel is a real tear. That really made me lose everything right there. That's a fucked-up feeling that you will not want to feel. For real, for real, for real. You can stress that when you write about me. That's some shit. And I was, like, three and a half. And it leads to everything. It leads to your mother abandoning you and leaving you with your uncle for four years. A psychologist can look at that for you. You're not a psychologist, are you? Your questions are intimate like that.

No, though I guess I've studied psychology.
RZA: Let me ask you: Most of these questions you ask me, is it because you want to know or do the people want to know?

Both. Why do you think people read biographies all the time?
RZA: It's just that these kind of questions sound like police questions to me. There's one part of me that says I don't want to expose this stuff. But I got a habit of telling the truth. We're talking about my pain and shit as a child, and it's like, why would fans want to read that? At the same time, I'm so-called successful. I made it to a level that a lot of brothers want to make it to. I don't mind manifesting this stuff because they can think, "I was fucked up in the same way he was fucked up." One day, we'll probably get past the level of articles though, man.

So what did you do this one for? You didn't have to.
RZA: I did it for my team. If my team is there, I'm there. And I've been reading that motherfucker [*Rolling Stone*] since I was eight years old. I had that shit in my motherfucking house. My motherfucking cousin had it in his motherfucking

house. If I have a chance to be in that motherfucker on the cover, my cousin's going to see that shit. That's the MC in me talking right there, wanting to be the best. You gotta control that side of you. It's a bad motherfucker.

[JUSTIN TIMBERLAKE]

Since I wasn't having much luck getting Pharrell Williams of the Neptunes on the phone, I made an emergency call . . .

What made you choose to work with the Neptunes on your new album?
JUSTIN TIMBERLAKE: I think, as much as I wanted to show the world something, Pharrell and Chad did, too. I have labels put on me, and they have labels put on them. So we're kind of in the same boat. They have this label on them that they are the hip-hop beat guys, but when people hear this album, they're going to realize that they're musicians.

Do you ever think, I'm just a white guy, people aren't going to—
TIMBERLAKE: No, no, I never. I mean, that's just something that comes along with it. I just do the music that feels good to me. I don't make music for the critics. I make my album so people can put it in their car when they go to work and just play it. Honestly, I could give two shits when the media tries to say something. People say stuff all the time. That's their job.

But then why are all your album titles responses to critics: *No Strings Attached*, *Justified*?
TIMBERLAKE: I think it's my Monty Python-style sense of humor. Come on, man, let's be honest. If I made such an effort to keep my business of the past year private, then why would I bring it out in the lyrics specifically, you know what I mean. I get questions all the time, "Were you thinking about so-and-so* when you wrote this?" And that's exactly what I wanted people to do. There's this side of me that sees everything for what it's really worth and wonders if I can manipulate it a little bit. I think that anybody who's in my shoes does that. You look at Elvis: They said, "Don't shake your hips on *Ed Sullivan*!" And what did he do?

Do you think hip-hop, like Elvis and rock and roll, has created a generation gap?
TIMBERLAKE: It's funny, me and my dad were talking about this the other day. My dad had never heard Coldplay, so I was playing him the record because I thought

---
* Britney Spears.

Attention

Calling all SINGLE WOMEN
between the ages of
SEVENTEEN and TWENTY-SIX,
PROPER in APPEARANCE,
PRECISE in DICTION, with
ARM LENGTH of over
32 INCHES, a NEW CAREER
awaits in TELEPHONY.

Apply Today.

Call a REAL HUMAN at 310-927-0192.

GOOD PAY.
GOOD MEALS.
GOOD
SURROUNDINGS.
GOOD WORKING
CONDITIONS.

The Live Person
Call Center is looking
for qualified operators.
Do not let the machines
like the Ansa Fone put
human beings out of
business. Become part
of the movement to bring
the soothing warmth of
the human voice back
to message taking now.

he'd really like it because Yes is his favorite band. Well, he loved it, and we started talking about that. And he said, "At the end of the day, music is just music, you know."

When you were growing up, did he not like the music you were listening to?
TIMBERLAKE: I'm just getting to the age where I'm really okay with getting along with my parents. I went through the whole rebel thing. We sat down and listened to Coldplay—that was a big step.

One last question: When you call Pharrell, does he call *you* back?
TIMBERLAKE: Eventually.

[THE STANDELLS]

"I'm gonna tell you a big fat story, baby," the Standells began "Dirty Water," their 1966 hit that had three chord changes and enough snarling attitude to become one of the most frequently cited precursors of punk rock. Just before the band's first reunion since breaking up three decades earlier, original keyboardist Larry Tamblyn discussed its unexpected legacy.

How did the band start?
LARRY TAMBLYN: We were just basically a top forty cover band. That's what you did at clubs. We played for a while at the Oasis Club in Hawaii, and we alternated with a Japanese variety show. They had comedians, dancers, kabuki actors, and this guy who was the Japanese Pat Boone. And we came on right after the stripper. Mikimoto was her name.

How did you evolve into the dirtier rock and roll style you ended up playing?
TAMBLYN: We moved back to California and while we were playing at a club called the Peppermint West, we read an article about this unknown group called the Beatles. It was before they really hit this country. And they had the long hair and everything, so we all grew our hair long. Somewhere in one of the teen magazines, it shows us as the American Beatles because we were the first group to do this. So we were soon booked for a couple weeks in Las Vegas at what was then the Thunderbird Lounge as America's answer to the Beatles.

Were you signed at that point?
TAMBLYN: We were signed just around that time. We were playing at a very popular club on the Sunset Strip called PJ's, and this man came in by the name of Burt

Jacobs. And he said, "If I can get you guys a deal with Liberty Records, will you sign with me as a manager?" We said, "Sure," and signed with him. Then we came to find out later that he was a bookie, and he would take all these people's bets over at Liberty Records. That's how he got us on the label, because they owed him so many favors.

Then you moved to Vee-Jay?
TAMBLYN: In fact, Sonny Bono produced us there. And Cher sang in the background on a couple of songs. At that time, Sonny and Cher hadn't really taken off yet. But nothing much happened there, and Vee-Jay kind of folded.

Did you think "Dirty Water" would be a big hit at the time?
TAMBLYN: That happened when we signed with Ed Cobb and Ray Harris as producers. And the way Ed presented the song to us, we weren't too impressed with it.* It wasn't until eight months later that it started getting airplay. This station in Orlando, Florida, started playing it and it rose to number one there. Then it spread up the coast and didn't get here to California until much later.

How did that affect the band?
TAMBLYN: We were in Seattle, doing the same old top forty stuff for a bunch of drunks, and they booked us right from that nightclub to do our own tour, starting in Florida. And so we flew to Florida and got off the plane and there was this huge crowd of screaming teenagers out there.

I mean, you talk about a thrill. They were pulling at our clothes and it was great. Then right after that tour, we went back to LA and then were on the Rolling Stones tour. I believe it was 1967.

How long did you tour with the Stones?
TAMBLYN: We were on for a good couple of months, and that was crazy. By then, "Dirty Water" was in the top ten and we were very well known. When we played outside Boston, they had a big riot. Everybody was rushing at the stage, and they shot off tear gas. It was like Vietnam, you know. We had to drive through a cloud of tear gas in the bus to get out, and everybody was choking and gagging.

Did you ever have problems touring because of your image?
TAMBLYN: Yeah, we developed this really raunchy image. I remember an instance when they wouldn't let us in a hotel because we had long hair. And actually on one

---

* Cobb also offered the band the song "Tainted Love," later a hit for Gloria Jones and then Soft Cell, but the Standells turned it down.

tour, at some town in the South, there were a bunch of good ol' boys that came after us with their twenty-twos.

Why was that?
TAMBLYN: It was because their girlfriends were hanging around the hotel and they didn't like it (*laughs*). The long hair was kind of a symbol of freedom and it really incensed some people.*

[CHER SCENE 2]

There's a saying among those who work around Cher: If there's a nuclear war, only two species will survive—the cockroaches and Cher. The story of the making of her song "Believe," which charted at number one in over twenty-two countries, gives a clue to her durability and longevity, as well as an unusual case study of the creation of a hit and the resurrection of a career.

From its inception to its release, "Believe" took some nine years and required the combined efforts of more than six songwriters. There really aren't that many pieces to the song—a simple verse, a repetitive chorus, an electro-disco beat, and the gimmick of Cher's voice broken up by an effect that makes her sound like a robot. So why did it take so many people and so much time to come up with a four-minute pop song?

BRIAN HIGGINS [**songwriter**]: I wrote the first draft of the song nine years ago. I was at my flat, where I have two keyboards in the bedroom, and I'd just come back from my job selling advertising for a paper company. I didn't sit down to write a song about anything, and the lyrics and the melody just flowed out at the same time. I wish I could bottle it.

Five years later, Higgins's career as a songwriter began to blossom, and practically every time he met with a pop star, manager, or record executive, he played them "Believe." But no one was interested.

In the meantime, Rob Dickins, the chairman of Warner Music in London, began

---

* The British band the Pretty Things claim to have racked up an estimated sixty-one convictions around the same time. According to singer Phil May, most of these were due to the band's long hair. "People would look at you and take a swing at you," he recalled. "They thought that obviously we were homosexuals or perverts or transvestites. And we were considered dirty. But what they didn't realize is if you have long hair, you have to take more care of it than someone with a crew cut. We were taking three showers a day."

planning Cher's next album. At the time, Cher didn't have a record deal in the United States.

ROB DICKINS: I wanted to do a dance record with Cher. She didn't. I thought her greatest following was in the gay community, but she kept making macho rock ballads. I thought, "Why don't we make a high-energy record?" She said she didn't want to do that because there are no songs in dance music. I said, "There are songs. Leave it to me to find them."

CHER: He said, "I want you to make a dance album." I said I didn't want to. But I have that problem: If someone says I want you to do something and I'm not sure, I usually just say I don't want to do it.

DICKINS: When I was trying to get the songs together, I was in the record company office and I bumped into a songwriter called Brian Higgins in the corridor. If the phone had rung in my office or if Brian hadn't been in the corridor at that exact moment, we wouldn't be having this conversation.

I asked him to put a couple songs together for me. Instead, three days later, a tape came with sixteen songs on it. I lay on my bed and put the tape on and listened to every song. He's from a school of modern songwriters who just write choruses under the belief that if you don't like the chorus, what's the point of the rest of the song? So everything on the tape was basically one-minute choruses. The ninth song was "Believe."

Dickins liked the melody and thought the lyrics about surviving heartbreak would resonate with Cher, so he called Higgins and asked him to complete the song.

DICKINS: About a week later he comes in with the finished song, and it's terrible. I've got this great chorus and this terrible song. So I told him, "We're taking it away from you." He says, "What do you mean?" I said, "You've done no justice to your own song."

Dickins sent "Believe" to a studio run by producer Brian Rawling, and asked him to do justice to the song. A songwriter who worked at the studio, Steve Torch, took a crack at the verses.

DICKINS: I went down to the studio when they finished, and it was still terrible. I said, "What is wrong with all you people? I've got a hit chorus and none of you can write a song?" Brian said, "Give me another chance."

This time, Brian Rawling brought in someone else on his staff, Paul Barry. But Barry's first three attempts at the song were rejected by Dickins and Cher.

PAUL BARRY: I remember one version in particular that Cher didn't like. My son had just been born and I was ecstatic. One lyric Cher said was total garbage. She said, "You're too happy. The song is essentially sad, asking, 'Is there life after a broken heart?'" She was pretty blunt.

Around this time, Dickins was asked to leave his job at Warner Music as a result of a personality clash with one of his superiors.

DICKINS: I'd been with the company for twenty-seven years. It was a tough thing. So that was probably why I was so relentless with the song. The focus of it all was that they took my job away from me and this was going to be my last record at Warner, so I was going to show them.

Finally, Barry, with help from another songwriter at the studio, Mark Taylor, turned in verses that met Dickins's approval. However, Cher still wasn't happy.

CHER: The second verse was pitiful. It was a repeat of the same idea from the first line. And I thought, "Fuck that, you can be sad for one verse, but you can't be sad for two." That night, I was lying there in my bathtub with my toe in that little faucet, playing around with the words, and it came out in one line. I thought, "I've had time to think it through / And maybe I'm too good for you." It was so much better—though I didn't get writing credit for it.

While Cher was tweaking the lyrics, Barry and Taylor began putting together music for the song, adding a drum track, a keyboard melody, and a bass line. Dickins, of course, still wasn't happy. He didn't like the eight-bar section of the song before the final chorus (known as the middle eight or bridge).

DICKINS: I said, "In the middle eight, you're repeating the lyric line so many times. The point is to move the song along there."
CHER: He wanted them to change the bridge, but I didn't want to change the bridge. We're Leo and Taurus, so we go head-to-head.

However, Cher had another problem with the song.

CHER: When we got the song finished, the chorus was so great but the verses just kind of laid there. I kept singing them over and over again, seeing if there was something I could do. And finally I said to Mark, "I can't do it any better. This is as good as I can do it."

In the meantime, Auto-Tune, a new vocal tuning plug-in compatible with Cubase, a music recording and editing software, arrived in the studio, and Taylor decided to take a break and teach himself how to use it.

MARK TAYLOR: We'd only just gotten the toy. In the process of experimenting with how to use it, I took it further than it's comfortably supposed to go. It just so happened I had it looped around the part of the song that goes "life after love." So after we did it, we wondered whether we should play it for Cher or just keep quiet in case it made her angry that we were messing with her vocals. I was ninety-five percent convinced it would be a bad idea to play it to her. But something just snapped, and a couple of beers later we played it to her and she just freaked out. I was so close to not playing it. It's ridiculous the chance that goes into making these songs.

CHER: We high-fived. It was like some stupid *Rocky* film.

TAYLOR: It was late, and we were supposed to do mixes for the record company. So I banged off a rough version to send them because I thought it sounded all right.

Record company executives, however, had problems with the robotic Auto-Tune vo-cals: They didn't think Cher's voice was recognizable enough.

CHER: I had this meeting with Rob. He said, "Everyone loves the song but wants to change that part of it." I said, "You can change that part of it . . . over my dead body!" And that was the end of the discussion. I said to Mark before I left, "Don't let Brian change anything. Don't let Paul change anything. Don't let anyone touch this track, or I'm going to rip your throat out."

BRIAN RAWLING: So no one changed the track. That rough mix became the final version of the song.

DICKINS: When I was ringing Cher to tell her she was number one, she was in Milan doing some promotion. As the phone was ringing, all I could think of was me being fifteen and watching Sonny and Cher in bell bottoms on the pop pro-gram *Ready, Steady, Go!* I thought, "How great is this business that I'm going to ring this girl to tell her she's number one?" It was her first number one song in twenty-five years.

Afterward, I rang Brian and I told him, "We're number one, fantastic position—but the middle eight still doesn't cut it."

[THE NEPTUNES
SCENE 5]

A week later, the phone rings . . .

Hello.
PHARRELL: It's Pharrell. I apologize. Our time is very busy, and I can't help who organizes my shit. But at the same time, it has nothing to do with my interest in, you know, providing people with the information they need.

One thing I wanted to ask was that I remember hearing somewhere that you thought the Stereolab song "The Flower Called Nowhere" was the best song to get head to.
PHARRELL: Yeah, it's the fucking chord changes, man.

Thanks. That's all I need.
PHARRELL: What?

Actually, I had to turn the article in today.
PHARRELL: You did it already?

You're off the hook.
PHARRELL: Really? You got what you need?

Yeah, I talked to Justin Timberlake. I just needed one more quote from you for the end of the story.
PHARRELL: I see.

[CURTAIN]

ACT SEVEN

— OR —

TAKE YOUR DRUG DEALER TO WORK DAY

— SYNOPSIS —

Enter Neil Young, who is not available when people need help, though Bonnie Raitt will be there, Ryan Adams will tell them to fuck off, and Russell Brand will take a bath with them, especially if they're old bleeding junkies, though Nusrat Fateh Ali Khan prefers that people bleed at his concerts, &c.

[**NEIL YOUNG**]
SCENE 1

The most predictable thing about Neil Young's career has been his unpredictability. His frequent shifts of mood and mind have meant that every statement he makes, he may one day retract; every style of music he plays, he will eventually disavow (only to return to it again in the future); every musician he plays with, he could some day desert (and then collaborate with again years later); and every drive he takes may never reach its destination.

It was a sunny afternoon, and Neil Young was twisting up and down the hilly roads of Mountain View, California, in a pristine 1959 Lincoln Continental. One hand on the wheel, the other near his aching back, he was on his way to his chiropractor's office in San José.

NEIL YOUNG: What's happening with my back now is a result of me not stretching before I play. I have a very heavy guitar and I lean way over when I play. It transfers to my back.

Suddenly, Young hits the brakes and the convertible screeches off the side of the road. Then he gives the wheel a mighty turn to the left and within seconds he is on the road again, heading back in the same direction he came from.

Did you change your mind?
YOUNG: There's no way I'm going to make it to San José and back here again, especially during rush hour. No matter how much you need to do something, sometimes you just have to change your mind. And it's okay to change your mind.*

People say that when you're in a stressful or bad situation, you tend to disappear. Do think that's true?
YOUNG: Yeah, I think that's true. Sometimes that's the only statement I can make.

And what kind of statement does that make?
YOUNG: Well, you know, usually that's not the first thing I do. It's probably the last thing I do.

---

* Frank (Poncho) Sampedro, who plays guitar in Young's band Crazy Horse, on Young's driving: "You'll notice that Neil didn't make a left turn, he made a hundred-and-eighty-degree turn. We have a saying, the few people who work around Neil, that he never turns corners, he ricochets around them."

So is it because you're avoiding a problem or because the problem can't be solved?
YOUNG: Well, it's that I don't have the time to solve it. Sometimes I walk. Generally it's big situations that I walk out on.

I notice people often quote things you've said in the past, then try to make you live up to them.
YOUNG: That doesn't always work.

And they get obsessed with the way you change from record to record—
YOUNG: There are new bands all the time. The music is changing. Sound is reinventing itself all the time. So it's logical that someone is going to make different records. They're open to what's going on in the world and what's happening. So it just *seems* that I make records that are different, but they really aren't. I mean, really, I've been singing the same song for thirty years and I just sing it differently every time. You know, it's just a matter of perspective, I guess.

Are you ever influenced by whether an album is successful or not, critically or commercially?
YOUNG: I don't pay attention to it. That's what I've learned. I keep moving. Don't bother to read it. If you do read it, don't take it seriously. People are liking the records now, but I'll have more peaks and valleys. I'll put some other record out and people will say it's a piece of shit. They'll laugh. It's inevitable. It just goes up and down, and the tops are not really that much better than the bottoms. So long as you're moving.

Young soon parks in front of the Mountain House, a wood-cabin restaurant where he started the aborted trip half an hour earlier. He heads inside, gets a Coke from the soda fountain, and sits at a table in front of a log-burning fire, where he discusses the legacy of the sixties.

YOUNG: The pessimistic outlook that bands have today and the angst, this is a part of what we created for our children. They're reflecting it back at us, and now we have to live with it. And they have a right to be pessimistic. It's not as easy to grow up now as it was in the sixties. The world is a much more dangerous place. There are a lot less dreams being realized.

Perhaps your most often-quoted line is, "It's better to burn out than to fade away." But it's often been misinterpreted, like in Kurt Cobain's suicide note—
YOUNG: I don't know. I don't want to talk about that.

What I was going to ask is what it meant to you.
YOUNG: I think the idea is: Keep on going. Burn! Go! Keep going or you'll disappear. Now you can take it to an extreme, and some people have taken it to the wild extreme. But the real truth of the matter is that all I'm saying is: If you want to go, go! Go big. Try to do it. To me this is important in whatever I do next. And what I do next is as important as anything I've ever done. More important.

Is it difficult, especially when you're outspoken on different issues, to handle all the requests that come in to do charitable work and benefits?
YOUNG: You got to be selfish. You have to say no. You have to say, "I'm not available," even though you may not know why you are not available. You have to retain the part of you that is most important for the art, for the work that you're doing in your life. So you give all your energy to the art and if there's anything left over, then you can give it to some of the people who want you to do stuff.

[*Continued . . .*]

[BONNIE RAITT]

When it comes to benefits and charities, Grammy-winning blues and country singer Bonnie Raitt's philosophy is the exact opposite of Neil Young's. This became clear when Raitt was eating lunch at the Sunset Marquis in Los Angeles and a small blond boy scampered past her table.

BONNIE RAITT: Aww. Do you have kids?

Not yet.
RAITT: Me neither. I mean, I love kids, but I'm glad I don't have to take on that responsibility twenty-four hours a day.

What do you think is more important to society in the long run: leaving a legacy through having children or through your music?
RAITT: They're both important. Having children is an incredible commitment, which I take so seriously that I wouldn't want to do it in a half-assed way. That's why I chose not to. It's not fair to the kid if you're not going to be there in a major way, which would mean stopping tours. I understand that once the kid is around, those decisions come real easy. But I feel that my job is to mother the causes that I'm involved in.

I've rarely heard anyone say that.

RAITT: Hey, listen, I'm definitely in the minority. But every morning I wake up and I have my job. I think if you have kids, that priority gets changed. And with me, it's already so hard to say no. No matter if I say yes to five organizations and benefits, there are still thirty that I have to say no to. And that's what I go to bed with at night, thinking, "What's going to happen to that woman who said her Native American art department was going to close if I don't do this show?"

I interviewed Neil Young, who does benefits and is often the only popular artist writing a song about certain issues. But he doesn't have that same guilt when he doesn't do something.

RAITT: Yeah, I think some people have a bent to act when they see something wrong—like it really, really bothers them. I have to say that the driving force behind everything to me is an almost rabid need to be equal. I don't know whether it's because I came up in a feminist time or I just couldn't stand watching white people step on black people in the South. I can't stand bullies, you know. Some psychologist could probably unravel that. But the same thing that drives you crazy is what makes you want to be able to help. Like, if you see a kid go over and kick a dog, it's really hard not to want to go over and kick the kid. "How do you think that feels, buddy?"

Maybe that's why you don't have children.

RAITT: I have to fight that rage. For a long time, I just thought I was a peaceful Quaker passive person, but I've had to come to terms with a lot of anger and rage.

When you were in your drugs and drinking phase, do you think you needed them to perform?

RAITT: That used to be true for me. I'm really grateful that I didn't kill either myself or somebody else. I really used to think I needed to be messed up to sing the kind of music I sing. And, you know, in my twenties, I hated the way I sang. So I drank Jim Beam. I thought it would pickle my voice somehow. I don't regret all those years, but I was one of the lucky ones that could say no to it and not miss it that much.

So what made you decide to get sober?

RAITT: People saw me keeping it together and didn't know I had a problem until I started getting puffy in my middle thirties. And that probably saved me, because at some point, professional pride gets in there.

[RYAN ADAMS]

After a day spent interviewing singer-songwriter Ryan Adams, one can pretty regularly predict what the last words of his answers are going to be, no matter what subject he's discussing.

On America

Not to be like an arty fuck or anything, but I don't agree with our social situation here. I don't agree with our politics. I don't like the way people are treated. I don't like the way our children are raised. I fucking hate being from here. It's like, "Fuck off. See ya."

On Christina Aguilera and Britney Spears

I really hate that whole mixed-message thing. A whole generation is like, "Look at me, I'm sexy. But wait, no, I'm not sexy. I'm not having sex until I get married. Look at my tits, but don't look at my fucking tits. You are perverted." It's just like, "Oh, fuck off."

On Bonnie Raitt

I got to meet Bonnie Raitt yesterday. Man, she is so classy. I got to tell her about hearing one of her songs on the jukebox in this weird moose lodge, and I played it over and over. I was sitting next to this construction worker, and then I just said, "Oh, excuse me," and started bawling. I was so fucking completely destroyed from this gal. Bonnie was like, "Damn, man," and she was out the door. I was like, "Wait, I've got more soul destroying stories to tell you." She was probably like, "Fuck off."

On Los Angeles

Look, I can be shallow, but that's not going to be my experience in Los Angeles. My experience is going to be: I'm going to be harder on myself than I've ever been. I'm going to be better to myself than I've ever been. I'm going to be smarter than I've ever been. I'm not going to like go, "Let me go pick up some stupid actress and go fucking hang out and be a moron.* Isn't the sunshine great?" It's just like, "Oh, fuck off."

---

* Adams went on to date Winona Ryder and Alanis Morissette among others in Los Angeles before marrying singer and actress Mandy Moore.

On Reality

I run into less and less people who are able to quit playing it cool and just be for real and just be scared and just be fucking lonely and just be on the fucking edge for a moment. Like, let the storm cook up and let it cool down on its own—as opposed to people that just want to stand in the middle of a thunderstorm and say, "This isn't happening. I'm really not wet." It's like, "Fuck off and go be somewhere else."

On Drugs and Alcohol

If you get destroyed and someone really hurts your heart, and you don't have an option but to go out with a buddy and have a couple of drinks and talk things out, that's one thing. But I don't like to raise my glass up unless I'm celebrating something. I don't really see the point in doing drugs if they're damaging to you. Otherwise you're just a fucking loser. And I've already been that guy. Tired of that fucking guy. It's like, "Fuck off."

On Ego

I'm tired of people parading themselves around like they're the cock of the roost. It's like, "You aren't shit." When you start thinking you are, then you definitely aren't. It's like, "We aren't kings in this world. No one is ever really fucking king. Fuck off."

[NOEL FIELDING]
SCENE 1

Sporting tight pink pants and a Pia Zadora haircut, Noel Fielding sat in the back room of a dive bar in Camden with his girlfriend at the time, Dee Plume, and Courtney Love, who was uncharacteristically silent and attentive as he spoke.

The phrases that best describe Fielding are *infectiously good-natured* and *restlessly creative*. Throughout the night, he rarely shut off his surreal sense of whimsy. When he sat down, he spied a remote control on the table, picked it up, pointed it at a moose hanging on the wall, and tried to control it with the device.

Later, when we adjourned to a concert by Australian rockers the Vines and a bouncer gruffly told Fielding, "You're going to have to walk downstairs," he replied: "Aww, and I was gonna fly."

It wasn't easy for Fielding to watch the concert in peace. Girls asked him to sign their stomachs, random students told him they'd modeled their lives after his, and groups of teens chanted his nonsense songs in his ears. All of this came as a surprise to a guy who tends to compare the accessibility of his television show *The Mighty Boosh* to an esoteric record album.

Did you ever expect to have this kind of reaction?
NOEL FIELDING: We didn't expect it at all. When we went on tour, it was a bit like being the Beatles. We got chased by lots of girls, and they brought me loads of presents and tried to get on our bus and there was a lot of screaming. I've never had that before. My mates' bands have had it.

Did you ever want to be a rock star?
FIELDING: Probably since I was seven. My dad's best friend engineered or produced [Gary Numan's] "Cars," so I went with him to get his gold disc at some ceremony. Gary Numan was the first real-life pop star I'd ever seen. He was in the corner with a white face and a really weird sort of grey suit. And I thought: "Wow, who's he? He's not a real man. He's a spaceman." And I thought, "Wow, that could be your job? How cool is that?"

I have only one journalist-type question: If somebody watches your show and they say, "Wow, that was really . . . *something*," what would you want that word to be?
FIELDING: "Insane. Insane. What the hell was that? How's that supposed to be fucking funny? Was that a dream?" That's what I hope actually. When we first came out, it was a bit like a sort of difficult album. People felt like they were missing something, but they weren't. That's why children get it because children are open. They just go, "Yeah, cool. I like this."

As long as it stimulates them.
FIELDING: Yeah, if you say to a kid, "There's a rabbit in there made of ham and basically it won't come out unless you dress up as a pirate," they go, "Alright, I'll go get my pirate hat." I love that about kids.

Have you done much acid in your life?
FIELDING: I did quite a lot when I was young, but I stopped. I had a really good time with it and then I started not having fun. I thought, "That's enough. I've done enough."

When was that?
FIELDING: I had one experience when lots of foxes came and sat right next to us and their eyes were really sort of blue, sort of like lights, and we were sitting on a hill. Me and my mate and his girlfriend. We were listening to a little tiny stereo

really quietly. And they just sort of sat there innocently under us, like we were doing a show and they were an audience. About six of them. We were just looking at them and going, "What's this?" And it was like they were just quite happy to sit there.

COURTNEY LOVE: Were there actually foxes there in real life?

FIELDING: Yeah, and I thought, "It's never going to get any better than this—to have an audience of foxes—I've got to stop now." It was really frightening actually.

LOVE: But you connected with them.

FIELDING: And they said, "Write the Boosh." Actually, no, they didn't. This was way before then.

How did you get the show on television in the first place?

FIELDING: We couldn't get on telly at one point. A lot of TV people liked it, but they said, "What the fuck is this?" Like we'd write scripts where eagles would take us away, and they said it was going to cost millions and we'd need Terry Gilliam. But then Steve Coogan from Baby Cow saw us in Edinburgh, and said he loved it and wanted to make a TV show. So he sold us as a hipper Vic and Bob. (*To Love:*) You'd be great in the Boosh. You should do a bit in the Boosh.

LOVE: I'll totally do it.

FIELDING: Steve always comes in and says, "I really want this part." And we say, "You can't have it." He goes, "I'm not really cool enough to be in the Boosh, am I?" We think it's funny that he got us a show and we won't let him be in it. He says, "It's really cool. My status would go up."

DEE PLUME: He's never been cool. That's just the way it goes.

FIELDING: We do really take the piss out of him, a bit like kids do with their dads.

[*Continued . . .*]

[STEVE COOGAN]

Five moments from a day at the Edinburgh Festival Fringe with Steve Coogan . . .

MOMENT ONE

In a café, Coogan hands me a DVD of The Mighty Boosh *that his company, Baby Cow, produced. A woman walking by notices this and stops in her tracks.*

RANDOM WOMAN: That's such a great show. Have you ever seen it?

Coogan looks up at her, waiting for her to recognize him. When she doesn't, he says proudly . . .

STEVE COOGAN: I produced it.
RANDOM WOMAN (*unimpressed*): Do you work for Baby Cow?
COOGAN: (*Scrunches his face like he's just tasted spoiled milk and doesn't respond.*)

––•––

MOMENT TWO

On the way to a comedy showcase where he's a presenter, Coogan complains that his assistant and co-producer Lindsay is always undermining him—telling him, for example, that she ran into his ex-wife and she looked fantastic and happy.

When he enters the theater, Coogan is instantly consoled by two women in their thirties, who rush to his side and ask to take photos with him. Afterward, he explains . . .

COOGAN: Fourteen years ago, when I won the Perrier Award [the festival's top honor for a comedy show], I slept with both of them. That was probably the greatest moment of my life. You come here an unknown, and in four weeks the acclaim just grows until you win the big award, and it's like taking off in a rocket ship. It's like an entire career compressed to four weeks. After that, nothing was the same anymore.

––•––

MOMENT THREE

Coogan walks onstage to present the night's winners and looks at the expectant audience. His speech is as follows . . .

COOGAN: If you're expecting anything funny from me, you're not going to get it. I'm not performing—just announcing an award.

When he announces second place, which goes to a lesbian comic, he leans in to kiss her. She pulls back and offers her hand. He gives her a dirty look and begrudgingly shakes it.

After the show, he bemoans his notoriety. But then he remembers that when he arrived in Edinburgh a few days ago, he met a woman and was about to bring her to his room when a female comedy executive pulled her aside and warned, "You know about his reputation, don't you?"

COOGAN: In the end, that actually ended up helping. I think it made her curious.

––•––

MOMENT FOUR

At an industry party afterward, he sets his sights on a blond comedian, who talks constantly about her career. They adjourn to the Loft Bar, because he has an appointment with a beautiful black-haired drug dealer with missing teeth. Suddenly, he is accosted by a tall female fan with elfish ears and pointy canine teeth. She pulls a festival pin off her jacket, then holds the sharp end over her cigarette lighter and starts heating it up.

FAN: Will you carve your intials into my arm?
COOGAN (*stutters*)**:** W-w-why?
FAN: I want a tattoo.
COOGAN: No. No, sorry. I don't think I can do that. (*He walks away, then turns to me and explains:*) That's how you get stalkers.

MOMENT FIVE

The night ends with Coogan, the drug dealer, the blond comedian, and several other comics and hangers-on in my hotel room. Though there are five lines on the table, the focus is on Coogan, who is reciting comedy routines word for word—including ones he'd just heard that night. At times, he checks to make sure he has his audience's full attention, tapping people on the knee or grabbing their arm as he speaks. And he urges me to see a festival performer named Russell Brand, who was then unknown in America.

    After a five-minute monologue on the art of comic timing, I ask if I can bring out my tape recorder. Coogan presses the group to watch some of the shows he produced for Baby Cow with his partner, Henry Normal, and then consents.

COOGAN: When I met J.K. Rowling, the first thing she asked was if Henry Normal was a real person.

I've noticed that even though you're a lot different than your characters, there are still a lot of similarities.
COOGAN: Except I've made myself look as bad as possible in all the characters I play on television. I think that all the characters I do overestimate themselves and are weak. There's an insecurity about them. They have to be flawed to be funny. And I like doing deeply flawed characters, because that's humanity. Then when people meet me in real life, they're surprised by how good-looking I am.

Though when you make yourself a character, he's still very flawed.
COOGAN: That character is kind of a slight pastiche of me. Some of it is true. I don't need to try to convince people I'm perfect. I don't give a shit. I really don't. It's like, "Yeah, I've got issues. Lots of people have issues. I've got issues and I use them in my work." Once you arrive at that, it's a more relaxed place to be—especially with your relationship with the media.

So what do you think of Russell Brand?
COOGAN: I like Russell. He's got an instant gratification about him and his attitude, and you get it straight away. It's like the Sex Pistols couldn't have done a second album. A second album makes them by nature not the Sex Pistols. So it remains to be seen if it's style or substance, but he may well be more than that, because he's very smart. I certainly could learn a trick or two from him on how to handle the media. What he's done very, very well is to use his flaws and spin them into idiosyncrasies that make him interesting. There's a part of me that goes, "Fuck, I wish I'd thought of that."

I think a lot of the most creatively interesting people are slightly dysfunctional.
COOGAN: And I like to include myself in that.

[RUSSELL BRAND]
SCENE 1

Russell Brand dances to the lip of the stage near the end of one in a string of thirteen sold-out shows in Edinburgh, Scotland. He tosses back his long jet-black hair, and flippantly asks the crowd if they have any questions. The fans take this request at face value and erupt screaming. Women beg him to take off his clothes, to kiss him, to . . .

"I want to fuck you," yells one girl near the front.

This isn't rock and roll. This is comedy.

At this point, Brand had yet to make his debut in the United States, but it was already blindingly clear that he would become a star here. The sexually prodigious Brand went on to sleep with three women after the show that night. When he left Edinburgh, a leading British tabloid paid his local landlord to take pictures of the condom-covered floor.

His press comment: "Anyone who knows me will be aware that I'm a keen balloon animal enthusiast."

With the help of British comedian Steve Coogan and his assistant Lindsay, I tracked Brand down for his first American interview.

When I talked to Steve, he said you'd actually been doing comedy for a long time, but would get fired from most of your jobs until you got clean.
RUSSELL BRAND: Yeah, that's right. I worked for MTV when I was about twenty-five. I was addicted to crack and heroin at that time and was . . . I've always had some quite destructive tendencies and I was unstable. I had no off switch. I was unable to manage it. Up until then, I'd never had money in my life and as soon as people gave me money, I just hit the "fuck it" button and blew up.

Personally or professionally?
BRAND: Both.

What would be an example of professionally?
BRAND: On September the twelfth, 2001, obviously the day after the attack on New York, I went to work to interview Kylie Minogue and I went in there with my drug dealer, Gritty. He looked like a drug dealer—complete with gold teeth—and he asked me to show his kid around. I went, "Yeah, of course. No problem."

Take your drug dealer to work day was the way I later framed it. So I went to work that day with Gritty and his son, Edwin, and we were both sort of high. I was all dressed in a combat jacket, with white pants kind of like pajama bottoms and a long white top that went down to my knees. I had a fake beard on, and a towel on my head held on with a bit of string. And I was walking around MTV that day and everybody was like, "What the fuck are you doing?" I was like, "Come on, it was yesterday. Get over it."

So I interviewed Kylie Minogue dressed in that outfit, and I introduced Kylie to my drug dealer.

She let you interview her in a bin Laden costume?
BRAND: When I was interviewing her on camera, they made me take off the beard and the combat jacket, but I was still wearing this sort of tunic.

That's just a bad idea.
BRAND: It's because I was dead to everything. I was using all the time, at home and at work. I was smashing stuff up and jumping from moving cars after interviews with these boy bands and lots of crazy stuff with dead animals.

What would you do with dead animals?
BRAND: I was fixated with dead animals and death. The driving ideology behind what I was doing was pretty safe, right? And I felt that people were spellbound, like

they'd been hypnotized and had to wake up. So I would do things to wake them up. Like I'd have a load of dead rats or dead chicks, like baby birds, onstage. And I'd smash them up with a hammer and then throw them into the audience and go, "Why are you disgusted? I've just rearranged their atoms. They're dead already. Nothing's happened. You're being shocked by nothing."

They let you get away with that at MTV?
BRAND: It sort of led to lots of chaos, in fact, for MTV, especially after the bin Laden incident.

And then you started doing some other weird show, right?
BRAND: I started doing a TV show where my idea was to challenge cultural taboos. And one was that, because I didn't grow up with my dad, I had a boxing match with my dad to look at the idea of the Oedipus complex. Another one was that I had a homeless junkie come and live in my house with me. I shared my bed with him to see why we're disgusted by poverty and homelessness.

I think people are more disgusted by lack of hygiene than anyone's income or living conditions.
BRAND: That's why I ended up having a bath with this old deranged bleeding junkie. Me and him just sat naked in the bath.

[*Continued . . .*]

[NUSRAT FATEH ALI KHAN]

He may not be a household name, but Nusrat Fateh Ali Khan was one of the world's biggest stars, both figuratively and literally. Weighing in at 350 pounds, he had spent most of his life turning an esoteric form of music—*qawwali*, the singing style of Pakistan and India's Sufi mystics—into an international buzzword. He collaborated with Eddie Vedder; Joan Osborne studied under him; and Madonna showed up at his concerts to watch him sit cross-legged onstage and let loose some of the world's most entrancing vocals.

   In his home country of Pakistan, drugs and alcohol weren't necessary at his sold-out shows for over ten thousand fans. The music itself brought spectators into trances, leading to tireless fits of dancing during which inspired audience members renounced their worldly possessions—money, watches, jewelry—by showering Khan with them.

Wearing a loose-fitting gown and glowing with charisma, Khan arrived two and a half hours late for our scheduled lunch at a Pakistani-run restaurant in Manhattan, proving that sleeping the day away is a universal trait among most musicians. He was accompanied by his manager and acolyte, Rashid Ahmed Din, who not only translated for what would ultimately be one of Khan's last interviews, but occasionally chimed in with his own opinion.

Do people ever get hurt when they go into trance at your concerts?
NUSRAT FATEH ALI KHAN: A lot of people damage themselves. Sometimes they break their knees or legs, but they don't realize it at the time. They only know when they are out of the trance. Once, back in 1979 when I first came to England, one guy was dancing and he hit his forehead against the stage, and it made a mess. He was in a real trance, because he kept dancing.

What do you do with the money and valuables that people throw onstage?
KHAN: I usually give [them] to charity or poor people. There's a big cancer hospital opening in Pakistan I've been collecting money for, and there are a lot of people who used to perform with my father that no longer have a source of income. If there's any money left over, I divide it among the rest of the group.

What puts people into trance: Is it the lyrics or the rhythm?
KHAN: It is the words, the delivery of the words, and the rhythm that affect people—all together. The first thing that affects people is the lyrics, then the rhythm makes it stronger. But if you read the words, they won't put people in a trance. If they are sung, they will put them in a trance.

Is there a certain way they need to be sung?
KHAN: Yes, the technical qualifications make the difference. Like every time I repeat something, it is in a new way. This way, with a good voice, a rhythm, the lyrics, and the improvisation, everything comes together and builds up more the trance. If I just repeat it in a normal way, it will not put people into such a deep or long trance.

I'd heard of singers who were able to bring about storms and fire through ragas. Is the same true of your music?
KHAN: Those stories are based on the truth. The people who used to do that were Sufis. They were away from this world. Materials were nothing to them. So what they used to do had effects. But today our practical life isn't so good, so it cannot bring those effects.

RASHID AHMED DIN: I do think Nusrat can do that. A few years ago, he was in Toronto and it was a sunny day—very hot. And when we started singing, it started raining. And it has happened in other places so many times. But it can't be proven, and it depends on the situation. Sometimes the throat will be good to sing but the mind will not be working so well and he can't do it. Other times the mind is working but the voice isn't. You need the two things together to have an effect.

When was your first performance?
KHAN: My first performance was at my father's funeral. I wasn't going to perform, but then I had a dream in which my father told me to sing, and he touched my throat and awakened my voice.
DIN: The music affects the singer in an equal way that it affects the audience. I remember whenever his father got deeply affected after singing, he used to put himself in a dark room for days. After his father died, there was one classical singer that was singing so well that Nusrat's uncle got so affected he tore off his clothes. Sometimes when performing, Nusrat will cry or the improvisation goes so well that he will stick to one number for maybe four hours. So we have to tell him to stop.

I've noticed your music is used a lot in Hollywood movies during scenes of drug use and violence. How do you feel about that?
KHAN: I was displeased with the Oliver Stone movie. They took religious tracts and put them in the wrong place.* They weren't very appropriate for those scenes. When someone uses something that is religious and associates it with drugs or sex or violence, it reflects badly on my reputation.

A year after this interview, Khan died of cardiac arrest in London at the age of forty-eight.

[GENESIS P-ORRIDGE]

One of my first interviews was with Genesis P-Orridge—the leader of Throbbing Gristle and Psychic TV, the founder of industrial music, and the first hero of mine I'd ever met. I was nineteen and working on my first book, for a small, academic

---

* In the film *Natural Born Killers*, Khan's singing was used as the backdrop for a violent prison riot.

publisher called *Semiotext(e)*. I was joined by my college roommate, Scott, because I was too scared to meet P-Orridge alone. I think that's all the background necessary to introduce the following—except for the fact that I sat on the table to do the interview, which would have been fine if . . .

GENESIS P-ORRIDGE: Get off the table, you creep. You're actually sitting in front of the video camera (*much laughter at my expense*). This is the man who is editing *Semiotext(e)* with his brain, but obviously doing television with his ass (*more laughter*). We want to know why you stuck it on the lens.

I get off the table and sit in a chair.

So your bus broke down today?
P-ORRIDGE: Did it?

That's what your publicist said.
P-ORRIDGE: No, no. We made that up because we wanted to lie in this morning for a nap (*more laughter*). We actually got three hours of sleep in a bed—well, on a mattress on the floor, which is a bed to us. It was the longest sleep we've had in a week.

So do you see your new record as pop or experimental?
P-ORRIDGE: Well, I actually think this LP is experimental and pop. There's a track on it, "I.C. Water," which is about Ian Curtis.* And that song just got voted single of the week in *Sounds* in England. So there's pop music on it, despite what *you* may think. And then the track "Bliss" is a nine-and-a-half minute track with the Master Musicians of Jajouka. It uses very, very high frequencies, which hopefully are the ones that release endorphins at great volume. So that is quite experimental.

So you're remaining in both worlds at the same time?
P-ORRIDGE: I'm in lots of worlds at the same time (*more laughter*). People often wonder which world it is at any given moment, and I'm not sure anymore. I'm a born again psychedelian.
SCOTT: What do you do to keep your imagination flowing free? Any advice for young burnout people out there?

---

* Singer for the dark-rock band Joy Division who hung himself at the age of twenty-three.

P-ORRIDGE: For young cynics? Gosh, I've been doing it so long it's a way of life really. Surround yourself with people who stimulate you. I don't know. There's a guy called Art Kleps, who was at the Castalia Foundation for Psychedelic Research with [Timothy] Leary and everybody, and I was reading his book [*Millbrook*] just before I left England. He says that people often think when they take things like LSD or empathogenic drugs that they're actually developing telepathy with other people and they know what people are going to do. But in fact they're learning to read synchronicity better. And that ties in with what the Native Americans say, which is that there is always a story being told to you by every situation—and every object that you're surrounded by is telling you something if you start to look carefully.

SCOTT: So the best way for you to do this is . . .

P-ORRIDGE: I think the trick is to keep your ears and eyes and all your receptors open, willing to see what's being said to you. There are always incredible things going on. You're all doing it now (*we laugh nervously*). See? It's a lifetime's work, basically, to develop the imagination and keep it. And it's something that you have to decide when you're young and sacrifice all else to.

I wanted to ask about the holosound stuff?*

P-ORRIDGE: Why do you want to ask me that? It's boring! No, that was eight years ago. I never talk about eight years ago. Holophonic sound? Ask me about Brion Gysin.†

I recently got a cassette that was released of Brion Gysin's recordings of the Master Musicians of Jajouka.

P-ORRIDGE: Yes, they released it without telling the Master Musicians, but we got in touch with both parties and sorted it all out. It's amicable now. We are going to be doing a whole album with the Master Musicians of Jajouka and Bachir [Attar, their leader] sometime this year and it will be quite interesting.

Brian Jones‡ was the last person to really investigate their music and release it, so I'm just gonna keep out of swimming pools for a while (*pauses*). Did you understand that joke? Brian Jones died in a swimming pool just after he finished the album, before it was released. Doesn't know his pop history (*clucks his tongue at me*).

---

* Holophonic sound is a technology that creates three-dimensional audio, like the acoustic equivalent of a hologram. One of its supporters was Paul McCartney, who unsuccessfully tried to buy the exclusive rights to use it.
† A writer and close associate of William Burroughs, who opened a restaurant in Morocco chiefly so he could hire the Master Musicians of Jajouka and regularly hear them play trance music.
‡ Rolling Stones guitarist who was found dead in his swimming pool at the age of twenty-seven.

I knew that, but I wasn't alive then.
P-ORRIDGE: That doesn't matter. I wasn't born when Napoleon was around, but I know that he lost (*more laughter and humiliation*).
SCOTT: We better let you get back, I guess.
P-ORRIDGE: I guess I better go write a *pop* song (*mockingly to me*). You know, there's a track on the album called "S.M.I.L.E." and . . .

Is that the pop song?
P-ORRIDGE: No, that's the ballad (*laughs at me again*). And in the background, you hear this moaning sound and then you hear a baby crying. That's actually the tape I made of Paula giving birth to [our daughter] Genesse. But I was thinking of our children or any children as being really, very simply, the future—genetically and literally.

Do you have any predictions for the future?
P-ORRIDGE: I do (*laughs*). At the end of it when we're all gone, the sea will still go in and out even if it's purple—and some form of life will continue and the stones and rocks will still be there. The planet will be here for a long time. And we're nothing really. We're (*snaps fingers*) just like that. Forty thousand years is nothing. Hardly worth a mention. We're so pompous. We think that human destiny is all-important and it isn't. It'd be nice to leave something behind that generated respect. (*Whispers theatrically:*) But will we?

What do you think?
P-ORRIDGE: I doubt it. Some of us will and that's enough.

One month later, I received a letter from P-Orridge. Despite having made fun of me throughout the interview, he wrote: "I don't know why, but I feel you should write my autobiography with me." I was too intimidated at the time to follow up, so the project never happened. But seven years later, when I actually began a career writing autobiographies, I often recalled that he was the first person to believe in me—before even I did.

Years later, P-Orridge began taking female hormones and got breast implants in an attempt to physically resemble his second wife, Lady Jaye Breyer, who died soon afterward of a previously undiagnosed heart condition.

[THE MASTER MUSICIANS
OF JAJOUKA]

For many centuries in the Rif mountains of Morocco, the Master Musicians of Ja-jouka have been playing trance music on pipes and drums. In the process, they've attracted not just the infirm from nearby villages looking to be healed by the music, but also the patronage of writers and musicians like Paul Bowles, William Burroughs, and the Rolling Stones. On the eve of the group's first-ever trip to perform in America, I spoke to Bachir Attar, who'd inherited the leadership of the Master Musicians from his father fourteen years earlier.

I've heard that Jajouka music is cursed. Can you explain?
BACHIR ATTAR: We say that Jajouka music can wake the devils from the ground. This is because somebody married a devil woman, and the devils offered my father thousands of kilos of gold to go perform at the marriage. My father didn't want to go, because if you go to another world under the ground or in the sky, you might lose your mind or never come back. So he said no. But now we know that wherever we play the music of Jajouka in the world, the devils will be listening and dancing.

In what context is the music traditionally performed?
ATTAR: We have a ceremony every year for Boujeloud.* And then we play the music every Friday to honor this saint, Sidi Ahmed Sheikh, and for sick and crazy people who have lost their minds. And after we play, the people become normal in their lives. We've been doing it for thousands of years. It's like a hospital. Many people who come have gone to doctors in Europe and not been cured. Then they stay in the village and we tie them up and we play the music every week, and they feel better.

A lot of people first heard of your music through Brian Jones. Do you remem-ber him coming to the village at all?
ATTAR: I was almost five years old when Brian Jones came and I remember it like yesterday. He was the first hippie to come to the village, and the first white person I saw that I can remember. Everybody loved him. We didn't know who the Rolling Stones were, but he had this coat like a skinned goat, these wild pants, and big hair. Other people played me the music of the Rolling Stones then, which was the first

---

* A half-man, half-goat deity (similar to the Greek god Pan) representing fertility.

music I heard that was not Moroccan. At that time, I said I wanted to be like Brian Jones. At the same time, it inspired me to start learning and playing the music of Jajouka. So coming to America, it's like a long dream coming true.

[TIMOTHY LEARY]

After the interview with Genesis P-Orridge, he gave me a reading list, which included *Flashbacks* by Timothy Leary, the sixties countercultural guru who I soon after managed to pull aside at a festival where he was speaking.

Where did your slogan "turn on, tune in, drop out" come from?
TIMOTHY LEARY: I actually didn't invent that. That slogan was given to me by [the media theorist] Marshall McLuhan. I was having lunch with him in New York City. He was very much interested in ideas and marketing, and he started singing something like, "Psychedelics hit the spot / Five hundred micrograms, that's a lot," to the tune of a Pepsi commercial. Then he started going, "Tune in, turn on, and drop out."

How do you interpret those words?
LEARY: Everyone puts a meaning on it, but "turn on" to me means to go within and turn on your inner light. Then "tune in," to us, meant to tap into what we're doing here and tune it back in. And "drop out" is the oldest statement. "Drop out" means drop out of conformity. People thought when we said "drop out," we meant just lie around, smoke grass, and listen to the Beatles. Well, that's not what we meant at all. Drop out means change.

Do you have any worries about being publicly known as someone who takes illegal drugs?
LEARY: Just the way a Catholic goes to communion once a year, I try to take every illegal drug once a year. I'm in favor of legalization of all drugs for adults. Man, other people believe that also. But if you have any kind of a salaried job, you can't go around in public saying that.

It's been more than twenty years since the psychedelic movement. Do you believe it lived up to its potential?
LEARY: The problem with the psychedelic movement was that once millions of people began learning how to open up their consciousness, there were no metaphors, no models, no language to tell them what to do with it. The thing about psychedelic drugs and plants and foods is that they were always taken communally.

With marijuana, you pass it around. This isn't true with heroin or cocaine. Can you imagine anyone at Woodstock shooting heroin or smoking crack? These are lonely experiences: You lock yourself in the bathroom. So we intuitively went back to the communality and shamanic traditions and pagan rituals of the past. That's why we had communes.

What part has music played in your explorations?
LEARY: I have been fortunate enough to live through several generations of music, and I pride myself on the fact that I have known and hung out with and gotten high with some of the finest musicians since the sixties. Some of the first people that were probably doing experiments with me were Miles Davis and the jazz bassist Charlie Mingus. And I remember Dizzy Gillespie holding his horn and kissing it in my living room. There's no question that music is the way society evolves. Poets have changed lives more than politicians.

With a video camera running to capture the moment, Timothy Leary died of complications from prostate cancer in his Beverly Hills home in 1996. He was seventy-five. According to one of his sons, his last word was "beautiful."

[RAVERS]

For a *New York Times* story, I went to a four-day rave called Even Furthur in a campground in Wisconsin. These are a few of the things I overheard that weekend.

"Dudes, my last brain cell is already hanging on the edge, and it's only Friday—or Saturday."

"The last thing he did was drink a glass of orange juice. And now he's in a mental institution and he thinks he's an orange."

"I just saw a circus in a raindrop."

"I hate brushing my teeth when I'm wasted. I keep brushing other things."

"Can you see if my ear's bleeding? This fat set of speakers fell over on me."

"Does anyone have some milk—or vitamin B12?"

"I can't find my car. Man, I don't even know if I drove it here."

[MEAT PUPPETS]

Backstage at New York's Beacon Theatre, Curt Kirkwood and Derrick Bostrom of the Meat Puppets were sharing a bong. Elsewhere, Howard Stern was practicing guitar to join the band for its song "Lake of Fire," famously covered by Nirvana on its *Unplugged* album.

In a nearby room, the third member of the Meat Puppets, Curt's younger brother Cris Kirkwood, smoked a joint. He was pissed off and ranting about his mother's boyfriends and husbands, seven of whom he claims beat him, his brother, and his mother. One, he recalled, doused the house with gasoline and set it on fire with them inside.

"I'm stuck between a pinhead weasel midget who drums like a wind-up monkey and a fucking burned-out hippie beanbag brother and a marriage I've been forced into," he concluded. He took a giant drag off the joint. "I'm probably going to blow my head off soon."

I was on assignment to interview the band for *Rolling Stone*, but Cris was in no shape to be interviewed. So I decided to talk to Curt, who was dressed in the remnants of the band's *Rolling Stone* photo shoot: a vinyl miniskirt, torn stockings, a red bra, smeared lipstick, and giant hoop earrings.

Have you written many songs while you were on acid?
CURT KIRKWOOD: Oh yeah, all the time. I keep my trips in my mind, though. They don't affect my personality that much (*belches*). Fucking Dr Pepper.

Do you ever trip with the specific intention to write a song?
KIRKWOOD: Our whole first album was expressly intended to be recorded on acid, and it was. We didn't know for sure if there were any of our favorite psychedelic albums that had been done while the people were blown out. We just had to make one that we were sure of. The first album was done conceptually while using that stuff, and then the second one was done not so intentionally with a whole shitload of MDA, which was kind of like a predecessor to ecstasy. We had about an ounce of that shit, and did the record largely with its help.

Does tripping affect the way you play live?
KIRKWOOD: Yeah, yeah, definitely. To us. I don't know about to the audience, though.

How is it different?
KIRKWOOD: The guitar neck bends. It bends all the way over. That's the one thing I've always been able to put my finger on. [. . .]

Did you ever shoot guns?
KIRKWOOD: Yes.

Do you still?
KIRKWOOD: Uh-huh, it's a lot of fun. I've done it since I was a little kid. In Arizona, you can just go outside of town and you can have a scenic afternoon in the desert and blast stuff. The respectful people don't shoot the cactuses. When we were kids, we went out and shot anything that moved. But we still never shot cactuses. The cactuses just don't reproduce like bunny rabbits. Bunny rabbits are kind of like flies. You can waste them. There's no shortage of those fuckers.

Have you ever seen a dead body?
KIRKWOOD: I've seen it too many times. Yeah, it's just ugly. I mean, the first one I saw was when I was five. My friend drowned while we were swimming. That was kind of freaky. It didn't really bother me.

Was there anything you could have done about it?
KIRKWOOD: I did try to pull him out, but he was too heavy (*takes a big bong hit*). I can just see the picture of myself in my mind, trying to pull him up the steps of the pool and watching him bounce back down because I couldn't get him up. As soon as he got toward the surface, gravity took over and (*coughs*) . . .

Did you have to tell his mom what happened?
KIRKWOOD: What happened was I got tired of trying to get him out by myself, so I went and told his parents—who were eating lunch at a restaurant not fifty feet away—that he was asleep in the water. And they flipped. My mom dove into the pool with her clothes on and pulled him out, but they were never able to resuscitate him. I'm sure that colored my next few years considerably, though.

Did you feel guilty?
KIRKWOOD: No, not at all. I never did.

A few years later, the Meat Puppets broke up for roughly a decade, during which the brothers didn't even see each other. In that time, Cris Kirkwood's wife died of an overdose and he was imprisoned for eighteen months after he grabbed a security guard's baton and started beating him with it. The guard, according to the Associated Press, shot him in the back.

[NOEL FIELDING]
SCENE 2

After the Vines concert, Noel Fielding adjourned to the lobby of Claridge's Mayfair hotel for drinks with Courtney Love, Julian Barratt (the other half of the Mighty Boosh), and dark-comedy actress Julia Davis.

As they ordered exotically named champagne cocktails, a large man walked by. Fielding instantly recognized him as comedian Lenny Henry. He followed him to a nearby table, and was struck speechless by what he found.

Sitting there was Henry's then-wife Dawn French along with Jennifer Saunders, her husband Adrian Edmondson of *The Young Ones*, and Jools Holland.

DAWN FRENCH: We were just talking about your show.

NOEL FIELDING: So do you all always hang out together like this?

FRENCH: It's Lenny's forty-eighth birthday.

LENNY HENRY: Why don't you join us?

Fielding, Barratt, and Love sit down, but Davis hovers uncomfortably around the table, until she finally walks over to French.

JULIA DAVIS: I just wanted to let you know the reason why I didn't do the women of comedy special you invited me to.

FRENCH: It's okay. You don't have to explain.

DAVIS: It's just that I like your work and would want to do it, but I guess I don't like talking about myself in that context.

HENRY: You see, all of us here, we're all from the eighties and nineties. This (*gesturing to Davis and Fielding*) is the new generation.

ADRIAN EDMONDSON: I don't know if it really changes. I think it's a five-year cycle that repeats itself, so it just seems new and edgy when it comes round again.

COURTNEY LOVE: But Julia is different. She doesn't have any desire to be liked when she performs. There's no one like that in the States at least.

DAVIS: I don't have any desire to be likable. I know people do hate my stuff for that very reason. But I have no desire to, you know, do a comfortable sit-down cozy thing.

LOVE: Because—

DAVIS: Because I think my comedy is quite angry.

Davis takes a seat and French holds court for an hour. Afterward, Henry's party turns in for the night and the younger comedians head to Love's hotel room. A baggie full of white powder is passed around, which someone explains is pure MDMA. Soon, various friends and hangers-on join the party, and start dancing to classic rock songs until Barratt puts on a post-punk She Wants Revenge CD and kills the mood. When Dee Plume catches her boyfriend, Fielding, doing a popper in the bedroom, it is the last nail in the coffin of the party.

DEE PLUME: He's been partying every night and is sick because of it. (*To Fielding:*) Come on, you have to do a radio show with Chris Morris tomorrow.

[RUSSELL BRAND]
SCENE 2

What were some of the other ideas you explored on your show?
RUSSELL BRAND: Well, I said, "You know the only reason we can sleep with prostitutes is because of anonymity. If we got to know a prostitute, would we still be able to sleep with them?" And to examine that, I went and lived with this woman who is a prostitute. I got to know her and her family.

They were all smackheads, and I was addicted to smack at the time. And this amazing thing is, I was out in the garden with her boyfriend going, "You've got to get clean, mate." He was crying. I was crying. I've got it all on camera. And then his little daughter comes running out—his three-year-old daughter—and she was sitting on his lap. He enshrouds her in his pullover so that her head and his head are coming out of the fucking pullover like a Hydra. He pulls her in closer and they're both crying. I'm going, "You've got to get clean, mate." Then we stopped rolling and I was like, "Come on, let's have a use-up."

That's horrible.
BRAND: It gets worse. At the end of the three days with that prostitute and getting to know her, I was like, "All right, I've got to know you and you're lovely people. Here's fifty quid. Let me fuck you now." And she was a wreck of a prostitute.

How did they respond?
BRAND: They broke down. It destroyed the moment. I got annihilated, you know, and that show couldn't even be broadcast because it was too intense. I've still got it. For another one, I went out with this young BNP [British National Party] group—these Nazis—and ended up fighting with them, and they wouldn't let us

film them anymore. I tried to seduce an old lady, and did all these mad things to sort of challenge the way people thought.

Did it work on that level?
BRAND: Well, I did all of these things, but I wasn't well. I was having a breakdown, really. I got all these homeless people in the studio and it was a Sunday afternoon show, and I read out porn on the air. I was like, "Hey, if you're homeless, I'm the agony uncle for all your homeless needs." Of course no one phoned up with homeless problems because homeless people don't have radios. It was all filth and like anal sex, and they sacked me there and then. So I lost that job.

Is that what made you get clean?
BRAND: That happened later, after I got sacked from another job. I was doing a movie with Steve Coogan, David Walliams, and Rob Brydon called *Cruise of the Gods*. I only had a little part in it. I was mental at that stage, and we were on a cruise ship in the Aegean Sea. And before Steve even got there, I was going out to, like, these lap dance clubs in Athens, where I was like fingering the dancers and wanking and all sorts of stuff. And I ended up getting into a fight with the guy who owned the lap dancing club and he sort of punched me in the face. Then we were in Istanbul and we went to a brothel and fucked these prostitutes, and I ended up breaking this prostitute's phone on the wall.

How did that happen?
BRAND: I was sleeping with this prostitute and she kept answering her phone, so I picked up her phone, smashed it on the wall, then went back to the brothel and demanded my money back from these fucking Turkish blokes. I was lucky not to get killed. And I found out there were also dancing girls on the boat, so I fucked one of the dancing girls and the daughter of one of the passengers on the cruise ship. And the producers found out about it all and sacked me.

Did you throw a fit when that happened?
BRAND: I think they knew I would. So Steve's brother Brendan gave me a lift to the airport, saying, "No, you're just getting a week's shore leave. You're getting a week's holiday. You've been doing really well." I didn't even get it. I was going, "Do you want me to bring you back anything from England when I come back?" And Brendan said, "No, no problem." As a friend of mine put it, I was like a dog being taken to the vet to be put to sleep.

So how'd you finally get clean?
BRAND: Yeah, the point of all that was that I went totally mental. I lost everything, and my addiction totally got out of control. And then I got with this new manager, John Noel, and he forced me to go into a treatment center. I went there for three months, got clean, and was on some methadone to get off heroin and sleeping pills to help me sleep. I did it for three months, and then I came back and was like a timid and fragile old man. But eventually I got used to being a normal person again.

[*Continued . . .*]

[SPARKLEHORSE]

For a few months, Mark Linkous, the laconic singer who records as Sparklehorse, thought his first album would be his last. While on tour, he collapsed in a London hotel room after mixing Valium with his antidepressant medication. When the paramedics came over twelve hours later, they found him unconscious with his legs bent underneath his body. When they straightened his legs, a surge of potassium shut down his kidneys and heart. Linkous was dead for several minutes before they were able to revive him. He spent three months in the hospital, followed by six months in a wheelchair, before walking again with the help of leg braces.

Dog howls.

MARK LINKOUS: Shut up! What's the matter with you? Calm down.

So you were saying . . .
LINKOUS: Sorry. Yeah, I just took a whole bunch of pills, uh, and just like collapsed in a hotel room in London.

Did you do any writing while you were in the hospital?
LINKOUS: No, I couldn't write. I mean, I was really frightened that when I, like, flatlined for a few minutes, the songwriting cells in my brain died from lack of oxygen or something, but . . .

But?
LINKOUS: But I was on so much medication that I couldn't think straight.

Did being confronted with the loss of something you take for granted give you any new thoughts on life or what you're supposed to be doing with it?
LINKOUS: Well, yeah, it did. It confirmed in a way that I'm supposed to be here to make records, just because so many people wrote to me about how much my first record affected them.

In your songs, you like to mess with the sound of your voice and the instruments . . .
LINKOUS: Yeah, I just kinda like destroying it sometimes. Like with "Happy Man." I wrote that song before [my previous album]. So I put all this radio static in there.

Because?
LINKOUS: I was tired of the song. I wanted to, in a way, sabotage it. [. . .] I went to Memphis recently though and recorded, I guess, a friendly version of "Happy Man." It sounded pretty good.

Are you going to add that to the record?
LINKOUS: I think that's just for radio. The record label wanted it.

So you unsabotaged it?
LINKOUS: There's this really expensive motorcycle that I want, so . . .

When you sing about only needing "water, a gun, and rabbits," what's the idea behind that?
LINKOUS: Well, just that the way the world is, things get so complicated and move so fast. And I'm even guilty of acquiring all these possessions that I really don't need, like five old motorcycles. And then there's all this stuff that comes with having a house and health insurance and just all that bullshit. Sometimes I just feel like all I wanna do is just go up and live in the mountains and . . . and eat rabbits.

Are you worried about getting dropped or lost in the shuffle because of all the changes at your record label?
LINKOUS: If you start thinking about that kind of stuff, you'll just get depressed and want to hide or something.

Do you think touring with Radiohead influenced you in any way?
LINKOUS: Uh, it didn't really influence me. I mean, they said "No Surprises" was their Sparklehorse song, but I mean we could never compete with them. They're

just great at making those big majestic pop songs, you know, and our thing is being kinda small and pathetic.

In 2010, Linkous was at a friend's house in Knoxville, Tennessee, when he received a text message that upset him. He walked outside shortly afterward and fatally shot himself in the chest with his rifle. He was forty-seven. The contents and sender of the text were not disclosed.

[RADIOHEAD]

There are some bands that one gets to watch evolve into something much greater than anyone could expect, and Radiohead is one of them. At its first performance in New York, it was an apparent one-hit wonder, playing to a crowd familiar with not much more than its new single "Creep." When it returned to New York on its own tour after releasing *The Bends*, it had proven itself as a jittery, powerful band to watch closely. And by the time of Radiohead's visit to New York before the release of its third album, *OK Computer*, it was clear that it was one of the most important bands of its time. Sitting in the backseat of a van on the way to a photo shoot on the Brooklyn Bridge, Radiohead singer Thom Yorke struggled to put his music into words.

It took me a lot of listens to sort of penetrate the record. It's very—
THOM YORKE: It's a weird record. When we first gave it to Capitol [Records], they were taken aback. I don't really know why it's so important now, but I'm excited about it.

What do you think everyone's hearing in it?
YORKE: It's got an atmosphere of its own. It kind of throws you, and I think that's a good thing. When we were recording it, we just had this sound in our heads and . . . I don't know.

What was the sound?
YORKE: This sounds kind of *Spinal Tap* or whatever, but (*sighs*) when we were recording the new album, we had this sound in our heads, the sound of resonating glass and metal and sort of . . . It's a bit difficult to explain. It's sort of a cross between Marvin Gaye's *What's Going On* and Miles Davis's *Bitches Brew*. Sort of quite dense but also quite clear. This is kind of all in retrospect. I'm looking on it like you are, because we took a good year to do the album and I couldn't really explain what we were doing to anybody then.

It's surprising that you recorded the album in so many different places, since it has such a consistent sound.

YORKE: Basically, that was mostly to do with one of these amazing old reverb plates that we bought and took everywhere with us. It's like the size of a very large car and it kept breaking. But it was everything. To me it was like the sound of a really, really large railway station or airport. And that's what I wanted to hear.

Have you heard the rap song that uses the chorus from "Creep"?

YORKE: It excites me that we've got to the point where the song is public property. Anything we do will end up like that, really. I mean, we were in . . . Where were we? I think it was Bangkok. And we walked into a bar and sat down, and this band played "Creep" right in front of us. We all stood up in front of the band and clapped along, looking them in the eye. And they just thought, "Who are these people we don't know?"

They didn't recognize you?

YORKE: Yeah, it's great to be able to walk away from it as well. Like it's now the property of some Thai cover band, you know.

Is there an older band that you look to as a model of how to keep making important music that matters?

YORKE: We've been touring with R.E.M. And it was very inspiring to think you could actually do all of these things and not turn into a bunch of wankers.

[R.E.M.]

Early on, probably with the Led Zeppelin article, I learned to avoid interviewing members of a band together. If you talk to them all at once, they no longer speak for your benefit, but for the benefit of each other. With some bands, that means lots of private jokes they've accumulated on the road. With R.E.M., who insisted on doing this interview together as equals, it means a fear of even calling themselves a band in case another member disagrees. At the time, the group was grappling with the departure of its original drummer, Bill Berry, who suffered a brain aneurysm while touring and, after recovering, decided to become a farmer and spend more time with his family.

MIKE MILLS [bassist]: You've been around for a while: What kind of band would you say R.E.M. is? A rock band? What do we play? Do we play rock and roll? What would you call us?

If I had to broadly generalize, I'd say a rock band.

MILLS: I have to answer that question a lot. When people ask me what kind of music I play, I usually say, "The kind of music I play."

PETER BUCK [guitarist]: We were a punk band and then we were a new wave band and then we were college rock, whatever that was. We don't even have college degrees. And then there was indie rock. We're not indie.

MILLS: We're all those things and then some.

MICHAEL STIPE [singer]: I don't even know if we're a band anymore. I almost feel like we're a musical collective at this point. I'm not really sure.

MILLS: I'd call it a group. Combo is good. Collective just sounds pretentious.

STIPE: I didn't mean it to sound like that.

BUCK: We are three guys who write songs together, and then there are other guys who help record it. And we don't know who the other guys are from record to record.

STIPE: It's a revolving door, but the glass is on the outside.

BUCK: I don't know what we are, and I can't worry about it. But I do think about it: Where do I fit in? What I have to realize is, I can't keep up with trends. As exciting as it is when I listen to DJ Shadow, it would be so stupid to go that way or to go techno.

MILLS: Maybe we'll wear baggy pants and wear our hats backward.

BUCK: I was talking to Neil Young about it and he was talking about a tour in Europe in '87 where he had to cancel every other show because he couldn't sell more than a hundred tickets. In the last two years, he's been selling sixty thousand seats. It comes and goes.

MILLS: As long as you do great work, you're going to be rewarded.

BUCK: It's a great journey where we're going, and I firmly believe that if we keep strong as a band and keep our vision, somewhere down the line we're going to sell ten million records. I'd love to be fifty years old and have people go, "Jesus, these guys have never made a bad record." And then all of a sudden, you're legendary. We're not legendary yet. We're between being new and being legendary. We're stuck right there.

[NEIL YOUNG]
SCENE 2

Sometimes you meet musicians on a good day and get a great interview. Other times, you meet them on a bad day.

Are you doing a video for the single?

NEIL YOUNG: We're doing a video, but we're not in it.

What's the concept?
YOUNG: I don't know. We're not there.

Is "Fallen Angel" about a stripper?
YOUNG: I think everybody's got their own picture.

What was your picture?
YOUNG: My picture's *my* picture.

And you're not going to share it?
YOUNG: No.

You're turning fifty this year—
YOUNG: It's going to be a big party.

Do you have any thoughts on turning fifty?
YOUNG: I can't help it.

That line you wrote on the new album, "On the ocean people my age, they don't do the things I do."
YOUNG: Yeah.

What does it refer to?
YOUNG: Oh, I don't know. This stuff came out one time.

It wasn't in reference to anything specific?
YOUNG: No, just the way it is. I wrote it late one night, early one morning.

When you were up in Seattle, did you meet other musicians or anything?
YOUNG: Yeah, I met quite a few musicians from different bands.

Have you stayed in touch with anyone?

YOUNG: I'm not really the best communicator. But when I see them, I'll know who they are.

——◆——

At what point in your career could you basically do what you wanted artistically without anyone saying no?

YOUNG: Well, sometimes you want to do things and it doesn't work out. Usually it turns out that it wasn't a good idea anyway. But there are other ways of doing things. So I still feel like I can do things that I want to do. Doesn't seem to be going away.

And at what point in your career did you get that freedom?

YOUNG: When did I begin to do that? That's a good question. It must have been a long time ago.

——◆——

Do you still find yourself limited much technically as a musician?

YOUNG: No. I mean, technically I'm limited. I don't have the greatest chops in the world. But I don't care.

——◆——

So what made you decide to do this interview to promote the album?

YOUNG: You know, just show that it can be done. Just do it. Didn't do it for the last album or the one before that—or the one before that. It's good not to do too much.

——◆——

After the interview, Young walks to a parking lot, where a photographer and a TV cameraman are waiting for him. As he sits there being manipulated into different positions, he grows more and more uncomfortable, until he thrusts a long middle finger menacingly in the direction of the TV camera and speaks to the public.

YOUNG: You better buy my goddamned record, fools.

[DOLLY PARTON]

One night, I happened to catch country singer Dwight Yoakam on a talk show. The host kept asking questions about his new album, but Yoakam had other things he wanted to discuss, such as, if I recall correctly, the theory that dogs are closer on the evolutionary scale to humans than apes are. He was so enjoyable to listen to that I became a fan on the spot. Conversely, artists who spend an entire interview trying to steer the conversation back to a product they're promoting tend to have the opposite effect, no matter how charming they try to be. This is part of the mind game of the interview: Most established musicians wouldn't be doing it if they didn't have a new release to promote, but most interviewers wouldn't be talking to them if they weren't interested in their past and getting to know the person behind the songs.

I notice you changed some of the lyrics to Neil Young's "After the Gold Rush" on your new album.
DOLLY PARTON: I wasn't certain what it was about, so I needed for myself to make it a little clearer. In the original, it said something about a queen, so I changed it to a king, like Jesus. And then there were a couple of lines about, "I felt like getting high" in the original. And I said, "I felt like I could cry."

You don't want any drug references in your songs?
PARTON: I thought, well, with this anti-drug thing going on, people would jump my ass for saying I felt like getting high. Did you ever know what the song meant?

I think it's something about how we're destroying the environment.
PARTON: It's such an abstract song. I think nobody ever knew what that song meant, not even Neil Young. So I just tried to personalize it a little bit so it would make more sense, and I could explain it if someone asked me what it was about. Now, to me, it's about the second coming or an invasion of the aliens or whatever. I figure if there's a second coming, it's going to be coming in a blaze of glory in some kind of spaceship (*laughs*). Were you fascinated with the fact that I did "Peace Train," the old Cat Stevens song?

Yeah, and then you added [South African Zulu singers] Ladysmith Black Mambazo to it. How did you first hear of them?
PARTON: Actually, I found them on TV. I heard a Life Savers commercial on TV,

so I called my producer and said, "Whoever's singing that Life Savers commercial is who I want on 'Peace Train.'" So it turned out to be them.

I visited Dollywood recently, and it's impressive because so many musicians have talked about opening an amusement park, but few have ever done it.
PARTON: Dollywood is a theme park, not an amusement park. It's really about preserving our Smoky Mountain heritage. People don't realize that. And we're up in the top five of all parks, including Disney.* Anyway, it's just a good location, so I was lucky and, I'd like to think, smart to start it when I did. I always wanted to take something back home and provide a lot of jobs, because there's a lot of poor people in that area.

I don't know if this is true or not, but—
PARTON: This interview is about the music, I think.

I was just going to ask if you were in some kind of accident.
PARTON: What? No! Are you talking about Barbara Mandrell?[†]

No, I was talking to your publicist. I'm sure she wouldn't get it confused.
PARTON: No, you must have . . . The only thing it might have been is that three months ago, I had some laser peel on my face. And I came out of the clinic with a veil over my head only because I had about a foot of Vaseline on my face since it kind of burns your skin. So they got a picture of me with this veil on my head and then the tabloids all had headlines saying, "Dolly scarred for life from some bizarre surgery," and all that shit. But that's a lie. There was nothing. I was back at work in the studio when that article came out.

Your publicist was saying all they talked about on the Jay Leno show was the plastic surgery and some accident and you were upset they didn't discuss the album—
PARTON: I have never had an accident. It just must have been that. We don't even need—

Okay, we can get back to the album. [. . .][‡] Thanks so much for taking the time to talk.

---

* A spokesman for Dollywood, as well as spokespeople for the International Association of Amusement Parks and Attractions, were unable to confirm this statistic.
† Twelve years earlier, Mandrell was in a car accident. She broke several bones and suffered temporary memory loss and speech difficulties.
‡ Fifteen minutes of question-and-answer about her new album omitted.

PARTON: Thank you for taking time to talk to me because I'm the one that's asking for the favor. So I hope it turns out good. If not, well, I'll kick your ass when I see you. Maybe I'll see you the next time I'm in New York. I'm up there a lot.

I hope you like the article. Don't beat me up.
PARTON: Yeah, okay, but if I don't, I *will* beat you over the head like a little pup.

THE WHITE STRIPES
SCENE 1

Jack and Meg White, the ex-husband-and-wife duo known as the White Stripes, peered tentatively out of the doorway of their dressing room at the MTV Movie Awards at the Shrine Auditorium in Los Angeles. Sharon Osbourne stood in the hallway, and she was not happy. Apparently, Eminem's bodyguards had dared to ask her to remove her children from the corridor so the rapper could pass by. "Crack a smile, little boy," she cackled as Eminem and his muscular entourage walked past. "Keep your head down. Don't look at me."

As the bodyguards and Eminem stared at the ground obediently, Jack and Meg shook their heads in disbelief. "We've slipped into some other dimension," muttered Meg.

"I can't even fathom why they asked us to perform here," Jack grumbled. "I hate award shows."

This reluctant relationship with their success is what makes the White Stripes—who were about to walk down the red carpet for the first time in their lives—among the most difficult kinds of musicians to interview. Not only are they worried about being in the spotlight, but they're even more worried about being judged and criticized by old friends and enemies for being there.

Since you guys first met each other, has Jack changed much?
MEG WHITE: I think we're about the same. It's hard to tell because we live our lives so close to each other that people on the outside would be able to tell easier than we would.
JACK WHITE: What should change, even if we had only sold a thousand records or a million records? I mean, should anything change? I don't think it should really.

Hopefully something changes. Hopefully you learn from your experiences and grow and change for the better.
JACK: I suppose so, yeah. You can become a better person. Usually those kinds of

success things have the opposite effect. People become worse—more cocky and egotistical. I think we both have remained the same.

Where do you guys actually live in Detroit?
JACK: In the city. We both live in the city.

Which part did you grow up in?
JACK: In southwest Detroit.
MEG: I live near the college, like closer to downtown.

Did you—
JACK: We don't really want to talk about our childhood stuff.

Not that it matters, but it's interesting that you broke eye contact when you said that.
JACK: It's not like that. I don't like to get into that because it kind of gets involved in the whole white rapper *are-you-really-from-the-hood?* kind of thing. [. . .] The whole point of the band isn't, are we really brother and sister or are we husband and wife? And are you really from the city or are you just pretending you're from the city? Or did you like sandboxes as kids or the monkey bars?

I do think there's a difference between asking what underwear someone wears and asking about the way they were raised, because that affects who they are as artists.
JACK: I guess so, but how many times have you heard Jewel say, "I lived in my car for a year?" Okay, I'm sorry you lived in your car for a year. But I'm not going to bow down to you and say your poetry is amazing because you lived in your car. Big deal—millions of people do that all the time. And if we say things like that, I don't want them to be misconstrued as, "Oh, love us because we grew up in the poorest neighborhood in Detroit." I don't like that.

So instead, you sort of want to maintain your mystique?
JACK: Well, I don't know. I'm afraid to discuss that. I mean, if the topic of discussion is that the White Stripes want to maintain their mystique, that's a destruction of mystique in itself (*chuckles*).

Maybe you've internalized past criticism, because a lot of times when I ask a question, I notice that you take it in a negative way as a judgment. Like when I asked if you'd changed at all, you assumed it was for the negative.

JACK (*laughs*): I don't know. It's true. Even if I feel that I'm a better person now than I was two years ago, I'm not going to say it because people will make the judgment of, "Oh, look who's got a lot of money and success now. That's why you're so happy."

Okay, let's play what if: What if everyone knew everything about you—every little thing from where you came from to your favorite color to the details of your personal life, just like they know everything about their favorite Backstreet Boy?
JACK: Right.

What would happen?
JACK: Then we'd be completely dead.

[*Continued . . .*]

[JEWEL]

"Sometimes I want to take that Volkswagen van and affix it to a burning cross," Jewel said when we first met at the Four Seasons Hotel in Manhattan, referring to the story about how she lived in her van when she was a struggling singer-songwriter. "I just feel like a comic book."

When I started writing articles, I read a lot of magazines for inspiration. And an article that always stuck out was a profile of Neneh Cherry in *Details* that opened with the singer in the female writer's bed. As a surrogate for the fan, I thought, a profile writer can't get much closer to the subject than that, though the following article would turn out to be my nadir as a young, impressionable journalist.*

And so it was that, after an interview that began in New York and seemed to be winding down at a benefit in San Diego, Jewel made an offer I couldn't refuse. "You should spend the night at the house," she suggested.

At her mother's ranch house, I stripped the guest bed of its myriad of pillows and prepared to go to sleep as she talked with her mom in the kitchen. As I was lying under the covers, flipping through a glossy color picture book of Alaska, Jewel walked in wearing a green zipper sweatshirt and crawled under the covers with me. This was it: my Neneh Cherry moment. The tape recorder was dutifully started.

JEWEL: As a kid I had a Mormon pamphlet, and it said you had to keep an arm's length away from a woman in bed and a husband couldn't spoon his wife for more than twenty minutes.

---

* Not counting, of course, the time I thought *nadir* meant *peak*, and in the Ryan Adams profile called his former band Whiskeytown "the nadir of alt-country."

WANT TO FIT IN
WITH THE
POPULAR CROWD?

HOW?

with
SANITIZED

TAPE
WORMS

*These Little Friends will
Help You Lose Weight
so People can See
the Real YOU:
Beautiful, Charismatic,
Dateable. No Strict Diet
or Tedious Exercise
Necessary. Just Swallow
These Hungry Fellows
and Let Them do
the Eating for You.
The Fat You Consume
Doesn't Have to
End Up in Your Body.*

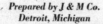

She flips onto her side and begins discussing women, insecurity, and body image.

JEWEL: When I left Alaska and went to LA for the first time, the women there looked like bonsai trees or something. You know, they were all trimmed and coiffed. And just to see those women with those lips, like this (*puffs out her lips*). I can't believe it. No one's allowed to grow old now.

They end up looking so hard on the outside.
JEWEL: I know. I took Pilates for a while, and I got so scared off. These house-wives would come in, and they were just ripped. Where I was raised, it was like women should have hips and breasts. And they were naturally vital and they built their own houses and they milked their own cows. They were these radiant older women. In LA, it's such a sad thing.

Do you think that if you're forty and still doing photo shoots constantly, you'll ever consider plastic surgery?
JEWEL: I don't want to grow old in the States at all. I want to go back to Alaska. So few women do it with grace. I feel like, just thank God for Bonnie Raitt. That's why I realized recently, "Jewel, you better get a grip now on who you are and what you are, because it'll be so ugly if you're hitting forty and still trying to be eighteen."

The problem is that most people think of aging only in terms of losing looks, not in terms of gaining wisdom and understanding.
JEWEL: Yeah, and plus it would be so embarrassing to be on your deathbed . . . I think about this. I don't know why.

Everyone does.
JEWEL: I just don't want to get on my deathbed and realize the whole focus of my life was off by a degree. It'd be so embarrassing to realize that, like, I got caught up in what was frivolous.

I think most people are caught up in things that don't really matter, including both of us.
JEWEL: That's heavy. My best friend just died of cancer. It was wild. It really makes you re-question everything. I question things I never thought I'd question. It won't come out in my writing for a long time. It happened kind of quick—over maybe four months at the most—and it just made me think, it's not okay that I got successful in four years. It isn't all right.

Why is that?
JEWEL: I don't know how to describe it. It's just that I went from, you know, welfare to being an incredibly rich magazine cover girl in four years. It's insane, and it's not success. I don't know why, but her dying really hit me hard that it doesn't matter at all. It just doesn't.

So what do you think does matter?
JEWEL: The quality of your life and the quality of people's lives is all that matters. There were people next to me living in their cars or sleeping on the street corner, and they're not rich in four years. And I'm not any more deserving of it just because I have a talent the world thinks is worth giving a ridiculous amount of money to. That doesn't make it all right for me.

I don't know. That sounds like guilt. You worked for it.
JEWEL: It still doesn't strike me as fair when all those people are still worrying about things like clothing and shelter. It doesn't strike me as right. I guess I realize that, ultimately, when I look back on my life, I think I'll define my success as that I bring other people with me.

A few minutes later, Jewel's mother, Nedra Carroll, walks into the room to tuck her in.

NEDRA CARROLL: Is this an example of sleeping your way to the top?

[DJ JUBILEE]

When Louisiana was briefly the nation's hip-hop capital, rappers on local labels like Cash Money cruised New Orleans at night in their own helicopter, sporting jewelry worth tens of thousands of dollars. Meanwhile, DJ Jubilee, the regional star who first popularized many of the catchphrases those rappers brought to the pop charts, was rising at 5:30 a.m. every morning to take the school bus.

By day, Jubilee taught special-education classes at West Jefferson High School in New Orleans. But in the evenings, he ruled the dance clubs and block parties, acknowledged as the master of a call-and-response booty-shaking style of hip-hop called bounce. The New Orleans rapper Juvenile took the title and chorus of his popular single, "Back That Azz Up," from a local hit of the same name by Jubilee. And Master P released a hit with his group the 504 Boyz, "Wobble Wobble," also lifted from a DJ Jubilee lyric. In all of these cases, Jubilee received neither royalties nor credit.

On a Monday morning, DJ Jubilee sat behind a teacher's desk in the school's special-education room, wearing a white T-shirt and a large pendant promoting his label, Take Fo' Records. On his calendar was a George Eliot quote he often turns to for inspiration: "Keep true, never be ashamed of doing right." Sitting next to him was a student, Chad, who was wearing protective headgear.

How long have you been working with Chad?

DJ JUBILEE: I've been with him [for three years]. We're buddy-buddy. I know everything he does. He comes from a background where his mother's gay and his dad doesn't want him. When he gets sick, I tell other kids, "You don't know how fortunate you are to have everything working."

So what kinds of things do you teach him?

DJ JUBILEE: He only just learned my name last year. (*To Chad:*) What's my name?

CHAD (*slowly, grinning*): Jubilee.

DJ JUBILEE: How old are you?

CHAD: Seventeen.

DJ JUBILEE: He's twenty-one, but he has the number seventeen stuck in his head. He has a problem with seizures. There's another student here who's partially blind, and another one who's really smart but is schizophrenic and is always laughing at the voices in his head. We try to teach them the basic survival skills they need: their name, address, the date and time, and what holidays are coming up. We want to teach them the concept of being streetwise.

Do they know your music?

DJ JUBILEE: They all know my music. (*To another student, Glenn:*) What are the names of my songs?

GLENN: "Get Ready, Ready," "Back That Thang Up," "Do the Jubilee All." When's your next album coming out, Jube?

DJ JUBILEE: In the summer.

How do their parents feel that, by night, you're performing at these really sexual parties?

DJ JUBILEE: They all love me. I'm a positive guy. I don't smoke. I don't drink. I don't do negative things to fit in with other people. I don't even drink a wine cooler. But it's much harder to keep kids positive now. We're outnumbered: There are more negative role models than positive role models. And it's going to take a long time to recover the ground we've lost. I'm fighting that, and it hurts me just to see kids lose their lives like they do in some of these neighborhoods.

Is it dangerous for you to be out that late in your neighborhood, especially since everyone knows you're carrying DJ and studio equipment?
DJ JUBILEE: I could sit in the hood all day and not fear anything. The community loves me so much.

How much do you make working here?
DJ JUBILEE: I make some nice money. Between teaching and DJing and record sales, I make between twenty-three and twenty-four thousand dollars a year. Plus I get insurance and benefits and a medical plan.

How do you feel that some of the rappers who are using your music walk around wearing jewelry worth more than that?
DJ JUBILEE: I like my job. I've been here for six years. I do my songs here. I wrote my last three hits at this desk.

Pats a notebook lying open on his desk.

But you must sometimes get upset seeing your lyrics on the pop charts without your name next to them?
DJ JUBILEE: At one time I had writer's block because every time I said something on the microphone, people took it and would put it on albums or start saying it at parties. They'd always claim to be the originator or the person who turned me on to it. So I'm fighting to keep my mouth closed. They used to ask me in interviews where I got my ideas from, and I'd say second line parades or high school dances. And then the next day, all these rappers would be out there looking for new ideas. And now somebody just got another one.

You mean another one of your songs?
DJ JUBILEE: The 504 Boyz got "Wobble Wobble." It's like I'm feeding them information to use in their hits. I saw Master P on TV and they asked him, "What's the meaning of 'Wobble Wobble'?" And I could have kicked the TV. He said, "It means when you're hanging out with your boys, you're wobbling" (*pauses, shakes his head*). You go say "wobble, wobble" to a girl, and you watch what happens.

Ten years later, DJ Jubilee was still teaching special ed at West Jefferson High School while continuing to record, DJ, and tour.

[LUDACRIS]

The occasion was the first (and last) annual Ho'lympics, an epic competition in which two great powers—the hip-hop nation and the mass media—engaged in a fierce battle of wits, brawn, and libido. Representing the hip-hop nation was Ludacris, the crown jewel of the Dirty South, with over ten million albums of fast-rhyming twang sold in his name. Representing the mass media was me. The odds were clearly on Ludacris, especially when he appointed his assistant to act as referee.

Before the games began at his palatial new three-story home just outside Atlanta, Ludacris noticed my belt, which had a silver orb-shaped buckle that doubled as a cigarette lighter, and raised the stakes.

LUDACRIS: Lemme see that belt? (*I show him how it works.*) I want that.

I bet you do.
LUDACRIS: I'll tell you what: If I win today, I get the belt.

What do I get if I win?
LUDACRIS (*scans room*): Jam Master Jay's tennis shoes! *

CHALLENGE #1: ONE-HANDED BRA UNHOOKING

Before a small crowd of assistants, recording artists, label employees, hangers-on, and Ludacris manager Chaka Zulu's ten-year-old son, the first competition is set up. Five women kneel on a black leather couch. We stand facing them, ready to be timed on how fast we can unhook their bras with one hand behind our backs. There will be two rounds.

LUDACRIS: Man, who thought of this idea? Oh, it was me.
REFEREE: Ready?
LUDACRIS: The only reason you might win is because girls always be taking them off for me.

---

* Jam Master Jay, the thirty-seven-year-old DJ for Run-DMC, had recently been shot and killed while in a recording studio in Queens.

In the first heat, Ludacris's time is 1:36 and mine is 0:45. The second round goes much better for Ludacris.

LUDACRIS: How was that?
REFEREE: Eighteen seconds.

Ludacris runs through the room, throwing his fists into the air, galloping into the foyer, and punching the walls—until I score eighteen seconds as well.

LUDACRIS: Damn.
REFEREE: That's a draw then.
LUDACRIS: I'd just like to thank lady number three for making this possible.

SCORE
Rapper: 1
Writer: 1

CHALLENGE #2: HIP-HOP SCRABBLE

Did anyone bring a Scrabble board?
LUDACRIS: I have one. (*Runs upstairs and fetches a still-wrapped deluxe edition of the game.*) I have a lot of stuff like this, because I like entertaining.

Ludacris settles at a table near his home theater, the Ludaplex, and spreads out the Scrabble tiles. He hands the instructions to the referee. The rule: Only hip-hop lingo can be used. Thus, words like "here" and "there" are not allowed, but "herre" and "thurr" are golden.
    Ludacris draws seven tiles, arranges the letters on his board, and claps his hands together. Slowly, he lays his first word onto the board: N-E-G-R-O.

LUDACRIS: That's a hip-hop word right there!

I lay down an even longer word, S-E-R-V-I-N. Ludacris parries with M-O-F-O.

CHAKA ZULU'S TEN-YEAR-OLD SON (*to Ludacris*)**:** What's a mofo?

LUDACRIS: It's somebody who's crazy.

I lay down C-R-A-Z-Y. Ludacris then lays down the letters N-I-G-G-A-S. And so it goes: Ego, Ride, Real, Fo, Raw, Nann, and Punann—until I lay down the word H-O-Z.

LUDACRIS: That ain't right. It can only be spelled H-O-E-S or H-O-E-Z.

What about the Juvenile song, "Hoz Ain't Nuthin' But Hoz."
LUDACRIS: Referee!

The reference is checked online, and the word is validated. Ludacris then lays down J-E-N.

How is that hip-hop?
LUDACRIS: Like "Jen From the Block," the J. Lo song.

"Jenny From the Block"?
LUDACRIS: Same thing. And that's a double word score, you bastard.

The referee allows it, and Ludacris takes the game, 256 to 236. There is such a thing as a good winner, but Ludacris is not one. As he snatches a victory chicken breast from the hands of a Def Jam employee, he gloats . . .

LUDACRIS: Y'all are at a loss for words. I beat you in Scrabble!
CHAKA ZULU'S SON: I'm thirsty.
LUDACRIS: Aww, let the little nigga have a drink.

SCORE
Rapper: 2
Writer: 1

CHALLENGE #3: FORTY-OUNCE SKEET SHOOTING

Ludacris walks along the side of his lake with a .22 caliber rifle in his hands.

LUDACRIS: There's two things in life: to be scared or prepared, and I'm prepared like a motherfucker.

A Def Jam employee, unable to find any forty-ounce beer bottles at the store, purchased a case of Corona instead. But every last drop has been guzzled already. So a diet root beer pyramid is erected instead. Ludacris stands at the ready, lovingly polishing the muzzle of his rifle.

LUDACRIS: We live by the motto: I wish a motherfucker would.

He fires off his first shot, and demolishes both the first and second row of cans. With three more shots, the entire pyramid is eliminated.

LUDACRIS: Beat that!

With the first shot, I knock off the top can alone. The second bullet eliminates the second row, and a third shot explodes the rest of the diet root beer. It is pure luck, because never in my life did I think I'd be a better shot than a gangsta rapper.

SCORE
Rapper: 2
Writer: 2

◆

CHALLENGE #4: ATV RACING

Chaka Zulu gives me a quick riding lesson since I've never ridden an all-terrain vehicle before, and the race around Ludacris's lake is on. Actually, race wouldn't quite be the right word for it. Let's just say that Ludacris wins by about twenty-five bras.

SCORE
Rapper: 3
Writer: 2

◆

THE AWARDS CEREMONY

Ludacris sits in the corner of his rec room and discusses the details of the ceremony with Chaka Zulu for several minutes. Finally, he stands up, ready to receive his accolades. Bra model #4 comes by with a gold medal for Ludacris and a silver medal for me.

LUDACRIS: Why are you getting the platinum medal?

It's actually silver. The winner gets gold.
LUDACRIS (*pauses, thinks*): In hip-hop, that's platinum. So I should get the platinum medal.

Bra model #4 hangs the winning platinum around Ludacris's neck, the hip-hop nation having defeated the muckraking press. As I walk away with the ignominious gold medal around my neck, Ludacris stops me.

LUDACRIS: You forgot something.

I reach under my jacket and give him the belt from off my pants. Fair is fair.

THE WHITE STRIPES
SCENE 2

Occasionally, I'm under orders to do or ask about something specific when I write a story. Some artists, like Ludacris, enjoy playing along, no matter how ridiculous the concept. Others rankle at even the simplest suggestion.

So *Rolling Stone* has a sidebar they do with all their features now. And for this one, they want to run a list of your five favorite albums or bands.
JACK WHITE: Is it a little *Teen Beat* square at the corner of the page with, like, my favorite top to wear (*laughs derisively*).
MEG WHITE: (*Laughs derisively.*)

I hate to ask you to do this after everything we've talked about.
JACK: Just tell them that we were complete jerks and refused to do it (*laughs again, joined by Meg*).

They'll make me put something in there. We could discuss a couple of the songs you cover and why you chose them instead, and do it in a meaningful way.

JACK: I don't know. Whatever you think. Those little things always look stupid to me.

I know you pick the songs you cover for good reasons.

JACK: I'm scared of that, because I don't want attention because of the coolness factor of what songs we pick to cover. I don't want people to say that we think we're cool because we play [Dolly Parton's] "Jolene." That's not why we do it. We don't try and make a joke out of it or anything. That's scary territory.

I don't think it would seem like that. But it's up to you. I would imagine it would just be you saying where you first heard the song and the impression it made on you.

JACK: Let's pick something else.

MEG: What about bands in Detroit?

JACK: Well, I don't know. I'm sorry. I don't mean to be a negative kind of guy, but we are in such a stupid spot nowadays. If we start saying how good Detroit bands are, it will be like we're perpetuating the new-Seattle-scene idea. It's pathetic.

You're way too much fun to be with.

JACK: This is war, man. This is war. We've been thrust into a position that we never asked for. We never asked for all that jazz. I feel it's my duty to not bow down to all that.

Can I quote* Joseph Campbell here?

JACK: Please (*laughing*).

By rebelling, you're just bowing down to the system in a negative sense. You're still allowing the system to control your behavior.

JACK: See, you're gonna walk away and say, "You know, the White Stripes, they're gonna get in a lot of crap 'cause they are going to have to keep fighting all these people—and it's gonna end up exploding on them."

I'm not thinking that. To be honest, I'm thinking that at some point later, all

---

* Paraphrase.

these battles of yours are going to seem kind of silly because they don't really matter.

JACK: Yeah, but, look, man, if you go interview Blink-182 and they tell you about which one of them like, uh, pulled the other guy's pants down on the tour bus last night—that's an element of popular culture that we don't have in our brains and we don't want in our brains and we don't want ever around us. If you want to know about how we are and how we relate to everybody, this is how we relate to everybody.

I've noticed that, and maybe this is human nature, but you could receive a thousand compliments and one criticism, and you'll only remember the negative thing.

JACK: I do have a thing where I like to learn from bad examples. I like to learn what not to do. So I can appreciate the bad comment. I think it's more appreciated than a hundred good comments.

[RUSSELL BRAND]
SCENE 3

What's interesting is that usually a person with your personality and goals and sexual appetite would go into rock and roll, but you chose stand-up comedy instead.

RUSSELL BRAND: Yeah, because I went to drama school and wanted to be an actor. But I couldn't help it: People would laugh at me. I've never, because of my childhood, ever felt cool. I have never felt accepted. I've always been odd and geeky and people always laughed at me, and a lot of the times when that was not my intention and I was trying to be cool. But now I realize that comedy is in me. It is essential to me. It is this thing that I'm sort of good at.

Like when you talk about Prince in your show embodying rock and roll?

BRAND: I say that very deliberately so that at least one percent of the audience thinks that maybe I embody comedy, because I feel like I am it. When it's going well for me, when I'm in contact with it, I feel it's something that I can completely embody, without any obstacles or boundaries. I feel like I'm happy being funny and happy being foolish. But I suppose the other thing is that I do feel like I'm exposing myself and, for example, [singer and activist] Bob Geldof called me a cunt or whatever, and things like that have been humiliating.

Do you think you get that reaction because rock stars are supposed to be arrogant, but maybe comedians aren't?

BRAND: I think that there's an integral difference. When a rock star is onstage, they're saying, "Look at me, I'm fucking gorgeous. I'm going to fuck you with my mighty cock." When I'm onstage, I'm saying, "Don't look at my little dinky. I've got it tucked between my legs like Buffalo Bill from *Silence of the Lambs*."

I think some people like Howard Stern do that, but with you, there's a certain androgyny and a certain sexual swagger that I haven't seen in comedians, but I have seen in David Bowie or Mötley Crüe.

BRAND: I see. I understand. That is something I am sort of keen to convey, and since meeting you it's something that I've thought about, like, how does that come across to a set?* It is like one long seduction routine, and I suppose I do want people to be left with the idea that, "Yeah, that person knows how to fuck." I want to make it clear that I'm not going to get confused and baffled by the sight of a naked woman. But that is kind of inadvertent, really. It wasn't sort of . . .

But you do seem to go out of your way to make that point.

BRAND: Well, I was doing a question-and-answer session at the end of a big gig like the one that you came to, and one girl was asking a question. And she said, "Russell, I want to fuck you. How would you fuck me if you fucked me tonight?" And I go, "Well, let me look at you." And she stood up and turned around and she had like a nice ass. And I go, "I would lay you on the floor with your legs quite close together and I would lick your asshole and your pussy till you're wet, and I would fuck you in your pussy and fuck you in your ass" (*laughs*).

That's pretty direct.

BRAND: But there's a comedic element to that, to describing what I would actually do, right? Because it was just entirely honest. And people cheered and enjoyed it. And it was so fucking outright mad, because that is what I would have done, you know.

[CURTAIN]

---

* A set is slang for a group of people that pickup artists approach. I had mentioned to Brand that his show, with its sexual boasting, seemed to intentionally be a seduction to inspire women in the audience to sleep with him.

ACT EIGHT

OR

CANNIBALISM IS THE ANSWER

SYNOPSIS

Enter the Mafia, who threaten a journalist while Sacha Baron Cohen claims to be more gangsta, so Paris Hilton won't sleep with him when he goes undercover to battle bigotry along with the Upright Citizens Brigade and Stephen Colbert, though Hanson's afraid, Steely Dan's too old, and Ozzy Osbourne's fucked up, &c.

[THE MAFIA]

In the markets of the small mountain towns surrounding Reggio di Calabria on the Southern tip of Italy, a musician named Mimmo Siclari can often be found selling cassettes from the back of his van, as he has for several decades. The tapes, many of which he produces himself, are emblazoned with explicit covers that depict men shot in the heart, grieving widows, and pools of blood. The cassettes themselves are transparent, because only see-through tapes are allowed in prison, where many of the fans of his cassettes can be found.

Siclari does not sell gangsta rap or heavy metal: He sells folk music. And his cassettes are representative of a very unusual and specific folk tradition, *il canto di malavita*, which translates literally as songs of a bad life. More colloquially, the songs are known as Mafia music.

For more than a hundred years, Calabrian Mafia members have developed and sung *malavita* songs among themselves, traditionally at feasts celebrating the admittance of a new recruit, the release of a member from prison, or after a particularly successful act of vengeance.

"Whoever took the liberty to neglect their duties, I'll slaughter him like an animal," run the lyrics to one song. "And if someone dares to talk, I'll whet my knife for him."

I traveled to Calabria and visited with various Mafia dons to learn about the tradition. Before the first interview, however, my guide, Francesco Sbano, laid down some ground rules.

GROUND RULES AND ORIENTATION

1. Do not mention the names of the villages I take you to or identify the people you interview.
2. You may take notes, but you can not use tape recorders or cameras.
3. We will be controlled from the beginning to the end of the trip. They will know where we get our lunch, where we get our dinner, and where we sleep.
4. We will meet a lot of people, and you will never know whether most of them are Mafia members or not. They are just people of respect.
5. This is very important to me: I am not married, but I have a big family. There will be consequences if an interview or article does not go well.

INTERVIEW #1

We meet Mimmo Siclari at a market where he's selling cassettes. Though he doesn't appear to be in the Mafia, he's largely responsible for the spread of its music outside the ranks of the mob, thanks to his tireless dedication to discovering and recon-structing the songs. Often, he was not allowed to record or transcribe the lyrics when they were recited by Mafia members, so he would remember as much as he could and piece each composition together from several different people's reminiscences.

What drew you to this music?
MIMMO SICLARI: It was a beautiful world because of the idea of respect and honor. And once I found a tape of Fred Scotti* and it sold very well, I knew it was possible to sell this type of music, so I searched for more.

How did you first hear it?
SICLARI: One day, a man asked me something in the special language of the Mafia.

What did he ask you?
SICLARI: He asked me under whom I was working. And I was astonished to dis-cover through him and then through others that these songs—these words—were a reality. I discovered that the songs were speaking about true life, about a world where the people get their rights by fighting against a government that is just a ghost. I perfected the music and put everything in rhyme, and the people were excited when they discovered the authenticity.

——◆——

INTERVIEW #2

In the hills outside Reggio di Calabria, a long table is set up in a secluded clearing, where a Mafia feast is in progress. Some thirty men dine on wine, meat, and cheese as musicians perform *malavita* music on guitar, percussion, and a bagpipe-like instrument made from a goatskin and played by blowing into the leg.

One man, in particular, stands out—dancing, playing the goatskin, and telling stories. Sbano explains that this is a Mafia don who's seventy-six, and legendary for having been the only mob member to escape a recent police raid during which

---

* One of the most famous *malavita* singers, Fred Scotti was killed in the seventies for his interest in a mob member's girlfriend.

nearly sixty others were arrested. To my surprise, the musical don agrees to an interview, but only on condition of anonymity. As soon as it comes time to talk, however, the garrulous old man suddenly has nothing to say.

How did you first hear of *malavita* music?
OLD DON: I don't know *malavita* music.

But you were playing the music just now . . . ?
OLD DON: I have never heard *malavita* music before. Just *tarantella* [traditional dance music].

Okay, I get it. Is this how you've survived for so long in this world?
OLD DON: Next question.

The following interview with some of the other musicians doesn't go much better. Evidently, the only people who ask these men questions are the police and informers.

Do you ever worry about your association with the Mafia?
MAFIA MUSICIAN: It is safer this way. If someone steals my car, I go to the boss, not the police.

And what happens to the person who stole your car?
MAFIA MUSICIAN: Where do you live?

In America.
MAFIA MUSICIAN: Where?

Um, New York.
MAFIA MUSICIAN: But what address?

What do you want that for?
MAFIA MUSICIAN: I visit New York a lot. Maybe I will come see you.
OTHER MAFIA MUSICIAN: A visit like this (*raps loudly on the table three times*).

Everyone laughs but me.

INTERVIEW #3

The following afternoon, Sbano drives to an ice-cream shop in a nearby village, where we meet the head of a local Mafia family who is identified as one of the number two men in the region's mob hierarchy. He wears Champion-brand shorts and has a tattoo on his leg of a snake wrapped around a dagger and a skull.

How important is the music to you?
NUMBER TWO GUY: The music is a very important tradition for the people. It's like pasta. The Mafia without the music is like dishes of pasta without salt. The salt is the music of the Mafia.

From what I understand, the songs aren't just music, they're a way to communicate messages and teachings.
NUMBER TWO GUY: The songs are in code. Like hearing about a boat with "five plus seven" on it means five members and seven rules of society. Everything is code. When the Mafia gets a new member, every jail gets a telegraph. The telegraph says that a new flower has been born and gives the special name of the flower. So everyone hearing his name knows who he is if he comes to jail.

What does your tattoo signify?
NUMBER TWO GUY: If you see a snake, it means that you know the language of snakes, the language of honor. The skull means that you're not afraid to die.

His phone rings. The ring tone is Michael Jackson's "Smooth Criminal."

⬥

INTERVIEW #4

Later that day, we meet the man who supposedly runs the entire local Mafia. He is also wearing Champion-brand shorts, with a matching Champion shirt. On one of his arms, there's a tattoo of a winged lion. Birds chirp noisily in cages throughout his apartment as his wife makes a martini for him.

Have things changed a lot in the Mafia since you started?
NUMBER ONE DON: Once upon a time, it was very different from today. Then, respect was the most important thing. When the society had problems, they resolved it with each other and without involving other people. Most of the time,

the problem was resolved with a knife or a piece of wood. Nobody died—it was enough to get a bit of blood. And then the next day, they were all together again, drinking wine. Today, everything happens because of money. But I don't want to talk about that.

What made everything different?
NUMBER ONE DON: New times have brought cocaine and heroin. The tradition of today is to try to keep the village free from drugs and new problems, and this is very hard. I don't know for how long I can control them. The new Mafia uses the old Mafia to keep in power—and most of the old Mafia are dead because they wouldn't work with them.

Is there anything you can do about it?
NUMBER ONE DON: Whoever tries to keep the tradition alive risks not only his life, but his whole family's lives. If you want to explain what the Mafia is doing today, there is no song explaining this. Who can understand somebody who goes on the street and kills somebody like an animal? You can only explain respect and honor. There are no songs about murder and drugs, because there is no argument there. Money has no argument.

Why is the music important to save?
NUMBER ONE DON: It's tradition. Some days ago I heard a song that was playing, and I was nearly crying after the song. It's very strange, and maybe you can't understand, but you don't sing the songs along with other people. You feel what the song says. It is a lesson.

How would you define a man of honor?
NUMBER ONE DON: It can sound a bit hard, but a man of honor is a neutral person keeping the honor of his family and the rest of the families. So if someone makes a mistake in the family, you must react. You don't have to kill your sister, but if the mistake is so big, the man of honor must react in an extreme way. This is what makes a man of honor—authority to make that decision.

[SACHA BARON COHEN]
SCENE 1

When Sacha Baron Cohen came to America to film his first TV show here as the character Ali G, a parody of a white suburban wanna-be gangsta, I called HBO

and asked to interview him. They explained that he didn't do interviews out of character, but I could watch a taping and then e-mail him questions.

Hello.
ALI G: Easynow West Staines Massiv indahouse a'ight.

In England, how have the people you've interviewed responded after the show has aired?
ALI G: Me get a lot of calls from de geezas I iz intraviewed, not realy to chat but mostly dem goin menstrual axin if dey can have deir VCRs and hifi's back, a'ight.

Which was your favorite interview?
ALI G: It woz when me went to hexamine sumfin called "sexism" (which for all de ignoranuses out dere readin dis means when u iz racialist to bitches). Me intraviewed someone called Naomi Wolf—who iz an incredible hintelectual, a very hindependent finker, and surprisinly thin and good-lookin for a lezza.*

When did you start rapping?
ALI G: Checkit when me came out me mum's poom poom bush me immediately started cryin in a jungelistic riddim. Me first word woz "ho." Infact in de maternity ward a few of de really fly mums woz so hattracted to me dat dey arksed de nurses to let me have a go on deir nips.

Are you interested in recording an album?
ALI G: De troof iz me spent yearz tryin to get a recordin contract. Back in de day dey said "no, u got a bad voice," "you have no riddim," "your ears are too big for your face." But we all know de real reason. Racialism. Just look around, de record industry iz full of it. Tell me has u ever seen a black man succeed in de world of rap? I arrest me case.

Who is Sacha Baron Cohen?
ALI G: He iz some fool goin around tryin to be me, probly coz he iz tryin to lay some pipe wit all de hotty-botty hoes dat I aint never gonna touch coz I iz 120% faitful to me Julie innit. By de way if any fly hoes has read dat and iz turned on by it, and wanna hexperience de real Tower of London den give me a ring on me cell 917-428-3819. Dat number can also be reached by any of u out dere who iz got a

---

* At the time of this interview, Wolf was married to former Bill Clinton speechwriter David Shipley.

chronic need for a herbal remedy a'ight. I iz gotta go coz me Julie iz waitin and I iz losin me stiffie. Respek ya nana. Wesside.

[*Continued . . .*]

[PARIS HILTON]

In 1999, shortly after moving to Los Angeles to cover pop culture for the *New York Times*, I ended up in a room with someone I'd never heard of before. She seemed to embody young Hollywood. She didn't want to be an actress, a singer, or a star—though she would soon become all three. The art form she'd chosen to embrace was partying. She was with a model friend of hers and talking about performing a sex show together for someone named Artie the previous night, then taking dirty photographs afterward. In the background as we spoke, the movie *Saving Private Ryan* was playing. After this conversation, she proceeded to get drunk on Midori sours (each with six cherries in the glass), make out with David Faustino of *Married . . . with Children*, take a hit of ecstasy, play Britney Spears songs practically nonstop, and have a threesome. Maybe she said what follows for provocation and shock value. Maybe she didn't. You decide . . .

PARIS HILTON: I had a breast job when I was fourteen, but my mother made me take them out.

How old are you now?
HILTON: I'm eighteen.

Are you working?
HILTON: I'm thinking about posing for *Playboy*. They love famous people's kids.

Like who?
HILTON: I don't know. And the only reason I'd do it is because when my dad finds out, he'll pay me double the money not to do it.

Later . . .

HILTON: I went out with that guy last night.

Which guy?
HILTON (*points to an actor in* Saving Private Ryan): We were making out, but then we went somewhere where it was bright and I saw that he was black and made

an excuse and left. I can't stand black guys. I would never touch one. It's gross (*pauses*). Does that guy look black to you?

How black does a guy have to be?
HILTON: One percent is enough for me.

[RACISTS]

While stationed in Nashville for the *New York Times,* I received a call from a friend named Kim, who was on tour with the Charlie Daniels Band. The group had just performed at a new outdoor amphitheater in an obscure Tennessee town called Skullbone.

KIM: It was like going back in time. I've never been so scared.

What happened?
KIM: We got into town around two-thirty, and Charlie went somewhere for lunch with his wife. Somebody in the restaurant went up to him and started talking about the show and said, "They don't like blacks out there." Charlie's a good Christian and said, "I don't like that attitude at all." They said, "That's the way it is. There are no blacks allowed there."

What was the venue like?
KIM: The people in line, even fourteen- and fifteen-year-old boys, were wearing these T-shirts with racist slogans. They said like "whites only" or "nigger family tree" with a tree with nooses hanging on it. After Charlie's first song, he says, "I don't like people that hate people," and the crowd got a little riled up.

Were there any problems?
KIM: We got out of there pretty quick. Backstage, when Charlie was getting ready to get onstage for the encore, he said, "When I'm done, be on the bus and we are getting the hell out of Skullbone." I met this guy Allen who owns the place. He said he had five shows lined up for next year, and Lynyrd Skynyrd is the first one. But I don't think any of the bands know what kind of place this is.

I call a number of people in the concert industry, including Steve Hauser of the William Morris Agency, who booked the Charlie Daniels Band tour, to see if any of them have heard about a whites-only amphitheater in Skullbone. None of them have any idea what I'm talking about.

STEVE HAUSER: We had heard of this little amphitheater down there that was putting on shows, but we hadn't heard anything like that. The show was run to a T. There would be a buzz in Nashville if something like that was going on.

Did you do any research yourself into the place?
HAUSER: As long as they provide sound and lights, we don't really check anything else.

A book called Tennessee's Last Kingdom *by Skullbone historian Ernest R. Pounds confirmed the legacy of the town, known locally as the Kingdom of Skullbonia.*

TENNESSEE'S LAST KINGDOM [**book excerpt**]: Rumor has it that a bunch of "Niggers" were hanged in the Skullbone area many years ago. This is the reason that for many, many years, no blacks would dare set foot in the Kingdom of Skullbonia. It is still an unwritten rule that blacks are not to become permanent residents.

When the next season of concerts starts at the Skullbone Music Park, I drive to the double bill of Nazareth and Eddie Money to expose what's been going on. After parking in the lot, I take a hayride with other ticket-buyers to the front gate. On the other side, an ominous black flag with a giant skull-and-crossbones on it hangs over the stage. There are two roped-off areas on the grounds: one for minors and those who don't want to be around alcohol; the other for Hells Angels. Nearby, I find the park's owner, Allen Blankenship, a large man with a blond mustache, a hefty gut, and denim overalls.

How did Skullbone get its name?
ALLEN BLANKENSHIP: Back in the twenties or thirties, they used to have bare-knuckle fistfighting here, and it was illegal to hit below the jaw. It was all head punching. So that's how Skullbone got its name. I love the area. They've always been known for being tough boys in Skullbone. I'm not saying we're still trying to hold a claim to that. We're just good ol' boys.

What made you start a concert venue here?
BLANKENSHIP: One night, I was sitting down here in the holler and I got to thinking, "I'm turning forty and this is my life dream. If I want to do it, this is the right place." This was nothing but an overgrown swamp right here. You clapped your hands and it went dead, so I realized that this is great acoustics out here.

How did you get the money together to make it happen?
BLANKENSHIP: I'm by no means a rich man. My wife broke a couple of lamps over my head, probably had two or three breakdowns, and said I was nothing but a glorified gambler. But I took my life savings and dumped every bit of it into this dream.
WENDY [his wife]: I see his vision a lot more now. He's so focused. His throttle is always pulled out. But he gets crazy because there aren't enough people coming sometimes.
BLANKENSHIP: Here's the way I think as a promoter: For tonight's show, Eddie Money has a ton of hits. But the women like Eddie Money. Old rule of thumb: Where there's a woman, there will always be two men. But men find him a little too wimpy, so let's give them Nazareth. That way you're appealing to both sides of the crowd.

What do you do for security if anyone gets drunk and out of hand?
BLANKENSHIP: We used a security firm from Nashville for a while, but I'm not using them anymore because they brought that city attitude into our country atmosphere. They didn't know how to relate to the good ol' boys. So I talked my friends from around here into getting bonded and insured.

The main concession stand, the Skullshop, is operated by Blankenship's mother, Mona McNeely. She sells ceramic skulls there as well as flasks, playing cards, flashlights, drumsticks, and bandanas, all emblazoned with a prominent skull-and-crossbones logo.

How do you feel about selling all these skulls?
MONA McNEELY: Actually, I don't like them. I'm a Christian and I go to church. And I don't particularly like some of the words these bands say, either.

As the show begins, the amphitheater fills and other merchants set up shop. At one concession, a vendor sells iron crosses. His T-shirt also bears the logo of a cross and reads, "The KKK is getting bigger. Aren't you glad you ain't a nigger?" A concertgoer nearby wears a T-shirt with an image of a hooded Klansman and the words, "The Original Boys in the Hood."

VENDOR: We used to sell more things here, but Allen told us not to sell blatantly racist stuff anymore in case someone takes a photograph and it gets in the news and people get the wrong idea. I'm going to give you this. (*Holds up a cap with a gold CSA—Confederate States of America—insignia on it.*) You could take this back to the city and wear it, and the niggers wouldn't even know what it is.

A biker joins the conversation and invites me to smoke crank with him at campsite four, then smiles and lets me know one more thing about the party . . .

BIKER: No niggers.

A few yards away, another vendor is selling less racist biker paraphernalia.

What do you think would happen if any black people in the community came to the show?
VENDOR: I'd advise against it. It's not a good idea. They're liable to get beat up. Last year, there were two blacks in the alcohol-free area, and when the sun went down, people started saying things like, "Those two trees there look mighty sturdy to me." They got out of there pretty quick.

After the show, I meet Eddie Money in his tour bus and ask if he noticed anything strange about the show. He says he was shocked by some of the fans, particularly one who had a picture of a black man's head tattooed on his arm with a circle around it and a red line through it. During the short interview, Money behaves bizarrely, often forgetting the name of the town and calling it Headbone or Crossbow.

EDDIE MONEY: You better be careful out there.

Do you often get invited to these things?
MONEY: For some reason, I don't know why, the bikers love me. They always want me to play their rallies. I fucking hate them.

You do?
MONEY: But I really enjoyed the show. I thought it was an amusement park when I saw the name. I thought I was doing a Tampa Bay Buccaneers show. It rained all day, but people still came. And we did two thousand dollars just in T-shirts. The pulled pork was the best I've ever had.

But don't you feel weird or wrong performing at a place with these kind of prejudices?
MONEY: They may be a little backward in their attitude—you feel like Bobby Kennedy is still the attorney general—but God love 'em. I had a good time.

Later, Blankenship invites me for a drink at the Southfork Bar and Grill, nicknamed the Cut 'n' Shoot, because that's what customers there often do. At the bar, the windows have Confederate flags as drapes and the chalkboard reads, "Happy birthday Nigger Joe."

A girl named Krystal says about black people, "You can't look them in the eye. If you look at them, they like you." Her friend Eric says the problem with black people is that they think they're superior to everyone else. As they speak, the jukebox is not playing Molly Hatchet or Lynyrd Skynyrd. It is playing DMX and Nelly.

Blankenship orders a beer and says he is looking for other ways for the music park to make money. He's planning a Halloween horror trail, a Christmas lights drive, company picnics, and a Civil War reenactment.

What battle are you planning to reenact?
BLANKENSHIP: I don't know what battle it's going to be. But it's going to be one the Confederates won, because we can't have it no other way here in Skullbone, you know what I'm saying.

The Skullbone Music Park soon closed due to financial problems, and Blankenship sold the property in 2008.

= [**UPRIGHT CITIZENS BRIGADE**] =

On a few occasions, I've intended to report a story, but been roped into becoming part of it instead. This happened when I went to meet the Upright Citizens Brigade, who were sitting in a hotel basement in Aspen, Colorado, plotting a prank. At the time, the improv-comedy quartet was relatively unknown, though acknowledged by insiders as one of the best undiscovered comedy troupes in the country. They'd traveled to the U.S. Comedy Arts Festival in Aspen hoping to get a television show. And after the festival, not only did they land their own series on Comedy Central, but one of their members—Amy Poehler—eventually became a household name, moving to *Saturday Night Live* and then prime-time television and film.

At ten a.m. that morning, group member Ian Roberts had visited stores in town and asked them to sign a petition censuring the U.S. Comedy Arts Festival for not allowing a family-values act called the Hong Kong Danger Duo to perform because of racism. With some badgering, he succeeded in getting employees from several stores to sign it. Two hours later, the group wired me with a hidden microphone and camera, and sent me into the stores along with the *New York Times* photographer.

Hi, I'm from the *New York Times*. And we're doing an article on a group performing at the comedy festival here called the Hong Kong Danger Duo. Maybe you've heard of them?

EMPLOYEE ONE: Someone was in here earlier saying they weren't allowed to perform.

Exactly. And that's why we're doing this story. I was wondering if it would be okay to do a photo shoot here with them?
EMPLOYEE ONE: I'm not sure. I'd have to check.

Members of the Upright Citizens Brigade enter the store as the Hong Kong Danger Duo, wearing jump suits, crash helmets, and goggles. Note that there are three of them.

EMPLOYEE TWO: You can't do this here!

The Hong Kong Danger Duo starts trying on clothing, rolling on the floor, squirting water on each other, and harassing customers.

AMY POEHLER: We are Hong Kong Danger Duo!
MATT BESSER: You can't escape our danger!
EMPLOYEE ONE (*to me*): You have to get them out of here . . .
EMPLOYEE TWO: You're all going to have to leave!
POEHLER: What? You kick us out because we're not from your country?
BESSER: This is racism!
POEHLER: You racist like festival.

Look, is it because they're Asian? Is that the problem? *
EMPLOYEE ONE: No.
BESSER: You don't have problem when white people come in your store and try on clothes.
POEHLER: Yeah! You bad person.
EMPLOYEE ONE (*to me*): I need you to understand that I'm not a racist. They're scaring away the customers.

═══ [**SACHA BARON COHEN** *SCENE 2*] ═══

An Escalade stopped in the middle of Sixty-fifth Street on the west side of Manhattan and a tall, awkward mustachioed man in an ill-fitting blue-gray suit emerged.

---

* The members of the Upright Citizens Brigade are all Caucasian.

In the past month, through a series of press stunts and blanket advertising, this man had turned himself into a household name in America: Borat.

It was Halloween, and hundreds of Borats were roaming the city streets in costumed adulation of the spurious Kazakh journalist, but this Borat was the real thing. A throng of movie publicists, photographers, collaborators, and assistants closed around him as he headed toward the escalators that lead up to the Walter Reade Theater, where an advance screening of his self-titled movie was about to start. He paused at the foot of the escalator, turned to me, and extended a hand. "Hi," he said in a deep, genteel British accent incongruous with his mustachioed visage. "I'm Sacha."

And with this one word—"Sacha"—he informed me that I was being let behind the curtain, into the mind of the man playing the buffoon, into the very private world of England's most popular enigma, Sacha Baron Cohen. Since reaching star status in Britain in 1998 with his other alter ego, Ali G, Baron Cohen had never done an interview in his home country as himself and had never done an interview this extensive anywhere.

I'm surprised you agreed to do this.
SACHA BARON COHEN: It's scary to me, but I felt safe with you. I remember you coming to the studio. That was like four years ago. You were the first major journalist that showed interest and I really appreciate it. Did you like the movie?

I did.
BARON COHEN: Yeah, it would have been bad if you didn't.

I don't think I've ever laughed so much in a movie theater.
BARON COHEN: Really? It was hard. I mean, it was a hard film to make. You actually know more about the process than . . .

Most people?
BARON COHEN: Yeah, more than anyone who's not actually part of it. That's a disaster. Terrible for me.

Because you don't want anyone knowing how you get the people you interview to believe it's real?
BARON COHEN: I think it does work like a magician giving away his tricks. It's going to make it harder for me to do it in the future if people know how we do it.

Do you think that if you were just yourself that you could stay in situations as awkward as you do in the film?
BARON COHEN: I think I'd find it hard to do. You can hide behind the characters and do things that you yourself find difficult.*

Out of curiosity, were you raised in a strict environment?
BARON COHEN: My parents were incredibly loving, and I think that gives you the strength to go out into a crowd of people who hate you (*pauses*). Probably, if you want to analyze it.

What did your parents do?
BARON COHEN: My dad owned clothing stores. My mother was and still is a fitness and aerobics teacher—and so is my grandma, actually. She created her own style. My grandma was originally a ballet dancer in Nazi Germany and left in—I don't remember—and went to Israel.

By the way, can you please not mention my parents' names? A few years ago, I had death threats from some neo-Nazi groups and I don't want anything that I do to jeopardize the safety of my family.

I understand.
BARON COHEN: Weirdly enough, the Anti-Defamation League came out . . . Have you seen the statement they made? I mean, do you find the movie anti-Semitic?

No, I didn't.
BARON COHEN: It's been banned from all Arab countries as well. They're not picking up the movie.

I'm kind of glad, because when you watch it and see all the Americans cheering for destroying Iraq, that would probably make them hate us more.
BARON COHEN: I mean, I wanted them . . . I would have liked the movie to be seen in Arab countries. Because I think part of the movie shows the absurdity of holding any form of racial prejudice, whether it's hatred of African-Americans or of Jews.

As Baron Cohen continues talking, a waiter places a complimentary appetizer in front of him. He bombards the waiter with questions, until he's certain the ingredients are kosher, then digs in.

---

* For example, from later in the interview: "We thought it would be funny if Borat had a penis that went down to his knees. Unfortunately, I haven't been blessed with a comically large penis."

Is your family upset at all by the mock anti-Semitism in the movie?
BARON COHEN: They love the humor. My grandma actually saw the movie two weeks ago. She's ninety-one. She saw it in Israel, at a midnight screening in Haifa. And I called her up and said, "Listen, I want to warn you, it's a really extreme film and I really don't think it's a good idea that you go and see it." And she said, "Listen, I am your grandmother and I make the decisions." So at four a.m. in the morning, she called me up and told me that she loved it.

What's interesting about Borat is how far people are willing to go along with things that are racist or anti-Semitic.
BARON COHEN: Borat essentially works as a tool. By himself being anti-Semitic, he lets people lower their guard and expose their own prejudice, whether it's anti-Semitism or an acceptance of anti-Semitism.

I remember when I was in university, I studied history. And there was this one major historian of the Third Reich—I think he's called Ian Kershaw—and his quote was, "The path to Auschwitz was paved with indifference." I know it's not very funny being a comedian talking about the Holocaust, but I think it's an interesting idea that not everyone in Germany had to be a raving anti-Semite. They just had to be apathetic.

[STEPHEN COLBERT]

When meeting Stephen Colbert, I expected that he'd either be in the character of the ironically egomaniacal star of his late-night political comedy show, *The Colbert Report*, or be the witty, sarcastic, politically opinionated intellectual that he probably is in real life. But the Stephen Colbert I met was neither of those characters.

He was Ned Flanders.

He was wearing a short-sleeved pink dress shirt tucked into khaki pants—his street clothes. When he spoke about his improv-comedy approach to the show and how he lives by the improvisational decree of saying yes to everything, he was earnest, gentle, and well intentioned—words one would never use to describe his on-air persona. He didn't swear, preferring exclamations like "gosh," "shoot," and "boy." And on his computer, there was a small printed sign: "Joy is the most infallible sign of the presence of God." It was not meant sarcastically.

You teach Sunday school?
STEPHEN COLBERT: I teach the seven-year-olds. I'm the catechist for their first communion.

When I interviewed Sacha Baron Cohen, he said that what enables him to go into situations where an arena full of people hate him is that he knows he has the faith and stability of his parents behind him. Is that true for you when you play this sort of buffoon on your show?

COLBERT: Probably, in some regard. I think all the time about something my mother said to me many times as a child: "In the line of eternity, what does this matter?" In that regard, I'm very hard to embarrass. I really don't mind making a fool of myself, because I have some sense of who I am beyond this fool—I hope. And I think some of that comes from my mother. I don't actually believe that the present social norm is some sort of eternal truth.

What do you mean by "the present social norm"?

COLBERT: Like how you're supposed to look. For example, I have khaki pants on and a pink button-down shirt. Completely preppie, because that's just how I'm always dressed, I have no personal sense of fashion. It doesn't matter to me at all. Regard for people's appearance or regard for social norms are fine pastimes, but they have no meaning. I don't mind looking like an idiot or being ugly. That helps me a lot. [. . .]

Did you ever go through a period where you lost your faith?

COLBERT: Yeah, it was a college angst thing. But once I graduated from college, some Gideon gave me literally a box of *The New Testament, Psalms and Proverbs* on the street in Chicago. I took one and opened it right away to Matthew, Chapter 5, which is the opening of the Sermon on the Mount. That whole chapter is essentially about not worrying. I didn't read it—it spoke to me, and it was an effortless absorption of the idea. Nothing came to me in a thunderbolt, but I thought to myself, "I'd be dumb not to reexamine this."

What caused you to go through that dark period?

COLBERT: Well, I had very sad events in my childhood. The death of my father and my brothers [in a plane crash] was understandably a shattering experience that I hadn't really dealt with in any way. And there comes a time when you're psychologically able to do so. I still don't like talking about it. It still is too fresh.

Do you think experiencing that has helped what you do in any way, or made it more of a challenge?

COLBERT: Not to get too deep here, but the most valuable thing I can think of is to be grateful for suffering. That is a sublime feeling, and completely inexplicable and illogical. But no one doesn't suffer. So the degree to which you can be aware of your own humanity is the degree to which you can accept, with open eyes, your suffering. To be grateful for your suffering is to be grateful for your humanity, because what else are you going to do—say, "No thanks"? It's there. "Smile and accept," said Mother Teresa. And she was talking to people who had it rough. That's not how you make jokes, though.

[HANSON]

To many, the three squeaky-clean blond brothers in Hanson seemed like a teeny-bopper fabrication when they first emerged, paving the way for the Backstreet Boys and 'N Sync. However, they were more than that, and those who looked closer discovered that they were actually talented, self-motivated musical savants.

"I swore I'd never do another music video again," director Gus Van Sant said as he prepared to shoot their latest video. "But I love their music." Elsewhere on the set, Danny Goldberg, the president of the brothers' record label, prepared to give them a lecture on Woodstock as part of their home-schooling program.

Sitting in their trailer, the brothers discussed the other subjects they'd been learning. But where Stephen Colbert was open about his religious beliefs, the Hanson brothers, who are evangelical Christians, were a little less forthcoming.

Do you have Bible classes?
TAYLOR HANSON [age 15]: Yeah, we study that some, too.

What's your favorite part?
TAYLOR: In the Bible? I guess . . . I don't know.
ISAAC HANSON [age 17]: I don't know. That's not . . . I never really actually thought about that.
TAYLOR: Er, you know . . . I mean, we're just . . . We're always reading it all.
ISAAC: (*Starts to speak, then stops himself.*)

Did you have something else to say?
ISAAC: Oh, oh, I'm sorry. I was. . . .
ZAC HANSON [age 12]: It takes a while to read. (*They all laugh.*)
TAYLOR: It's like reading four *Atlas Shrugged*s.

Do you pray every day?
(*Awkward silence. The brothers look nervously at each other.*)

Are you guys embarrassed about the religious stuff?
ZAC: You know . . .
TAYLOR: We like to keep it, you know, on the side, because people . . . It gets . . .
The thing is, it kinda gets in people's way, like even if—
ZAC: Sometimes.
TAYLOR: —even if it didn't matter, you know, people would go, "Well, I don't like
them 'cause, you know . . ." So we like to keep it, like, to the music. The music is
what we do.

A lot of people already give you a hard time, though.
TAYLOR: The thing is, whenever you're liked in any way or anything does well, I
guess you're hated just as much.
ZAC: Somebody wishes they were you.
TAYLOR: It's like on the Internet, you have tons and tons of Hanson fan websites.
You also have tons and tons of Hanson hater websites. It's just people's opinion.
You can't say, "Hey, you have to like us."
ISAAC: Plus everybody has their own opinion. And if they don't like the band, they
don't like the band.
TAYLOR: If you like us, that's cool. If you don't, that's even cooler.

And then there are all the rumors . . .
ISAAC: Yeah, we were gay. We were in car accidents. We've done everything.
ZAC: I was dead and they were in comas. Ever since then, I've felt a little lighter.
TAYLOR: The night our newest sister was born, thirty minutes afterward, it was
on the radio.
ISAAC: It's actually quite scary.

Do you feel like you're missing out on a part of your childhood?
ZAC: You could look back on all of this and say, "I didn't get to see my friends as
much, and I didn't get to mow the lawn and get ten dollars, and I didn't get such
and such." Or you could go, "I got to travel around the world, perform for thousands of people, go to the Grammys, get MTV Europe awards."
ISAAC: Oh geez, I'm so deprived. I was abused as a child.
ZAC: I was abused by getting to stay in nice hotels.

[STEELY DAN]

Backstage at the Grammy Awards, Donald Fagen and Walter Becker, core members of the seventies fusion-rock band Steely Dan, looked genuinely befuddled as they stood in front of the press clutching Grammys—their first such awards ever—including one for Album of the Year.

"Think they'll take these things away from us or make us give them back?" Fagen asked before thanking Eminem—the night's predicted winner—for taking the heat away from them over the risqué lyrics on their album *Two Against Nature*, which includes themes of incest, misogyny, group sex, and statutory rape.

Afterward, I talked to them separately about their unexpected honors. Here are some highlights.

Is it strange that thirty years after the bulk of your work, suddenly you're getting so many awards and accolades?
WALTER BECKER: Well, I think that's a pretty typical pattern. We're getting a lot of credit just for surviving and persisting and doing more or less the same kind of music, which, depending on who you talk to, is either considered a kind of integrity or a failure of imagination—or both.

You do, however, change things up by singing "Let's roll with the homies" on the new album.
BECKER: Yeah, that's right, Neil. That's exactly what I feel. We may not be in the mainstream of musical thought, but we're willing to co-opt any catchy expression that comes along, however silly.

The Grammys were interesting, because *Two Against Nature* was just as taboo in parts as the Eminem record, but because the lyrics were cloaked in a more adult-sounding music, nobody really noticed it.
DONALD FAGEN: It's easier for us to sneak it in, I guess because of the various pop forms we use. And the fact that we're so old, nobody cares.

But the subject matter can be even scarier coming from adults rather than younger artists, because kids will be kids.
BECKER: I think using the word adults in regard to Donald and I always should have a footnote of some sort.*

---

* Becker on being an adult: "Clearly some of the processes have taken place, but not others. I don't know why that is."

Maybe because the music business is sort of a Peter Pan world, people in it never grow up.

BECKER: Oh, it definitely is, and it insulates one from a lot of the experiences that perhaps would have produced some sort of adulthood. Donald and I have been doing this since we were teenagers. And we had a business manager before we had any money or anything. Neither one of us has ever balanced a checkbook, I feel safe in saying.

And for some reason, being in the music world tends to keep people looking younger. Somehow, you two are the only exceptions to that.

BECKER: I think that's probably true, although it keeps us thinking younger.

I was kidding.

BECKER: But it is true that when you get to be our age, it sort of produces a not-too-desirable effect and you're sort of left wondering, "Gee, why am I still in a rock and roll band?"

[OZZY OSBOURNE]

Before he became reality television's favorite grumpy old man, Ozzy Osbourne battled abuse of uppers, alcohol, and acid. He was kicked out of bands, barred from the offices of his own record company, and forced to submit to rabies shots. He was charged with inciting teenagers to suicide, attempted murder of his wife, and urinating on the Alamo memorial. Yet somehow, through these events both tragic and ridiculous, the heavy metal pioneer not only survived but thrived.

What do you think of the latest round of Senate hearings on music lyrics?

OZZY OSBOURNE: Don't they realize what they're doing? In my opinion, by having these hearings in the Senate, you're gonna get some garage band that goes, "Wow, that's success! If they can get in the Senate with that, we'll write a song called 'Kill Your Mother Twice.'" I have never consciously sat down with the sole intention of doing anything like that.

Though you were sued after two different teenage suicides . . .

OSBOURNE: I was watching this lawyer that was suing me for that McCollum guy* being interviewed on VH1. He said, "It's like Nuremberg." And I thought, "This

---

* Jack McCollum sued Osbourne because he thought subliminal lyrics in the song "Suicide Solution" were responsible for his nineteen-year-old son's suicide. The court ultimately ruled that the song was not responsible for the death.

guy must be strung out on acid. He needs psychiatric help." He said, "You can honestly hear Ozzy say on the record, 'Get the gun, shoot, shoot.'"

Which you never said.
OSBOURNE: I can put my hand on my heart and swear on my children's fucking lives that those words were never said. You can misinterpret me as saying that: I've got an echo effect and I'm going, "shhht, shhht," and it's bouncing from speaker to speaker. I'll state with my hand on a stack of Bibles—whatever fucking religious Bibles you want me to use—and solemnly swear that that song "Suicide Solution" was about me drinking myself to death just after a friend of mine, the original singer from AC/DC, died from alcohol. A lot of guys in this business have died of drugs and alcohol.

Do you ever feel responsible when people do stupid things because of your music?
OSBOURNE: Never felt responsible. No way. The last thing I say at my concerts most nights is, "Make sure you go out and get home safely, because I want to see your asses next year and rock them again." If my intention was to do songs that anyone would harm themselves with, why would I say that?

I was talking to someone who said they were doing a movie about your life. Is that true?
OSBOURNE: I don't know who's going to do it, what my part of it is, or what the deal is, but I know that something is going on. But if the movie does come out, I don't want it to be like the fucking Doors film or the fucking *Rose*, I want it to be as it was. Because there was a lot of excitement. I always equate it to: If you're the strongest man in the world and if you throw a stone as high as you can, it's gotta come down just as far, you know. There's been a lot of highs and a lot of lows.

Have you ever thought of doing a book?
OSBOURNE: I had a book deal a while ago. But I gotta go around to a lot of old friends and ask them to jog my memory. If I have one regret, it's not keeping a daily journal, you know, because I've been fucked up all the time.

So you've forgotten everything?
OSBOURNE: I'll remember certain things, but there's a ton of shit that I don't remember. People will say to me, "Do you remember this?" And I'll go, "Oh, fuck."

So how do you keep—

OSBOURNE: Thanks to my wife. My wife is my biggest fan and my biggest adviser—and the one I love. I mean, half of Ozzy is Sharon, you know. I don't come up with these fantastic ideas and get all the logistics together. I have the easy job. I just go up there and entertain and do interviews, and fucking hang around hotel rooms all day long. She's like a workaholic. She hasn't got a figure like Pamela Anderson, but I don't care because she's my wife and I love her more than anything in the world.

QUEENS OF THE STONE AGE

There are certain rules on the road. And Queens of the Stone Age had just accidentally violated one. They discovered this when their two tour buses pulled into Los Angeles, finally home after a long, blistering tour that involved roadies brewing a lot of psychedelic mushroom tea.

On bus one, singer Josh Homme and temporary drummer Dave Grohl of the Foo Fighters struggled to find matching shoes and pack up remaining bottles of liquor for home use. Bassist Nick Oliveri, who'd taken the second bus with his girlfriend Deborah, walked on board, scratching his bald head.

NICK OLIVERI: Hey, has anyone seen Deborah?

DAVE GROHL: No, wasn't she traveling with you?

OLIVERI: Yeah, but we stopped at a rest stop, and she got off the bus and didn't get back on. So I thought she was on your bus.

GROHL: Nope, haven't seen her.

OLIVERI: Oh shit!

GROHL: Yeah, man, I think you left her at the rest stop.

THE FUNERALS

THE ORIGIN

It was a crazy idea that began, as most crazy ideas do, at the end of a long night of drinking. At a house party in Iceland, polishing off the last of the beer and whiskey, the members of a Reykjavik band called the Funerals decided to embark on a tour of the country.

The idea was crazy for several reasons, not the least being that it was October and the roads were blanketed with snow and ice. Beyond that, the country outside of Reykjavik is only barely populated. And the only bands that regularly leave the capital are pop cover bands that play music for revelers to drink, dance, and sing along to. The Funerals, in contrast, are a slow, sad country band—probably the only such group in Iceland—that plays songs about being pathetic and scared of teenagers.

According to Ragnar, the singer, the band originally formed after he broke up with his girlfriend of five years. "She took away the TV, so we couldn't watch TV," he explained. "So instead we started playing guitars and writing songs. I'd never written songs before."

Because a journalist would be joining them on tour, the Funerals decided to name it the "Almost Pathetic Tour," a combination of the film *Almost Famous* and the title of its album, *Pathetic Me*. Before the tour even began—one week after the drinking binge that started it—it had already lived up to its name. This occurred when Ragnar tried to rekindle his romance with his TV-taking ex.

RAGNAR: I made dinner for my ex-girlfriend at my house, trying to get her back. But then I played her our songs, and she walked out. It was strange to make music that you get in a fight over.

What songs did you play her?
RAGNAR: "Unappreciative Man" and "Rich Bitch."

———◆———

THE BAND

Ragnar, vocals and guitar—and the first male ever to graduate from Husstjornar-skolinn, an Icelandic school for housewives.

Thor, drums—grandson of the doctor who delivered Ragnar.

Doddi, keyboards—son of a priest who invented the ubiquitous cocktail sauce served at restaurants in Iceland. Employed as a janitor's assistant.

Lara, accordion and vocals—joined the band because her boyfriend, Doddi, took a nap during the recording session, so she ended up singing instead.

Vidar, bass—known for passing out drunk most nights while kneeling on the ground, then suddenly waking up and punching the closest person in the stomach several times before passing out again.

Olaf, guitar—says that while playing a solo, his mind often drifts and he finds himself thinking about eating a sandwich.

OLAF: It's a little surprising that I'm even in this band. I never understood country music.

But you must understand country music now.
OLAF: No, I'm not any closer.

TOUR PREPARATION

Before going on the road, the band stops by Iceland's national radio station for an interview. The sliding glass doors at the studio happen to close directly on Ragnar as he's walking through, an omen for the tour to come. Within hours, more bad luck strikes: The tour bus driver calls to say he'll be late because the bus has already broken down and Thor, the drummer, crashes his car into a brick wall on the way to meet the band.

DODDI: There's no sense in going on a tour like this. People just want cover bands. They're going to hate us.
ARON [manager]: It's okay. Everything that starts out a little bit shaky usually ends up really good.

A dirty white tour bus with a faded rum advertisement on one side wheezes into a hotel parking lot several hours later to pick up the band. One of the windows is shattered and there's still trash in the coffin-like beds from the last occupants. It is spewing so much exhaust that the hotel manager runs outside to complain that the fumes are going to kill his guests. The six-member band and its four-person entourage cram into the tiny bus and stop at a liquor store for supplies.

VIDAR: We can only perform drunk.

FIRST SHOW—GRUNDARFJORDUR

Krakan is a family restaurant in Grundarfjordur, a town of 952 people. The owner feeds the band asparagus soup, lamb, and beer as an older, conservatively dressed crowd trickles in. Slowly, song by song, the band wins the room over, until the small audience is on its feet, whistling and clapping for an encore. When Aron approaches the restaurant owner for a cut of ticket sales after the concert, he is given two packages of home-smoked fish as payment instead.

SECOND SHOW: SKAGASTROND

Kantrybaer is an imitation country and western saloon run by a famous national eccentric known as the Cowboy of the North. As the band arrives, the Cowboy of the North sits in a booth upstairs, playing his own songs on the radio station he owns. Downstairs, the band sets up on a stage with a somewhat disturbing backdrop mural of cowboys shooting Indians dead.

Unfortunately, that evening a local man is holding a party for his fortieth birthday and two fishing trawlers have recently set sail, resulting in low attendance. Nonetheless, the audience—a dozen people and a dog—is still moved, especially when Ragnar performs a song about watching his mother after her divorce, with the sad refrain, "I'm so tired of watching you cry."

THIRD SHOW: AKUREYRI

The following night, the band arrives in Akureyri, the largest city outside greater Reykjavik (population 16,000). It is therefore a disappointment when only three people show up to the concert. Nonetheless, the band pledges to perform its best show— and delivers.

OLAF: I've done a hundred rock and roll shows, but tonight I did the best show of my life. And for what? For three ladies in Akureyri. Isn't that the story of my life?

Afterward, the band adjourns to a local bar, where Ragnar proves that his lyric "I'm still afraid of teenagers" is no joke. While talking to two local boys, he insults the rapper Ice-T, which evidently rubs one of them the wrong way. Soon, the boy is shoving Ragnar and bouncers separate the two before further violence can ensue.

FINAL SHOW: REYKJAVIK

After a long bus ride, with a bathroom break on the side of the highway during which the northern lights can be seen in full splendor, the Funerals arrive in Reykjavik just in time to set up for the final show of the tour. To the band's surprise, the club is packed with fans.

THOR: I'm worried we're not going to be able to perform tonight.

Because you're tired?
THOR: No, because we're too sober.

Nonetheless, the show is a success. Audience members say that it is the best Funerals show they've seen, prompting them to view the band less as a joke and more as a major new addition to Reykjavik's vibrant music scene. More important, Ragnar's ex-girlfriend shows up and she leaves with him that night hand in hand.
At his mother's house the following day, Ragnar explains . . .

RAGNAR: I was so happy that I couldn't sleep. I just kept looking at her all night and smiling. So I learned two beautiful things on this tour: the first is that I'm in love, and the second is that I can combine music and love.
THOR: And we also learned a third lesson: that we can play sober.

[ICE-T]

Sometimes the best moments in a celebrity profile occur when the person is talking to someone else. This happened at one of the first music conventions I went to while I was in college. I was interviewing the rapper Ice-T for a cover story for a music magazine called *Option*. But far better than the words I had with him were the ones he exchanged with a female college student in the audience who accused him of being sexist during a panel discussion that also included Chuck D of Public Enemy and jazz guitarist Sonny Sharrock.

ICE-T: Well, let me explain something to you. My fight is not between women and men. My fight is between women and feminist women. Take my album cover with the girl in the string bikini: Half the girls look at it and say, "Damn, I wish I was on the album cover." And other girls say, "That's a terrible thing," because they wish they looked that good in a bathing suit and they have a problem. I don't understand what you think is so sexist about a woman in a bikini.

WOMAN: What about a man in a bikini?

ICE-T: I would put on a bikini if I got enough requests, baby, but I left my shit at home. And I got more girl fans than guy fans. When I don't make a sex record on my album, the girls complain, "Ice, tell me how you want to fuck me."

CHUCK D (*incredulous*): Yeah, Ice-T is a rock and roll god.

WOMAN: But you insult women.

ICE-T: What's insulting to women? Alright, let me ask you: If I say to you girls in here tonight, "I want to get butt naked and fuck," is that insulting to women? Some of them might want to fuck me, goddamnit. If a woman says she wants some dick, is she insulting a man? You know, c'mon, get off of that shit.

If I make records about raping girls, shooting girls, pouring gasoline on them—even though I have one about killing my mother, which I think I can kill my own motherfucking mother if I want to—that's one thing. But I'm not attempting to do that. I'm not out to hurt females. I happen to love females, because I have yet to find anything I can do with a man in a hotel room (*various exclamations from the audience*). If that's sexist, I can't help it. I'm just into sex.

He stands up and thrusts his crotch in the direction of the audience, as if to illustrate what he's discussing.

WOMAN: Oh, god.

ICE-T: I'm sorry, man. C'mon, all I'm trying to do is be really honest. It would be nice if I could make records saying all men are nice and like to treat their women well. But as soon as you leave here, the guys are gonna say, "Did you see her tits?" That's how men are. You would like for us to be different, but we can't because the evil dick doesn't let us. These women who are nodding their heads, I just gave you the best public service announcement you will ever get. Do not think, "All guys ain't like that." Bullshit! They just want to fuck all the time.

Sonny Sharrock drops his head into his hands as Chuck D shakes his head in disbelief. Ice-T picks up a magazine on the table, leans back in his chair, and starts reading it nonchalantly.

[COPYEDITORS]

In a preview of weekend concerts for the *New York Times*, I wrote about a double bill by the groups the Friggs and Jackass. When I picked up the paper the next day, the preview just mentioned "two bands" and, although the description remained intact, the actual names of the groups were nowhere to be found in the story. Evidently, a copyeditor found their monikers obscene and simply removed them. It was just one example of the many challenges of writing about rock, hip-hop, and popular culture for the *New York Times*.

On another occasion, I wrote about a shady corner deli where "neighbors used to hear the sound of crack addicts having sex in exchange for free drugs." When I looked at the paper the next day, the sentence had been changed to read in its entirety, "Neighbors used to hear the sound of crack addicts."

Here are a few more examples of how decency standards are enforced at the paper of record.

Editing an article that quotes the Courtney Love lyric, "I'm eating you / I'm overfed" ...

COPYEDITOR: We have to remove that quote.

What's wrong with it?
COPYEDITOR: It's about oral sex.

The whole article hinges on that lyric.
COPYEDITOR: If you want, I can run it past the news desk and see what they say.

Ten minutes later ...

COPYEDITOR: The news desk says it's about oral sex.

———◆———

Editing a concert review in which singer Francis Dunnery describes himself as "complete scumbag white trash from the north of England" ...

COPYEDITOR: We can't use the word scumbag.

Why is that?
COPYEDITOR: Because it refers to a condom.

What's wrong with condoms?
COPYEDITOR: It's a family newspaper. You and I might like to talk about scumbags, but that's on our own time.

———⋅—⋅———

Editing a Rage Against the Machine review . . .

COPYEDITOR: You write here that the band has lyrics attacking misogynists and homophobes.

Yes.
COPYEDITOR: Did the band say homophobes?

No, that's my summary of the lyrics.
COPYEDITOR: We have a rule that homophobes is a word that can only be used by homosexuals in the newspaper.

Isn't that a double standard?
COPYEDITOR: There's also the case of the religious right. We don't want to accuse anyone of having a clinical psychological condition that is the cause of their actions.

———⋅—⋅———

Editing a review of the English group Laika . . .

Why did you remove the sentence where the singer's talking about how men carry an assault weapon in their pants?
COPYEDITOR: Because it's obscene and this is a family newspaper.

But there aren't any obscene words there.
COPYEDITOR: It's implied.

Come on. There were dead bodies on the front page of the paper the other day. That's much more damaging to a child.
COPYEDITOR: You sound like you're pissed off that we're taking this out. But you can either stay pissed off or realize that we'll never print something like this, so don't even bother trying again.

———◆———

Editing an article in which country singer Steve Wariner recalls Garth Brooks signing autographs for "twenty-four hours straight without a pee break" . . .

COPYEDITOR: We're going to have to send that to the news desk.

Because of the word *pee*?
COPYEDITOR: Yes, it's scatological.

Ten minutes later . . .

COPYEDITOR: What do you want to say instead?

You mean the word *pee* is unacceptable?
COPYEDITOR: Let's not argue about it.

———◆———

Editing an interview with Master P . . .

COPYEDITOR: Is there any reason why you wrote g-a-n-g-s-t-e-r?

Yes, because whenever I write *gangsta*, you change it to *gangster*.
COPYEDITOR: Well, Al [Siegal, *New York Times* standards editor] has okayed the use of the word *gangsta*. He found a precedent for it in a 1924 review. So you can use it now.

———◆———

Editing the interview with Mike Tyson, in which he says, "We made the industry, but we have no control over the destiny of the music" . . .

COPYEDITOR: It's not clear what the referent for "we" is.

It's obviously African-American people.
COPYEDITOR: Okay, let's change it to, "Speaking of black people, Mr. Tyson said, 'We made the industry.'"

No, don't do that.
COPYEDITOR: It needs a referent. It's not grammatical.

It sounds racist. And my name's on the article.
COPYEDITOR: Then give me another referent to use.

I don't know.
COPYEDITOR: Well, who is he talking about if not black people?

Just anyone involved in the culture that rap comes from.
COPYEDITOR: Okay, then let's make it, "Speaking of the rap world, he said, 'We made the industry . . .'"

————◆————

Editing a review of an Irish-themed music festival with the sentence, "On the main stage, Hootie & the Blowfish—the very name of which evokes a sudden desire to yawn and move on to the next article—rigidly jammed through a version of 'Black Magic Woman' that seemed longer than the lines for the Portosans" . . .

COPYEDITOR: I just don't think it works.

What's wrong with it?
COPYEDITOR: The last few words.

They don't make sense to you?
COPYEDITOR: The mandate here is not meaning and content, which is fine, but taste.

What if I said longer than the line at the Guinness tent?
COPYEDITOR: That's fine.

But that's perpetuating an Irish stereotype. Isn't that worse?
COPYEDITOR: Maybe, but it's acceptable.

Despite the copyeditors' efforts, a few obscenities still made their way into articles, starting with the Eazy-E song "Nutz Onya Chin." The word "pussy," used as an insult, also ended up in the paper. No one seems to have noticed it yet, so if you're the first person to successfully find it and e-mail me the article at manofstyle@gmail.com, you'll win a well-worn copy of Lenny Bruce's How to Talk Dirty and Influence People.

[U2]

When reviewing music, hate mail is to be expected. But every now and then, it comes from an unexpected source. After a negative review of a Phil Collins concert, the singer and drummer handwrote a two-page screed on stationery from the Peninsula New York hotel that began by admitting, "It was not a good show but not for the reasons you gave," and ended with a less restrained, "Well Neil, fuck you."

More creatively, in response to a critical piece about a U2 tour, Bono sent a teddy bear stuffed with women's panties and a condescending note. However, after reading a positive review of a subsequent show, he sent a friendly letter with a cute illustration. So when I met Bono for the first time at a Miami party after writing about the U2 album *All That You Can't Leave Behind*, I wasn't sure what kind of response to expect.

BONO: You were very generous with your review.

I don't think I was. It's a great album.
BONO: I was going to write you a letter after I read it. I actually didn't think it was fair to the album. It missed the dark parts of the record.

It was more of an essay, using your album as a jumping off point for the idea of musicians trying to find a purpose and meaning in their success.
BONO: Yes, and in trying to prove your thesis, you didn't really review the record. It's not all "don't worry, be happy." "Grace" has darker subject matter.

That's true, but—
BONO: In the end, I decided not to write the letter. The piece was well-written, but not that well-written.

Were you happy with the *LA Times* review?
BONO: That's LA. When we go to LA, everyone is always saying how great you are. But in Dublin, you get in the cab and the cabbie will tell you your new album is shite.

For the next hour, Bono talks about everything from U2's origins playing Ramones covers to James Joyce to the Bible to the band's reputation for arrogance.

BONO: The problem is that when we get nervous, we get smug.

Suddenly, U2's manager comes over and warns Bono that his voice is getting hoarse and he needs to take care of it for his tour. But Bono keeps talking, until his manager suggests adjourning to a quiet bedroom nearby.

   In the room, Ed Kowalczyk, singer from the rock band Live, is lounging with two conservative-looking guys who appear to be in their early twenties. They introduce themselves as Shawn Fanning and Sean Parker, the founders of Napster, which at the time is the scourge of the music industry for almost single-handedly spreading illegal music downloading across the globe.

BONO: I'm not worried about what they're doing.

Really? I was with Trent Reznor one night, and he was practically crying about it.
BONO: At some point, I know I'm going to have to start reaching fans directly instead of going through the record label. I'm not looking forward to it, but it's an inevitability.
SHAWN FANNING: A lot of artists want to work with us. The problem is that the music labels are suing us instead of trying to find a way to use us in a way that would benefit the artists.
SEAN PARKER: We want to get artists royalties from the downloads, but the labels won't even discuss it.
FANNING: If the record industry destroys Napster, people are going to move to a noncentralized server like Freenet, which is going to make it even harder to stop.
BONO: You should talk to Chris Blackwell. I think he could help you out.*

The group continues to talk about music downloading, with Bono acting very positive about it, though it is unclear if he really feels that way, until finally . . .

FANNING: We're going to the beach.
BONO: What's on the beach right now?
FANNING: Girls.
PARKER: Yeah, girls.

---

* Chris Blackwell, the founder of Island Records (which U2 recorded for), responded, "If you don't like a grocery store, you can't just burn it down. You need to have a new way of selling groceries to people first." Bono later had his own problems: A future album of U2's was leaked on Internet file-sharing sites when he played advance tracks too loudly at his home and a fan outside recorded them on his cell phone.

Fanning and Parker leave.

BONO: They're twenty, they're millionaires, and they're tearing apart the record industry. And what are they doing tonight? They're going to pick up girls. I think we're getting old.

[BILLY CONNOLLY]

Scottish comic and actor Billy Connolly's talent for improvising shows where he talks about whatever's on his mind, with no script and no off button, evidently extends to his interviews. We went for dinner, drove all over LA, and spent hours in a cigar shop, where the conversation below took place. By the time he was finished, I had recorded hours of Connolly pontificating on everything from cannibalism to teaching children masturbation to dolphin rape,* but only one moment of anything real.

When you were younger, were you able to pontificate on anything, like you do now?
BILLY CONNOLLY: That came about in my teens. I found I could have a little angle on things different from the other guys, and it would meet with howls of laughter. The problem was that men liked it very much, but it scared women away. I had to get a rein on it in order to have girlfriends. Clever humor scares women.

Why do you think that is?
CONNOLLY: Because they're frightened you're going to humiliate them. A guy who's prepared to wear his brain on the outside is terrifying.

Do you ever worry that by just speaking whatever's on your mind, you're going to go over the edge and say something that gets you branded as racist or sexist?
CONNOLLY: I find myself sometimes inadvertently going too far when saying something I think is very funny. And people would say it's maybe racist or sexist, but I really couldn't give a fuck.

Is there an example of when you went too far onstage?
CONNOLLY: I did a thing about junkies and said we should eat them. You know, putting all these junkies in jail and rehab is a waste of time and money. Ay, what

---

* "Every bloody nature program you see blames humans for everything. That's not the truth. Dolphins rape, you know. And they gang rape."

we should do is, instead of going after the dealers, because they're good at what they do and the people at the top are hard to find, we've got to kill the junkies. We advertise free heroin and when they come to get it, we'll kill them and we'll eat them. Because undoubtedly half the world isn't getting enough food, and cannibalism is the answer. If all the starving people get to eat one person, we'll solve two problems overnight.

Does comedy serve any purpose for you as far as influencing society?
CONNOLLY: I use it to entertain. It has no other use. It's frippery. It's small. But by the fact that so few of us have it, it's just very, very entertaining and cathartic.

So then ultimately it's a selfish act, just wanting to get laughter as this form of approval?
CONNOLLY: Ultimately, I find everything is a very selfish need. For me, it's to get nearer to the microphone than everybody else and to be a somebody, to count. Not to live and die and be unnoticed is what I'm kind of driven by.

That's very honest of you to say.
CONNOLLY: It is, but you know, I just have this desire, this painful drive, to be remembered. I remember as a comparatively young man thinking that that's what heaven was, being remembered well—and hell was being remembered as a bastard.

ACT NINE

OR

STABBING YOUR MOTHER
FOR A NUMBER ONE ALBUM

SYNOPSIS

ENTER TRENT REZNOR,

WHO HAS WRITER'S BLOCK

BECAUSE HE'S TIRED OF SCRAPING HIS SOUL,

though Robyn Hitchcock cures his block with

HELP FROM A DEAD BODY,

WHICH IS WHAT DJ MARLBORO ACCIDENTALLY CREATES WITH HIS DANCE MUSIC

WHILE KAZEM TRIES TO STOP THE KILLING

AND KHALED'S FRIENDS

are murdered by fundamentalists, &c.

[NINE INCH NAILS]
SCENE 1

The best time to interview musicians is not when they're promoting a new album. The best time is when they are in the throes of creating a new one—and wrestling with the material, questioning their self-worth, and not reciting rehearsed answers. I learned this when I drove to a cliffside house in Big Sur on the California coast, where Trent Reznor had just moved in an attempt to write a Nine Inch Nails record he was supposed to have completed a year earlier. It was not a good sign for his fans that inside the boxes he was unpacking were two video-game consoles and dozens of games.

So which game is better: Quake or Doom?
TRENT REZNOR: Quake technology is far, far superior to Doom.

Do you ever go to gamer forums on the Internet under an alias and post messages asking for help when you're stuck?
REZNOR: Oh yeah, totally. I'm a cheater. And I'm a video game addict. I could have written fifteen more records in the amount of time I spent playing Doom. [. . .]

Is it fair to say that you suffer from writer's block?
REZNOR: I inherently am kind of lazy, and I'm afraid to really push myself and write because I'm afraid of failure. When I was doing *The Downward Spiral*, I was kind of freaked out and [producer] Rick Rubin, who's doing the new album with me, was trying to talk to me. And I just wanted to kill myself. I hated music. I was like, I just want to get back on the fucking road because I hate sitting in a room trying to . . . trying to . . . uh, how do you say this? . . . Just scraping my fucking soul.

Can you elaborate on that process a little?
REZNOR: You have to scrape it to where it's so painful that you get that revelation, you know what I mean. And it's exploring areas of your brain that you don't want to go to. The great moment is when you write something down and you go, "Fuck, I can't say that. I don't want people to know that." It's so naked and honest that you're scared to let it out. You're giving a part of your soul away, exposing part of yourself. I avoid that. That's why I write one song a year. I hate it. I hate it.

But there must be a feeling of accomplishment when you do complete a song?
REZNOR: I love it when it's great, but I hate that feeling of sending a tape out to someone and it's like, "I just cut my soul open. Here it is. Check it out. Criticize it. Are the lyrics shitty?"

Though you *can* learn and grow through constructive criticism.
REZNOR: My skin's not thick enough. I don't fit into the rock star mold because I really don't have the fucking thick coat to deal with what comes with it. The fame shit—I don't like it. I'd rather just write music and disappear. None of my friends are rock stars. I'm not dating supermodels. I don't want to live in LA.* I don't want to be that.

Do you worry that between your last album and when your next album comes out, in those three years—
REZNOR: If the music still matters? If I'm pertinent anymore? That's a real factor to think about, but that's the challenge—making something that matters. That's a real thing to think about. I can only do what I can do. (*Car horn blares outside. He yells at his girlfriend:*) What the fuck are you doing? (*Then continues:*) If it works, it works. If it doesn't, it doesn't.

This is a journalist-type question, but would you tear the wings off a butterfly to be guaranteed that your next two albums will go to number one?
REZNOR: I don't give a fuck. I do and I don't. I'm not bitching about the fact that I can rent this house and pay the gas bill and not worry about that shit, but it's also nice sleeping at night knowing that I did it on my terms. So, yeah, if the next record came out and sold five copies, would it depress me? Yeah, it would.

Actually, the reason I asked that was because someone asked me if I'd tear off the wings of a butterfly for a trip around the world, and I said no. Then they asked if I'd squash a cockroach for the trip, and I said yes. So I found it interesting.
REZNOR: I would stab my mother for a number one album, yes.

[*Continued . . .*]

---

* In 2007, Reznor purchased a four-million-dollar home in Beverly Hills, and soon after moved in with a singer and *Playboy* model he was dating.

[SCOTT WALKER]

Scott Walker is among the finest, most enigmatic American pop baritones of the late twentieth century. At the height of his fame in Britain in the mid-sixties, hordes of fans mobbed him everywhere he went, tearing off his clothes, pulling out locks of his hair, sinking their fingernails into his flesh, even removing upholstery and mirrors from his car as souvenirs.

In his home country, however, after two top forty singles with his former band, the Walker Brothers, he dropped out of sight, and the four spectacular solo albums he recorded in England in the sixties remained practically unknown in America. So when I heard he would be releasing his first new album in eleven years, I contacted him for what he said was the first major American interview he'd ever done.

People have said you're terrified of singing, and I was wondering what they meant by that.
SCOTT WALKER: I do have a terror of singing. That's one of the reasons I don't perform. I want to do the vocal as quickly as possible, because that's going to be the one that's closest to the vocals in my dreams.

So the fear is more of not being able to replicate what you hear in your head than of hearing your own voice?
WALKER: I'm terrified of the approach. It's like a Zen thing: If I get it wrong when I try it, it drives me insane. I even had an arrangement with the studio so I could call up on the day I felt like singing it and go in. I don't even own any of my own records, and I would never listen to them. They would drive me crazy. They drive other people crazy, but not for the same reason.

If you usually do the vocals in one take, then what makes the recording take so long for you?
WALKER: The lyrics are the thing that takes everything. If I get the words, the words will create the track for me. They'll tell me everything, almost down to the cover. I try to keep the vocal quite neutral. There's not a lot of heavy emotion on one side or the other. In the sixties and seventies, I'd sing with quite a lot more emotion.

Why did you eliminate the emotion?
WALKER: It's a way to try to get people to focus on the lyrics.

But at the same time, you won't explain your lyrics to anyone?
WALKER: I had to work at it, so they should too.

[ROBYN HITCHCOCK]

For over twenty years, Robyn Hitchcock has been one of England's finest songwriters—at least for those who enjoy songs with titles like "My Wife & My Dead Wife" and "(I Want to Be an) Anglepoise Lamp." At the time of this interview, I'd just seen him perform half a dozen new, unreleased songs that held up to his best material, and was surprised to learn afterward that he wasn't signed to a record label and hadn't released a new album in three years.

How many songs do you think you've written since your last album [*Respect*]?
ROBYN HITCHCOCK: After *Respect*, I got very menopausal. I think I was just burned out. My father had died, and I'd been unsettled from traveling a lot. Then I moved to the States and lived in Washington, DC for a bit with somebody I was going to marry. But it didn't work out, and I just didn't write anything for eight months. I felt like maybe this was it: I was gonna have to do painting instead.

What got you writing again?
HITCHCOCK: I came to terms with the fact that she belonged in her world and I belonged in mine. So I went back to my world in London and started writing again. I'm probably now back up to about forty songs, which means I'm about ready to get a record out.

What was the last idea or experience that made you think of writing a song?
HITCHCOCK: Well, I was in Rio recently. And there was a corpse on the beach when I got there at sundown. It was lying there very still with flies on its wrists and ankles, and a towel over its head. It wasn't just motionless, like sunbathers and sleepers are. It was just still. You could tell it was dead. It was the first time I ever saw a dead human (*pauses*). Funny, that's what I'm gonna become one day, and I've never seen one.

So what song did that turn into?
HITCHCOCK: Actually, what's funny is I didn't write anything about the corpse. I went back to the hotel room and I wrote . . . Actually, I don't know if I wrote or not. I think I wrote a song about a pulse.

So the corpse didn't actually inspire a song directly?
HITCHCOCK: No, it didn't.

Oh, okay.
HITCHCOCK: I just mentioned it in passing.

Right, because I'd originally asked—
HITCHCOCK: It's something that I would have written about in the past, but not so much now. I went out swimming a couple of days after on the same beach after they'd taken the corpse away, and I noticed that the sea was first full of dead leaves and then full of kind of medical plastic things. And then something just bobbed up to me and it was a severed fish head.

And so you decided not to write a song about that?
HITCHCOCK: You know, again, it's the kind of thing I would have had in a song in the past, but I don't know now.

Have you ever written a song that you felt uncomfortable performing live, that you maybe thought was too—
HITCHCOCK: Too clever or too sappy?

Whatever—too clever, too sappy, too corny, too immature.
HITCHCOCK: I never tried anything *that* corny. I've been fighting clichés in lyrics. Although I wouldn't do some of my earlier stuff now because I think it was a bit misogynistic. Some of the people I liked when I was younger were pretty misogynist, and I sort of put their records on loud if I was angry with my girlfriend or pissed off at my mother. I don't know whether it's the same for women with men, but I think there are ways in which women are much more frightening than men. And I kind of felt resentment toward certain women who can get through the cracks in your shell in a way that a man can't. A man can punch you out, but a woman can kind of seep in like acid.

It sounds like you're much better now . . .
HITCHCOCK: The truth was that I didn't like people anyway. I was, you know, a white, middle-class kid from a wealthy background and I used to *hate* myself. I didn't want to be human. So I went and spent a long time kind of ranting in the undergrowth—or feeling like a severed head, as if I was walking along with no head but carrying my head floating in the air like a balloon. It was up in the air, unattached. Or I'd feel like an angel's head sewn onto a baboon's body, which I think is pretty much the human condition. But now I feel a bit more human and less harsh.

What do you think made you turn that corner?
HITCHCOCK: You know, I just couldn't accept humanity. And now that I'm at least halfway through my life, I figure there's no point in actually trying to stamp on the rest of it like a cigarette end. I might as well enjoy what I've got left.

[DJ MARLBORO]

It was Sunday evening at an open-air community party in the Cidade de Deus (City of God), one of the most dangerous *favelas* (shanty towns) in Rio. DJ Marlboro, two cell phones in hand, moved through the crowd. A pregnant woman asked him to kiss her belly, beautiful dancers gave him their phone numbers, and a nine-year-old begged him for a recording contract. On the perimeter, the drug dealers had already amassed, carrying machine guns, AR-15 rifles, and shotguns, selling coke and weed at the entrance.

An hour later, DJ Marlboro was making another appearance. This one was at a club in the poor Duque de Caxias neighborhood, where spectators ringed a balcony, gawking at the spectacle on the dancefloor below. There, two elevated podiums were set up in the middle, each manned by a security guard. They watched as men linked up in chains—their hands on each other's shoulders in a line—then swept through the crowd like slam-dancers at a punk club. Sometimes, when two different *trenzinhos* (little trains) met, they exploded in a rain of punches and kicks. When this happened, the security guards leaped off their podiums, broke up the trains, and the ritual began anew.

This is the realm of the *baile funk* (funk ball), perhaps the most controversial dance scene in the world. The following took place at the final stop on DJ Marlboro's itinerary: the *favela* Rio das Pedras, where a wall of more than a hundred white speakers and subwoofers blasted the homegrown electronic booty music.

How do you feel about the violence on the dancefloor at some of the parties?
DJ MARLBORO: I feel like that guy who invented the airplane, and then the Second World War disappointed him when he saw the planes being used to drop bombs. It's not that bad yet, but I worry it could be like that.

What did you think when you saw the first *baile de corredor*? *
DJ MARLBORO: I thought, "It's going to be hell." It's an energy that you can't stop. But I understand the attraction that violence can have: It's a way to show your friends that you're strong.

Has all the negative press affected the parties?
DJ MARLBORO: We had five hundred *bailes*, and about fifty of them were *bailes de corredor*. But after all the press, some of the justices outlawed *bailes* to people under eighteen. So a lot of the non-*corredor bailes* closed because of that.

A rapper named LG, a former drug trafficker in a Wu-Tang Clan shirt, exits the party and joins the conversation.

LG: I made a lot more money with drugs than I do with music.

How much money did you make?
LG: About a thousand dollars a month. But I saw a lot of friends and relatives get killed. When a spray of bullets flew over my head and almost killed me during a *favela* shootout in 1995, I realized that everything ends from one second to the next. I thought, "How could I use my life better?"

A baile funk MC, Mr. Catra, comes by, and a heated debate ensues about whether the music should stay true to the ghetto or evolve so it can be accepted by a wider audience.

DJ MARLBORO: I'm concerned about the quality of music. Quality is longevity, and the voice, the equalization, and the grammar of the lyrics all still need to evolve. This national funk is still very young. But the promoters just want to play what people like, like "Pokémon Rap."

---

* *Baile de corredor* translates as corridor ball. At these parties, club patrons choose which side of a club (side A or side B) they want to enter. Between the two sections is a three-yard space known as the corridor of death. On each side, teenagers from rival gangs line up and face off, strategically sending squadrons of *funkeiros* into the opposing line flailing with their feet and hands, and trying to drag enemies across the corridor for a beating. When the fighting becomes too violent, a security guard with a leather belt wrapped around his fist will charge into the crowd, whipping *funkeiros* off their feet, often so hard that huge welts form on their bodies.

What's that?

DJ MARLBORO: It's a boy who's maybe twelve years old singing about how a girl invited him to see the *Pokémon* movie. But he says he would rather go to a hotel room with the girl and play with her private parts.

MR. CATRA: But that is the reality of the *favelas* and the kids today. What is happening is that our sound is completely original now. It is not a copy of American music. Only the beach is the same as Miami.

Suddenly, a gunshot penetrates the air and people start running. A police officer handcuffs a teenager, pushes him roughly into the back of his squad car, and races off as the crowd starts to converge angrily on the car. A few blocks away, we see another police car. Alongside it is a black tarp covering what appear to be two bodies. Rivulets of blood are leaking from beneath the tarp and flowing down the sidewalk.

DJ MARLBORO: This happens too much. These people are going to ruin the opportunities for the music before it gets a chance to evolve.

[DISC JOCKEYS]

A week before the following interview, one of the disc jockeys at Radio Zid, Karim Zaimovic, was wounded by a rocket-propelled shell. Another disc jockey was killed by an explosive, one was wounded while riding his bike, and a third was shot in the leg.

This was life for the volunteer disc jockeys of Radio Zid (which means "wall" in Serbo-Croatian), who were committed to bringing alternative music to Sarajevo during the Bosnian War. Every week, disc jockey Srdan Vuletic walked an hour from his home near the front line in order to broadcast music by his favorite bands. Like many of the DJs, he had to cross either a dangerously exposed park (in which the trees had all been cut down for firewood) or a soccer field (which had been converted into a graveyard) to get to the station. Because of a ten p.m. curfew, when he came to the station to broadcast at night, he had to stay there until dawn.

Did Karim survive?

SRDAN VULETIC: He has brain damage but is alive in a coma.*

---

* He died from his wounds five days later.

What happened?
VULETIC: He was walking in the center of Sarajevo and a shell exploded. It was from one of those multi-rocket throwers that launch ten or twelve shells.

What motivates you to take these risks just to play music?
VULETIC: We love music, and we want to share with the community all the stuff you cannot hear on the government stations. People who are working on the radio are real heroes, because most of them risk their lives just to get there. There is shelling, there are snipers in the streets, there is chaos, and all the time, the radio still goes on.

Do you play English and American bands, or local music?
VULETIC: We play both. Hundreds of new bands have sprung up in Bosnia since the war started. It's a paradoxical situation. In these depressive times, everyone wants to expend energy doing something creative.

Have many of your DJs been drafted into the army?
VULETIC: The government tried to enlist several of our disc jockeys recently. I'm not sure if it was random or in retaliation for something they said in protest on the air. So they went into hiding until we could convince the government that they were journalists and not eligible for the draft.

So—
VULETIC: So in the end, they were saved by a little station.

When the war ended, Radio Zid stopped broadcasting. Many of the disc jockeys were hired by other local stations, while Vuletic became a film director. His first full-length feature won the Golden Iris Award at the Brussels Film Festival; his second was selected to open the Sarajevo Film Festival.

[KAZEM AL SAHER]

Kazem Al Saher is not only Iraq's biggest pop star but also one of the most popular singers in the Arabic world, a dashing romantic who has sold over thirty million albums. As the United States was preparing to go to war with Iraq after 9/11, he chose to do something that his friends and family warned was dangerous: tour America.

At his first tour stop, the Palms Casino Resort in Las Vegas, where casino owners the Maloof family are big fans, he sat down to discuss his decision.

Is this the first interview you've done in English?
KAZEM AL SAHER: Yes. For the past two years, I've been studying English for two hours a day, three days a week.

What made you decide to tour here?
AL SAHER: I want to show people that Iraqis are all very true. They want peace. They have the right to live like everyone else. They give me respect and love in Iraq, so I can't forget them. I have to make the world remember them.

Do you have any security while you're here?
AL SAHER: I didn't think about it. My friends didn't want me to come here now. It's a difficult time, but I'm here for peace. If you listen to my music, that's the message. They offered me bodyguards for when I'm onstage, but I said no. I like to be with my friends or by myself.

Were you in Iraq during the last Gulf War?
AL SAHER: I was in Baghdad for forty-one days during the Gulf War. There was no electricity and no petrol. I had to bike two or three hours to see my friends. But I composed my best songs in this time. I put my music in one room and slept in another room at the end of the house, so that if the house was bombed, either me or my music would survive. I wrote a note that I put with the music, asking if someone found it, would they please put it out.

If you could talk to President Bush, what would you tell him?
AL SAHER: Think about the people, think about the children, about the innocent people. Please don't forget about them. Don't let them suffer. I saw Kofi Annan on a plane once, and I gave him a CD and wrote "Don't forget about Iraqi children" on it. I want to know that my children will be safe. And I wish that for everyone else in the world.

And what would you tell Saddam Hussein?
AL SAHER: *(Laughs and looks down.)*

Would you get in trouble if you said what you really thought?
AL SAHER: *(Silence.)*

[KHALED]

Blessed with a voice that calls to mind a flower wavering in the breeze, Khaled is known as the king of rai, the dominant form of pop music in Algeria. And for this, Khaled has been condemned to die. Islamic fundamentalists claim that the lyrics of rai are too sexually explicit, condone alcohol, and lead the youth astray.

As a result, not only was the music banned in taxis and coffee shops, but two rai stars were murdered: Cheb Hasni was shot at point-blank range near his parents' home and Rachid Baba Ahmed, who produced several of Khaled's hits, was machine-gunned to death outside his record store in Oran. Even at a concert of Khaled's outside Algeria, a fundamentalist hurled a tear-gas grenade onstage. Speaking through a translator, Khaled was discussing his two favorite topics—women and alcohol—when the conversation began to turn more serious.

What's the most extreme emotional reaction you've ever gotten from an audience member?
KHALED: The biggest reaction I get is the women who throw their bras onstage. It's true. I like it when I see this liberty and I see girls from my homeland who are a bit free. We always have restrictions in Algeria.

Is it true that you're banned from playing in Algeria now?
KHALED: I'm often invited to play, but because of the situation, there is not much that I can do. Because if I go there, there will be fights or maybe a crazy person is going to put a bomb in the crowd.

When was the last time you were back in Algeria?
KHALED: In 1990. I went back to Oran, where I was born, because I was feeling nostalgic and wanted to see everybody there.

How did you find the city had changed since you'd left?
KHALED: It wasn't as happy as when I was a child there. What is happening now was already beginning in 1990. The people had aged. It wasn't like a massacre, which is what it is now. There was a small fear at the center of things.

Why do you think they target rai music as evil?
KHALED: It's not only rai. It's any type of music. Even the vendors of music in the street, if they open their stalls, they will be killed. If they see a home with television

antennas, they harass the family. Even people in sports who are world champions, they leave Algeria because they can't live there. They want our female runners to compete wearing hijabs.*

Do you have bodyguards or protection?
KHALED: I know I'm at the top of the list of the well-known people the fundamentalists want to kill. I don't have bodyguards, just tight security during concerts. Even so, I get scared. It could happen anywhere.

Are you worried about your family there?
KHALED: At times I lose sleep over it, but I am always in contact with them. I call them frequently.

Were you close with Rachid Baba Ahmed?
KHALED: Yeah, he is somebody very close. He was a singer and a producer, but he didn't give a damn about politics. Two months before his death, I tried to talk him into moving to France. But he said, "They won't touch me." He was trusting life a lot. But he got killed because these people have no respect for human beings. They kill well-known people just to gain publicity.

We're returning to the Middle Ages. These people don't respect anything. I am a Muslim, too, but you must respect all religions. It's so completely chaotic in Algeria. We never know whether it's the extremists doing something or the military doing it to stir up the movement against the extremists.

Does the situation affect the music you're making?
KHALED: I don't know how it's going to translate into the music yet, but it is something that definitely gets to me. What I'm thinking about a lot is the fact that kids are now involved in this movement and a lot of them see people being shot for nothing. I'm astonished when I see young people, like twenty or twenty-two, who have their whole lives in front of them go on the sacrifice missions.

What do you think will happen to your culture and music in the future?
KHALED: The women are the strongest now in this. They are the ones who have the balls to answer and demonstrate and do things like that. So maybe with them, there is a future. They are ready to go and fight because they are fed up with it.

---

* The person transcribing this interview noted here: "The tone of the interview has gone from a joyful, laughter-filled conversation to a somber tone at this point. I can't understand Khaled, but the tone in his voice brings tears to my eyes. Very sad. A little hopeless sounding."

[GWEN STEFANI]

As No Doubt walked down the red carpet at the *Billboard* Music Awards in Las Vegas, paparazzi screamed not for the band but for "Gwennnn," who obliged them by opening her fur jacket and sticking out her chest, which was covered by just a teeny bikini top. She gave a big patronizing smile, her body a bone for the dogs. Later, a teenage fan ran up to band bassist (and singer Gwen Stefani's ex-boyfriend) Tony Kanal. "Man, I love your band," he said. "You're my hero. I have to ask you something: When you guys first got together, did you just think, 'Wow, she is hot!'?" Kanal didn't answer.

Over a Japanese meal the following week in New York, Stefani wrestled with the concept of being a sex symbol.

So you were saying about the new record . . .
GWEN STEFANI: Yeah, I think it's a cool record. It does have a sexiness and a hipness that we've never had before. The thing about the sexy side, for me, is that I earned it (*laughs*). I feel like I didn't play my cards too soon on that because I never felt comfortable.

When did you start feeling comfortable with that side of yourself?
STEFANI: It wasn't until, like, two years ago that I felt comfortable wearing high heels, because when you're on heels—dude, you should try it—all of a sudden you're sexy. It doesn't matter who you are. It just gives you a different way you walk. I never felt old enough before. I think I finally feel like there's a side to me like, "I'm a woman now," which is cool. It's fun.

That's pretty good—you're thirty-two.
STEFANI: Yeah, I never felt really strong growing up. I think it was the way my parents raised me, in this really Catholic way. And maybe being insecure about being the girl in the scene back in the day. I didn't know where I fit in. All the women around me that I could look at were in bands like L7 or Hole. And these were hard girls. They were angry and they were pissed, and I didn't really feel like that. And then the other ones were these folky girls. So there wasn't really anybody, until I discovered Blondie. She was sexy and she wasn't ashamed to just be rocking out. And to me, that's having it all because we all want to be sexy, even guys do. It's in human nature, because we've gotta have babies.

It's interesting, because when we went to the *Billboard* awards, you would vamp and show skin and give the photographers what they wanted, but you'd do it sort of tongue-in-cheek.

STEFANI: I think the whole being sexy thing, to do it seriously is just a joke. The only time it ever becomes serious is when you're one-on-one with the person you love, and then you can't be silly about it—other than saying, like, "Come on, dude. I mean, have you seen me when I wake up in the morning?" Nobody's perfect. I don't get it. I don't get the whole thing.

WAITER: Everything okay? Did you like the noodles?

STEFANI: Yeah! It's so weird to think that noodles came from Japan, right? And then they somehow made it to Italy and turned into pasta.

One thing I've noticed after talking to you is that you're a very traditional person.

STEFANI: It's from my family. You'll meet my mom, and you couldn't get more traditional.

What does your brother do?

STEFANI: My brother was always an artist—since the day he was born—and he always got all the attention. He would win all the awards at school. I didn't have to do anything, because I had him. That was my claim to fame.

Were you popular in school?

STEFANI: I was always a pretty passive person. I was a one-on-one person. I had my one best friend, and I didn't have lots of girlfriends. I never have. I can still name all of my best friends: the three girls from growing up, my first boyfriend—who was the first guy I kissed—and then Tony. And that's it. There's not much before the band. I wasn't doing drugs or having premarital sex or anything.

Were you more of a studious type?

STEFANI: I was always a really good girl, but I was really bad at school. So I decided that once I graduated, I was going to start over again. I went to college, and I took it really seriously. I wanted to, like, get smart. I took every class from the very beginning: beginning English, beginning math. It took me a long time.

What did you want to do with that education?

STEFANI: I guess I never had any dreams and never really thought that far ahead.

At that point, I just decided, "Okay, I'm going to take art for my major, and then I'll decide what I'm going to do with it after I explore it." But then we went on tour, and that was that. I never headed back. I didn't have to fucking decide.

The waiter returns.

WAITER: This is the last thing. Usually after finishing your food, you drink this to your health.
STEFANI: Okay, I need the health stuff. (*Downs the drink in seconds.*)

[NINE INCH NAILS]
SCENE 2

When the interview began stretching late into the night, Reznor invited me to sleep over. Fortunately, unlike Jewel, he preferred separate beds. While cleaning off the pillows and papers, I noticed an envelope. Scrawled in black pen on it were the words "new songs." I didn't open it, though I did notice that it was very thin.

Do you ever regret dropping out of college?
TRENT REZNOR: I went through a phase after Nine Inch Nails got signed and I was living this dream lifestyle that all my friends from high school envied. And I thought for a while, "You fucking idiots. Why buy into this bullshit concept of you graduate from college, panic, marry your fucking college sweetheart, and buy a condo that takes you thirty years to pay for?"

I had this real shitty, bullshit attitude. And when I went home to where I grew up for the holidays, I looked at my sister's whole world, which is ten minutes from where she grew up—my only sister. And at one point I really got into shit about, like, "You don't know how big the fucking world is! It's limitless. How can you sell yourself short by this stupid reality that you've accepted?" And then I realized, fuck me, man. I'm more miserable than all of them.

Accepting others' life choices is something most people only learn with age.
REZNOR: Maybe it is age, because I feel differently now than I did before. When I first got signed and got all this praise and got treated like a fucking freak—and it was everything I ever wanted—I treated a lot of people shitty because I could. The whole music business, it trains you to be an elite son of a bitch and nobody . . . I don't know. It's my own thing. I just . . .

No, no. Go on.
REZNOR: David Bowie—I was afraid to meet him because I'd met Prince and some other people I really liked, and they were assholes. And it broke my fucking heart because I couldn't look at them the same way anymore. But Bowie, he's a fucking gentleman and a great guy. So I've spent many a miserable night talking to people I hate for that same reason. But I'm the luckiest fucker in the world, man.

In some ways.
REZNOR: In a lot of ways. I'm not happy, okay. And that's my own fucking mental fuck-up. But I don't take for granted the situation I feel fortunate to have fallen into. I think I deserve it. I think I worked my ass off to get here, but at the same time I know there's a big degree of luck involved.

Yeah, do you ever feel like—
REZNOR: Like *fuck it?*

No, not like fuck it. More like—
REZNOR: Because I do, actually. [. . .] My head's just wrong. There's something wrong with me. I'm not trying to be Mr. Tortured Artist Guy. I wish I could be more content with the situation I've got. It's a complicated situation, and I see contemporaries—my peers—who are very happy in the situation they've got. But my head doesn't work the same way.

But is being content something one should necessarily strive for?
REZNOR: It's not about being content. It's about: What if everything you ever wished for in your life and never thought you'd get, you got—and it still sucked? That's the thing. I look at Oasis: dumb idiots just living life. Not to be shitty to them, but I guess the lowest strive for being an asshole and stupid. You know, ignorance is bliss and there's a truth to that. I guess I don't want it, but at the same time I always wished I could fucking fit in and just escape.

The idea of fitting in is a delusion. No one really fits in.
REZNOR: I guess I want it and I don't want it at the same time. When I went to high school, I was a fucking misfit freak. I thought, "When I go to college, I'm going to join the fraternity. I'm going to be the most normal fucker in the world." Two months later, I'm an outcast. It's something I've had to come to terms with

in my own head. That dream of fitting in is bullshit, I know that. But at the same time, it'd be nice just once to just . . . What I'm saying is so stupid right now.

Do you ever think that you don't deserve all the popularity you've gotten, that maybe your fans are deluding themselves and you're not all that?
REZNOR: I'll say one thing here: When Nine Inch Nails first got signed, I didn't know how to do interviews. I really still don't. I talk too much and I say stupid things. At the time, my heroes were Jane's Addiction, among others, and I'm reading where Perry [Farrell] was a male prostitute and had this junkie lifestyle. And I'm like, "I smoked pot when I was eighteen once."

Right, but—
REZNOR: I'm boring. I'm not this icon. I love Kiss for the same reason. Gene Simmons had a cow tongue grafted to his. That was the greatest shit.* And I kind of made this pact with myself that I would just be honest. I am thirty-one. I grew up in Pennsylvania. I wasn't a male prostitute. I'm not gay. My tongue is my own.

[*Continued* . . .]

[DAVID BOWIE]

Ask just about any male rock musicians who they want to be like when they're older, and their answer is always the same . . .

Every time I interview a new, younger musician, they always point to you as an example of aging gracefully—
DAVID BOWIE: Agh!

What does that mean?
BOWIE: I must say it never occurred to me. I think forty was much worse for me. It really was a period where I knew it was a struggle to let go of what I thought was imperative about being youthful. And it's not a coincidence that it came at the same time as my great depression about my writing—in 1987. That whole period for me was extremely difficult, but after getting through that and relaxing into a new plateau of age [at fifty], all I can say is it's quite possible to be just as

---

* And, unfortunately, not true: Simmons's tongue is real and Farrell was never a male prostitute.

happy, content, and satisfied with one's lifestyle at this age as ever it was in the young twenties. In fact, for me in particular, I think I'm a lot happier now than I was then.

When you were in your early twenties, was there someone who was a model for you?
BOWIE: It was William Burroughs. He never stopped thinking, and that really impressed me. And of course Picasso: You can't look at Picasso and not be completely inspired. He was always playing with his mind and his reactions to life, and it was always fresh and childlike. I think it's the element of being continually astounded by what this world can do. Once you lose that sense of wonder at being alive, you're pretty much on the way out. [. . .]

What about the Velvet Underground? Do you remember the first time you heard them?
BOWIE: Oh, yeah. I'd had a manager in the mid-sixties who'd been on a trip to New York and had met Andy Warhol, who gave him a demo of the Velvet Underground's first album, which he brought back to me and said it was hideous and probably the kind of thing I'd like (*laughs*).

And he was correct.
BOWIE: I adored it and—this is a funny thing—started doing a couple of the songs from the album onstage. So I was actually doing Velvet Underground covers before the album came out. I definitely covered the Velvets before any other artist on earth. I still have that acetate with Warhol's signature on it. Is that great? I always kept my vinyl because I'm a vinyl freak. I love vinyl.

Had you ever been to America yourself yet?
BOWIE: I really didn't know any people at all in America. I still don't (*laughs*). I was totally on my own when I first went there around 1971. I was just stuck in my hotel room. Paul Nelson, my publicist at Mercury Records, would come over and bring me albums. So I told him about this huge love I had for the Velvets and that they were such a big thing in my life and I thought they changed my whole sensibility about how I wanted to write my particular kind of rock music. I wanted some kind of sensibility that the Velvets had, but I wanted it to come out in an English way.

And he said, "In that case you might want to go to the Electric Circus." I said, "What's that?" And he said, "That's a big thing here in New York, but it's in

FACIAL
Rejuvenation

its last night. It's closing down. And the last act on the last show is the Velvet Underground." I couldn't believe that I was going to be seeing the Velvet Underground.

Is that when you first befriended Lou Reed?
BOWIE: Not exactly. I went to the Electric Circus, and I went backstage afterward and knocked on the door. I met [Velvets bassist, keyboardist, and violist] John Cale and asked if I could speak to Lou Reed. And Lou Reed came to the door and we talked and talked, and I said how much I admired him.

Anyway, I saw Paul a day or so later and I said, "Thank you so much. That just made my trip." I couldn't express my gratitude for getting to speak with my hero.

He laughed and said, "You know something?" And I said, "No." He said, "Lou Reed left the band. You were speaking to Doug Yule, his replacement" (*laughs*). He never fessed up that he wasn't Lou Reed. He just became Lou Reed for the duration of our conversation.* I was talking about his damn songwriting and how I'd come all the way from England (*laughing so hard he can't speak*) . . .

And that was before the whole glam thing started . . .
BOWIE: On that trip to New York, I was definitely long-haired. I was kind of a goofy guy at that time. And I stayed that way until I got back to England. I know that I cut my hair in January 1972. The whole glam thing gelled into place for me at that time. Very distinctly. Anybody who knew me in January '72 would have seen a major change in me (*pauses*). Have you seen the Henry Darger exhibit yet at the American Museum of Folk Art?

No.
BOWIE: Oh, God, you *must* go and see it! I took Lou Reed, and he was blown away.

Is Henry Darger the outsider artist?
BOWIE: Exactly. He died in his early eighties. All his life he was a shiftless, strange, reclusive man in Chicago. He had an apartment there, and when they broke in after he died, they found he'd written a nineteen-thousand-page manuscript based on this alien force coming and making child slaves out of a planet of goodness and light. And he accompanied this with ten-foot-by-four-foot paintings

---

* Bowie most likely didn't meet John Cale either. Cale had left the Velvet Underground over two years earlier.

he'd made all over his room. There's an exhibition of it, and I'm telling you it's the most riveting artwork.

I'll definitely go see it.
BOWIE: Please do. I assure you that you will respond. You'll see what I mean.

[MINGERING MIKE]

The story began one morning in a Washington, DC flea market, where two men came across a box full of strange hand-painted album covers. These men were known as diggers, the term used for those obsessed souls who dig through boxes at thrift stores and garage sales in search of rare record albums.

When they pulled the records out of the sleeves, they were surprised to find that the discs were made not of vinyl but of cardboard. Each had been cut in the shape of a record, with grooves and a label painted on. The inner sleeve was a shopping bag meticulously taped together to hold a record, and a few albums even included shrink wrap, price stickers, and fake promotional quotes. Altogether there were thirty-eight albums, nearly all credited to an unknown musician by the name of Mingering Mike and dated between 1968 and 1977.

What these two diggers had found was a cache of seemingly nonexistent music: The covers purported to contain film soundtracks, benefit records, double albums with gatefold sleeves, protest songs, and even albums of Christmas, Easter, and United States Bicentennial music. In short, they had discovered an outsider artist.

As soon as I heard about the discovery, I called the two diggers—Dori Hadar and Frank Beylotte—and made them promise not to talk to anyone else from the press until I arrived. By the time I landed in DC a few days later, they had tracked down Mingering Mike, who was so shy and reclusive that he refused to divulge his real name or let his face be photographed for the article. All he would allow me to print was that he worked as a security guard somewhere in DC.

How did you find him?
FRANK BEYLOTTE: Fortunately, in addition to picking up the fake albums and tapes, I also picked up as many personal letters and photo albums as I could. Some had names and addresses of people he was in contact with.
DORI HADAR: So we tracked down one of his cousins and went to his place in

Landover, and I knocked on the door and tried to explain that I was looking for Mingering Mike. He was very friendly, and I left my number with him. I don't know if he ever gave it to you.

MINGERING MIKE: Yeah.

HADAR: He did?

MINGERING MIKE: Mm-hmm. I was at my job and I don't ordinarily call my phone and pick up messages. And something just told me to do it that day.

HADAR: Oh, and you heard his message on there?

MINGERING MIKE: I said, "What?" I didn't believe it. Afterward, I talked to a couple of my buddies and they said, "Yeah, right, just be careful."

So you never called back?

MINGERING MIKE: No.

HADAR: We didn't know if his cousin even gave him the message, but he had told us that [accidentally says Mingering Mike's real name] lived in the Southeast. Whoops, I'm sorry.

MINGERING MIKE: You didn't hear nothing!

HADAR: I'm so sorry. He didn't want to tell me where you lived exactly. But then I went back to the office and I looked up your name. Because I work as an investigator for a law firm of criminal defense attorneys, I have resources at my disposal, so I found your street number.

BEYLOTTE: We couldn't find a phone number, so we just went there.

If you had a phone number, would you have called?

HADAR: I probably would have gone in person, because for my job, if you call somebody, it's very easy for them to blow you off. It's very hard to just close the door when you're face-to-face with someone.

BEYLOTTE: We were really nervous about showing up out of the blue: Here are these two white guys walking into a not-so-great apartment complex with no way to get in. We had to bang on the door, and people were looking at us.

MINGERING MIKE: I heard something clicking outside. Probably their knees.

What did you think when you saw them?

MINGERING MIKE: I said to myself, it could only be limited possibilities: bill collectors, police, or a summons.

HADAR: We knew it was you immediately, because we had your picture and we recognized you. Then, when we mentioned the album covers, your eyes kind of lit up.

BEYLOTTE: It was like we were talking about your children.

MINGERING MIKE: When they told me that the things were put up for auction, I said, "But those were my babies."

How did all the records end up at the flea market in the first place?

BELOYTTE: A lot of times, flea market vendors acquire their wares from a storage facility that's auctioning off the possessions of someone who hasn't paid their bills. They bid on the entire contents of a unit and then take it right to the flea market and sell it. So he fell behind on his payments for the storage space, and thought he had something worked out with the management. And then it was auctioned off.

HADAR: I told Mike that I had posted some of his album covers online and there was this overwhelming response and people loved his artwork. He was very quiet. I said, "I really think I might be able to help you do something and realize your dream here."

What was your original dream with the albums?

MINGERING MIKE: I was writing music. But I felt like just writing music wasn't enough. I wanted to go a little further than that and make the records. And then like if it all came together one day, I'd be ready.

How did you get the shrink wrap on your albums?

MINGERING MIKE: I took it off records I'd bought. It took me about an hour to put it on each album.

So how do feel about finally being discovered now?

MINGERING MIKE: It would have been a dream come true if it happened twenty years ago. But now it's strange. Overwhelming.

Since this interview, Mingering Mike's album covers have been displayed in several art galleries; he's released an album of actual music, Super Gold Greatest Hits; *and a book of his artwork was published by the Princeton Architectural Press.*

[CHARLES GAYLE]

If you ever see Charles Gayle play saxophone, you'll never forget it, because he blows—blows music apart, blows clubs to pieces, blows minds wide open. He is, without doubt, one of the most powerful free-jazz saxophonists of his time, signed to a Swedish record label and occasionally flown to Europe to perform. Despite his acclaim, however, at the time of this interview, Gayle had been homeless for over fifteen years, making money by playing in the streets and subway stations of New York.

After convincing an editor to let me write about Gayle, I searched for the saxophonist in subway stations, left word with his friends, and checked club listings, but he was nowhere to be found. After a few weeks passed, I began to worry, until one day my phone rang. It was Gayle calling from a pay phone to explain that he'd been sick for two months with hepatitis A (which he'd caught from the mouthpiece of a horn) and was recuperating in a squat on New York's Lower East Side.

A week later, wearing a gray overcoat, a blue baseball cap, a few days of white stubble, and a large crucifix dangling from a string around his neck, he met me for coffee.

How are you feeling?
CHARLES GAYLE: I'm good now. But when I had that hepatitis, I thought I was going to the other side. I said, "Okay," and I made my peace. But it didn't happen. I just alerted a few people to let them know that I don't know what's happening and I may not be around anymore.

Have you always been playing in the street for money?
GAYLE: I used to draw sketches on the street and I had jobs a couple times, but basically I was always playing for money.

In the Times Square subway station?
GAYLE: It's only for the past two or three years that people have been allowed to play in the subways. Before that you had to play in the street, no matter when it was. I was able somehow to even play through the winters outside. Sometimes it would get so cold, my horn would freeze.

So what would you do?
GAYLE: I don't know what I'd do. I'd just stand there and look at it, I guess.

Where do you stay when you need shelter?

GAYLE: I live in a squat on Ninth Street. I don't want to stay in that place, but what else can I do? It's either that or the street. But I'm trying to get off the streets, man. Otherwise I'm gonna go out like this. I got a couple things in my mind about doing something this year, to make a move one way or another because I don't play enough here.

What about California?

GAYLE: The edge is off there. I just want to feel that edge, man.

Do you make more in the clubs or on the street?

GAYLE: The truth is, I don't make hardly anything. I make enough to eat. That's the truth. In the clubs, I split the money three ways—with the bassist and drummer—so if I get forty dollars, I'm lucky. When I play outdoors, it's like five to six days a week—outside or in the subways or somewhere—and I get seven dollars or five dollars. Ten dollars is a good day—an excellent day. I've got to stand there all day to get that. Sometimes I don't hustle the right places, but after a while, where am I gonna go?

Has anyone ever stolen your horns while you're sleeping?

GAYLE: I sleep with them on the street, and I've never had my horn or nothing stolen.

What else do you own?

GAYLE: All I have is my horns and a few changes of clothes. That's it. The only book I read is the Bible. I read the newspaper, and that's just because it happens to be my thing. But, see, that's the key to playing free, because I can afford to be free.

After you play, would you rather have a standing ovation or would you rather empty the club?

GAYLE: To answer that one question, I'm gonna dance on my feet right now, because it's a good one. In a way, I would want to be able to empty the place out, you dig? To me, a lot of times when they empty the club, it's a form of ovation too, because you can pop somebody's head and they can appreciate it.

I've seen people walk out of your gigs, including the president of your record label, but have you fully emptied a place before?

GAYLE: I feel like I'm not radical enough in my playing, just through that horn.

I'm gonna be more. I want to do that. I want to put something out here that's so heavy that cannot be denied. Yes, every time I would like to empty the joint—just be that unsettling. Yeah, I'm gonna work on that.

What would you do if you came into a lot of money?
GAYLE: I don't know what would change, man. I'd get a little place. And I got some kids, so I'd give them the money. I don't think nothing would change. I feel all right. I really do, man. I feel very strong somehow. So maybe I'm where I'm supposed to be.

Since this interview, Gayle has recorded more than twenty-six albums for various labels, in addition to appearing on recordings by several rock and jazz legends. He eventually made enough money as a professional musician to rent his own apartment in the East Village.

[TOM PETTY]

Tom Petty sat in his Malibu home on a warm summer afternoon, sipping from a mug of cold coffee and wearing a suede fringed jacket, brown moccasins, and black socks. From a distance he looked like he hadn't changed in a quarter of a century, but up close his face was etched with deep lines of experience. Only his pale blue eyes (which he rarely made eye contact with) and a sporadic sheepish smile betrayed signs of vibrant life. Every few minutes, he arched his back like a cat, extended his arms into the air as far as they would go, and stretched his bones. He then froze in that position for several awkward seconds, occasionally dropping his cigarette to the floor.

This is the longest amount of time that's ever elapsed between albums for you. What took so long?
TOM PETTY: You know, that didn't occur to me until recently. I don't know if I was just fed up with it all or what, but I just didn't really feel compelled to run out and do another record. I just thought, "I am going to take my time." Then someone told me the other day that it's been three years.

It's actually been four years.
PETTY: Has it been? Four years? That's a long time. I'm surprised that I waited that long. But I have to honestly say that I didn't even notice the time going by. And it

didn't take long to make the record, just a few months. I guess I was touring and I took my time writing.

The songs on the album all seem to have similar themes about drifting lost in the world and looking for something solid to hold onto.
PETTY: What is that song [on my album]? It's got the line, "It's hard to say who you are these days but you run on anyway, don't you?"

"Saving Grace"?
PETTY: Yeah, that's kind of how I see these times. There are a lot of people who aren't sure who they are anymore, so they're just trying to keep their head above water because things are moving really fast these days. There is a lot of information flying around and a lot of people staring into their palms (*pauses*). I don't know why I took so long [between albums]. That really staggers me that it took so long.

I remember just before you moved out here, people were worried about you because you'd split up with your wife and were living in a shack somewhere.
PETTY: Yeah, I was living in a pretty rundown shack. I didn't mind it. It was in a part of the Pacific Palisades in the woods. And I was living back there and had chickens and all kinds of shit. In some places, you could actually see the daylight coming through the walls of the cabin. But it was my bachelor pad, you know. I had a big adjustment to make, and maybe they were right to be worried about me. I had a lot of free time in that period, and it wasn't the best period in my life. But I am through that. I came out the good side.

What was the wake-up call that made you try to clean up?
PETTY: Oh, yeah, well, you know, it was: One of us is dead.* It's like, "Shit." Yeah, that's a big wake-up call. I've lived life pretty hard. I took an adult portion of life and squeezed it into a very short amount of time when I was younger. We lived hard, we didn't sleep much, we traveled all the time. In this job, you don't realize that you're getting older. Then, probably around the time I got married again, I said, "I am going to try and act my age now." I'm still coming to terms with it a little bit, but it's not bad.

---

* Bassist Howie Epstein, who died at age forty-seven from complications due to heroin addiction.

What's been the most difficult part to come to terms with?
PETTY: The thing that's tough about it is you realize you have a limited amount of time left. That's the first time that ever dawned on me: "Oh shit, you're going to run out of time." That's one of the reasons I don't want to spend the rest of my life touring. I've done it. You can do that and then look up one day, and a lot of your life has gone by and all you did was go around doing rock and roll shows.

Between the Internet, satellite radio, and satellite television, there are way too many media and promotional outlets now that take up artists' time also.
PETTY: It's more than I am going to deal with, I'll tell you that. I am straight up. Actually, this is it for me. This is the last interview I am doing, because I have to live life. I can't spend every day fulfilling the needs of the label or the media in order to promote the record. You know, I love the record and I really care about it, but there is a point where you start to not like yourself (*laughs*).*

I have tried to explain this to the label. I am sure it comes from the life I've lived, but my mind is so delicate that I can't take being part of that. It's just like hanging around after a show to meet people. I can't do that.

If you'd embraced it more, you may have been even bigger, but you'd be much less happy.
PETTY: I say if things were any bigger, I couldn't deal with it. If I was more famous or more successful, it would be too much.

These pop stars today that really spend all their time promoting themselves, but that's all they know, I feel sorry for those people because someday they're going to look up and see what they spend their lives doing and it's going to burn them out. Your shit will burn out. So this is it for me. This is the last interview I'm doing for a long time.

Look at the Sly Stones and Captain Beefhearts. They don't talk to the press and they're still legends.
PETTY: Yeah, I can see myself that way very easily. As a hermit out in Malibu.

---

* Note that this interview was one of the few he'd done in years, and the record that he was promoting, *Highway Companion*, not only hadn't been released yet, but he hadn't finished mastering or sequencing it.

[SYSTEM OF A DOWN]

With long, stringy hair receding off a high forehead, bulging bug-like eyes, and the posture of a baboon, Daron Malakian—songwriter and guitarist in the Armenian-American hard rock band System of a Down—makes for an unlikely rock star. Sitting in his two-story home in Glendale, California, he flipped the cap off a bottle of medical marijuana labeled Night Queen and began packing a glass pipe as he talked about his proclivity for staying indoors for months at a time.

When you were younger, were you more social?

DARON MALAKIAN: Yeah, I think I've become a lot less social. Say I walk into a place, I feel like five people might know who I am and five people might not. And it's kind of like made me a little bit uncomfortable. I see a different guy in the mirror than what they see. I see Daron. And I forget that Daron is someone who plays in this band that so many people love. So whenever someone walks up to me, they have to understand they are probably talking to someone that is ten times more nervous than they are.

Do you really think so?

MALAKIAN: I do. My palms get all clammy (*laughs*). I don't have that kind of confidence. The only time I have that confidence is when I'm onstage. When I'm onstage, that Daron can do anything and can say anything [. . .]

Have you ever been on any psychiatric medication?

MALAKIAN: There was a time in my earlier twenties when I was having a lot of panic attacks and things like that. They tried to put me on those drugs that make people plastic—Prozac and shit. But now when shit gets too much for me to think about, I meditate. I can't say that I'm a constant meditator, but I know how to slow my mind down if I need to.

So what do you do when you think super-dark thoughts, like about hurting someone?

MALAKIAN: I've had—not to get into too many details, but I've had dark moments in my life. As a child I had a lot of dark, dark moments. I had to be an adult very quick. I was drinking coffee at AA meetings at nine years old. I'm used to it, man. I've done acid once in my life, and I watched *The Exorcist* and everyone in the room with me was freaking out. And I was like, "I'm not comfortable, but I know how to handle this, because I've been in hell before."

Hell in what way?
MALAKIAN: I knew it wasn't that different from being a child and feeling scared or feeling alone or whatever. Like because I have skulls and shit like that, my girlfriend is afraid to sit in my house alone. But to me, I see these things almost as a form of spiritual protection. I just feel very comfortable around that kind of mood, that kind of vibe. With that said, I love going to Disneyland. And Dodgers games.

I didn't peg you for a sports fan.
MALAKIAN: I've always liked sports. In the eighties, I was crazy fucking insane about the Lakers. If you ask me what the biggest influence is aside from my dad, the honest answer from me would probably be Kareem Abdul-Jabbar, more than any musicians. Just because I looked at the way he carried himself, his style, how he conducted himself, the role he played for the team. I really look up to Kareem Abdul-Jabbar—and not just because he's 7'2".

That's a really cool answer.
MALAKIAN: I long for conversations sometimes. Like I said, I don't get out and about too much. So sometimes it's nice to talk to someone that isn't an idiot.

[HENRY GRIMES]

In avant-garde jazz circles in the mid-sixties, Henry Grimes was one of the most respected bassists working. Trained at Juilliard, he performed with legends like John Coltrane, Thelonious Monk, and Miles Davis in his youth before going on to play on some of the most seminal albums of the free jazz era.

But around 1968, Grimes disappeared. For over three decades, nobody in the jazz world heard from him. Several reference works even listed him as dead.

And that's where the story of Henry Grimes might have ended if it wasn't for a determined fan from Athens, Georgia, named Marshall Marrotte, who discovered Grimes thirty years after he'd disappeared.

Grimes was living in a one-room efficiency in downtown Los Angeles. Not only did he no longer own a single musical instrument, but he had never seen a CD before and was unaware of the deaths of many of his colleagues, including his legendary former bandmate Albert Ayler (who was found floating in the East

River in 1970). Marrotte helped Grimes find a bass, booked him for his first concert in New York in three decades, and gave me the number of a pay phone in the lobby of the transient hotel where Grimes was living.

Did you ever think you'd be making music again?
HENRY GRIMES: I expected that I would be. I didn't know when or how exactly, though.

What made you stop in the first place?
GRIMES: Because economically, I was in no shape at all. My money was down to nothing. It was really just that kind of a thing. Economically, I wasn't in tune. So I came to California where the sun shines. Mostly that's the idea. I didn't want to be subjected to the cold. I find that in LA, with the heat and everything, it's okay.

What happened to your bass?
GRIMES: I sold it to a violin maker here. I was working with a group led by [pianist] LaMont Johnson. That was the last group I worked with. So I sold my instrument.

And did selling it help you survive?
GRIMES: It wasn't enough, but I still sold it anyway. I was feeling that's what I had to do, so I just did it. It permitted me to get a very good view of everything.

Was it difficult to let go of music like that?
GRIMES: I wasn't worried about it. All I knew was that I got out of New York and that cold weather. That was the only thing I was looking at.

What did you do for money in the meantime?
GRIMES: I was doing a lot of physical labor: working as a janitor in a Beverly Hills Jewish temple and in a school. And I was working in a bowling alley in Long Beach. In between those jobs, I did a little construction work. It keeps me in shape, you know.

Did anyone know you were a musician at those places?
GRIMES: No one knew.

Did anyone seek you out in that time and try to get you into music again?
GRIMES: Nobody was able to get in touch with me until Marshall called and found out where I lived. He did good detective work.

Were you aware of all the musicians you'd influenced?
GRIMES: I didn't really know. I was amazed, because I listened to some of the CDs [of my music] that Marshall and others sent me. At the time, I didn't pay that much attention to them, but when I listened to them again two weeks ago, it was amazing what I heard. There was more to it than I ever realized.

Maybe you needed that distance from it to appreciate it.
GRIMES: I think that's why I left and went into isolation, because when I heard that music, it was fantastic. Sometimes you have to uncloud your perceptions. Your emotions can get in the way and get you in a lot of trouble or hassle. And you can either let them bother you or you can find a way to get something out of them.

Do you have any regrets about all the time you haven't been on the scene?
GRIMES: All I know is that it happened. I'm working on straightening things out now. But I'm back for good.

True to his word, when I checked in with Grimes seven years later, he had been working constantly, playing concerts in over twenty-three countries, teaching at schools and conservatories, and appearing on more than a dozen albums. Though no one was certain at the time why Grimes originally disappeared, it was later disclosed that he had a nervous breakdown, and was hospitalized for several years and treated for mental illness.

[JAMES TALLEY]

"All things unfinished or in turmoil around me are reminders that I'm still alive."
—Quote hanging on wall in the office of James Talley

In the seventies, James Talley was one of the most eloquent spokesmen for the working man, rural life, and the resilient human spirit, recording one powerful album after another for Capitol Records. Fans placed him in the lineage of Jimmie Rodgers and Woody Guthrie. Jimmy Carter even invited him to perform at his inauguration ball. But when I met him for an interview two decades later, Talley, the voice of the blue-collar worker, was behind a desk in Nashville selling real estate.

JAMES TALLEY: Who would have thought that a populist songwriter like myself would be doing this? I mean, I never thought it in my wildest dreams.

Where did you think you'd be now instead?
TALLEY: I suppose years ago, I hoped to be at the point today where I could sell out shows in a few hours. But it didn't happen that way. And if it doesn't happen that way, then you go on another way. Or you do like Phil Ochs and you kill yourself.*

Did you ever think about doing that?
TALLEY: You know, I probably thought about that a time or two during some of the really dark periods. But then you say, "Well, if I do that, who's going to take care of my kids and my wife? And maybe, just maybe, I might still create something good here. I just have to hang on, keep the faith."

So what derailed your career?
TALLEY: I don't know how much tape you want to spend, but when I left Capitol back in 1979, I still owed them three more albums. I was working with a manager at the time who convinced me that I should be doing something better. I was very young and naïve. I never saw a lawyer my whole life. And when I left Capitol, they deleted my catalog,† which wasn't something I had anticipated.

How did you finally get the rights back to your music?
TALLEY: In 1990, when *Rolling Stone* voted my first album as one of the essential albums of the seventies, I thought, why not see who was at Capitol and try to get the albums reissued?

My mother was a tenant farmer; her father didn't even own the land. When you see where she came from, you realize the incredible determination it took for her to get a college degree, become a schoolteacher, and teach for thirty-eight years. She taught me determination by example. And those guys at Capitol know I'm one determined son of a gun. They never met anybody as tenacious as me. I wasted over nine years of my life until I got those albums back.

---

* In 1976, at the age of thirty-five, popular protest singer Phil Ochs hung himself after a long period of alcoholism and mental illness.
† In other words, the label stopped manufacturing and distributing his records.

Did you try to get signed to another label?
TALLEY: I didn't shop it anywhere else, because people aren't interested in releasing music from a fifty-five-year-old performer. So I decided to start my own label. I funded it from real estate at first, then I had to take out a loan to put out the Guthrie album.*

Even if you were younger, I don't think you could have gotten signed to a label in Nashville today, because they don't really put out traditional country anymore.
TALLEY: I know. Life is not like they make these records in Nashville. It's not supposed to be slick. It's supposed to be rough and brilliant. The heart doesn't move to the click track; life doesn't move at one constant tempo. Life's full of times when you fell down and skinned your knee, when your wife left you, when your girlfriend threw your clothes out in the front yard, and when you had your car repossessed or wrecked. It is not perfect.

So have all the ups and downs to get your music out been worth it to you?
TALLEY: You do wonder and you do despair, and you do go through some incredible pain and suffering. You risk your fortune. You mortgage your house. You take what little you've been able to accumulate and put it on the line to do something because you believe in it (*sighs*). Lord, I wish at one point in my life I had been in the right place at the right time. But if you don't give up, all things are possible.

Ten years after this interview, Talley was still selling real estate while recording and releasing albums on his own label.

[NINE INCH NAILS]
SCENE 3

Over breakfast outside the next morning . . .

Do you ever worry that something or someone is going to cut short your life or your career before you've said everything you have to say?
TRENT REZNOR: Through my own self-destructiveness or through a random act of violence?

---

* One of the best folk cover albums of its time: *Woody Guthrie and Songs of My Oklahoma Home.*

Either.

REZNOR: There's the whole romantic notion of Ian Curtis, or for that matter Kurt Cobain, burning out before they've said what they have to say. But I don't really think about it much. I've got a long ways to go in terms of what I want to accomplish personally. I've got a lot more I really want to say. I'd be sad if I was dead tomorrow though (*laughs*).

When you go on a big drug binge or something, do you ever worry, "What if I've gone too far? What if I'm losing a part of myself that's important to my creativity?"

REZNOR: I have thought that. I've been on binges at times where I wonder, "Why am I doing this? Am I going to lose the gift I have? What's the point of even doing it?"

And the point, like any person who does drugs, is to escape. I think the nature of the whole rock situation creates such a surreal and potentially pressured I-need-to-get-away situation that many people turn to drugs and follow that cliché. And that thought is what snapped me out of it: It's not original, you know. I've got to think of a new thing: No one's jumped off a building.*

I'm sure someone has.

REZNOR: You know what I mean: no rock stars. But I'm better than that. So once in a while, I just slap myself in the face and say, "You're a lucky motherfucker. You're in a great situation. What are you bummed out about, man?"

Has your success made you more paranoid?

REZNOR: It absolutely has. It's made me not trust people at all. Everyone you meet, you've got to assume it's about what you can do for them. I've been fucked by a lot of people who have been close to me. They'll ask to come out on the road with me and film the show, and then say, "Hey, I've made a compilation tape of every moment that you were an asshole. And I think I need a couple hundred thousand dollars in reimbursement." Shit, like, I got baited into a fight the other day and I threw a glass into a guy's face. And he goes, "Hey, you've got a lawsuit, motherfucker."

---

* Note to Puffy Combs: It's not just me. See also Marilyn Manson, scene two, last answer.

How did he bait you?

REZNOR: It was a friend of a friend, and he shows up late at night uninvited and drunk, being an asshole, insulting my company, and then takes a piss in my hotel doorway. I snapped and (*mimes throwing glass into guy's face*) . . .

Who do you consider your real friends?

REZNOR: I don't have that many close friends. It's not that I'm paranoid. It's just that I'm not open to it really. Years ago I was with a girlfriend and we met a guy in a band, and he was really cool.

Who was that?

REZNOR: Actually, it was Billy Corgan. And he really struck me as a nice guy. We exchanged phone numbers. And a couple days later, she said, "Are you going to give him a call?" I thought, "Maybe." But I knew I wasn't going to. She said, "That sucks, because that's someone who could be a friend." And I wasn't open to it. I just know me, and I knew I wasn't going to find the time. (*Makes noises mimicking small talk with Billy Corgan.*) The reason I even remember that is because it struck me as odd. I started thinking, "Why do I behave that way?" [. . .]

How much of what's going on pop-wise do you view as competition?

REZNOR: I watch MTV and I think it sucks and I think most videos are shitty. But I want to be aware. I have to be aware. I want to know that the last No Doubt video sucked so I don't do it myself. Since I'm aware of the business element of things, I get to feel a little competitive. For example, I like Beck now. But when he first came out, I felt that *urrggh*, just purely from a he's-the-competition point of view—not that we're doing the same thing. I felt stupid even feeling that. But I wanted to not like him. And then I was like, "Your shit's good."

The tape recorder is getting wet. Does it usually rain lightly like this all morning?

REZNOR: We can go inside.

[*Continued* . . .]

[BECK]

Lounging in his tour bus, Beck tells the story of a concert he performed. It was the last show on what had been a disappointing tour, and he and his band were determined to get their final audience on its feet and dancing. Yet no matter how hard they tried, the people in the front rows remained seated. Before the encore, Beck and his band met backstage and said they weren't going home until the entire audience was dancing. They came back out and tried everything, even attempting to pull people in the front row out of their seats. When that failed, Beck did something very uncharacteristic: He yelled "fuck you" into the mic, spit at the audience, and stormed offstage.

It wasn't until after the show that Beck discovered the concert had been a benefit for the disabled, who were given free front row seats.

I picked up a newspaper review of your show in Houston. Guess what overused word was used to describe you?
BECK: Oh no. They probably said something about how I do really bad Elvis moves. They really think I'm doing Elvis, but it's not Elvis at all. That's just really lazy.

They didn't mention that.
BECK: Was it *wacky*?

No, though they may have used that.
BECK: *Slacker*?

No, it's a word that's used almost exclusively to describe you.
BECK: Most words they use to describe me really turn me off. Like if I read it, I would not like this person at all and would not seek out his music.

I'll give you a clue. When you played in New York, you changed the chorus of "Asshole" to this word because you said it was just as offensive.
BECK: Oh, *manchild!* Of course. I started substituting that because every review I'd pick up would say "manchild Beck." What do I have to do? I've got hair on my chest, you know. I'm twenty-six. I mean, granted, I look young. I always take it as a little disrespectful. It's like I'm not to be taken seriously. We don't like to read the reviews. It bums you out. You feel so defeated. You put so much into it and you make sure everyone has a good time, and then someone just shuts it down.

There are so many misperceptions about you . . .
BECK: So many, oh my God.

So how do you want people to perceive you?
BECK: Uh, well, that's a hard one, because human nature says that you don't want to be categorized with *Beck* stamped on your forehead and sealed in hot wax. [. . .] There are so many people out there who are going to make you feel like you don't ever want to pick up a guitar again. Everywhere you turn, there's somebody saying "I dig what you're doing," and then you turn around and there's a few other people over there saying you don't deserve to live. Literally.

Who said that?
BECK: I mean, you might want to check out the Kurt Cobain article in your magazine where the journalist was saying she wishes it was me who had killed himself instead. In hindsight, I can see it as a snide thing to say, and sometimes it's hard not to resist. But there's no way you can't take that hard somehow. After I toured and that whole thing, I just went back in and stuck to the music. Otherwise I was never going to want to play music again.

[GARY WILSON]

In 1977, a twenty-four-year-old musician from Endicott, New York, named Gary Wilson released an odd and wonderful proto–new wave album called *You Think You Really Know Me*. The self-released album quickly found a cult following. In his single "Where It's At," Beck even sings about how Gary Wilson "rocks the most." As the reputation of the album grew, fans naturally sought out its creator. A few even hired a private investigator to find him. But no one could find any trace of Wilson's existence since the early eighties.

Then, one day at the *New York Times*, I received a call that Wilson had been found, but didn't have either a cell or home phone. So I went to meet him at his job: working the graveyard shift behind two layers of bulletproof glass at an adult bookstore and peep show in San Diego.

He was short and pale, with his hair pulled back in a ponytail. He agreed to give his first interview in over twenty years and told me to meet him at his apartment the following day.

Why don't you have a phone?
GARY WILSON: Sometimes they bring bad news. Or they pull you away from

something. It would be nice to have it for emergency reasons, but it works out pretty well. If someone wants to get a hold of you, they will.

Do you see yourself as a recluse?
WILSON: I really am, actually. I'm pretty private. But, you know, that's just the way I am. You get older, too, and things calm down a little bit and you don't go out as much.

Have you saved any copies of your album?
WILSON: Well, I used to break and smash my records onstage—just snap them in half and throw them. And then one day, I realized I didn't have any more.

What were your old shows like?
WILSON: Sometimes we'd pick up props and things to smash and throw onstage. When I was doing more experimental stuff, I had to be careful because a lot of guys in the band ended up needing stitches. We used to dump ten to twenty pounds of flour on ourselves. But then at some radio benefit in Seattle, I got so much flour on me that for months I was scratching my eye. From then on, I had to wear goggles onstage if I used flour.

Later, Wilson leaves for the Rancho Bernardo Inn, where he plays a monthly show with a lounge band that covers songs like "The Girl from Ipanema" for mostly elderly patrons. During a break between sets, Wilson discusses his upbringing.

Were you more social when you were younger?
WILSON: In school, I was in the Dion fan club. I had hair just like him. But one day at the pool, a bunch of guys jumped me, held me down, and cut my hair off. And one time I had a whole book of poetry when I was in high school or junior high. But some girl took my book and ripped it up and threw it away. It's funny, too, because it didn't affect me too much.

What were your parents like?
WILSON: I got along with my parents well. My mother passed away when I was nineteen, but my father is about eighty-three or eighty-four. I haven't seen him in twenty-four years.

You should see him again while you can.
WILSON: Yeah, you're right. I'd probably regret it if I didn't see him. [. . .]

When was the first time you went to Manhattan?
WILSON: I went once when I was seventeen. I ended up sleeping under a building, then hitched a ride on the New Jersey turnpike to get home. A nice Asian woman picked me up. She stopped at McDonald's and picked up hamburgers, but I couldn't eat mine because it had a pickle on it.

A pickle?
WILSON: I like things plain. I'm a plain guy. I only eat one meal a day, and I don't eat vegetables or fruits.

Is that when you tried to get signed to Columbia?
WILSON: That was later. I went into Columbia Records in New York, and snuck past the doorman and the guard. Then I turned my coat inside out and put a turban on and tried to give my tapes to people. They figured that since I was inside somehow, I must be all right. I never got a deal though. They didn't quite know where to put me or what it was. That's why it's funny that things kind of switched around in twenty-five years, and now I guess people have been looking for me. I guess times have changed a little bit.

It's interesting how most of the songs on the album are avant-garde musically, but thematically they're love songs about women.
WILSON: All the women in my songs are real, except I did have a mannequin named Cindy I'd drive around with. A lot of my new songs are about Linda. I was just dreaming about her. I haven't dreamt of her in thirty or forty years. She was one of my first girlfriends from eighth grade. I hope she didn't pass away.

Is there anything you've seen working in the adult bookstore that's shocked you?
WILSON: I guess so. I saw a guy in one of the booths smeared in his own excrement like a commando. That was pretty avant-garde.

Since his rediscovery, Wilson's album You Think You Really Know Me *was reissued, followed by an additional recording of lost and rare material, a documentary about his life, and his first albums of new songs in twenty-seven years.*

[NINE INCH NAILS]
SCENE 4

We walk inside and sit on the couch with Reznor's dog Daisy, who farts almost continually throughout the interview . . .

Marilyn Manson gets onstage and does theater, whereas when you get onstage it's more of an in-the-moment emotional thing.
TRENT REZNOR: Well, there are times I feel the guilt that everyone in this twenty-thousand-seat arena paid twenty bucks to see me and I owe them a fucking good show. And I know if I throw this guitar that someone's going to scream, and you start to rely on things like that. I hate to even admit that. But I think what I've gotten criticized for the most doesn't deserve to be criticized because it was real.

Like Woodstock?
REZNOR: When we walked onstage at Woodstock, I'd never been more nervous in my life than for that show. And we just fucked off and got all muddy before as like a pressure release. Then I realized five minutes into the show that I can't play guitar because there's so much mud on the fucking strings and I can't see because my eyes are burning. I'm slipping. Everything's shitty. But I walked offstage and I started crying, because in the end I really felt like I connected. It wasn't until I saw the tape later that I realized how terrible we sounded.

Most musicians judge their shows by technical standards, though the audience usually just wants an authentic experience.
REZNOR: If you connect, there's this weird feeling similar to when you hear a song and you get goose bumps. To take your bleakest, darkest, most alone moment, and see everyone screaming it back at you—wow, that kind of makes all the bullshit worth it. Every time singing "Down In It," I want to kill somebody by the end and I mean it, you know. And I have to get rid of that character, whether it means I drink half a bottle of tequila before I walk onstage or whatever. And then afterward I'll get offstage and call home and be nice and polite, because I just screamed for two fucking hours. I got it out of my system, you know. *(To dog:)* Daisy, what just came out of your butt? [. . .]

Why do you think *Spin* chose you as the most vital artist in music?
REZNOR: I don't know. I've no idea. And, honestly, it was more flattering than some other award. Like when I got a Grammy. Okay, I beat Jethro Tull this year for best hard rock something video with rubber pants on. But I was pretty shocked

when you told me, "Hey, you're number one." I was like, "Is this good?" Because I can already read the letters the next month saying, "Fuck that, man. Why didn't you choose so-and-so?"

Of course, no matter what—
REZNOR: I'm not saying I don't deserve it. It's nice though to have some kind of mainstream media appreciation. So it's flattering. It's nice to know that . . . I don't know what the fuck I'm saying. You know, I'm just the guy that had mud on at Woodstock. I'm a footnote in rock history. "Where are they now: the nineties."

Do you ever wonder, "How am I going to make sure I'm a chapter and not a footnote, and I still matter in the next decade?"
REZNOR: I don't know. When you think about the rock world, there's a window of time where what you do has pertinence and meaning. I hope ten years from now I'm making soundtracks or producing or something. I don't want to be putting mud all over myself at the fucking Sands lounge in Las Vegas.

[**CURTAIN**]

ACT TEN

OR

WHAT EVERYBODY NEEDS TO GET
TO SLEEP IN THESE TROUBLED TIMES

SYNOPSIS

Enter Death,

because one day we're all going
to go, and we can't always choose
when or how, but we can choose
what we do until then, &c.

[DEAD PEOPLE]
SCENE 1

One afternoon, I was in the elevator at the *New York Times* with the editor of the obituary section. A copyeditor turned to him and remarked, "It's so sad when someone dies."

He looked at her, uncomprehending for a moment, and then replied curtly, "It's just another peg for a story."

In my ten years at the newspaper, I turned in many stories to that editor. Sometimes I'd write obituaries for people just months after interviewing them. Other times I'd write their obituaries while they were still alive: If Bob Dylan was sick or Courtney Love was on a drug binge, the editor would request one in advance—just in case.

Unlike him, though, I found writing obituaries stressful, because I wanted to make sure that I did justice to these people's lives, knowing that their family might read the article in search of some consolation, some sign that their loved one's time on this planet had truly mattered to others.

The following are excerpts from much longer obituaries I wrote for the newspaper.

DARREN ROBINSON

Darren Robinson, also known as the Human Beat Box, the 450-pound member of the rap group the Fat Boys who was known for vocally mimicking the sounds of a drum machine, died on Sunday at his home in Queens. He was twenty-eight.

The cause of his death was cardiac arrest during a bout with respiratory flu, said Charles Stettler, who named and managed the band. Mr. Robinson was rapping for friends when he fell off a chair and lost consciousness. . . .

GLENN HUGHES

Glenn Hughes, who sang in a leather biker outfit with the disco group the Village People, died on March 4 at his home in Manhattan. He was fifty.

The cause was lung cancer, according to press reports.

Mr. Hughes, who grew up in the Bronx, was working as a toll collector at the

Brooklyn-Battery Tunnel when friends dared him to respond to an advertisement seeking "gay singers and dancers, very good-looking and with mustaches." The person who placed the ad was the French-born producer Jacques Morali, who, after watching a group of macho men dancing in a Greenwich Village nightclub, decided to put together a disco group in which each member represented a different fetishized American male stereotype. . . .

WENDY O. WILLIAMS

Wendy O. Williams, the leader of the 1980s punk band the Plasmatics, a group more famous for its destructive onstage antics than for its music, died on Monday at her home in Storrs, Connecticut in what officials called a suicide. She was forty-eight.

The cause was a gunshot wound to the head, said a spokeswoman for the state's Chief Medical Examiner.

Born in Rochester, NY, to an Eastman Kodak chemist and his wife, Ms. Williams got her first taste of fame tap-dancing on *The Howdy Doody Show* at age six and her first, but not last, run-in with the law at age fifteen when she was arrested for sunbathing nude. She left high school soon after and hitchhiked to Colorado and later Florida, making money selling crafts and working as a lifeguard. She drifted through Europe, bartending, dancing, and getting arrested for shoplifting and passing counterfeit money. In 1976, she landed in Manhattan as a performer at Captain Kink's Sex Fantasy Theater, where she met Rod Swenson, a Yale graduate who ran the sex shows there.

Mr. Swenson became her manager in 1978 and helped her put together the Plasmatics. [. . .] Ms. Williams, with a striking blond mohawk and wearing a nurse's uniform, electrical tape, or just shaving cream, would attack guitars with chainsaws, fire shotguns at amplifiers, and destroy television sets with sledgehammers. At one performance, she leapt out of a Cadillac moments before it exploded and plunged into the Hudson River. . . .

ROBERT PILATUS

Robert Pilatus, a member of Milli Vanilli, the German pop duo forced to give up its 1990 Grammy Award when it was disclosed that the pair did not sing a word on its album, died on Thursday in a hotel room in Frankfurt. He was thirty-two.

The cause was a heart attack, according to Frankfurt Police. Though his producer, Frank Farian, told German reporters that Mr. Pilatus had been mixing pills with alcohol, an autopsy has not yet been performed.

Milli Vanilli represented one of the most extreme rise-and-fall stories in pop music. The duo's first album in 1989 generated three number one singles, sold some ten million copies, and gave the pair the license to brag in interviews that they were more talented than Bob Dylan and Paul McCartney. The album earned them a Grammy Award for best new artist the following year.

But when an army veteran in his forties stepped forward and announced he was the real singer on the album, Milli Vanilli's career took a sharp downturn. The band returned the Grammy at a humiliating press conference, broke up, and went into therapy. The following year, Mr. Pilatus cut his wrists, mixed pills and alcohol, and tried to jump out of a ninth-story Los Angeles hotel room. "The hardest thing to take was kids in a school bus sticking out their tongues at me," he once said. . . .

[*Continued . . .*]

[LORETTA LYNN]
SCENE 1

Country singer Loretta Lynn grew up quickly. At age thirteen, she was married. When she was fourteen, she was a mother. By the age of twenty-nine, she was a grandmother. So perhaps it makes sense that at age sixty-five, she was already grappling with death.

Do you know that it's been more than fifteen years since you last performed in New York?
LORETTA LYNN: Well, I just started going back on the road last year, because my husband was down for five years before he died. He had sugar diabetes, and I didn't know it kept you from hearing or seeing. He kept telling me he couldn't hear the music anymore. So I was with him, and I didn't work.

I think the last record you released was in 1993, with Dolly Parton and Tammy Wynette . . .
LYNN: I talked with Tammy just two nights before she died, and she was feeling great. We talked for a long time, you know. We were planning on going and tour-

ing the big coliseums: me, her, Merle Haggard, and Johnny Cash. Johnny's in bad shape, you know.

Yeah, I heard.
LYNN: And so she was real happy about touring and she went out and bought a bunch of new clothes and, well . . . I guess God knows what happened.*

In a very short amount of time, you've experienced a lot of loss.
LYNN: Yes, I lost twelve people in four years, and that's not counting Tammy. I lost two brothers, uncles and aunts, and one first cousin who was raised with me like a sister. It was really rough. And also there was Conway [Twitty]. Me and Conway never said a cross word to each other his whole life. My husband loved him. He came to see [my husband] Doo, and I went down to get him. And when I got to where his tour bus was parked, they come dragging him in the hospital and blood was coming out of his mouth. It was a terrible sight.†

That's so sad.
LYNN: And he was trying to look at me and there wasn't any way he could see me. His eyes . . . You know, it *was* sad. It's still hard on me. I can't watch him and me singing together today. I miss him so much, you know. And Shel Silverstein, you know he died. He had a massive heart attack.

I didn't know about that. I grew up with a lot of his words.
LYNN: Sixty-six years old,‡ the night before last. He wrote "A Boy Named Sue" for Johnny Cash.

And if you think about it, Owen Bradley also died recently.
LYNN: Oh yeah, and he was my producer for all my life. Not all my life, because I started singing when I was twenty-seven years old. [. . .] I had four children in school before I ever started singing. I was just a mother. It was very hard for me to get out there and sing. My husband said, "Sing for two years and we'll make enough money to build a home and you can quit." Why, two years from the day I started we was making enough to eat on, and that was it (*laughs*). It don't happen overnight like it does today. It's been three years now since I lost him.

---

* Wynette died at the age of fifty-five in her home. Though the doctor said the cause was a blood clot in her lung, three of her daughters had the body exhumed because they believed it was due to injecting prescription medications. Their claim could not be proven.
† Twitty, who recorded several hit duets with Lynn, became ill while touring and soon after died of an abdominal aortic aneurysm.
‡ Silverstein, a poet, illustrator, and songwriter who wrote several of Lynn's hits, died at age sixty-eight.

You were with him for over forty years—
LYNN: Yes, it would have been fifty years this year.

Tammy sang "Stand By Your Man," but was divorced four or five times. Your songs are more about independence and women's rights, but you ended up standing by your man.
LYNN: Well, I think that's the way you're supposed to do it. I think when you sing about something, it should be for real. Whatever life is about is what you ought to be singing about. I mean, we're still honky-tonking. When love and honky-tonks and the Bible go out of style, it's over. Men still cheat, they still lie, they still run around, and they still go to bars and drink. So all you have to do is update the language—and, you know, maybe the melody just a little bit.

[*Continued . . .*]

[CHUCK BERRY]
SCENE 1

Chuck Berry is arguably the most important figure in rock history. His pioneering hits provided a template for the Beatles, the Rolling Stones, and thousands upon thousands of other rock bands. He also happens to be rock's original bad boy, having served three prison terms: one for armed robbery, a second for transporting a minor across state lines for immoral purposes, and a third for tax evasion.

Along the way, he developed a reputation for being bitter, cantankerous, and difficult to deal with—and rarely, if ever, submitting to interviews. "He's a very private person," explained Bob Lohr, his pianist for over fourteen years. "As long as I've been playing with him, he's only done three or four interviews that I know about."

So it was with little hope of success that I called Joe Edwards, who runs Blueberry Hill, a St. Louis restaurant and club where Berry has a monthly residency, and requested an interview. Fortunately, Edwards caught the eighty-three-year-old Berry in a good mood and, the following month, I flew to St. Louis to meet the legend.

"If he doesn't like you or is uncomfortable, the interview will probably only be five minutes," Edwards warned when I arrived. "And talk slowly. He gets frustrated when he can't hear and might walk out."

As we sat at a table in the back room of Blueberry Hill, the interview began shakily. But when the conversation turned to gambling, Berry began to open up.

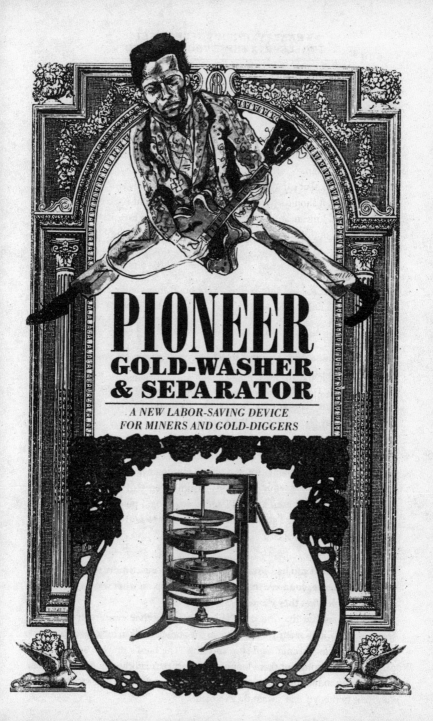

PIONEER
GOLD-WASHER
& SEPARATOR

A NEW LABOR-SAVING DEVICE
FOR MINERS AND GOLD-DIGGERS

CHUCK BERRY: I play a slot machine, and the day before yesterday I had four jackpots. I was sitting there waiting to see if I could get five. Now if that's greedy, I'm greedy. Like I wonder if there's anything beyond raising the roof on a show. Is there more? And if so, I want to try! If that's greed, yeah, I have a bit of greed.

You could also see that as ambition.
BERRY: Well, I have lots of ambition, hm-mmm, yes!

When I laugh at his joke, Berry suddenly removes his sunglasses, puts in a hearing aid, and breaks into a broad smile—and the whole mood of the interview changes.

BERRY: I can already feel that you're a very good interviewer and these kind of interviews last a little while. And we'll get into some things that I've been wanting to say for years!

Great, because one thing I wanted to ask is: People always say you invented rock and roll. Do you agree with them?
BERRY: No. I've tried to say it, too. There's Louis Jordan. There's Count Basie. Nat Cole, for sure. This guy Joe Turner. There's Muddy Waters, Blue Eyes [Frank Sinatra], Tommy Dorsey. I loved their music.

Their music inspired you, but most of them didn't really play rock and roll.
BERRY: I go back to mathematics, and there's nothing new under the sun. So I just feel I got my inspiration, education, and all from others that came before me. And I added my . . . I don't even know if I added anything. I played what they played and it sounded different, I guess. It means something to a lot of people, but I don't know what it means to them.

My thought is that you had your influences, but because you're so good at reading your audience, you were the first one to pick up on what was in the air and give the people what they wanted.
BERRY: That last line that you said, "give people what they want," that's true. I'm searching for who is attentive out there in the audience. I can look around and be singing "My Ding-A-Ling" and stop and sing "The Lord's Prayer" because some people will be sitting out there looking like they're from church. There's certain songs—and thoughts for that matter—that almost make tears come to their eyes. I'd give it to them if that's what they wanted.

So maybe your audience invented rock and roll and you were the first one to listen to them and understand what they wanted and give it to them.*

BERRY: That's very good. I don't know if I know it, but I would try and get it to them. You're right there. Hm-mmm.

Berry is interrupted by the ringing of his iPhone. Dick Alen, his booking agent for more than five decades, is calling about a possible concert with Jerry Lee Lewis.

BERRY (*to Alen*): You called in the middle of an interview—you know, the thing that Chuck Berry doesn't do.

After the call, the thing that Berry doesn't do resumes . . .

People who've worked with you say, "Chuck Berry doesn't understand how important, significant, and influential he is."

BERRY: I've heard that. It's one of my beliefs that I'm just a small portion of music. It's like the sun and a blade of grass. There's grass all over the earth, but for somebody to pick out me? I appreciate that . . .

I think you're looking at it from a different perspective. They're thinking of just rock music, not all the music in the world.

BERRY: I think they're talking maybe about what I've done, and not just me. 'Cause I'm a baaaaaad boy (*laughs*).

[*Continued . . .*]

[N.W.A]

In the midst of recording a new album, Eazy-E, a former member of N.W.A, the group that put gangsta rap—and Compton—on the map, was hospitalized. Four weeks later, he was dead of AIDS—the first mainstream rapper to die of the disease. Before he passed away, he told friends he was uncertain how he'd contracted HIV. However, he had fathered seven children with six different mothers, so safe sex definitely wasn't his forte.

For rappers who always said their music was intended to expose the realities

---

* In many of the theaters Berry played, he later explained, the whites were on one side and the blacks on the other. And the whites responded well to black music (the blues) while the blacks responded well to white music (country). So, in part by trying to please both audiences simultaneously, rock and roll came to be.

of life on the streets, his former bandmates seemed to have trouble facing his illness and death. Each of these interviews took place separately—MC Ren and DJ
Yella on the phone, Ice Cube over lunch in Beverly Hills, Dr. Dre on a video set.
Note that when they originally left N.W.A, Ice Cube and Dr. Dre had vehemently
dissed Eazy-E in their lyrics, while MC Ren had publicly distanced himself from
his former friend.

Did you reconcile with Eazy-E before he died?
ICE CUBE: Me and Eazy reconciled. We weren't friends anymore, but we weren't
enemies. The last time I seen him was at a club out in New York called the Tunnel
three months before he died.
DJ YELLA: The last time I saw him was at a convention in Vegas in January. After that,
I just talked to him on the phone. He'd always disappear and I wouldn't see him.
DR. DRE: We made peace, and we were talking about doing something on his
album.
MC REN: Me and him weren't talking for two years, and then right after Dre and
Cube did "Natural Born Killaz," he called and was like, "Man, let's do a song together." At first I thought he was bullshitting, because he be running around a lot
and doing crazy shit. But I called him back and we started working on it. We did
that shit in three days. A week later, that's when he went in the hospital. Something
brought us together to do that shit.

Did you visit him in the hospital?
ICE CUBE: We went by the hospital, but he was unconscious. I didn't want to
just go in there and look at him, so I told him I'd be staying in a hotel down the
street. Then I said to his wife, "If he wakes up, call me so I can come back down."
But he never woke up.
MC REN: I was supposed to call him a couple days after we came out the studio, but
when I finally called him, he wasn't calling me back. Then I called somebody else
and was like, "Where he at?" And they said, "He's in the hospital. He's getting out
tonight." So I thought I'd call him the next day.
DR. DRE: When I got to the hospital to see him, he was already in a coma. So I
never talked to him.

Did you know he had AIDS?
MC REN: In the studio, I knew something was wrong with him, but I didn't know
it was that. Because when we were working on the song, he would be coughing a
lot. He would cough for like five or ten minutes straight, like he had bronchitis

or something. Then he'd stop for a while and then he'd start back again with this hard cough. I was just thinking, "Man, you need to quit smoking that weed." I didn't think it was that.

Have you known anyone else who's died of AIDS?

MC REN: A couple people I grew up with found out after that.

DJ YELLA: When I was younger, somebody on my street died [of AIDS], but they was sick for months and lost a lot of weight. It's nothing like what happened this time. It's scary. It even opened my eyes. If it got him, it can get anyone. He wasn't gay or nothing like that. So it proves a point: It don't discriminate. It don't matter how much money you got or nothing.

Did you go to the funeral?

DJ YELLA: I was the only one [from N.W.A] who showed up. It was here in LA. No excuse: I went. I can't say too much about why everyone else didn't come. I'm mastering my record this week. My album is dedicated strictly to him. I felt I could do that because I never turned my back on him. I was there in the beginning, and I was there putting dirt on him when nobody else was around in the end.

[LIONEL RICHIE]

In the 1970s, Lionel Richie performed with the Commodores, moving from saxophonist to lead singer as the group shifted from funky pop to ballads. In the early and mid-eighties, he was one of pop's most successful singers, crooning five number one hits. But by the end of the decade, Richie had disappeared. So when he suddenly resurfaced years later, I decided to find out where he'd been.

What made you return to music after ten years?

LIONEL RICHIE: I woke up one morning and realized that my well was full again. The reason I took off in the first place is that I did sixteen years straight in a row, from my Commodore days through my solo days. There's a word called *burnout*. And one day, before I got to that point where I was going to completely just wipe out, I was walking off a stage with this Oscar in my hands. I had just finished singing "We Are the World" and I had just performed at the Olympics in front of 1.6 billion people. And I said, "You know what? I'm going to take a vacation."

And your well filled back up during that time off?

RICHIE: I must admit I was only going to take a year off and go back to work, but what happened to me was, during that year off my father became very ill. And I wasn't going to go back to work because I wanted to be with him through his illness. Well, his illness lasted two and a half years. Once he died, then I went through a divorce. And from there, right when I was doing my greatest-hits package and planning on following it with a new album, my best friend walks up to me and says, "I have AIDS and I'm dying of AIDS." It devastated me, and I wasn't about to leave him. Once he passed, I said, "Let me get up, get back to work, and never use the word vacation again."

Have you thought about putting these experiences into a book?

RICHIE: I did decide to write about what I experienced in climbing to the top. And finally when I got there, I discovered what was at the top. You know what was there?

No, I don't.

RICHIE: Nothing. Not one thing. What was at the top was all the experiences that you had to get there.

[CHUCK BERRY]
SCENE 2

You said earlier there were a couple things that you wanted to talk about?

CHUCK BERRY: Let me see. I don't know, but I think I don't have as long as I perhaps feel I have to be here. And I want to do something that I know will last after I leave. In other words, I want to do another "Johnny B. Goode" in action or deed, something as powerful as "Ding-A-Ling" and not—what's a song that didn't do anything—"Blue on Blue." Leonard Chess* named that, you know, and it did nothing. [. . .]

So what are your plans for the new album?

BERRY: You know, as much popularity as I have had since my last album was out, I don't think it would be blasting like Michael Jackson or anybody. But, boy, it would sure buy six or seven yachts at least for people. Because everywhere I go, I

---

* With his brother, Phil Chess, Leonard founded Chess Records, the label that Bo Diddley and Chuck Berry, among many other blues and rock legends, recorded for.

get that look—you know, "Is that him?" It would be good for my kids if I'm not here.

Let's say it happened and the money came, what would be the first thing you would do with the money?
BERRY: Which kids? They'd do different things. My son would buy a Mercedes, that's for sure. [My daughter] Ingrid would buy a home in the South because she doesn't like the weather here. Who else?

What would *you* do with it?
BERRY: Oh, me! I thought you said what would my kids do. In the first place, I can tell you what I wouldn't do with it. I wouldn't put it in stocks. I would put it in real estate . . . Oh here, I can give you the percentages: Ten percent would go to Haiti.* Then the next ten percent would go to trying to develop something from a company that I will start. Then there's a lot of things that prisons need. I saw, you know, prisoners,† and a lot of them, man, they ought to give them the gas right away. I would put that there. Just make it plain so if you don't follow this gift [of rehabilitation], you know, gas him! Gas him or her. And then, with most of the rest, I'd wait to find out if I got any other ideas.

[*Continued* . . .]

[ROADIES]

To some, the idea of being a roadie conjures up tantalizing visions of a permanent backstage pass to wanton women, copious drugs, and eternal reckless fun. But after going on tour undercover as a roadie for several weeks, I discovered that the reality was a lot different than the fantasy: When you wake up at eight a.m. to start putting together a show and don't stop working until one a.m., after the concert is over and the gear is packed back in the trucks, there's not a lot of time or energy left over for decadence. And even when there is, most nights the tour bus leaves the moment work ends, en route to the next city to deliver the dream anew to another five or fifty thousand people.

It takes a certain kind of person to choose a life of hard, stressful work and

---

* Where an earthquake had just killed an estimated 200,000 people.
† During his collected five years in prison.

constant movement over the stability of a day job and a normal family life. And one of those people is Bill, who has been a production manager—in other words, the head roadie, responsible for coordinating nearly every detail of the setup, staging, and breakdown for each show—on big tours for over two decades.

BILL: I'm fifty-one now. I'm getting too old to do this.

Do you ever think about stopping?
BILL: All the time. But it's too late now for me to stop. I don't know what else I'd do. I think sometimes that I'm becoming irrelevant and wonder what I'm going to do next. But it's the only thing I know how to do. So I clutch onto it like grim death. You can't sit still for a second because there's a hundred guys waiting in the wings, ready to stab you in the back to take your job.

But with all the skills it takes to do the job, from accounting to managing people to understanding production, there are probably a lot of different jobs you can do.
BILL: I don't know. If I go into the real world, no firm is going to hire me with my résumé working with rock bands. And I wouldn't want to work most places, because I don't want to wear a suit.

So you prefer being on the road . . .
BILL: I don't have a love affair with the road. I'd love to be home all the time, but I just can't. I go home and there's nothing to go home to. Nobody's waiting for me at the airport. I have nobody there but my dogs. This [the band's entourage] is my family now. But I don't have any illusions: If I quit being of any use to them, it's not like they're going to take care of me in my old age. I'll be out the door.

Did you have any aptitude for school when you were younger?
BILL: I had the highest SAT scores in the state of Missouri. I got an 800 in math and 710 in English. Big colleges tried to recruit me. But I wanted to be in a rock band. And I have no regrets because I followed my heart. I went to my high school's twentieth reunion, and everyone was all fat and boring and had families. I was like, "Ha!" But I'll have to pay the piper one of these days. Right now, I'm putting it off. Jeff [a guitar tech] and I always talk about getting old and ending up sharing a tenement together, with just a bare lightbulb swinging from the ceiling and nobody visiting us.

What are the things about the job that make it worth the sacrifices?
BILL: I make a good living, I wear T-shirts and jeans to work, and people take me seriously. I was in the bus bathroom the other morning, hacking and clearing the old lungs like you've probably heard me do every morning. Then I grabbed some coffee and got ready to step into the morning chaos. That's what I love, going from solitude to chaos. I love waking up at eight a.m. and hearing the sound of chain motors and cases going down the ramps. And it sounds stupid, but there's a feeling of power you get when, just before the show, you give the order for the lights to go out and the audience just erupts.

Do you have any kids?
BILL: I have a daughter who's thirty-one now. She has two kids, and we have a strained relationship.

And your wife?
BILL: She died.

Did you meet her at a concert?
BILL: I met her at a bar when I was nineteen. I was in a band back then. We were together for ten years. It was a stormy relationship.

Was that because of her or you?
BILL: Me. I'm not an easy man to be with. I was a young guy. I wasn't ready to be tied down. I was wrong.

Are you ready now?
BILL: I guess I'm still not ready. There's a disconnect that happens from living alone all the time.

Do you ever feel bad about not being there for your daughter?
BILL: All the time. But my ex-wife moved with her to Florida when she was twelve basically to punish me. She tried to keep us apart. Then [my ex-wife] got sick with Hodgkin's disease. I was weirded out by the whole disease thing, and the alienation with her made it even more awkward.

Did you ever see her when she was sick or try to reconcile?
BILL: Well, her disease went into remission and I ran into her at a concert I was working at. It really weirded me out. She wanted to talk and make peace, and it

just wigged me out. I couldn't deal with it. I was cowardly. I had a show to do and asked her if we could just deal with it later. So she got drunk during the show and started berating me afterward in front of everyone. I couldn't take it and just walked away.

Did you see her again after that?
BILL: I never saw her again. The next day, she called and apologized and said she felt bad. She wanted to go to dinner that night. But I made up some excuse, and then left town the next day. A year later, when I was on the road, a friend called and said she'd died. I hadn't even known that the disease had come back.

How did you feel when he told you that?
BILL: It just hit me like a ton of bricks. I felt not like I'd killed her, but like she died thinking I hated her.

Do you have regrets about how you handled your wife's illness now?
BILL: I have to tell you that her death changed me. That's when I found spirituality. For years after that, I would talk to her every day.

In what circumstances would you talk with her?
BILL: Early on, I'd talk to my wife just about anywhere. I'd do it four or five or six times a day, just begging her to listen and begging for her forgiveness for the fact that we never managed to reconnect. I really did come to feel she was hearing me and that she's forgiven me (*pauses*). I don't know. Maybe I'm trying to rationalize what I did so I can live with myself. But we have a much better relationship now than we did when we were young.

Do you still talk to her now?
BILL: Once I came to terms with it, I talked to her less. It's been thirteen years now, and there are times when I talk to her every other day; other times months will pass. On a night off, most of the guys won't call me to go out. And I don't want to bring them down and make it so they can't feel like themselves around me. So sometimes I'll just be alone in the hotel room and talk to her because she's the only one to talk to, the only one who will listen. When my mom died, I talked to her a lot.

Did you have these kinds of conversations with her when she was alive?
BILL: I'm not good at talking. I never talked to her like this when she was alive. She got a raw deal from me. I thought that if someone loved me that much, there must

be something wrong with her. Her death probably did more to cause growth in me than anything else. I'm more comfortable in my own skin than I ever have been. I guess I finally accepted her love after she was gone.

Did you try to reconcile with your daughter afterward?

BILL: I tried to make it up with her, and we reconnected at the funeral. She came to live with me for a while. But she hooked up with this shady Eminem-looking guy. And while I was on tour, he went into my file cabinet and pulled out all my records and did these credit card scams.

When I got back home, they had moved into their own place. And I came over and grabbed him by the scruff of the neck and I was ready to do some damage. I was really angry. But then my daughter said, "Don't kill him. I'm pregnant."

That stopped me in my tracks. I just said to her, "Call me when you get rid of him," and left.

Did she ever get rid of him?

BILL: She's still with him. They have two kids now. I only hear from her when she needs money.

And do you give it to her?

BILL: I always give it to her, like a thousand dollars. Money is the only thing I can provide her with that she never had when she was growing up. It's not like she owes me anything: I was never there for her.

Have you ever met your grandchildren?

BILL: Never met the babies. She won't let me. I'd like to see them.

Do you think she's doing that out of revenge?

BILL: My cynical side says that's true. But I haven't given up on her. I still hope she'll come around. But I've got nine kids now. I sponsor kids as part of the Christian Children's Fund. I've done it for many years. You send 'em twenty-eight dollars a month. Except on their birthday, you send fifty bucks and you get a card. It's great: a cheap way to relieve myself of some of my guilt.

Did you ever see the movie *The Wrestler*?

BILL: That movie really hit home for me. That one and *Up in the Air*.

In what way?

BILL: The way he was trying to make it through the world and trying to find somebody to care about.

= [THE RED HOT CHILI PEPPERS] =

When a band of hard-touring, hard-partying delinquents grows up, gets sober, starts families, and finds spirituality, as in the case of the Red Hot Chili Peppers and its bassist Flea, something unexpected starts to happen: The rock and roll dream turns into a job—with very long hours.

Is it harder touring now that you have a family and you're sober?
FLEA: I like playing music for people, but the touring lifestyle sucks. I miss my daughter. I have a feeling of rootlessness that I don't like. It's very taxing physically being in a different city every day, travelling on buses and planes, and playing shows every night. For me, playing a concert is a huge physical output and outburst. Doing it night and night again and again exhausts me and wears me down, and I become very lonely, sad, and tired. And that's not a good threesome: I'd rather be loved, creative, and energetic.

It's an interesting contrast between the way you are onstage, when you're more of a wild animal, versus when you walk offstage.
FLEA: It's kind of like jacking off. Right after you cum, it's a big change of emotion: *Oh, it's so good because there's this beautiful girl, oh, and she's doing this and oh, oh, oh, now I'm lying around in my room with my cum on my belly.* It's a quick change. It can be like that going offstage sometimes (*pauses*). Did you ever make beans?

No.
FLEA: I'm cooking and need directions on how to make them.

Has all the touring affected your health at all?
FLEA: I'm definitely feeling the effects of physical wear and tear, of taking lots of drugs and being just wild all the time thinking I was Superman and could stand anything. I'm really conscious about my body now and trying to treat it like a temple and all that. And things I did before—I used to go into people's houses and rob them—I definitely feel like they're bad karma. I'm going to actually make an attempt to get in touch with people that I did wrong to, and try and set it straight for my own sanity.

Have you done that yet?
FLEA: I haven't done it yet. I just keep talking about it. *(To someone in background:)* Clara, get Mr. Salty off that thing. *(To me:)* Our cat Mr. Salty was about to eat Mr. Periwinkle.

Who's Mr. Periwinkle?
FLEA: Our fish.

What do the lyrics "love and music can save us" mean to you?
FLEA: I wrote those words—and in reviews, they single those particular words out as being stupid and corny and cliché and just ridiculous. I don't care what they say anyway. I think love and music can ruin you if you're scared.

What do you mean by that?
FLEA: People talk about love being painful and terrible and all that. I think it's only painful and terrible if you're scared of your own self. For me, that's when it was painful. The times of my life when I've been scared to love somebody are because I'm scared it's going to hurt when I get left alone or if they don't love me back the way I want them to. I've been through some terrible lows because of that, but it's only because I'm scared.

═══ [MERLE HAGGARD] ═══

Merle Haggard is the American dream personified. Born to a hardscrabble family, he lost his father at age nine, was in juvenile detention homes by the time he was thirteen, and was in prison for attempting to rob a bar at age twenty. Three decades later, with some forty number one country singles to his name, he'd become one of the most legendary country singers of his time and was even pardoned for his crimes by Ronald Reagan.

What's the most meaningful lesson you've learned about life?
MERLE HAGGARD: Honesty.

Why honesty?
HAGGARD: I don't know. It somehow or another just came to me *(laughs)*. It just seemed like the right thing to do.

Was there ever a point when you were less honest than you are now, like when you were in jail?
HAGGARD (*clears throat*): No, I always wanted to be honest. Ever since I can remember thinking about anything, I knew that that was necessary.

Was it a struggle or was it something that came easy?
HAGGARD: It's kind of like gravity. The first time I lied to somebody, I couldn't live with it for ten minutes. I had to straighten that out. I just didn't want that to happen. And the other thing is that I don't have that good of a memory. You know, if I lie to somebody, I'd have to remember it.

So when in life did you learn that?
HAGGARD: About the same time I learned gravity.

Really?
HAGGARD: Yeah, it was right around in there. I was real young when I realized. My father was my first idol and I heard him say that he couldn't stand a liar. And that went all the way through me.

But what about the small lies, like telling someone you're late because you're caught in traffic?
HAGGARD: I may be guilty of those and have used those to keep from hurting people's feelings and things like that. But I really have been working on that area and I find that when you take the time to tell the truth, it's usually more interesting. And a lie is obvious. I mean, if it's too good to be true, it probably is.

I was interviewing Chuck Berry and he put it in a great way: "There's nothing that stands up straighter than the truth."
HAGGARD: He's right. Lying is a terrible sin and something we're not supposed to do. And we should be happy to not do it. How's Chuck's health?

Chuck is in amazing health. He's really sharp.
HAGGARD: Well, ahh, I hope Chuck lives forever and I hope I get to meet him soon. He influenced everything. Of course, I've been a fan ever since he entered public showmanship. Even before he recorded.

What made you relate to his music when you first heard it?
HAGGARD: They didn't play black music on the radio and so I knew he was influenced by the same damn people that I was, and *that's* what he got out of it—and

it knocked me out. He didn't sound black to me. And when I found he was black, it was like, "So what!"

Right. Because—
HAGGARD: It's the way I felt. I'm not . . . I don't have any problem with black people. So what, you know? What's that got to do with it? The thing about Chuck Berry is, he was just as wild as he sounded.

[CHUCK BERRY]
SCENE 3

One of the reasons Chuck Berry does so few interviews is because he still carries the psychological scars from when public opinion vehemently turned against him in 1959. That was when he was convicted of violating the Mann Act (forbidding transportation of women across state lines for immoral purposes) by bringing a fourteen-year-old Apache prostitute he'd met in Texas to work as a hat-check girl in his St. Louis club. After he fired her, she ended up pressing charges in retaliation against Berry. Much of the press and even the judge at one trial condemned Berry not just for the violation, but for his race. When he emerged from prison, the Beatles, the Rolling Stones, and the Beach Boys were taking his songs, melodies, and riffs to the top of the pop charts. Yet his career and reputation—and psyche— never fully recovered.

You were saying you were anxious to do what?
CHUCK BERRY: Oh, I want to get that album out, yeah. And I want to try to patch some of the negative opinions that lie awaiting my assistance. I say assistance be- cause if there was a comeback, there would be things I could hand out. What do you call it, poor people, when you give . . .

Donations? Charity?
BERRY: Charity. I can hand out charity and it would appear that the negative things have faded, you know.

I've interviewed a lot of people, and many of them worry about the negative opinions and bad reviews and scandals. But if you don't pay them any attention, they go away. People don't remember for very long. All they remember is the music that affected them.
BERRY: Okay, I do that. See, but when you say they go away, somebody brings them back, you know.

But they don't bring them back with judgment. When the bad things first happened, people judged. But when they bring them back now, they're not judgments anymore, they're stories.

BERRY: Okay, if they have become stories, so much the better, so much the better.

Because you survived. Here you are . . .

BERRY: I have no problems. No worries either. But if they come back, the other thing is (*laughs to himself*) . . .

If they bring them back, they have no power anymore. You just keep doing great work. That's your job.

BERRY: You're saying something and I *hear* you. I hear you. So I just do good work after bad work. Is that what you're saying?

That's exactly what I'm saying. Everybody in the world who succeeds, people try to drag them down. Everybody.

BERRY: Oh, tell me about it! Tell me about Obama. Tell me about the mayor of Washington. Yeah. You know, it seems like sometimes you almost hit the bottom, but right now, after this talk, I may go up a little bit.

Did you notice that with Michael Jackson, everybody was calling him a monster, but when he passed away, all of a sudden everybody loved him again?

BERRY: That's the way I stop worrying, because I'm just a guy. How many guys have gone before me? I'm going to go. It's a matter of time. And if I'm going to go, what about that incident that I'm thinking about? Forget it! It's nothing. Our greatest worries are just really nothing. I'll tell you what: It would be better than not having them and just having nothing to do. It's like being the richest man in the world and having no place to spend it.

I've met those rich people and they're not happy because they're so worried about trying to keep their money. The more you have, the more you worry about losing it.

BERRY: What are you doing working for *Rolling Stone*?

Oh, stop it.

BERRY: You got another job? Because we could do fifteen minutes in Vegas.

JOE EDWARDS: Would you ever want to show him Berry Park?*

---

* Berry Park is his estate an hour outside of St. Louis—or thirty minutes with Berry driving.

BERRY: The way our friendship relations are, you could bring somebody out there anytime. [. . .] Yessir, because it's just there and I'm gonna keep the grass cut and all that. I'm a millionaire, but I cut the grass. And each time I cut it, it's my grass (*laughs and claps his hands*). And that is satisfying. Hm-mm-mmm.

It's interesting because every patch of grass has a story and you know the stories.
BERRY: Oh yeah, every blade. It's like a person. A blade is a blade: When it's cut in half, it dies, for sure. But the half that isn't cut springs back to life.

Did you just make that up about the grass or is that a quote from something? Because I think it's true about all the obstacles you've overcome.
BERRY: No, it came to my mind.

That's a great metaphor. Really deep.
BERRY: Like I said, we can do fifteen minutes in Vegas.

[*Continued . . .*]

[BO DIDDLEY]
SCENE 1

Reeling from diabetes, back problems, and a pending divorce, Bo Diddley was nonetheless brimming with energy as he took a cab around Manhattan, visiting guitar and stereo stores to buy new gear. He was in New York to celebrate the fiftieth anniversary of his first single, "Bo Diddley," which helped launch rock and roll and popularize its most famous rhythm, known as the Bo Diddley beat. Unlike Chuck Berry and Jerry Lee Lewis, the tirelessly inventive Diddley didn't have major scandals that derailed his career. But that didn't mean he was any happier about the hand that history had dealt him.

Do you feel that you get the credit you deserve for your part in starting rock and roll?
BO DIDDLEY: I was just looking at something on TV this morning and they named a bunch of people, and they started off with Elvis. Elvis was not first. I was the first son of a gun out here. Me and Chuck Berry. And I'm very sick of the lie. You know, we are over that black and white crap, and that was all the reason why Elvis got the appreciation that he did. I'm the dude that he copied after. And I'm not even mentioned, and I'm still here, seventy-six years old and feeling good and

still working. But I don't know how much longer I can stand by and see somebody else get all the glory that they got off of me.

Have you gotten any royalties for your own recordings?
DIDDLEY: I've been out here for fifty years, man, and I haven't ever seen a royalty check. There ain't no motherfucker in the United States that's going to be honest and pay you right. It's the American bullshit, I guess. I don't know what else to call it. But Elvis did not invent rock and roll. He didn't start rock and roll. He came two and a half years after me. See, and Little Richard said that he invented rock and roll. Richard is three years behind me. He's my buddy and I love him to death, but Richard just talks.

How do you feel when you turn on the radio station and you hear your beat being played by some band?
DIDDLEY: That I ain't getting a dime for it, and I'm sick of it. I am sick of it. I've got a lawyer that I call my pit bull because he's got an extra set of teeth, you know what I'm saying. I am not going to be nice about it when I decide to turn him loose.

Did you ever check to see if it's possible to copyright your beat?
DIDDLEY: *Boom bi didem boom ba didem bad did dum* is something that I came up with. They say, "Oh, that's public domain." That bugs me, 'cause I was young and dumb and didn't understand what the hell was going on. They told me that I can't copyright a beat. But that's a lie. If you can write it, you can copyright it.

When you were younger, what money did you survive on?
DIDDLEY: Working, like I'm working now. That's the way I survive. I own a piece of land, but I'm still waiting on somebody to make my mailbox look like a football. But after fifty years, it's not gonna happen. I've got people, and I can't name no names right now, but they know they had better get ready because I'm coming. See, I don't want just back royalties, I want interest—for fifty fucking years. I don't care if it ain't but ten dollars from the first year, I want interest on the ten bucks. All the way up to whatever millions I'm pretty sure that I'm owed. I figure there's about fifteen to twenty million dollars that I could have in my pocket. After fifty years, someone is living good off of what they stole from me and other cats.

You're a smart guy and I think you've always had common sense and defied convention—
DIDDLEY: Exactly. I'm smarter than the average bear.

So how did you end up getting ripped off so much?
DIDDLEY: I've been through it. I tell young musicians, "Don't trust nobody but your mama. And even then, look at her real good." You don't have enough time to talk to me about the shit that I know about. We have a few people mixed in that are bona fide one-hundred percent thieves. They live by scamming you. But, you see, all my great grandkids is growing up and when my ass drops out of here and goes, "Good-bye Bo Diddley," somebody is going to have problems, because they are more aggressive than I was.

[*Continued . . .*]

[JOHN HARTFORD]

One afternoon, John Hartford sat in the kitchen of his Nashville house, surrounded by a metronome, a microphone, a tape recorder, and three young bluegrass players. Through the room's small windows, all that could be seen was a picturesque stretch of Nashville's Cumberland River. Hartford was a bluegrass legend, riverboat pilot, and television host best known for writing one of country music's most popular songs, "Gentle on My Mind," performed by over two hundred artists.

It would have been a perfect moment if not for one thing: Hartford's doctors had told him he didn't have long to live. Complications from lymphoma (a cancer of the immune system), combined with anemia, a sinus operation, and a knee problem, had worn him down. In the little time he had left on this planet, Hartford had chosen to focus on one thing: fiddling.

JOHN HARTFORD: I tried to get real healthy about twenty or thirty years ago, and I think that's why I got health problems now. I tried to be a vegetarian and all that crap. I think it hurt me: One of my big problems right now is that I have anemia. My daddy was a doctor and he told me to be real careful at the time, and his words have all come true. Cancer has just about emptied my phone book. And I've got it, too.

Are you planning to do anything to support your new record or does that not really matter now?
HARTFORD: I don't think I'll be touring this time. I've probably only got two years left, and promoting a record is a lot less important to me than having a hell of a time with what I've got left.

Define "hell of a time."
HARTFORD: I love to play. It gets me up and gets me going. What I do is I sit over here at this table and I work on this tape recorder.* The reason I'm in the business is because I love to play and I love to explore where to go. What happens is you run up against a wall in your playing, and you start searching along the wall and you find this door down here. And you open it up and there's this beautiful garden on the other side, and you crawl through and all of a sudden every tune that you know becomes a whole new experience again.
YOUNG FIDDLER (*jokes*): Where can I find that door?
HARTFORD: There are so many of them. [. . .] And to be real honest with you, I have a terrible time with my records, all of them. Since we made *Good Old Boys* six or eight months ago, there are all kinds of little doors that I've found. In fact, I'd like to go back and re-record the whole thing.

You could spend your life remaking the same record.
HARTFORD: My ultimate goal is to rent my records rather than sell them. So when I get past a problem, I can call them back in and say, "Listen, we've remodeled this piece of material."

What draws you to the music beyond the problem-solving?
HARTFORD: I love the mechanics of the music. Roy Buchanan and I did a show for Don Kirshner[†] and got real close to each other. [Roy] had just come off the stage and played the goddamnedest blue-est, lonesome-est thing on the guitar I think I might have ever heard in my life. I was starting to reach for my jacket, I was getting so cold. I said, "What in the hell do you think about when you play the guitar like that?" He looked at me and said, "My mother's grave." He was dead serious, too. About a year later, he shot himself or hung himself.[‡]

A local banjo player enters the house and approaches Hartford, intending to shake his hand. But Hartford greets him by waving instead. Hartford has not shaken a hand for as long as anyone can remember. He is scared of someone bruising or breaking his bones. Among Hartford's other eccentricities are his writing style (he gives autographs

---

* By which he means recording music on the tape recorder, then playing it back and analyzing it.
† *Don Kirshner's Rock Concert* was a popular television show that aired live rock concerts before the music-video era.
‡ After being arrested for public intoxication, Buchanan, one of the greatest electric blues guitarists of his generation, was found hung by his shirt in his jail cell.

writing with both hands simultaneously in a beautiful script) and his preference for speaking by telephone instead of in person (because, he explains, "it's more like speaking into a microphone").

HARTFORD: I started fiddling for dances when I was thirteen or fourteen. Then, when I got old enough, I started playing in the honky-tonks. And that's where you saw rough stuff: people carrying guns and fistfights. I had a lot of that. I saw a guy back out of a tavern one time and swear that he was going to go get a gun and kill [banjoist] Doug Dillard. The next morning in the newspaper, we read that he'd been drunk and gotten a gun, come back, and gone in the wrong bar and killed somebody who didn't know nothing about it.

After the interview, the group at Hartford's house spends another three hours picking and listening to rare bluegrass recordings from the fifties. When the young musicians disperse, Hartford remains sitting alone, flanked by his microphone, metronome, tape deck, and instrument, still trying after almost fifty years of fiddling to get it right.

HARTFORD: I've been thinking today about leaning back on the beat real hard, kind of like water-skiing behind the beat.

Wow, you never give up.
HARTFORD: This is the pain in the life of a guy who considers himself a mediocre musician.

Shortly after this interview, while on tour in Texas, Hartford lost movement in his hands. He continued to host picking parties, which he watched instead of played at, until his death several months later at the Centennial Medical Center in Nashville. He was sixty-three.

[LEONARD COHEN]

One of the advantages of being a music journalist is meeting artists you respect and hearing their unreleased songs. Especially artists like Leonard Cohen, who can take up to a year to write a song and then another five or ten years to release it.

When I was at your house, you played a song that was fantastic. I think it was called "Tell Me That You Love Me Then."

LEONARD COHEN: Yeah, I played that for you. I didn't play "Lullaby," did I?

No.

COHEN: They really work now. I don't know why. The songs seem to become somewhat more relevant. That "Lullaby" song, I got that on my little laptop. I should go get it. Want me to go get it?

I'd love that.

Cohen scampers out of the room and returns moments later with a black MacBook, opens iTunes, and plays a slow dirge . . .

> *"Through a net of lies, I will come to you.*
> *When our dead arrive, I will wait there too.*
> *If your heart is torn, I don't wonder why.*
> *If the night is long, here's my lullaby."*

When the song ends, Cohen sits silently for several seconds before speaking.

COHEN: I thought "Lullabye" was just what everybody needs to get to sleep in these troubled times.

I was asking my father the other day if he's lived through a worse or more scary time than the present, and he said no.

COHEN: I tend to agree with your father.

Have you seen a period like this before?

COHEN: I don't really know what to say. I find myself writing about it and anything I write seems to be more authentic, though not necessarily more accurate or insightful, than any casual conversation.

In many ways, [your 1992 album] *The Future* picked up on what was in the air and became almost prophetic.

COHEN: I think that sensibility is nothing you can summon, but it really arises if you keep uncovering the song and trying to get beneath the slogan—either the emotional slogan or the political slogan. So much of the work that I hear, there's nothing wrong with it, but much of it has the feel of a slogan or an agenda that's

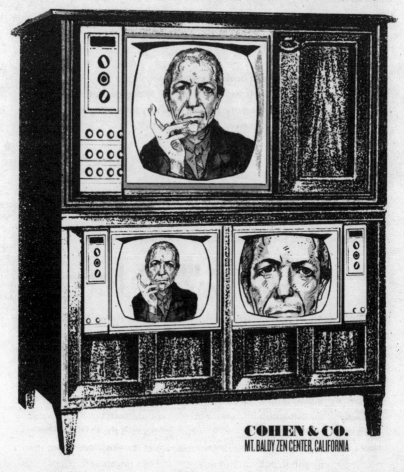

already been written. It's a perfectly good slogan, and there are interesting varia-tions in it. But if you're interested in forming yourself through your work, which I think is more interesting, then you have to keep uncovering and discarding those slogans until you get to something. When you have those moments where you inform yourself of something that wasn't immediately apparent, that's when it becomes interesting.

Do you enjoy the process of writing itself?
COHEN: I feel very distant when I'm doing it. I feel like there's someone across the room who is very diligently filling in the blanks of a questionnaire. It's hard (*pauses*). Check this out.

Cohen plays two more new songs.

Is all the legal stuff* done and behind you now?
COHEN: Yes, mostly, mostly. If we meet privately sometime, and I hope we do down the road, I'll tell you the story. It has a very, very interesting and O. Henry-esque ending. Are you in LA ever?

I live there now.
COHEN: Give me a call or come over.

By the way, I meant to thank you for turning me on to that movie website.† It's amazing that they have all that for free.
COHEN: And some of the porno channels are incredible, too.

[CHUCK BERRY]
SCENE 4

After three hours of talking, Berry took a break to see a lawyer because he was being sued over concerts he'd cancelled. Incredibly, he wanted to meet back at Blueberry Hill afterward to talk even more. When we sat down again that evening, his guard had completely dropped, and the Chuck Berry I'd been told to expect—bitter and stubborn—was nowhere to be found.

---

* Cohen had fired his manager, who absconded with crates of his memorabilia and most of his retirement fund. The legal battle that ensued decimated what was left of his savings.
† When I'd previously met Cohen, he showed me where to go online to stream free documentaries.

CHUCK BERRY: I ain't got nothing against faggots. Just don't fool with me! And also not only prostitutes, but women (*searching for word*) . . . lesbians. You know, it would be interesting to me to get right to the heart of why do they like their own kind. [. . .] I want to get into it because I want to know, does anybody think like I think about sex?

I'll tell you something: Everybody does.
BERRY: Huh?

Everybody thinks like you do about sex, but nobody admits it.
BERRY: Yeah, well how do we know, though, that what you're saying is fact?

The book that I wrote, *The Game*—
BERRY: It's got some of that in it?

It's *only* about that.
BERRY (*pounds table*): Oh, I am gonna enjoy that (*laughs and claps*). I'll pay somebody to read me this book.

The topic is always interesting.
BERRY: Mmm, this interview going to get goooood!

Sex is still such a big taboo in society, though.
BERRY: But in Hollywood, the cleavage now is dropping lower and lower, and this is in the last six months. Some men don't even notice it. And when a woman sits down, you know, you get a flash—whoosh! Even now, because when a woman bends over, you notice the cameraman pulls in like that so you look where you want to look. Oh, man (*claps*)!

Have you noticed that if a woman gets fake breasts, she doesn't mind showing them since they're something she bought and not something she was born with?
BERRY: Boy, I'd like for us to get into a discussion on TV, 'cause we could open up the category of thoughts that are allowed, you know. 'Cause they'll put you off TV if you get too blatant. Is that the word?

Yeah, blatant or explicit.
BERRY: But if everybody did it, who's gonna stop that? I know the kind of guy you are, (*lowers voice*) that's what I'm getting ready to say. I know how you can think

and you probably know how I can think, because there's nothing (*pounds table*) that stands up straighter than the truth.

This category must have been much more closed when you were younger.
BERRY: My dad used to do carpentry work all around South St. Louis. And in South St. Louis, a lot of men work away from home and the women keep the home. And here's the funny part: When I was young, I was pretty nice.

Not like now.
BERRY: I'm talking about nice-*looking*! Anyway, I would be helping Dad to fix a lock, and the women would bring some oranges or something. Not all women, but some women were forward. Firstly, Daddy would ignore them. I would wonder why Dad wouldn't laugh if she would laugh. They would flirt with my dad and make comments about me, and they would try to encourage him to say something for me. And he taught us not to say anything and not to smile. If you did, you'd get your neck broke. You'll find yourself in jail. When I was five, eight, and ten years old, relations weren't like that. You weren't even born. See, I'm talking out of your time. But he wanted to keep us alive.

Imagine what it was like when your dad was born.
BERRY: Oh, when he came up, well, they didn't get a chance to answer. They'd hang you in a minute. You know, I didn't know that you were educated . . . I mean sophisticated. Your sophistication is coming to realization, so to speak. You know a lot of stuff!

Thank you.
BERRY: Literally, you know a lot of stuff. There are a lot of things in life that people don't talk about. We've hardly said a thing about music since we've been in here, you know, but boy, when we got on the sex thing (*laughs*), you know we talked. And I can tell you a few things, because it's altogether different from what you might have [learned at] university. What's your company?

Rolling Stone.
BERRY: *Rolling Stone*! That's a sophisticated magazine. It's not as into sex as *Playboy* is, but it's way more into sex than *Discovery*.

True . . .
BERRY: You know, what's that yellow dictionary?

National Geographic?

BERRY: Yeah! But you can see a little of something in there. I used to look at that (*pounds table and laughs*). They show a little, because I remember looking at a lot of them. And of course *Playboy*. All the youngsters did look at *Playboy*. It was so graphic! It shows right what you want to see. Who ever heard of a nipple covering a whole page? But that was *very* interesting. I've never been that close (*laughs*). Oh, man, we could write a book about it.

[*Continued . . .*]

LORETTA LYNN
SCENE 2

Since you've sung about birth control and other women's issues, have you ever thought of doing a song about breast implants after your bad experience with them?

LORETTA LYNN: Well, I'm telling you what: I had a secretary that had this done. And I walked in my office one day and she said, "Look at this, you don't ever have to wear a bra!" And I'm very self-conscious about my bra straps showing or something, you know. And she said, "Look how big I am now!" And I said, "I don't want to be no bigger." She said, "Well, you'll never have to wear a bra again if you go get this done." So I went to have it done. They started it, but they ran into bleeding tumors and an ulcer so they didn't finish it. And when they tried to reconstruct the other side to match, I guess they used stuff that's not good for you.

Silicone?

LYNN: Yeah, I guess that's what it was. And it had busted and it went on my right arm, all the way down on my arm and the bones. They had to scrape it off my rib cage and everywhere. It still worries me, because this girl today has cancer and she's in chemotherapy right now. Hers never even busted. But see, she went in and had it three or four times. I would not want one of my girls to ever try that.

And that doesn't make you want to write a song about it?

LYNN: Well, you know, I hadn't thought about that, but that's a good idea. I could call it, "Don't You Think You're Big Enough?" (*Laughs loudly.*)

[BO DIDDLEY]
SCENE 2

"If I put the guitar down today or tomorrow, I would not starve," Bo Diddley said as he walked me through his Gainesville, Florida home—crammed with dozens of instruments and games he'd invented—to his home studio. "I know too many damn things. I can decorate. I can cook. I can do electronics and wire any kind of electric shit. I can figure anything out."

In the studio, Diddley sat behind a desk strewn with recording equipment, turned on a drum machine, and began singing mostly bawdy rhymes into a microphone for nearly two hours straight, providing a rare insight into the mind that helped invent rock and roll.*

BO DIDDLEY (*sings*): Two old maids was playing in the sand / One told the other, "I wish you was a man." / One said, the other said, "I ain't no man / But hold still baby, I'll do the best I can." (*To me:*) That's the stuff I used to do as a kid.

What are the lyrics from?
DIDDLEY: A friend at school wrote the song out for me on a piece of that lined notebook paper. My mom found it, saw it, and said, "Come here." I took a few steps toward her. She said, "Come closer." I came closer, but with one foot back so I could escape. She said, "If you run, it'll be twice as hard."

So she beat you?
DIDDLEY: That's right, she did. Now if you do that, you go to prison for child abuse. Man, my mom would have been in every one of them prisons. She used to beat me if I did anything wrong (*pauses*). But it worked.

The dirty lyrics you were doing before that, were they from "Uncle John"?†
DIDDLEY: Yeah.

You should consider putting that version of it out sometime.
DIDDLEY: Oh no, I can't do it. It's too rough.

---

* Keith Richards on seeing Bo Diddley in his impressionable youth: "He was there with that square guitar and he would go for it. I would see him come offstage and he would only have two strings left on that guitar. There was also that mixture of the tribal beat and almost New Orleans showmanship. He had [his guitarist] the Duchess with him, in that gold dress. She'd come over and give you a hug: 'Oh, baby, I love you!' I mean, being stuck between those tits when you're nineteen years old—wonderful."
† His legendary lost song, which was rewritten into the less ribald "Bo Diddley" for his first single.

If you think about it, Chuck Berry's biggest hit was "My Ding-A-Ling" and that's just as rough.

DIDDLEY: I'm working on something new to hit the public with instead. (*Picks up a guitar and sings an even more obscene song, then stops to make sure I'm appreciating it.*) I don't do this just for anybody.

Thanks. I'm enjoying it.

DIDDLEY (*sings*): I know a guy, a guy named Neil / He come way down here to hang out with me / He's got a little article and he's gonna write it right / And I'm gonna sing it, it's the way it's gonna be / He gonna start hanging out with me / Bo, Bo Diddley, do my thing / Gonna take him back to hear me sing.

He hits a button on a sampler and a screaming heavy metal guitar riff rips through the speakers. He begins yowling in a mock-metal style, but doesn't seem to be feeling it. So he stops, opens a drawer, and removes a wig of long, black Nikki Sixx-like hair, which he then puts on. He starts mock head-banging as he screams the lyrics with new, committed venom.

I didn't take you for a heavy metal fan.

DIDDLEY: People would be surprised at what I know how to do.

When the song ends, he removes the wig and patches one of his homemade stringed instruments into a guitar synthesizer. He plays Bach on it, followed by minor-key gothic-sounding orchestrations of his songs. Soon after, a twenty-year-old protégée of his named Tiffany arrives, and the two begin working on a new song.

DIDDLEY: I'm fifty years in the business right now, and it don't look like it's been fifty years. I feel very good and I'm happy. I've got a little problem with my toe, with that diabetes. So many people got that crap now. But I'm going to tell you something: Something's feeding it. It's a disease, but I think it's from fast foods. All of the grease and all the prepared stuff you get, even in the grocery store, has something to do with it.

Even with all that going on, your stamina is pretty impressive.

DIDDLEY: We aren't put together that great. Down here (*pointing to his legs*), I can't stand no more weight than the top of my body. But from here up (*gesturing from his torso to his head*), I'm not to be messed with.

After the story ran, Diddley called and thanked me in his own inimitable way. "If you were a girl," he said, "I'd fuck you." I tried to convince Diddley to release an album of his home-studio recordings, but he said he was in the middle of divorcing his fourth wife and didn't want to start a new project yet in case she was awarded any of the proceeds.

Less than two years later, Diddley collapsed from a stroke after a concert in Iowa. Later that same year, he had a heart attack from which he never fully recovered. He died in his home the following year at the age of seventy-nine.

[CHUCK BERRY]
SCENE 5

After an hour of almost solid sex talk, Berry asked to stay in touch.

CHUCK BERRY: You mentioned this evening that we could get together some other time. We're gonna have to, 'cause I'm gonna ask you some questions. But I don't do e-mail.

I'll give you my phone number, and anytime you want to talk . . .
BERRY: Oh yeah. In fact, I can fax you.

Great.
BERRY: Oh, yeah, we must talk. We've got a great relationship here. 'Cause, like I say, I'm gonna be asking you some things. If what I think is in that book, oh ho! I'll know then that somebody has written about it. Roll over Berry and send Strauss the news!

When people talk about things others are scared to talk about, I think that's what makes good art, good music, and good books.
BERRY: As long as it's entertaining and inspiring, I don't see why it shouldn't be known by more people. If there was nothing but love, there would be no wars. How could there be? And I would like to see a war of love. You know, instead of death or destruction, it would just be—mm-mmm—everybody running wild.

Maybe that's what the hippies tried to do.
BERRY: Oh, you know what, many of their traits are coming back to realization. Look how long it took miniskirts to come in. It took from the 1700s all the way

to 1970. That's two-and-a-half hundred years. There was a time when women's clothing was all layers and layers, way out.

Like those Victorian dresses.
BERRY: There's room to live in those (*laughs and hits table*). And I've thought about it! Whoo (*hits table again*)!

I think women's sexual fantasies are more wild than men's. Because men's fantasies are encouraged, but with women, their parents always say, "No, don't talk about that—that's bad." And so it's repressed, and then it just grows and grows—
BERRY: What do you mean grows and grows? (*Laughs at his pun.*)

That's what happens to men . . .
BERRY: I've seen some men look actually better to me because they have such large breasts (*laughs*). I call them breast chests. That's what it is, but in the first place it's flabby. If it's large . . . I don't even want to talk about it.

Don't talk about it. We won't go there.
BERRY: Yeah, let me ask one question. Don't laugh at this because it's not laughable, and I'm not . . . Yes, I am serious. You're not funny, are you?*

No, I'm not.
BERRY: Well, that's what I want to hear. I mean, I've talked to funny guys. Like do you know Little Richard?

Not personally.
BERRY: Anyway, he's for real. I know because I've been asked for . . . He came on to me once, you know. And it just doesn't make sense. I couldn't *believe* it! And he believes it. By that, I mean he doesn't deny it. Anyway, when I ask you that, it's only because you said, "We'll talk," you know . . .

Oh no!
BERRY: And I'm also a comedian. That's when I should have said it, but you kept talking.

See, I ruined it. Did you ever consider doing comedy professionally?
BERRY: Oh yeah, I wanted to be a comedian so bad. And I did that so much in high school, I couldn't get a girlfriend.

---

* Funny (fun·ny, adj. [archaic colloquial]): Of, pertaining to, or exhibiting homosexuality.

Do you still want to?
BERRY: Every time I get a chance. I'm still trying!

I'll let you go, but I had a blast. This has been one of my favorite interviews.
BERRY: Let's do it again!

[OLD PEOPLE]

At St. Paul's Episcopal Church in upstate New York, two dozen senior citizens sat, quietly preparing for a free meal. Paper napkins were distributed, followed by silverware and small brown bowls of Thousand Island dressing. Everything was moving in accord with the tempo of the aged, until David Greenberger pulled up a chair at the head of the long, rectangular table and shattered their serenity.

Greenberger is the publisher of *The Duplex Planet*, perhaps the world's longest-running fanzine, with hundreds of issues consisting solely of the results of his interviews with senior citizens. In the process, he has given many of his subjects an unexpected second career: as poets, record reviewers, artists, and cult celebrities. They've published books, recorded albums, written for magazines, and even designed album covers (including one for R.E.M.) as a result of Greenberger's friendship.

JAMES: Are you going to ask us more questions again?

Greenberger removes a sheet of white paper from his briefcase and looks down the table's gallery of wrinkled faces.

DAVID GREENBERGER: Who is the king of love?
JERRY (*smiles at his wife*): Leona.
LEONA: I'm not the king.
JERRY: Oh, you're not the king?
JAMES: She's the queen of love. (*To Greenberger:*) You answer: Who's the king of love?
GREENBERGER: I don't know. There's no right answer. It differs according to opinion.
JAMES: Rita, who's the king of love?
RITA: God, I don't know. I haven't met him yet. I don't know where he's hiding.

JAMES: Hang in there, Ri. (*To Greenberger:*) It sure as hell ain't me. Although I heard a song on television. It was put out from the movie *Dusty*. I think it was by Strait. What the hell's his name, Black Strait?

George?
JERRY: George Strait, that's it. It was called "No Greater Love Than My Love Is For You."* That was just beautiful.
MARIE: I have love all around me.
ELEANOR: I never heard of that.
JERRY: That sounds like some biblical thing.

In Greenberger's car thirty minutes later . . .

What's your goal ultimately in doing these interviews?
GREENBERGER: I want to teach people that aging and decline is part of the deal. That this is what's going to happen later.

Is it hard for you to see the people you work with die?
GREENBERGER: It's part of the process. I was seeing this guy Arthur Wallace. I knew him when he was dying. He was very outspoken about his radical political past, but in the last few months of his life, he was beginning to mix stuff up. I saw that it was not without purpose that this was happening. It seems that some sort of protective mechanism takes over when you get older. That's why people stop making sense sometimes in their old age. How else can you face dying unless you're a little confused about your circumstances? It makes the whole thing a bit more gentle.

[RAYMOND SCOTT]

Somehow, while interning at the *Village Voice*, I managed to talk the music editor into flying me to Los Angeles to interview Raymond Scott. It was my first big break. I could barely drive and I'd never been to LA before, but those were the least of my challenges. The person I was supposed to be interviewing could barely speak.

---

* Disambiguation: The movie is actually called *Pure Country*, Strait's character is named Dusty, and the song is "I Cross My Heart."

For most of his life, Scott was a man far ahead of his time. But when I met him in his Van Nuys home for his first interview in decades—and his last—time had caught up with him.

Though Scott's name may not be familiar to most people, his music definitely is: Watch almost any Bugs Bunny or Daffy Duck cartoon, and you'll hear the orchestra playing his syncopated, almost mechanical jazz riffs, especially if there's a scene involving things moving along a conveyor belt.

Scott came to fame as the leader of an eccentric late-thirties jazz combo called the Raymond Scott Quintette, recording evocative swing hits with titles like "Reckless Night on Board an Ocean Liner" and "Dinner Music for a Pack of Hungry Cannibals." Each new 78, which embodied his musical philosophy of "grab 'em by the ear," sold out within weeks. He went on to have one of the most varied careers in music: He started the first racially integrated radio band, led an NBC television orchestra, wrote a Broadway musical for Yul Brynner, worked for Motown Records, composed jingles for companies like Gillette and Pepsi, and became an inventor and electronic-music pioneer. In the 1950s, he actually pieced together a synthesizer, sequencer, and artificial-intelligence composing machine called the electronium.

The garage in Scott's Van Nuys home was filled with meticulously collected evidence of his Zelig-like career, including a recording of him auditioning (and rejecting) a young Bo Diddley. Sitting in their living room, Scott's wife, Mitzi, discussed the resurgence of interest in him.

MITZI SCOTT: I've been really surprised by the interest people have shown. Raymond got two fan letters and three requests for photographs since the CD came out. The fan letters were all from young people. One came with nut bread. (*Raymond Scott enters the living room in his robe.*) It's a reporter from the *Village Voice.* He's going to write an article about you.

Scott sits silently next to his wife.

Is it okay to ask him some questions?
MITZI: He has brain damage and can't communicate. He's had four strokes. I think the mental skills are there somewhere inside, and I know he knows he's brain-damaged. And he's very upset with that. He gets frustrated because he knows what's going on. In some ways, Raymond is very childish. If he doesn't get his way, he has a tantrum. There are no inhibitions.
RAYMOND SCOTT: S-s-sorry.

Is he doing any kind of rehabilitation?
MITZI: When he had his first stroke, I took him to the emergency room and he was perfectly lucid, joking with the nurses. While he was in the hospital, he had a second stroke. That really did a lot of brain damage. When he was recuperating at home, his vocabulary was coming back. He was learning how to write again. Then he had a third stroke and that did more damage. He was making progress after that, and then he had another stroke in July. Now I don't know if he'll ever be able to recuperate.

Does he remember the things he's done?
MITZI: There's a radio station out here that plays a lot of big band music. Sometimes they play his music. If he hears it, he'll say, "That's mine." It's really a terrible thing that all this has happened to him. He used to be such a smart man.
RAYMOND: Who is this?
MITZI: His name is Neil Strauss. He's from the *Village Voice* in New York.
RAYMOND: Oh really?

I show him the CD cover.

I'm here to write about your CD.
RAYMOND: That . . . that's me. It's w-w-wonderful.

Your music is very good. A lot of young people are listening to it now.
RAYMOND: S-s-sorry. C-c-can't talk.

Was he still composing orchestral and jazz music before his strokes?
MITZI: Oh yes. When he used to sit at the piano and compose, he'd play something for me and say, "Does this sound familiar to you?" And if I said, "Well, this part right here sounds a little like such-and-such," he'd throw it out. If it had the nearest hint of sounding like something else somebody had written, he would not use it.

Do you know much about the electronic instruments he invented?
MITZI: He was always interested in electronics. In fact he wanted to be an engineer. But when he graduated from Brooklyn Tech, his brother [CBS orchestra conductor] Mark Warnow thought that he had so much talent as a musician that he bribed him with a Steinway grand piano to go to Juilliard. But he never lost that interest in engineering. I think that's what took him into electronic music.

And he did electronic music for Motown for a while?

MITZI: He was head of research and development for Motown. What happened was that he built the electronium, and they had a piece on it in one of the Long Island newspapers and somehow a copy of that got onto the desk of [Motown founder] Berry Gordy. So Berry Gordy came out with an entourage of limousines and people to hear the electronium, which was wild. It didn't have any cabinet, just wires all over the place. He said he wanted one and he gave Raymond a contract to build one for him.

What did it sound like?

MITZI: Oh, it sounded so wonderful. And my mother, who didn't like electronic music, listened to it one time and it played this beautiful, moody music. She said, "God, it sounds like [Duke] Ellington." And it did. It was really a remarkable machine and it's a shame that he cannibalized it. He took so many parts out of it that it could never be put back together again. If he had just left it alone, it could still play. But now it's an empty shell.*

How did he feel when mass-produced synthesizers and computer programs that could make music came out?

MITZI: The year before his first stroke, he had bought a computer, a printer, and a piano keyboard. And he said, "You know, I can do everything with this that I did with the electronium."

Is there any way to hear his new music?

MITZI: That music is still in that computer somewhere and nobody knows how to get into it.

Raymond Scott gets agitated, stands up, and starts to leave the room.

RAYMOND: C-c-crazy.

A year and a half later, Raymond Scott died of pneumonia in a nearby nursing home.

---

* During an interview with Les Paul, the musician who helped develop the electric guitar and popularize multi-track recording, I mentioned Raymond Scott and accidentally set him off on a tirade. Evidently, the two were rival innovators. "He's light years behind," Paul snapped. "He used to come to my house to learn about multi-tracking. He had a non-synchronous seven-track [recorder] and he didn't understand it. He sure had some equipment though. I envied him."

[ZAPP]

During the interview with Lenny Kravitz in New Orleans, he took me to the House of Blues to see Zapp, the legendary band of funk brothers. Frontman Roger Troutman's pioneering use of the talk box—an electronic device he used to create the effect of robotic-sounding vocals—influenced countless hits and rappers like Snoop Dogg, Dr. Dre, and Eazy-E. Years after the show, I interviewed Troutman for the *New York Times.*

All of a sudden you're on all these rap songs. How do you feel about the music?
ROGER TROUTMAN: I make it a point to acknowledge that hip-hop is indeed an art form. I've never allowed the older generation—or the turned-off generation, because they're turned off to hip-hop—to influence my opinion of hip-hop music. When people finally meet me in person though, they find that I don't drink, I don't smoke, and I don't use drugs. There is a particular image that I'm trying to portray in terms of how I dress and my demeanor.

What kind of image is that?
TROUTMAN: Not completely, totally heterosexual. I'm not trying to look like an older guy who's over the hill, but I'm not looking like a young guy, either. It's flashy colors and the best of clothes and not just wearing something that's comfortable. Things that would impress me as a kid would be guitar players with a dazzling guitar or the shiniest shoes. And I loved to see the circus as a kid.

I hear you have a construction company that hires neighborhood youth to build low-income housing . . .
TROUTMAN: It was our idea—me and my brothers Larry, Tony, and Lester. It was not for profit but to give something back. Each of the guys in the group are extremely capable of putting up a house. Their principal position is taking the stage and dominating the stage as they do, so they learned this in their spare time. There is a need to clean up if you want to look great and take on the responsibility of being famous. I accept my responsibility and take it very seriously.

And what is that responsibility?
TROUTMAN: What can I say? I want to be the next black hero.

[DEAD PEOPLE]
SCENE 2

The most humbling lesson one learns when writing obituaries is that it doesn't matter how famous, obscure, good, evil, happy, sad, or healthy someone may be. In one instant, everything can change.

ROGER TROUTMAN

Roger Troutman, a renowned funk-music innovator who recorded with his brothers in the band Zapp in the early eighties, died on Sunday at the Good Samaritan Hospital and Health Center in Dayton, Ohio. He was forty-seven and lived in Dayton.

Mr. Troutman was shot several times in the torso and died during surgery, Sgt. Gary White of the Dayton police said. Mr. Troutman's older brother, Larry, a former bandmate and business partner, was found dead of an apparently self-inflicted gunshot wound the same day in a car nearby. Police said they were investigating the possibility of a murder-suicide. . . .

MARK SANDMAN

Mark Sandman, the leader of the idiosyncratic Boston rock trio Morphine, died on Saturday during a performance at the Giardini del Principe in Palestrina, near Rome. He was forty-six.

The cause was a heart attack, according to the Associated Press. Mr. Sandman collapsed in front of several thousand fans during a performance on the second day of a three-day festival that was part of the band's ongoing European tour. . . .

RANDY CALIFORNIA

Randy California, the lead guitarist for the virtuosic sixties psychedelic rock band, Spirit, is believed to have died on January second on the Hawaiian island of Molokai. He was forty-six.

Mr. California was body-surfing with his twelve-year-old son, Quinn, when an undertow swept him out to sea, said a spokesman for the Maui fire department. Despite land, sea, and air searches conducted by the fire department and Mr. California's friends, a body was never found. The search has been suspended pending any new developments, he said. Mr. California is missing and presumed dead.

Born in Los Angeles as Randy Wolfe, Mr. California began playing in folk and country bands in his early teens. On a trip to New York with his family at the age of fifteen, Mr. California changed his last name and began performing with Jimi Hendrix (then known as Jimmy James). When Mr. Hendrix went to England, Mr. California returned to Los Angeles and ran into his future bandmates at a love-in he had taken his stepfather to. . . .

MICHEL-MELTHON LYNCH

Michel-Melthon Lynch, bass player and drummer for Boukman Eksperyans, the best-selling Haitian band in the world, died on June fourth at his home in Port-au-Prince, Haiti. He was twenty-five.

The cause was meningitis, said his manager, Dan Behrman.

Though meningitis is a curable illness, friends and family members of Mr. Lynch were unable to locate in Haiti the antibiotics that could have saved his life. Antibiotics sent to Mr. Lynch by concerned parties in New York never arrived. . . .

JEFF BUCKLEY

Jeff Buckley, a folk, rock, and pop singer and the son of the folk musician Tim Buckley, died on Thursday in Memphis, the police said. He was thirty.

Mr. Buckley drowned while swimming in the Memphis harbor, said Lieut. Brenda Maples of the Memphis Police Department. His body was recovered Wednesday night after it was spotted from a riverboat.

Mr. Buckley and a friend had stopped by the harbor on their way to a rehearsal studio last week. Mr. Buckley was wading and swimming when a speedboat passed by, creating a wake. The friend, Keith Foti, said he turned away to protect the pair's stereo and when he looked up, Mr. Buckley had disappeared. The police and the harbor patrol searched for Mr. Buckley with helicopters, scuba divers, and foot patrols.

His body was not found until a passenger on the riverboat spotted it floating in the harbor near the city's main thoroughfare, Beale Street.

Mr. Buckley was born in Orange County, California. His father, whom he remembered meeting only once, was an influential, eclectic, and introspective folk singer who died of a drug overdose at age twenty-eight in 1975 . . .

SHANNON HOON

Shannon Hoon, lead singer of the rock group Blind Melon, died on Saturday in the band's tour bus in a parking lot in New Orleans. He was twenty-eight.

The cause was apparently an accidental drug overdose, said Chris Jones, the band's manager. An autopsy was performed yesterday morning but the results were incomplete. Recently, Mr. Hoon moved back to his hometown of Lafayette, Indiana with his girlfriend of ten years, Lisa Crouse, and a daughter, Nico Blue, was born to them this summer. . . .

[PAUL NELSON]

"His solitude, which he seemed to carry with him everywhere, even onstage, was in a way far more moving than the audience's enthusiastic acceptance of his work."
—**Paul Nelson, writing on Leonard Cohen, 1975**

Some consider Paul Nelson the nation's first rock critic, others its finest. Though firsts and bests can rarely be proven, one thing is certain: Nelson's influence on rock criticism and rock itself is extraordinary. As a college student, he loaned a middling young singer named Bob Dylan the Woody Guthrie albums that would determine the course of his entire sound, aesthetic, and career. While working at Mercury Records, he not only served as a mentor to Rod Stewart and David Bowie, but also fired the starter's gun of punk rock by signing the New York Dolls. And as a writer for *Rolling Stone*, his literary reviews cracked open the careers of Willie Nelson, Jackson Browne, and the Sex Pistols.

Yet, for the last fifteen years of his life, Nelson did not publish a single word. Instead, he dropped out of sight and worked in obscurity at a New York video

store until, at the age of seventy, he starved to death in his apartment. His body had been decomposing for several days before it was found.

His friends and fans all wrung their hands and wondered how an icon who was so talented, who had contributed so much to the culture, and who was so universally respected could go out like that. So a few weeks after his body was discovered, I began piecing together the story of his missing years, beginning with the end of his tenure as an editor at *Rolling Stone.*

KIT RACHLIS [former editor in chief, *Los Angeles* magazine]: There's no question in my mind that Paul was the first rock and roll critic. He precedes everybody.

DAVID BOWIE: He was the PR [public relations] man at Mercury when I met him. He kind of met me off the plane when I first went to New York. I guess it must have been around 1971, something like that. I would tie it to that year because one of the albums he gave me was *Loaded* by the Velvet Underground. Sometimes you meet someone casually who makes a big impression on you, and Paul made a big impression on me. He was one of the kindest, most generous men I've met inside or outside of the music business.

JANN WENNER [publisher, *Rolling Stone*]: He was a well-loved guy, but he lived in a mysterious corner of the office, where he had a little sanctum and nest. He was allied with us, but it was a separate world that he was in. He was a loner then, even when surrounded by his entire peer group. But he started to lose his drive and became less reliable.

GREIL MARCUS [rock critic and author]: Getting Paul to the point where he was satisfied with his writing and felt it did justice to whoever it was about was getting to be impossible. So I don't know if it's a matter of him deciding to give up writing as it is of writing receding from his grasp, to where his own standards exceeded his ability to rise to them.

TOM PACHECO [folk musician]: We spoke on the phone and he told me he was quitting *Rolling Stone.* Something about him not liking the new music and specifically about hating the new Billy Joel album, whichever one it was.

KURT LODER [former *Rolling Stone* editor and MTV correspondent]: The last time I saw him, he was leaving the [*Rolling Stone*] office with a hundred blank videocassettes, saying he wanted to find a job where he didn't have to think anymore. I think he gave up and was ready to go.

DAVE MARSH [rock critic and author]: If you ask me where Paul Nelson ran into problems as a writer, it was the day that he got his first Betamax, because then the movies he loved weren't something you could go to the New Yorker [Theater] and see once a week. You could see them every night. [. . .] He kept a distance from human beings that he didn't keep from records and movies. And the movies he's into are going to be on late at night. So now he's even more out of sync, and in terms of his clearly obsessive-compulsive tendencies, there you are: The rest of the world becomes less interesting than sitting there in the dark.

In addition to these factors, Nelson's mother had recently been diagnosed with a lymphoma in her neck.

MICHAEL SEIDENBERG [used bookseller]: I first met him in my bookshop. He had come in to sell books because his mother was sick, and all the money he had saved up from when he quit *Rolling Stone* was in the hospital fund. He came back one day for the thirty dollars I still owed him, and the shop was empty. I gave him the money, but he said, "Why don't you just use that thirty bucks for advertising?" It touched me so much to see someone in a desperate situation helping someone else out like that. After that, he kept coming to my bookshop. We were just two failing people.

JONATHAN LETHEM [novelist]: His mother died, and he spent a lot of money on it. And it seemed that was the hurdle he stumbled over: He went broke with medical bills. And when he came out of that world, he'd always say that he didn't like enough music to be writing about it.

One of Nelson's favorite haunts was Evergreen Video. Though it was technically a mail-order video sales company for film buffs, every now and then a cinema diehard would come in off the street.

STEVE FELTES [owner, Evergreen Video]: Paul ended up being one of the people to show up off the street. So one day, I'm checking out whatever films he's renting and I said, "You wouldn't be by any chance the Paul Nelson who published the *Little Sandy Review*?* I happened to be one of your subscribers." Then in '88 or '89, we moved down to the Village, and either I asked Paul if there was a job or he asked me if there was a job available. So Paul started working for me at nights.

---

* A folk music newsletter that Nelson and his roommate, Jon Pankake, began publishing while in college.

BILL FLANAGAN [**former editor, *Musician* magazine**]: He seemed to feel a relief that he could just go to a cool video store in Greenwich Village and get a paycheck for doing it without getting an ulcer. I have to agree: If it gets to that point where writing is eating a hole in your stomach, go do something else. I'd see him on Carmine Street pretty regularly, because he was always there smoking a Nat Sherman cigarette, wearing his sunglasses and beret.

GREIL MARCUS: I went to see him at the Evergreen Video shop to give him a copy of one of my books. For me, there was just tremendous sadness in Paul's quietness. There was something he said once about the family that he abandoned. There was a whole other life left behind that he could never return to. And that was all over him. He was a tremendously alone person. I wouldn't say lonely, but he was alone.

Though few of his friends in New York knew it, in his youth in Minnesota, Nelson had married the homecoming queen of his school and had a son, Mark, with her.

DORIS HOPER [**Nelson's ex-wife**]: We moved to Queens, but things didn't work out with Paul and I. So I left in 1969 and went back to my hometown, and he stayed out there. Paul stayed in touch for quite some time, then I guess he just forgot about us. I think that was part of his being in New York. He was getting lost in himself, but he wasn't a bad person. [. . .] You don't really get inside of Paul Nelson. Even I didn't really get inside of him. I found out more about him by reading what he wrote.

JON PANKAKE [**Nelson's college roommate**]: I remember shortly before we lost contact, he said something that was very heartbreaking: All he really wanted was to watch his son grow up, but he didn't think that was going to be possible.

MARK NELSON [**his son**]: I didn't see him much during my teenage years. And in college, I decided to look him up and see if he wanted to see me. I was living in Minneapolis with my mother and flew out to see him. It didn't really occur to me until I was on the airplane that I didn't know what he looked like and he didn't know what I looked like. So I decided I'd get off the plane and look for the most uncomfortable person I could find, and that was him.

STEVE FELTES: I stayed in his apartment for a while after I broke up with my wife. Paul had boarded up the windows and painted everything in the kitchen black because he slept from four or five in the morning until late in the afternoon. I remember seeing in the fridge there were probably four or five six-packs of Coca-Cola and the rest of the space was taken up with Reese's Peanut Butter Cups. And the kitchen sink was filled with old books. Paul was into collecting first editions, selling them when he didn't have money, and then buying them back again when he did.

In 1993, Kit Rachlis, who was editing the LA Weekly *at the time, tried to bring Nelson to Los Angeles, hoping that some work and a change of environment would help. He assigned Nelson stories on two of his favorite artists, Lucinda Williams and Leonard Cohen. Nelson did the interviews, then returned home to New York.*

KIT RACHLIS: The deadline passed. I called a week later, then a week after that— and never heard from Paul. I kept calling twice a week, saying, "It's okay. Just tell me how you are or where you are. If you can't do these pieces, it's not going to interfere or affect our friendship." Then one night at about ten-thirty, the phone rang and it was [film critic] Jay Cocks saying, "Kit, I'm calling for Paul. He's embarrassed. He's mortified. But he's just never going to get those pieces done."

MICHAEL AZERRAD [music writer and editor]: I offered him some work writing about his last musical love, bluegrass, and he said no. It was a lot of money, and I knew he needed it. I asked why, and he said he simply couldn't do it justice.

In the meantime, Nelson was growing unhappy at Evergreen as well.

MICHAEL SEIDENBERG: What upset Paul was when Evergreen Video moved to a street-level storefront and he had to deal with more mainstream people. He would get tired of people saying, "I don't want to think" or "I don't want to see a black-and-white movie." It really broke his spirit how many people looked at movies as some kind of distraction from life rather than as part of life.

In addition, living in the city became more difficult for Nelson. He was mugged walking home, and he was also held up in the store. The robber asked, "What should I do with you?" And Nelson suggested, "You could lock me in the bathroom." So that's what happened.

STEVE FELTES: When he was sixty-five, I sent him to get an ID and helped him open a bank account so he could get Social Security. Around that time, he totally fell apart for the first time. He was getting very curmudgeonly with the customers, especially when they asked for the wrong films. He was filing things in the wrong place, and he was getting more and more upset because people were less into *film noir* than they were ten years ago. I said he should really take time off. This was something he was not happy with.

MICHAEL SEIDENBERG: He would come to my house four or five times a week. Because he was losing his short-term memory, he'd check in with me to have some balance. He had some financial security because Steve had hooked him up with Social Security. But he'd lived hand-to-mouth for so long, it was hard for him to grasp that this check was coming and would take care of everything.

STEVE FELTES: There was a time he called me and said he'd locked himself out of his apartment. And he'd spent at least the last two to four nights sleeping on a park bench. He was staying in an illegal sublet that belonged to Michael's brother, and at some point he met the landlord and the landlord found out. A week and a half later, he got a lawyer's letter saying he was being evicted.

MICHAEL SEIDENBERG: From the moment I heard that, I knew that his days were numbered. I was going to have to find a place for him to live. And I'd run out of ideas. He wasn't getting any better, and I didn't think he could live on his own anymore.

One day, Nelson stopped by Seidenberg's house and randomly brought him a copy of the Little Sandy Review, *a Warren Zevon cover story he'd written for* Rolling Stone, *and a printed copy of a more recent interview he had done for rockcritics.com.*

MICHAEL SEIDENBERG: He saw the Zevon story as his crowning achievement, and he brought rockcritics.com to show that he hadn't been forgotten. He told me he was up all night going through every important event in his life. He couldn't stop. He didn't know what it meant. He'd been living in his past so vividly. I see now it was him summing up, even though I didn't realize what it was at the time.

STEVE FELTES: I called Michael because Paul hadn't shown up here for two or three weeks, and Michael said he hadn't seen him. He used to eat at Dallas BBQ every day, and we called them and they hadn't seen him. He didn't have a phone, so I went to Michael's apartment and we got the key for Paul's apartment. We knocked on the door and got no answer, so we put the key in and unlocked the door. There was a chain lock across the top. We were about to put our shoulders to it when Paul showed up and opened it.

MICHAEL SEIDENBERG: He was very thin. Paul was totally bald, and since I'd known him, I'd only seen him three times without his hat on. He went and sat in front of his boombox, which is where he'd sit. We asked if he'd been eating and he said, "Yes." Yet they hadn't seen him at Dallas BBQ. He was as if in a fog, yet he knew enough to lie to me. So Steve and I emptied our pockets, and gave him what we thought he'd need.

STEVE FELTES: It was a week to a week-and-a-half later when they found Paul's body, so he must have died soon after that. The medical examiner went in and said I couldn't go in because the body wasn't recognizable. It was the heat wave, and he lived on the top floor with a metal ceiling, so it was a hot box. There were rat droppings, so maybe rats had eaten him. They found the exact same amount of money on him that we'd given him. That means he didn't eat any more at all.

When they returned to the apartment after Nelson's body had been removed, Seidenberg and Feltes noticed something unexpected: a pair of baby shoes hanging near Nelson's bed. They belonged to his estranged son, Mark.

MARK NELSON: The last time we spoke, I told him I was getting married. My regret is that I don't believe that he was aware he had a grandson when he died.

DAVID BOWIE: Over the last eighteen months, I have been thinking about trying to get hold of him. I just wanted to ask how life was, you know, because life slips by. I had tracked him down to a video store that he was working at, but I never got to see him. And I kick myself as we always do when these kind of things happen. It stung me hard when I heard he passed away. Particularly so when I heard he was on his own. I was just amazed that some of his fellow writers didn't stay in touch with him.

ROD STEWART: How long ago did he die? . . . God almighty. Where was he when he died? . . . I missed the funeral and all that? . . . No. Did he starve himself on purpose? . . . Someone can't starve in this day and age. Was it a while before they found him? . . . That's grim, very grim. Jesus Christ, it's amazing how someone can slip out of your life and you think, "I wonder where they are now." And then to find out he was working at a video store. He was such a talented writer.

In the years before he died, many of Nelson's former colleagues either sought him out or bumped into him. And when they asked him what he was working on, he always said the same thing: a screenplay.

MICHAEL SEIDENBERG: It's a big question to all of us who were close to him: What was it exactly? Did it exist? He used to tell me details from it, and then he became angry, saying, "If they want to put Brad Pitt in it, I'm pulling this thing." Then he decided he'd just write it and not care what happened. In the end, the answers don't really matter. What matters is that it was there to keep him company. He was writing every night. And for the first time, he was writing for himself.

[**CURTAIN**]

[EPI
LOGUE]

In twenty years of writing, I'd never struggled more with a story than with the *Rolling Stone* article on Paul Nelson. As a workhorse for the *New York Times*, I'd turned around big features in a matter of hours. But that particular feature—which was written as a much longer story, not in the interview format used here—took three months. I missed deadline after deadline. Every word, every paragraph, even just sitting down to write was a labor.

On one hand, that came from my respect for Nelson and my knowledge that every one of the writers and critics I'd admired since I was a teenager would be reading the story. On the other hand, and more significantly, every word brought me closer to my own cautionary tale—or that of any writer, creative person, or dedicated follower of art, entertainment, or culture. Because it makes you ask: In the end, is it worth it?

After all, here was a man with better taste than most of us, a better writer than most of us, a better critic than most of us—and better didn't mean happier. All those books and videos he'd dedicated his life to collecting and consuming ended up as just junk to put in boxes and bring to Goodwill. As for his meticulously honed aesthetic, it lives on only through articles that are nearly impossible to find, most of them tied to cultural products that are no longer as significant as they seemed at the time.

The baby shoes hanging over Nelson's bed continue to haunt me, because as someone who's sacrificed personal relationships for the pursuit of culture and career, I know what they symbolize: the regret of someone who has spent his entire life with his priorities wrong. Nelson did not live for nothing—the sheer breadth and influence of his work bear that out. But he died with nothing, as alone as the Leonard Cohen ballads and fictional detectives he admired. It may be romantic on one level, but on every other level, it's lonely and tragic.

In reporting, editing, and reading the interviews included in this book—and examining who's miserable, who's happy, and why—I ended up learning as much about myself and my life choices as the lives and philosophies of the artists and celebrities I was profiling. Never having gone to therapy, I often used these sessions with people wiser, older, or more experienced than myself to work out my own issues and dilemmas. Looking back on the conversations, I can see specific quandaries I was trying to resolve for myself at different stages of growing up. And most have to do with trying to get closer somehow to the purpose of life and the secret to happiness.

Fortunately, it is much easier and less painful to learn from others' mistakes than our own. And the people in these pages have made just about every mistake there is. Reading their stories becomes a reminder of the importance of stepping back from our own day-to-day lives—and our anxieties, goals, obligations, regrets, and infatuations—and making sure we're doing the right thing from the proper perspective with what little time we have left. To expand on something Jewel said in her interview, hell is getting to the end of your life, and realizing you were off by a degree and your priorities were wrong.

So outside of the obvious lessons—don't marry your thirteen-year-old cousin, don't kick security guards in the head, don't loan Courtney Love money, and be careful not to get caught with those "Hindu good luck ashes"—here are a few instructions for living compiled from the common experiences in these interviews:

1. *Let go of the past.* Many of the people we consider legends, like Jerry Lee Lewis and Chuck Berry, remain so scarred by scandals, injustices, and regrets from decades earlier that they're barely able to appreciate their accomplishments. While you do have to deal with each and every problem in the moment, when it's over and done with, there's nothing you can do about it anymore. So focus instead on being great at what you enjoy, like John Hartford. And that, ultimately, is what you'll be remembered for. Unless you're Ike Turner.

2. *Fame won't make you feel any better about yourself.* Many celebrities who work hard for their success believe that celebrity and money will resolve their feelings of insignificance, insecurity, worthlessness, or disconnection. But, like Eric Clapton and Brian Wilson, they soon learn that rather than fixing one's flaws, fame—and the "leap of consciousness" it takes to deal with it—magnifies them. Especially when the drugs are free.

3. *The secret to happiness is balance.* People who spend every waking hour working, like Paul Nelson, or partying, like Rick James, tend to end up in crisis. At best, they get to a certain point in life, look around, and find themselves alone. At worst, they have a mental breakdown or end up in jail or die in tragic circumstances. Almost everyone who reaches a plateau where he or she is happy and comfortable says it's because of finding balance, creating boundaries, and dedicating each week to a mix of work, relaxation, exercise, socializing, and family—plus some alone time to do something contemplative, creative, or educational.

4. *Fix your issues now, because the older you get, the worse they become.* Another theme in these interviews is that people who grow up in stable homes with unconditional love, like Sacha Baron Cohen and Jay Leno, tend to stay out of turmoil, while others who suffer from trauma, abandonment, or neglect in childhood—and never resolve those issues—often end up sabotaging their career and their life.

5. *Derive your self-esteem from within, not from others' opinions.* The artists who are the most miserable are the ones who spend too much time reading—and believing—their own press. No matter how bad or good or right or wrong others may be, you're handing the key to your happiness to strangers when you're letting their words control your feelings. What Jack White and Trent Reznor haven't realized yet is that when people are talking shit about someone, their goal is not actually to make that person look bad, but to make themselves feel good.

6. *Say yes to new things.* Most of the rich and famous people in this book ended up that way by complete coincidence. Just trying something new one day or answering a classified advertisement or working hard with little reward set in motion a chain of events that led to them becoming household names. So rather than finding reasons not to do things, embrace Stephen Colbert's dictum of saying yes to everything. And then, when you do get famous, avoid burning out by embracing Neil Young's dictum of saying no to everything but your art.

7. *Live in truth.* This means not just being honest with others, as Merle Haggard and Chuck Berry advocate, but being truthful to yourself and who you are. The artists who last the longest learn to accept themselves as the flawed but striving-to-improve human beings they are. Even if it means believing you were on the moon speaking Almond to nut creatures, you'll soon find that, as Lucia Pamela did, people will play along and you'll die happy. Or institutionalized.

8. *Never say never.* Life takes many surprise twists and turns—some for the worse, some for the better. So never rule anything out as a possibility, especially if it involves the clichéd things that successful people do—unless, like Trent Reznor or Ryan Adams, you want to eat your words in the future. Most of the time when we vehemently detest something in another person's behavior, it's either because we recognize a part of it in ourselves or we're secretly envious.

9. *Trust your instincts.* Cher had an international number one hit because she trusted her intuition—and fought for it—while James Talley lost his life's work for two decades because he listened to someone else. Even if your decision turns out to be wrong later, at least you'll know that you did what was right and true for you in the moment, and you'll be less likely to have regrets later. This, however, is not always an easy thing to do, because it's a lot easier to blame someone else for a mistake than ourselves.

10. *Be happy with what you have.* I often think of Bo Diddley, who was not only one of the most important musicians of the twentieth century but a genuinely sweet person. He went to the grave bitter about getting ripped off instead of appreciating the influence he had and the money he'd earned. Not only did he get to make a living touring the world and playing music for a worshipful audience, but he had homes, horses, and dozens of grandchildren. He was also in danger of losing most of it to his litigious ex-wife, but that's another lesson.

11. *Everyone loves you when you're dead.* Because when you're dead, your happiness and accomplishments are no longer a threat to their belief system and self-esteem. You've been appropriately punished.

So let us raise a toast to the artists, celebrities, and crazy people of the world—to the ones arrested outside clubs for driving drunk and filmed yelling racial slurs at audience members and hospitalized for accidentally setting themselves on fire with crack pipes. Thank you not just for keeping us entertained with your mistakes, but for reminding us to be happy with who we are.

KEY

— = speaker was cut off mid-phrase by the line that follows.

. . . = speaker didn't complete a thought or sentence and trailed off, switched topics, or started talking to someone else.

[. . .] = portion of dialogue omitted or shift in time.

(*parenthetical comment*) = description of ongoing action.

[words in brackets] = additional information that was not part of the interview but may be necessary to understand what's being discussed, most often identifying details for a person the speaker is referring to.

In most cases, rather than consulting published articles, the original transcripts, recordings, or notes have been used to preserve the back-and-forth conversation and atmosphere of the exact moment. Several facts and transcriptions that were inaccurate in the original articles have been corrected. In a few cases, grammar and sentence structure have been corrected for intelligibility, and a small number of sentences or phrases that were repetitive, off-topic, or meandering have been silently removed— along with some of my own stammering.

ACKNOWLEDGMENTS

The following interviews were originally conducted for: *Rolling Stone* (Christina Aguilera, At the Drive-In, Sacha Baron Cohen scene two, Chuck Berry, Orlando Bloom, Russell Brand, Leonard Cohen, Stephen Colbert, Tom Cruise, Bo Diddley, Zac Efron, Game, Merle Haggard, PJ Harvey, Hugh Hefner, Incubus, Jewel, Lenny Kravitz, Lady Gaga, Hugh Laurie, Taylor Lautner, Jay Leno, Courtney Love, Madonna, Marilyn Manson, Meat Puppets, Paul Nelson, Pearl Jam, Tom Petty, Pink Floyd scene one, Andy Prieboy, Keith Richards, Chris Rock, Snoop Dogg, Soul Asylum, Ringo Starr, Gwen Stefani, Ben Stiller, Strokes, System of a Down, White Stripes, Who, Wu-Tang Clan), *New York Times* (Ryan Adams, Kazem Al Saher, Chet Atkins, Backstreet Boys, Sacha Baron Cohen scene one, Bon Jovi, David Bowie, Bruce Brown, Johnny Cash, Jackie Chan, Cher, Chic, Alex Chilton, Eric Clapton, Josh Clayton-Felt, Puffy Combs, Billy Connolly, David Koresh's Girlfriend, Disc Jockeys, DJ Jubilee, DJ Marlboro, Fleetwood Mac, Funerals, Kenny G, Grateful Dead, Lee Greenwood, Henry Grimes, Hanson, John Hartford, Robyn Hitchcock, Rick James, Jane's Addiction, Billy Joel, Ernie K-Doe, Khaled, Nusrat Fateh Ali Khan, Kraftwerk, Led Zeppelin, Jerry Lee Lewis, Love, Loretta Lynn, Mafia, Branford Marsalis, Jimmy Martin, Master Musicians of Jajouka, Curtis Mayfield, Paul McCartney, Mingering Mike, Joni Mitchell, Alanis Morissette, N.W.A, Ozzy Osbourne, Dolly Parton, Pink Floyd scene two, Pretty Things, Prince, ? and the Mysterians, Racists, Radiohead, Bonnie Raitt, Ravers, Red Hot Chili Peppers, R.E.M., Lionel Richie, Slayer, Slipknot, Smashing Pumpkins, Patti Smith, Sparklehorse, Britney Spears, Bruce Springsteen, Johnny Staats, Standells, Steely Dan, James Talley, Ali Farka Touré, Ike Turner, Otha Turner, Mike Tyson, Upright Citizens Brigade, Vanilla Ice, Wax Figures, Brian Wilson, Gary Wilson, Neil Young, Zapp), *Maxim* (Judd Apatow), *Esquire* (Neptunes, Justin Timberlake), *Spin* (Beck, Korn, Mötley Crüe, Nine Inch Nails, Oasis), *Blender* (Ludacris, Pink, Queens of the Stone Age), *Details* (Jordy), *New York Press* (Von Lmo, Monster Magnet, Lucia Pamela), *Option* (Ice-T, Charles Gayle), *Interview* (Moby),

Village Voice (Fake Bootsy Collins, Old People, Les Paul, Raymond Scott), and *The Source* (Snoop Dogg).

Special thanks to all the magazine and newspaper editors I've worked with, particularly the ones who first took a chance on me when I wasn't yet ready: Carol Tuynman, David Laskin, Mark Kemp, Joe Levy, Barbara O'Dair, and Jon Pareles.

Thanks, always, to Ira Silverberg, Cal Morgan, and Carrie Kania. And also to Jamie, Dan, Nick and Norah at Canongate. Thanks also to the following people who, among other things, read through hundreds of clips to help select and proofread the ones included here: Monique Sacks, Ingrid De La O, Krista Lauder, Kristine Miller, Randy Sacks, Christina Swing, Carolyn Berner, Sue Wood, Eleanor Starlin, Carola Madis, Gerda Sirendi, Kerli, Tiffany Sledzianowski, Aaron Berger, Jamie Sher, Miss Jones, Thomas Scott McKenzie, Chris Holmes, Matt Friedberg, Brian Schroeder, Alex Willging, Ama Birch, Britt Warner, Don Diego Garcia, Dr. Michael A. Turek, Dr. William Miller, Kristi Malenfant, Mark Fletcher, Matt Van Winkle, Nola Singer, Randall Mah, Ray Timmons, Ryan Smith, Selim Niederhoffer, Skylaire Alfvegren, Zoe Sara Allen, Zorine Rinaldi, Todd, IGS, MtG, and especially Phoebe Parros, who, in one of her more impressive feats of research, figured out Loretta Lynn's actual age. She's on Wikipedia correcting it now.

INDEX

oral sex (*cont.*)
    wife, 107–08; *see also* fear of,
        female genitalia
Orcs, 190

Pampers, 5, 13, 28, 290
Parkinson's disease confused with
    arthritis, 105
passage regretfully cut, 492
peace and love,
    being persecuted for, 121; as
        catchphrase, 121–23; in dreams,
        121; how to attain, 122; one
        second dedicated to, 121; respect
        vs., 122; struggling to explain,
        121–22
pee,
    Dave Pirner and where he will, 154;
        dogs and, 283; Incubus and where
        they will, 155; *New York Times*
        and, 409; Ozzy Osbourne and,
        251, 252, 399; in Shawn Crahan's
        face, 220; spiders' superior fluids
        to, 249; Taylor Lautner and where
        he will, 214–15; Trent Reznor
        offended by, 455; Tricky's aunt
        and where she will, 307; -wee
        Herman, 15
Peking opera school, 244
Philbin, Regis, 30
phone numbers, 291, 384
plastic surgery, 223, 269–70,
        316–20, 359, 364; *see also* breast
        implants
Polaroid photography,
    of journalists, 196; of rear ends,
        252
probably funnier if you were there,
    345
prosthetic limbs, 171
pus-filled vomit bags,
    168-69

rabbit haters, 347, 352
rationalizations for failure (real or
    perceived), 79, 168–69, 174–77,
    281, 286, 304–05
raw meat,
    and longevity, 224
readers who are frustrated by this
    useless index, *see* Xanax
Reagan, Ronald, 481
reincarnation, 48–49, 95, 132–33
rubber,
    hands, 109; pants, 460; shorts, 206;
    see also condoms
Russian spy plane, 42

Santa Claus, 168
    Marilyn Manson's personal, 185
SAT score, 476
Satan, 19, 94, 128, 129, 132, 179, 183,
    185, 206, 251, 343, 415, 448–49
sauce,
    barbecue, 13, 28; cocktail, 402;
    sweet-and-sour, 94
Scientology, 259–61
Scrabble,
    games that would have a different
        outcome if referee followed the
        rule that names don't count,
        369–70
scratch-and-listen, 31, 32
Sea-Monkeys, 170
serum, 92–93
shit,
    autograph requests while taking
        a, 206; Beck's, 455; covering
        Tommy Lee's bathroom walls in,
        251; feeling like a piece of, 136;
        lovey-dovey, 130; as metaphor
        for songwriting, 211; PJ Harvey
        accused of being full of, 93–94;
        rehashed, 266; Rick James taking
        a, 257; settling your own, 132;

SELECTED VISUAL INDEX

P. 339.

P. 360.

P. 382.

P. 394.

P. 339.

P. 411.

P. 418.

P. 422.

P. 429.

P. 431.

P. 436.

P. 443.

P. 449.

P. 456.

P. 466.

P. 468.

P. 485.

P. 487.

P. 489.

P. 509.